THE COMPLETE
Perennials
BOOK

Meredith® Books
Des Moines, Iowa

The Complete
Perennials
Book

PLANTING PLANS FOR SPECIAL GARDENS 60

INTRODUCTION

Formal English perennial borders have inspired many gardeners.

to maintain than shrubs, are a good substitute where you need a fast hedge. Perennials such as fringe cups, astilbe, or Russian sage provide as much interest and greenery as shrubs, without the overbearing size.

Good perennial partnerships involve more than aesthetics. The best plant companions are compatible in cultural needs, habits, or manner of growth. The best partners are cooperative, adaptive plants that share their space and resources well.

This book is full of clear, step-by step photographs and inspiring plant combinations. There are also many useful charts and tables. Information such as bloom times for different plants, how many plants to buy, and when to fertilize can be seen at a glance. You'll also find lists of perennials for special situations: perennials for damp soil, perennials that have variegated foliage, perennials for dry shade, and so forth.

Perennial gardening is a rewarding hobby that transforms your yard into a setting where fun, satisfaction, and beauty prevail. It also relieves stress! This book will help you reap the most from your efforts by showing you how to plan, design, and care for your dream garden.

Perennials are moving out of traditional beds and into larger roles in the landscape as foundation plants, ground covers, and mini shrubs. Plants such as lady's mantle and perennial geranium can cover ground and suppress weeds while putting on a floral display. Ornamental grasses, which are easier

PLANTING PLANS

This book features 15 plans for predesigned gardens. Each planting plan includes an illustration of the garden, a detailed description of the maintenance needed, a scaled plan with locations of specific plants, and a plant list. These plans are a great way for beginners to get started.

PREPARATION TO MAINTENANCE

One chapter is devoted to preparation, so when you finally do plant, you'll be more

English cottage gardens are characterized by loose design and a profusion of perennials, annuals, vegetables, and herbs.

Recent innovations in gardening, typified by swaths of bold perennials, combine the loose cottage garden style with the naturalistic effect of grasses and woodlands.

likely to succeed. Another chapter is focused on caring for your perennials. You'll learn where to buy plants as well as how to choose healthy plants, get them in the ground, and help them thrive for the years you can expect them to grow in your garden. Tasks including watering, fertilizing, staking, weeding, pruning, grooming, dividing, and propagation are described in detail, accompanied by how-to photographs.

An entire chapter is devoted to troubleshooting. Detailed information on identifying and solving a wide range of plant problems is given. Insect and animal pests, weeds, diseases, and environmental problems are covered. You'll learn about cultural practices that can keep plants healthier and about beneficial insects that help rid the garden of insect pests.

ENCYCLOPEDIA OF PLANTS

The extensive Encyclopedia of Plants describes more than 190 perennials. And they're not just flowers. Ground covers, ornamental grasses, ferns, and vines are included, as are perennials grown for their foliage alone. Every entry in the Encyclopedia of Plants includes scientific and common names, description of the plant and its peak time, hardiness zone rating, height and width at maturity, optimal light needs, type of soil required, and amount of moisture needed.

The encyclopedia also recommends how to incorporate each plant into your garden design and suggests other plants to grow with it. Plant-specific care instructions are given. Particularly outstanding varieties and related species are listed. Finally, noteworthy features are included, such as whether the plant is poisonous, has exceptional color during a certain season, is fragrant, or attracts birds or butterflies. Every entry

is accompanied by at least one large photograph of the plant.

MAXIMUM SATISFACTION, MINIMUM FUSS

Here's your chance to learn time-honored and cutting-edge techniques for designing with perennials and growing plants that will make your garden a showplace. The result will be a garden full of beautiful, healthy plants that you can enjoy with maximum satisfaction and minimum fuss.

This book offers something for all readers, from those who are just starting to grow perennials to experienced gardeners looking to broaden their knowledge and add interest to their yards.

The same cubic foot of earth can accommodate five or six types of compatible plants for ongoing drama. Early spring blooms give way to summer stars, which are then replaced by fall flowers.

Many people view their gardens as extended living space, even if set in small lots—another reason to buy and place perennials carefully.

12 STEPS TO SUCCESSFUL PERENNIAL GARDENING

With a little creativity, planning, and patience, an enticing, colorful perennial garden can be yours.

This book is filled with detailed information on how to successfully grow perennials. Use these steps as a handy guide. The chapter and page references direct you to specific text on the topic.

1. Put your imagination to work. You expect your home to look good all year, so why not demand the same from your garden? Cultivate spring, summer, and fall perennials for a succession of blooms and multiseason appeal. Some perennials offer blooms over an extraordinarily long season.

Most perennials produce flowers for a shorter period, but some provide more than one season of interest with flowers, fruit, fall color, and handsome foliage and form. (The Year in Bloom, pages 10–27)

2. Know what you want. Before you buy a plant or dig a hole, figure out why you want a perennial garden. Are you dressing up a foundation planting? Are you interested in attracting birds and butterflies? Do you want cut flowers all season long? Knowing your purpose saves time, money, and effort. (Designing With Perennials, pages 28–29)

3. Have a plan. Half the fun is dreaming up a design just right for your home. Decide which hues look best with your house color, which plants will go where, and whether you should change the site before planting.

If your project includes a deck, patio, or other structural feature, it's best to address those aspects of the garden before planting. (Color in the Garden, pages 42–49; and Preparing to Plant, pages 70–71)

4. Start small. Be realistic about the size of your garden. Don't take on more than you can manage. Gardening does take time, especially in the beginning.

5. Choose the right plant. Get to know your site first, then select plants that are naturally adapted to it. A lot of gardening work (and failure) stems from trying to fix a site after planting it with ill-suited plants. If you try to grow plants that aren't hardy in your area, you'll have to coddle them through every winter. Don't fight your site. Choose plants adapted to growing there. (Preparing to Plant, pages 70–83; Encyclopedia of Plants, pages 146–244)

6. Choose strong plants. Choose disease- and pest-resistant varieties to reduce fussing with pesticides and to ensure plant health. For example, although garden phlox and bee balm are susceptible to mildew, recent hybridization has created new disease-resistant varieties. (Choosing and Growing Perennials, pages 92–94; and Encyclopedia of Plants, pages 146–244)

7. Begin with good soil. Great flowers grow in great soil. Many yards have soil stripped of nutrients, robbed of oxygen, and compacted by heavy equipment during house-building. Test your soil to learn about its condition and what is necessary to improve it. You can accomplish gardening miracles by testing and amending your soil; nearly all soils can be improved by adding organic matter. (Preparing to Plant, pages 86–91)

8. Mulch, mulch, mulch. Mulching garden beds has several advantages. Mulch on a perennial bed cools the soil in summer, helping it stay moist. Mulch smothers weed seeds so most can't germinate; the ones that do are easier to pull. As organic mulches such as shredded bark decompose, they condition the soil. Mulched plants also stay cleaner and healthier because less dirt splashes onto their petals when the plants are watered. (Choosing and Growing Perennials, pages 106–111)

9. Regular maintenance is easy maintenance. Although mulched areas require less care, flower beds still need watering, fertilizing, deadheading, and weeding to keep them in tip-top shape. Get into the habit of spending small amounts of time in the garden regularly to prevent chores from mounting up. Just five to 10 minutes every morning can keep your garden fresh. (Choosing and Growing Perennials, pages 112–119)

10. Treat problems when they're small. Problems caught early tend to go away fast. Weeds are a snap to pull when they're tiny seedlings but a major project to remove after they grow deep roots. Watering flowers before they're stressed with drought prevents damage that can allow other problems to develop. Catching a pest outbreak in its infancy can eliminate the need for time-consuming and costly intervention later. (Troubleshooting, pages 124–145)

11. When in doubt, rip it out. Keep your spade sharp. Sometimes a plant simply doesn't work. The color is wrong or the plant sickens and dies. If that happens, be ruthless. Don't waste time babying plants that won't perform. Gardening is about trial and error. Divide healthy plants that outgrow their space or move them to a more suitable location. Put pest- or disease-ridden plants in the trash. Remove plants you don't like, giving them to friends who want them, and substitute others.

12. Don't worry. For easy gardening, attitude is key. Relax! Delight in the loose edges, casual abundance, and growing surprises nature has in store for you— the chance seedling, the too-early bloom, the unexpected combination.

If you strive for perfect neatness and rigid predictability, count on plenty of effort. The pleasant rough edges and happy accidents of nature are some of gardening's greatest gifts.

Perry's blue Siberian iris, a late spring flower, gracefully welcomes warm, sunny days.

THE YEAR IN BLOOM

If trees, shrubs, and vines are the workhorses of the landscape, then perennials are the stars. A well-chosen succession of perennials will supply gardens with months of colorful, ever-changing drama. Selected for overlapping bloom, perennials can create waves of color from early spring, through hot summer days, and into autumn until the first frost.

While most perennials bloom for shorter periods than annuals (a few all-stars bloom for two months or more), many boast handsome foliage that creates a strong and lasting contribution to the garden. Some perennials have summer-long leaves as colorful as any flower, and many can be as structural as a shrub or small tree.

A SUCCESSION OF BLOOMS

Perennial gardeners have the pleasure of pursuing their hobby through more than one season. Months before marigolds and impatiens start to bloom, lungwort, Lenten rose, and catmint will have put on a show in the perennial garden.

Long after annuals fade in late-summer heat, perennial asters, sedums, and Japanese anemones make their debut.

The coral bells you select for sprays of red flowers will please you with their durable winter presence. You can extend the season even further with arrangements of seedpods and dried foliage that dress a perennial bed through the winter.

FOLLOW NATURE'S EXAMPLE FOR LONG SEASONS OF INTEREST

Beautiful, long-flowering natural models offer the means and methods to achieve a year-long show. Consider the tallgrass prairie, the mountain meadow, or the woodland. Each displays its own tapestry of interwoven perennials, annuals, grasses, and bulbs growing almost on top of one another. Cut out a cross section of prairie sod and you'll see roots layered like a club sandwich.

In a garden, this is called "sandwich planting." Think of garden soil as a cube rather than a square foot, and the options for perennial combinations increase dramatically.

DENSE PLANTINGS YIELD WAVES OF COLOR

The same cubic foot of earth can house five or six (or even more) types of compatible plants that will perform in one wave after the other. As the low-growing early bloomers go dormant, larger summer stars arise to take their place. These eventually give way to the towering flowers of fall, many of which persist as striking, lovely skeletons well into winter. The result is a yearly drama of ever-changing beauty.

Perennials provide year-round pleasure. Clockwise from upper left: Alyssum and phlox brighten this bed in spring. Summer heats up with bolder colors. Fall brings more muted colors of aster and black-eyed Susan. Winter quietly shrouds pampas grass.

FIRST FLOWERS

Spring comes early to this water garden, announced by blooming primroses and basket-of-gold. The hostas are in leaf, but are not flowering yet.

In early spring, garden beds and borders green up fast. Sleepy perennials stretch skyward as temperatures rise. Some, the hardiest, begin to bloom as the snow melts. Others leaf out first, their fresh foliage quickly followed by plump buds and cheerful flowers.

Spring flowers are not limited to trees and shrubs or bulbs. Look to nature and you'll find plenty of perennial early risers, such as sweet violet and fringed bleeding heart. Dozens of other native species flower in spring, as do their hybrid cousins.

To learn which early bloomers are suited to your region and climate, spend some time at a local nursery or botanical garden. Mail-order and online catalogs will increase choices, as will plant swaps. If you live in a mild climate, your choices will be plentiful. Harsh winters present more of a challenge. Regardless of where you live, the hunt for early-blooming flowers that can extend the garden year can bring exciting rewards.

COMBINE EARLY BLOOMERS FOR IMPACT

To develop vivid, early color, arrange first-flowering plants in clusters, keeping together those with similar needs and colors. Instead of dotting them in sparse patches around the garden, group them in sufficient quantities to make an impact.

Take a cue from nature; your garden plantings can be literally sandwiched into the same piece of ground, so that your first flowers are followed by second and third waves of other plants in the same location. Consider tucking clumps of early perennials between larger, later-rising plants; they will bloom early and the foliage remains as a ground cover.

The anemone family is a terrific source for early color: fuzzy-budded pasque flower is excellent for well-drained, sunny sites. Lacy-leaved wood anemone spreads in blankets of white in shady locations. Blue star retains its attractive, willowlike foliage long after its clusters of blue flowers open in spring. And after the spring blooms of columbine have faded, the textured foliage continues to provide interest (and hide dying bulb foliage) throughout the summer.

SPRING BLOOMERS

FOR SUN
- Cushion spurge
- Globe flower
- Heartleaf bergenia
- Leopard's bane
- Marsh marigold
- Rock cress

FOR SHADE
- Bishop's hat
- Bleeding heart
- Blue corydalis
- Columbine
- Lenten rose
- Lungwort
- Primrose
- Sweet violet
- Wood anemone

Several plants of alyssum clustered together result in strong spring impact.

EARLY SUMMER COLOR

Lupine and iris stand tall in the early summer garden (left). Peonies, roses and lady's mantle weave among one another in an early-summer scene (right).

By early summer, many gardens are fragrant with roses, lilies, and honeysuckle; but apart from peonies, foxglove, and coral bells, perennials appear in short supply.

Some gardeners select flowers that bloom at approximately the same time for a garden filled with color. This creates a spectacular, but brief, display. Unfortunately, it also means little or no perennial bloom for the rest of the season.

Gardeners who prefer a longer duration of early-summer color plant for a continuous succession of bloom, with new flowers coming as spring flowers fade.

While this may seem to dilute the impact of the overall color scheme, it actually reveals more of the character of the plants. In general, even when the garden is planned and planted with bloom succession in mind, there will still be three or four peak periods during the season, interspersed with periods of quiet green relief.

Sequencers—plants that remain effective throughout the seasons—help bridge the gap between these peak periods.

Meadow rue, for example, makes a super sequencer; its airy scrim adds a sense of mystery to the small garden and screens sweeps of browning bulb foliage.

Ornamental grasses, mounded spirea shrubs, woolly lamb's-ears,

and Brazilian verbena are all excellent sequencers.

MAKE IT LAST

Many early-summer perennials can also provide you with decorative effects over additional seasons. In early summer, false indigo—with its sweet-pealike flowers in blue or white—doubles as a splendid foliage plant. Its lustrous blue-gray foliage partners pleasantly with long-fingered peonies and the slender wands of peach-leaf bellflower.

In shady sites, try clumps of foxglove and aster, which are long-blooming. Bellflower, too, lasts longer than a single season. And if spent blooms are cut back, the plants will likely send up a fresh flush of flowers.

EARLY SUMMER BLOOMERS

FOR SUN
- Bellflower
- Butterfly weed
- Common peony
- Delphinium
- Dwarf crested iris
- Oriental poppy
- Pinks
- Siberian iris
- Threadleaf coreopsis
- Variegated iris

FOR SHADE
- Chinese rhubarb
- Coral bells
- Foxglove
- Hardy geranium
- Lady's mantle
- Woodland phlox

Oriental poppies herald the first days of summer. Unfortunately, these gorgeous flowers do not bloom long.

A traditional summer border layers colors. Bright red astilbe explodes like fireworks in high summer (far right).

HIGH SUMMER DISPLAY

High summer is show time in the garden: To create that dazzling array of nonstop fireworks, pay attention to the average bloom time of your favorite perennials. Once you know how they behave in your own backyard, you can devise powerful combinations, interweaving flowers and foliage. When one plant finishes blooming, another can step in and take its place. Track performance in a garden journal or notebook and use the Bloom Season Chart on pages 26 and 27 to help plan your display.

HIGH-SUMMER PERENNIALS

FOR SUN
- Blazing star
- Daylily
- Hollyhock mallow
- Joe-Pye weed
- Queen-of-the-prairie
- Red valerian
- Sea holly
- Tree mallow
- Yarrow

FOR SHADE
- Astilbe
- Goatsbeard
- Hostas
- Japanese painted fern
- Lady fern
- Maidenhair fern

Well into midsummer, clusters of yellow and red yarrow flourish in this sunny spot.

PLANT A VARIETY OF PERFORMERS

The best way to enjoy an unbroken sequence of bloom is to develop a full palette of perennial color. Variety helps ensure that despite quirky weather, disease, or nuisance animals, something will succeed. Begin with plants that have staying power. Yarrow, sedum, daylily, and similar tireless plants come in a range of sizes and colors.

Don't stop with color. Group your choices by shape and texture as well. Many perennials are basically mound-shaped and need contrast to keep their own identity. Choose yucca, Chinese rhubarb, sea holly, and fountain grass for a textural change of pace.

SUN OR SHADE?

Sunny gardens can host a tremendous number of summer bloomers. Among them are many native flowers that grow larger and bloom longer than they do in the wild. Purple coneflower and blanket flower, black-eyed Susan and beard-tongue all provide multiple possibilities throughout the summer season.

Shady woodland gardens are often quite dry by midsummer. Where water is an issue, select drought-tolerant plants. If you have damp shade, dozens of perennials suit it, from spiky ligularia to bold rodgersia. Damp or dry, shade gardens can hold marvelous tapestries of foliage perennials such as hostas and lungwort. For contrast, mix in rounded and ruffled coral bells, and fine-textured astilbes.

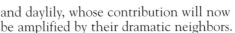

LATE BLOOMERS

As late summer melts into autumn, warm days and cool nights waken the hidden flames of foliage. Blue star and balloon flower turn to fiery gold. Variegated obedient plant blooms above foliage streaked with raspberry and cream.

EXTENDING AUTUMN

In order to have a good autumnal show, you must dedicate significant garden space to some of these late bloomers. It need not mean a summer sacrifice: If 10 to 20 percent of your plants offer strong fall flower or foliage color, they will carry the season. Keep in mind, many late performers are large plants with plenty of character. They are standouts. What's more, you can place them behind rebloomers, such as yarrow, blanket flower,

Black-eyed Susan blooms span two seasons, summer and fall.

and daylily, whose contribution will now be amplified by their dramatic neighbors.

To maximize your autumn display, group late bloomers in clusters and sweeps, and give them supportive companions (such as long-season foliage plants and additional reliable rebloomers), so the fall performers do not appear as an afterthought in the home landscape. Select fall flowers that can pull their weight over several seasons, such as sedum, black-eyed Susan, and calico aster.

NATIVE STARS

Native plants excel in the autumn landscape. The golden tassels of goldenrod burn against the sky, and asters haze the garden with smoky blue and purple. Varieties of native switch grasses, such as 'Heavy Metal' and 'Cloud Nine', shimmer like spun gold. Indeed, a host of other grasses bring glitter and gleam to fall gardens, from maiden grass such as 'Morning Light' or zebra-striped 'Stricta' to dwarfs such as Mexican feather grass and Japanese blood grass.

In shady gardens, bugbane and the white flowers of fragrant hostas scent the air. Rosy or creamy, Japanese anemone blooms long and hard in dappled light. Arching wands of toad lily are studded with tiny flowers. And when the foliage tapestry is turning golden, there are evergreen ferns and Lenten roses to carry on the spectacle through winter.

Crocosmia and sedum bloom together in the late summer (left). Pampas grass makes a spectacular addition to the fall garden. It's blooming with Helen's flower (right).

LATE PERFORMERS

FOR SUN
- Blue star
- Boltonia
- Goldenrod
- Hardy aster
- Helen's flower
- Plumbago
- Stonecrop

FOR SHADE
- Bugbane
- Cardinal flower
- Japanese anemone
- Monkshood
- Toad lily

New Zealand flax and lamb's-ears catch the first frost, while ornamental grass still stands tall.

THE GARDEN IN WINTER

WINTER INTEREST FOR COLD REGIONS

FOR SUN
- Black-eyed Susan
- False indigo
- Giant feather grass
- Globe thistle
- Joe-Pye weed
- Mullein
- Pinks
- Sea holly
- Stonecrop
- Yucca

FOR SHADE
- Barrenwort
- Golden grass

Winter in the garden does not need to be a barren time. The winter garden's subtle beauty lies in line and form. Cold-winter gardens can hold eye-catching shapes and textures. When sturdy, structural perennials are left to stand through wind, snow, and ice, the resulting shapes can work magic, transforming a meadow from stubble to sculpture.

The deep purple flowers and dark green foliage of Lenten rose look lovely in snow.

HOW TO MAKE A CHEERFUL SPLASH

Where mild winters are the rule (Zones 7, 8, and 9), the garden possibilities become far more plentiful. Evergreen perennials come into their own when earlier-blooming, brasher competition retreats. Grouped and given the support of compact border shrubs (evergreen herbs, rhododendrons, and dwarf conifers), even the least showy winter flowers can make a cheerful splash.

Winter is an excellent time to study the flow and follow-through of garden color. Journal notes will help you rule out the less suitable and rearrange better performers for winter appeal. Through selection and editing, you can develop your own winter perennial palette to enliven this underappreciated season. By leaving seed heads in place, you'll experience the moving color of birds visiting the winter garden.

As you expand your palette with off-season performers, you may need to make room by cutting back on spring- and summer-blooming flowers. Start by replacing plants that no longer thrill you, supplanting them with late bloomers. Take advantage of winter's down time to study specialty catalogs for plants to try. Before long, the flow of overlapping color will extend throughout the seasons.

Woodland winters are wonderfully quiet. Grasses whisper in the breeze, their hollow stems rustling softly. Blanketing snow emphasizes the graceful silhouette of purple coneflower, with its stems the color of burnt earth. Brown and burnished, the skeletons of Joe-Pye weed cast shadows on the snow, joined by native goldenrod.

TRACK THE SEASONS IN A GARDEN JOURNAL

If color themes are to change with the seasons, timing becomes critical. The chart on pages 26 and 27 is a good way to begin your color plan.

What happens in your garden is specific to your region and climate. The best way to track performance is by keeping regular records in a garden journal. You don't need to make voluminous notes, and you don't have to write in it every day; simply follow these guidelines:

■ Record what you've planted, along with rainfall and temperature.

■ Note what's in bloom when so you will have an idea of the general flow of each season through the year.

■ Take snapshots to remember where and when plants bloomed. Study them to plan new combinations.

■ Keep a calendar in the garage or shed in order to indicate your spray and fertilizer schedules from year to year.

■ Jot down the first and last blooming dates of all perennials each year. Patterns will emerge, and soon you'll be better able to combine plant selections to extend the season of interest.

Spring's succession: Roses, penstemon, spurge, and colewort mark the arrival of the new season.

Summer's succession: The same mixed border a few weeks later boasts a vivid new palette that includes crimson pinchushion, lily, and daylily.

WINTER INTEREST FOR MILD WINTER REGIONS

FOR SUN
■ Anise hyssop
■ Feather reed grass
■ Maiden grass
■ New Zealand flax
■ Pampas grass
■ Switch grass
■ Twinspur

FOR SHADE
■ Bergenia
■ Stokes' aster
■ Variegated Japanese sedge

Autumn's succession: As summer recedes, so do its star performers. But the ornamental grass is at its peak. As other colors become muted, the blue spruce gains prominence.

PLANTING PLAN FOR A THREE-SEASON GARDEN

For a garden that will appeal throughout the growing season, consider this three-season scheme that provides color from spring into fall. Although the color may not at all times match the intense impact of color found in spring or summer gardens, this planting doesn't fall short in either beauty or interest. The plan's strengths are the attractiveness of the individual plants and the pleasing associations of foliage and flowers.

All plants in this scheme were chosen for their long period of bloom (the roses, in fact, are varieties that flower in all three seasons). Rather than bursts and gaps of blossoms, there will be a continuum of flowers. The backbone of the garden is shrubs chosen for their foliage as much as for their flowers.

Perennials make up the remainder of the scheme, although the alternative selections list suggests three long-blooming annuals that you could substitute for some of the foreground drifts. Plants in the main list thrive in Zones 5 through 9, although in Zones 5 and 6 the floribunda roses will need winter protection and the beard-tongue may need replacing every two or three years. With the substitutions in the alternatives list, the planting will succeed in the dry-summer regions of Zone 10. In all zones, locate the planting in full sun (at least six hours daily) and give it routine garden watering.

Late winter and early spring are the times to perform basic maintenance in this garden. Prune roses, rose of Sharon, and bluebeard to shape and remove unproductive wood. Cut

'Apple Blossom' beard-tongue could be used instead of the 'Prairie Fire' beard-tongue called for in the planting plan.

PLANTING PLAN

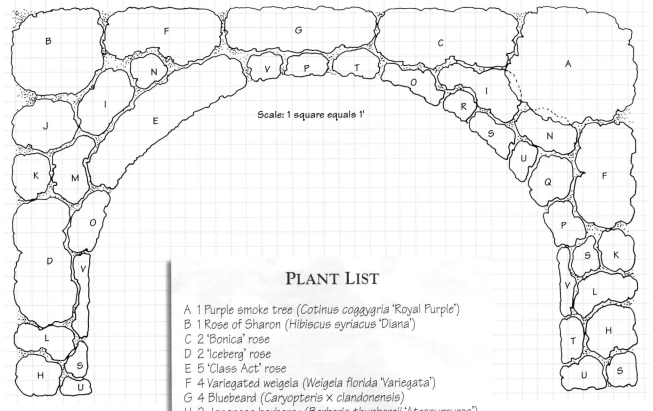

Scale: 1 square equals 1'

PLANT LIST

A 1 Purple smoke tree (*Cotinus coggygria* 'Royal Purple')
B 1 Rose of Sharon (*Hibiscus syriacus* 'Diana')
C 2 'Bonica' rose
D 2 'Iceberg' rose
E 5 'Class Act' rose
F 4 Variegated weigela (*Weigela florida* 'Variegata')
G 4 Bluebeard (*Caryopteris × clandonensis*)
H 2 Japanese barberry (*Berberis thunbergii* 'Atropurpurea')
I 6 Russian sage (*Perovskia atriplicifolia*)
J 2 Boltonia (*Boltonia asteroides* 'Snowbank')
K 6 Michaelmas daisy (*Aster novi-belgii*, tall blue cultivar)
L 6 Yarrow (*Achillea ageratum* 'W.B. Child')
M 5 Fern-leaf yarrow (*Achillea filipendulina* 'Coronation Gold')
N 7 False sunflower (*Heliopsis helianthoides* 'Summer Sun')
O 6 Threadleaf coreopsis (*Coreopsis verticillata* 'Moonbeam')
P 5 'Autumn Joy' sedum
Q 4 Daylily (*Hemerocallis* 'Evergold')
R 3 Daylily (*Hemerocallis* 'Stella de Oro')
S 14 Beard-tongue (*Penstemon barbatus* 'Prairie Fire')
T 9 Lamb's-ears (*Stachys byzantina*)
U 8 Leather bergenia (*Bergenia crassifolia*)
V 9 Catmint (*Nepeta × faassenii*)

ALTERNATIVE SELECTIONS (FOR ZONE 10)
B 1 Oleander (*Nerium oleander* 'Casablanca')
F 4 Tree germander (*Teucrium fruticans*)
G 4 Ox-eye daisy (*Leucanthemum vulgare*)
H 2 Fortnight lily (*Dietes vegeta*)
I 6 Glory bush (*Tibouchina urvilleana*)
N 7 Kaffir lily (*Clivia miniata*)
P 16 French marigold (*Tagetes patula*)
T 9 Petunia (*Petunia hybrida*)
V 9 Vinca (*Catharanthus roseus*)

*Note: The letters match the clump labels on the plan. The numbers represent how many of each plant are needed. If a clump label repeats, divide the plants among the clumps.

back the perennials that send up flowering stems from clumps or woody bases, and remove dead leaves. After the variegated weigela blooms, prune or thin as needed. Remove the spent rose blossom clusters.

VARIATIONS

A promenade path at the front of the crescent design will provide a pleasant stroll as well as a focal point at the end of the garden. An alternative is to cut the scheme in half, splitting the bed at the bluebeard (G). Either half becomes a corner bed and will fulfill the promise of three-season color.

Fernleaf yarrow with its long-lasting yellow blooms is a highlight of the midsummer garden. Out of bloom, it forms a nicely textured, gray-green mat.

PLANTING PLAN FOR A SUMMER GARDEN

Summer brings the fullness of the gardening year; it's in this season that the greatest number of plants flower in abundance. Summer also brings the warmest weather, signaling a time to take it easy (after you've attended to the watering) and enjoy the fruits of your gardening labors. This summer garden, therefore, features a shaded nook where you can sit, relax, and survey a riot of fragrance and flowers.

The shrubs and perennials in this summer border will thrive in Zones 5 through 9 and dry-summer Zone 10. All flower over a long period, some beginning in spring, others starting in summer and continuing into fall. The roses will provide color in all three seasons. Shrubs and perennials were chosen for this plan because of their relative permanence and lower maintenance needs.

They will flower year after year, except dusty miller, which will need replacing each spring in cold regions (Zones 7 and below). For this garden plan, there are two lists of alternative selections. The first lists shrubs and perennials that are especially suited to mild winters in the warmer parts of Zone 9 and in Zone 10. The second group features a set of summer annuals distributed through the framework of shrubs and perennials. All the annuals must be planted anew every spring—an opportunity for enthusiastic gardeners to vary the planting each year with new colors and varieties.

A cool green hemlock hedge forms the backdrop in the illustration, though a wall or fence could also provide an attractive background. The main plant list and the first list of alternatives include optional hedging shrubs. If you choose to plant a hedge, remember to allow space for it to broaden beyond the confines of the bed.

This is a full-sun planting. Each part of the garden should have at least six hours of daily sun during the growing season.

The plants need routine garden watering. In late winter or early spring, prune and thin the vines and shrubs (except for the smoke tree) to keep them shapely and productive. Clean out the dead stems and leaves of the perennials and remove the spent annuals. Divide and replant any perennials that are overcrowded. During the summer bloom season, cut back the spent flower spikes of delphinium and beard-tongue; this will encourage a second flowering.

At the height of summer, perennials are in full glory. Here, yellow yarrow and coreopsis partner with bright, white shasta daisies to complete the summer scene.

VARIATIONS

The predominant colors in this summer garden are pink, yellow, white, and blue—bright but not strident. For hot colors such as orange, red, and bronze, choose different cultivars of the shrub roses, rose of Sharon, bush cinquefoil, daylily, and coreopsis. Or select bright-colored annuals from the second list of alternatives.

If a double border is too elaborate for your space, you can plant either border as a rectangular bed facing a lawn or pathway. To do that, continue the front line to the back wall, past either the smoke tree (on the left) or rose of Sharon (right); finish off the front of the border with narrow drifts of coreopsis, and catmint, or both.

To make one long border, plant the gardens end-to-end, abutting the two 'Pink Meidiland' roses and eliminating the plants that overlap on the ends. This will give you an impressive bed 40 to 45 feet long, with the smoke tree at one end of the planting and the rose of Sharon and 'Ballerina' rose at the other.

Once cranesbill is established, it requires little care. It is available in a variety of colors and sizes. Plants do best in full sun but take light shade.

PLANT LIST

A 1 Purple smoke tree (*Cotinus coggygria* 'Royal Purple')
B 1 Rose of Sharon (*Hibiscus syriacus* 'Diana')
C 1 Jackman clematis (*Clematis × jackmanii*), trained on trellis
D 18 Canadian hemlock (*Tsuga canadensis*) hedge, planted 4 feet apart
E 2 'Pink Meidiland' rose
F 1 'Ballerina' rose
G 2 Bush cinquefoil (*Potentilla fruticosa* 'Katherine Dykes')
H 5 Bluebeard (*Caryopteris × clandonensis*)
I 15 'Pacific Giant Hybrids' delphinium
J 11 Fern-leaf yarrow (*Achillea filipendulina* 'Coronation Gold')
K 5 Shasta daisy (*Leucanthemum × superbum* 'Alaska')
L 6 Shasta daisy (*Leucanthemum × superbum* 'Snow Lady')
M 4 Russian sage (*Perovskia atriplicifolia*)
N 6 Baby's breath (*Gypsophila paniculata* 'Viette's Dwarf')
O 20 Beard-tongue (*Penstemon barbatus*)
P 8 Threadleaf coreopsis (*Coreopsis verticillata* 'Moonbeam')
Q 8 Daylily (*Hemerocallis* 'Winning Ways')
R 4 Spirea (*Spiraea japonica* 'Anthony Waterer')
S 10 Catmint (*Nepeta × faassenii*)
T 3 Cranesbill (*Geranium endressii* 'Wargrave Pink')
U 9 Lamb's-ears (*Stachys byzantina* 'Silver Carpet')
V 8 Dusty miller (*Senecio cineraria*)

ALTERNATIVE SELECTIONS I (FOR WARM REGIONS)
B 1 Oleander (*Nerium oleander*)
C 1 Jasmine (*Jasminum grandiflorum*)
D 18 Yaupon (*Ilex vomitoria*) or yew pine (*Podocarpus macrophyllus*)
G 2 African lily (*Agapanthus orientalis*)
H 5 Marguerite (*Argyranthemum frutescens*)

ALTERNATIVE SELECTIONS II (ANNUALS)
L 6 Vinca (*Catharanthus roseus*)
R 4 Flowering tobacco (*Nicotiana alata*)
S 10 Garden verbena (*Verbena × hybrida*)
T 3 Plume cockscomb (*Celosia cristata*)

Note: The letters match the clump labels on the plan. The numbers represent how many of each plant are needed. If a clump label repeats, divide the plants among the clumps.

PLANTING PLAN

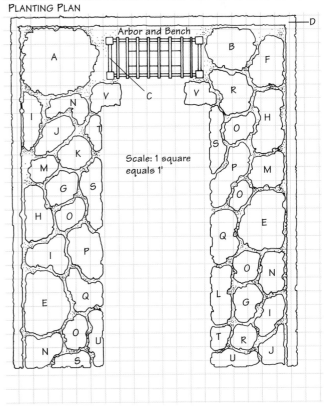

Arbor and Bench

Scale: 1 square equals 1'

PLANTING PLAN FOR AUTUMN GRASSES

No longer are grasses to be viewed as weeds or as plants to be sheared into subjugation as a lawn. Ornamental grasses—long on the periphery of horticulture—have come into the mainstream and are being recognized for their distinct beauty in form, texture, and color. This planting brings together the most commonly available grasses.

Featured are fountain grass in the foreground and 'Stricta' feather reed grass in the background. Both provide color and interest throughout the year and are particularly striking when they rustle in the wind over a thick blanket of snow.

Adaptability is characteristic of the grasses in this garden. Plants in both lists grow in Zones 5 through 9 and dry-summer Zone 10. The main list contains grasses that will prosper in a sunny bed; substituting the three alternate selections (including a grasslike sedge) gives you a planting to use in light shade. The best performance, in either case, will derive from well-drained soil and routine watering.

You'll find that this bed of ornamental grasses has relatively few maintenance demands. Aside from

watering during dry periods, an annual cleanup of dead leaves and stems is the only routine to put on your schedule. All but three of the grasses (blue oat grass, blue fescue, and tufted hair grass) and the sedge are deciduous, growing an entirely new set of leaves each spring. Cleaning up deciduous grasses is simple: Cut dead material nearly to the ground. With the evergreen kinds, pull out dead leaves from the clumps, though you can give unkempt blue fescue a close trim.

The timing for the annual cleanup depends on your climate and personal preference. The dead foliage and flower stalks may remain attractive, weather permitting, well into winter, so that you can delay cleanup, if you wish, until just before the start of new growth. In warmer areas, cut back dead leaves and stems any time from late fall to late winter or early spring. In snowy regions, leave the foliage and stems through the winter. Most ornamental grasses will thrive for years without dividing and replanting. The exception in this plan is the blue fescue: When clumps decline in vigor, dig them up and replant small divisions.

VARIATIONS

Although this planting is designed to wrap around a corner, you can make a simple corner planting by cutting off the wraparound. Draw a line from the corner fence post to the dot on

Although ornamental grasses look good in a garden all their own, they also work well as accent plants in mixed perennial borders, as in the case of 'Morning Light' maiden grass (above). Plant tall varieties in the back of the garden; then surround them with complementary annuals and perennials.

Colorful Japanese blood grass peaks in the fall.

the edge of the bed, then omit the plants in the smaller portion. Delete the purple moor grass (C), sea oats (I), three feather reed grass plants (B), and one drift each of the Japanese blood grass (D) and blue fescue (H).

PLANT LIST

A 1 Maiden grass (*Miscanthus sinensis* 'Gracillimus')
B 10 Feather reed grass (*Calamagrostis acutiflora* 'Stricta')
C 3 Variegated purple moor grass (*Molinia caerulea* 'Variegata')
D 9 Japanese blood grass (*Imperata cylindrica* 'Red Baron')
E 7 Fountain grass (*Pennisetum alopecuroides*)
F 5 Blue oat grass (*Helictotrichon sempervirens*)
G 4 Tufted hair grass (*Deschampsia caespitosa*)
H 12 Blue fescue (*Festuca glauca*)
 I 2 Northern sea oats (*Chasmanthium latifolium*)
J 1 Colorado blue spruce (*Picea pungens glauca*)

ALTERNATIVE SELECTIONS
B 6 Maiden grass (*Miscanthus sinensis purpurascens* 'Autumn Red')
E 7 Tufted sedge (*Carex elata*)
F 4 Golden grass (*Hakonechloa macra* 'Aureola')

Note: The letters match the clump labels on the plan. The numbers represent how many of each plant are needed. If a clump label repeats, divide the plants among the clumps.

PLANTING PLAN

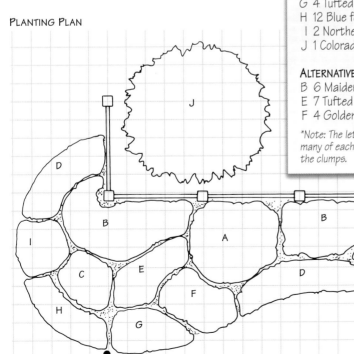

Scale: 1 square equals 1'

PLANTING PLAN FOR A WINTER GARDEN

In northern and mountain regions, where winter means a steady blanket of snow, garden color in winter is a sometimes thing, chiefly derived from evergreens, berried deciduous shrubs (before birds strip them), and the bright bark of certain dogwoods and willows. By contrast, gardeners in Zone 10 and the warmer parts of Zone 9 can plan for colorful flowers that will reliably enliven this least active but far-from-dead season. Between

Red twig dogwood and pampas grass shine in fall and winter.

these two extremes lie the regions where snow may or may not occur, comes and goes, or arrives late and leaves early.

The planting scheme for this winter garden was designed for Zones 6 through 8, especially the Northeast, eastern seaboard, upper South, and Pacific Northwest. Winter-blooming heaths and Christmas rose carry the banner of flower color in white and pink. The dogwood and Japanese maple present colorful stems and bark, while the European cranberry bush offers striking clusters of red berries on leafless branches that attract colorful songbirds all winter long. The cliff green, juniper, and arborvitae contribute foliage—respectively, bronze, purplish, and golden.

The alternative plant selections are appropriate for Zone 9 and also for most gardens in Zone 8. The warmer climate allows for an expanded range of flowering plants, including camellias. The alternative scheme retains the Japanese maple for its coral-red stems and bark, which are standouts. Foliage color derives from the dwarf heavenly bamboo and the dwarf golden arborvitae.

The main planting needs sun for at least six hours each day. To satisfy the heaths, the soil must be well-drained and moisture-retentive. The alternative planting needs partial shade or filtered sunlight for about half the day to accommodate the camellias and Lenten rose.

Minimal maintenance is a bonus with this planting. In fall, after the leaves have

PLANTING
PLAN

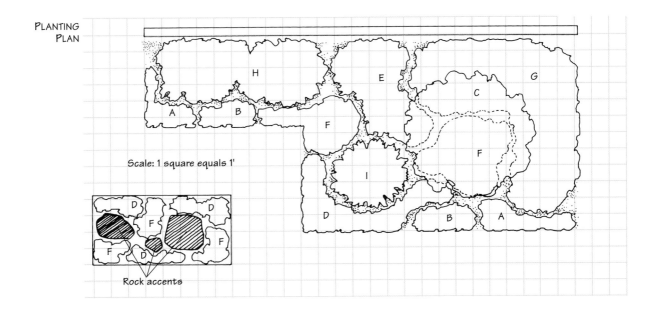

Scale: 1 square equals 1'

Rock accents

Look for small pleasures, such as this frosted seed head, in the winter garden.

PLANT LIST

A 9 Cliff green (*Paxistima canbyi*)
B 9 Christmas rose (*Helleborus niger*)
C 1 Japanese maple (*Acer palmatum* 'Sango Kaku')
D 9 Heath (*Erica carnea* 'Springwood') (15 in variation bed)
E 5 Creeping juniper (*Juniperus horizontalis* 'Plumosa')
F 14 Heath (*Erica carnea* 'Winter Beauty') (19 in variation bed)
G 3 European cranberrybush (*Viburnum opulus* 'Compactum')
H 2 Redtwig dogwood (*Cornus alba* 'Sibirica')
I 1 American arborvitae (*Thuja occidentalis* 'Rheingold')

ALTERNATIVE SELECTIONS

A 11 Lenten rose (*Helleborus orientalis*)
B 19 Viola (*Viola cornuta*)
D 24 Polyanthus primrose (*Primula polyantha*) (52 in variation bed)
E 10–Dwarf heavenly bamboo (*Nandina domestica* 'Harbor Dwarf')
F 19 Leather bergenia (*Bergenia crassifolia*) (31 in alternative bed)
H 2 Japanese camellia (*Camellia japonica* 'C.M. Wilson')
I 1 Arborvitae (*Thuja occidentalis* 'Rheingold')

Note: The letters match the clump labels on the plan. The numbers represent how many of each plant are needed. If a clump label repeats, divide the plants equally among the clumps.

dropped, rake off the ones that cover the low plants. In spring, clean out all unsightly and dead foliage on the perennials. After the heaths have stopped flowering, shear off the spent stems to keep the plants dense and compact. In the alternative planting, you will need to replace the violas each year in fall, but they may also spread on their own. Although primroses are perennials, in the warmest areas you will get the best display by setting out new plants each fall.

ALTERNATIVE DESIGN

This variation is deliberately small— a fragment of color to cherish during winter. The rectangular island bed is optional. As shown, it features a moorland patch of heaths and rock. However, it could just as easily contain a bench nestled among heaths (or Lenten rose and primroses), a place to contemplate these special winter-time offerings.

BLOOM SEASON CHART

Use this chart to help you plan overlapping seasons of bloom for color all year. Because perennials are listed in order of bloom, you can easily see at a glance which bloom together, which bloom in succession, and which bloom for extra long times. Remember that any bloom chart will be only a rough guide, as bloom seasons can differ according to the region, the weather, microclimates, and cultivars. Blue bars represent bloom seasons; orange bars represent fall foliage and fruit effects.

Plant Name	Spr. E M L	Sum. E M L	Fall E M L	Win. E M L
Basket-of-gold (Aurinia saxatilis)				
Bergenia (Bergenia cordifolia)				
Marsh marigold (Caltha palustris)				
Red barrenwort (Epimedium × rubrum)				
Cushion spurge (Euphorbia polychroma)				
Mediterranean spurge (Euphorbia characias)				
Lenten rose (Helleborus orientalis)				
Moss phlox (Phlox subulata)				
Bethlehem sage (Pulmonaria saccharata)				
Sweet violet (Viola odorata)				
Bleeding heart (Dicentra spectabilis)				
Luxuriant bleeding heart (Dicentra 'Luxuriant')				
Myrtle spurge (Euphorbia myrsinites)				
English primrose (Primula vulgaris)				
Columbine (Aquilegia)				
False indigo (Baptisia australis)				
Dwarf crested iris (Iris cristata)				
Cheddar pink (Dianthus gratianopolitanus)				
Woodland phlox (Phlox divaricata)				
Allegheny foam flower (Tiarella cordifolia)				
Lady's mantle (Alchemilla mollis)				
Blue star (Amsonia tabernaemontana)				
Astilbe (Astilbe × arendsii)				
Masterwort (Astrantia major)				
Yellow corydalis (Corydalis lutea)				
Japanese primrose (Primula japonica)				
Peach-leaf bellflower (Campanula persicifolia)				
Red valerian (Centranthus ruber)				
Twinspur (Diascia barberae)				
Foxglove (Digitalis purpurea)				
Bloody cranesbill (Geranium sanguineum)				
Johnson's Blue hardy geranium (Geranium himalayense × 'Johnson's Blue')				
Geum (Geum)				

Plant Name	Spr. E M L	Sum. E M L	Fall E M L	Win. E M L
Creeping baby's breath (Gypsophila repens)				
Stella de Oro daylily (Hemerocallis 'Stella de Oro')				
Coral bells (Heuchera hybrids)				
Bearded iris, early season (Iris hybrids)				
Siberian iris (Iris sibirica)				
Lupine (Lupinus Russell hybrids)				
Catmint (Nepeta × faassenii)				
Peony (Paeonia hybrids)				
Oriental poppy (Papaver orientale)				
Beard-tongue (Penstemon)				
Lamb's-ears (Stachys byzantina)				
Columbine meadow rue (Thalictrum aquilegiifolium)				
Variegated Solomon's seal (Polygonatum odoratum 'Variegatum')				
Coronation Gold yarrow (Achillea × 'Coronation Gold')				
Hollyhock (Alcea rosea)				
Goatsbeard (Aruncus dioicus)				
Hybrid sage (Salvia × sylvestris)				
Delphinium (Delphinium × elatum)				
Butterfly weed (Asclepias tuberosa)				
Speedwell (Veronica hybrids)				
Kamtschatka stonecrop (Sedum kamtschaticum)				
Mullein (Verbascum chaixii)				
Carpathian bellflower (Campanula carpatica)				
Common yarrow (Achillea millefolium)				
Maiden pink (Dianthus deltoides)				
Allwood pink (Dianthus × allwoodii)				
Baby's breath (Gypsophila paniculata)				
Daylily (Hemerocallis)				
Bearded iris, late season (Iris hybrids)				
Shasta daisy (Leucanthemum × superbum)				
Leopard's bane (Doronicum orientale)				
Threadleaf coreopsis (Coreopsis verticillata)				
Hardy geranium (Geranium psilostemon 'Bressingham Flair')				

Plant Name	Spr. E	Spr. M	Spr. L	Sum. E	Sum. M	Sum. L	Fall E	Fall M	Fall L	Win. E	Win. M	Win. L
Daylily, early season (*Hemerocallis*)				X								
Japanese iris (*Iris ensata*)				X								
Crimson pincushion (*Knautia macedonica*)				X	X							
Torch lily (*Kniphofia uvaria*)				X	X							
Tree mallow (*Lavatera thuringiaca*)				X	X	X						
Hollyhock mallow (*Malva alcea*)				X	X	X	X					
Golden lace (*Patrinia*)				X								
Chinese rhubarb (*Rheum palmatum*)				X								
Butterfly Blue pincushion flower (*Scabiosa columbaria* 'Butterfly Blue')				X	X							
Creeping verbena (*Verbena* hybrids)				X	X							
Sunny Border Blue speedwell (*Veronica* 'Sunny Border Blue')				X	X							
Feather reed grass (*Calamagrostis × acutiflora* 'Stricta')				X	X	o	o	o				
Tickseed (*Coreopsis grandiflora*)				X	X							
Blanket flower (*Gaillardia × grandiflora*)				X	X							
Frances Williams hosta (*Hosta sieboldiana* 'Frances Williams')				X								
Crocosmia (*Crocosmia* hybrids)					X							
Tufted hair grass (*Deschampsia caespitosa*)				X	X	o						
Globe thistle (*Echinops bannaticus*)				X	X	o						
Fleabane (*Erigeron* hybrids)				X								
Autumn Joy stonecrop (*Sedum/Hylotelephium* 'Autumn Joy'/'Herbstfreude')					X	X	o	o				
Yucca (*Yucca filamentosa*)					X							
Plumbago (*Ceratostigma plumbaginoides*)					X	X						
Queen-of-the-prairie (*Filipendula rubra*)					X	X						
Blue oat grass (*Helictotrichon sempervirens*)					X	X	o					
Purple moor grass (*Molinia caerulea* 'Variegata')					X	X						
Bee balm (*Monarda didyma*)					X	X						
Russian sage (*Perovskia atriplicifolia*)					X	X	o					
Rodgersia (*Rodgersia pinnata*)					X							
Stokes' aster (*Stokesia laevis*)					X	X						
Plume poppy (*Macleaya cordata*)					X	X						
Giant feather grass (*Stipa gigantea*)					X	o	o					
Monch Frikart's aster (*Aster x frikartii* 'Monch')						X						
Chinese astilbe (*Astilbe chinensis*)						X						
Bugbane (*Cimicifuga racemosa*)						X						

Plant Name	Spr. E	Spr. M	Spr. L	Sum. E	Sum. M	Sum. L	Fall E	Fall M	Fall L	Win. E	Win. M	Win. L
Purple coneflower (*Echinacea purpurea*)					X	X	o	o				
Sea holly (*Eryngium amethystinum*)					X	X			o	o		
Perennial sunflower (*Helianthus × multiflorus*)						X	X					
False sunflower (*Heliopsis helianthoides scabra*)					X	X						
Daylily, midseason (*Hemerocallis*)					X							
Rose mallow (*Hibiscus moscheutos*)						X	X					
Blazing star (*Liatris spicata*)					X	X						
Ligularia (*Ligularia*)					X	X						
Cardinal flower (*Lobelia cardinalis*)						X	X					
Gooseneck loosestrife (*Lysimachia clethroides*)					X	o						
Purple loosestrife (*Lythrum salicaria*)					X	X						
Switch grass (*Panicum virgatum*)						X	o	o	o	o		
Perennial fountain grass (*Pennisetum alopecuroides*)						X	o	o				
Garden phlox (*Phlox paniculata*)					X	X						
Pokeweed (*Phytolacca americana*)						X	o	o				
Balloon flower (*Platycodon grandiflorus*)					X	o						
Black-eyed Susan (*Rudbeckia fulgida*)						X	X					
Silver spike grass (*Spodiopogon sibiricus*)						X	X					
Anise hyssop (*Agastache foeniculum*)						X	o	o		o		
Joe-Pye weed (*Eupatorium purpureum*)							X	X				
Helen's flower (*Helenium autumnale*)							X	X				
Maiden grass (*Miscanthus sinensis*)							X		o	o		
Goldenrod (*Solidago* hybrids)						X	X					
Daylily, late season (*Hemerocallis*)							X					
August lily (*Hosta plantaginea*)							X					
Obedient plant (*Physostegia virginiana*)							X	X				
Monkshood (*Aconitum*)								X	X			
Hardy aster (*Aster*)								X	X			
Boltonia (*Boltonia asteroides*)								X	X			
Northern sea oats (*Chasmanthium latifolium*)							X		o	o		
Japanese anemone (*Anemone × hybrida*)								X	X			
Pampas grass (*Cortaderia selloana*)								X	X	o		
Meadow rue (*Thalictrum rochebrunianum*)								X	X			
Toad lily (*Tricyrtis hirta*)								X	X			
Kamchatka bugbane (*Cimicifuga simplex* 'White Pearl')									X			
Hardy chrysanthemum (*Chrysanthemum* hybrids)									X	X		

DESIGNING WITH PERENNIALS

To get the best performance from your garden, look at all aspects of a perennial, not just its pretty colors. While flower colors are important, it's the whole plant—texture, form, structure, and foliage—and where it will be placed that complete the picture.

Keep in mind that the same plant that belongs at the back of a border (a garden that is intended to be viewed only from one side) is the same plant that belongs in the center of a bed (a garden that has no structural background and that is viewed from all sides).

The kind of garden you choose determines its shape and placement on your lot. The purpose of your perennial garden and your expectations define its limits. A cheerful entry garden with a nicely landscaped front path will be visible to friends and strangers alike. A garden for meditating, on the other hand, requires privacy.

Practical considerations may also dictate your garden design. To create views from

In this informal garden, the natural form of the plants is apparent. Many of the plants spill into the pathway.

indoors, determine where you like to sit or stand when looking outside, and plant your vistas accordingly.

FLOWER GARDEN TYPES

A well-designed border works as a cohesive whole rather than a jumble of disconnected parts. Repeated forms and colors and balanced masses bring unity to border designs.

Perennial beds can be geometric or flowing in shape. They're usually meant to be seen close up. Beds lining patios, decks, and house foundations work best when planted for season-long interest.

Island beds add drama to the landscape. Large hostas massed beneath a small tree and seen from afar create a focal point in a large lawn. In urban settings, paving instead of lawn may surround geometrical islands of ornamental grasses, flowers, and shrubs, creating an approachable oasis of natural forms in a sea of gray.

FORMAL GARDENS: Style reflects a garden's mood. Formal gardens are architectural, extending the rooms of the

This formal garden features crisp edges and geometric lines. The plants are neatly clipped.

Stone sculpture is a focal point in this garden. It organizes the field of vision and gives a sense of scale to the plantings.

house they surround. A line drawn from a door to a distant bench or an urn can become the main axis of a formal garden. The simple formal garden has symmetrical balance, with plantings on one side of the main axis mirroring plantings on the other. In a formal garden, the gardener lays controlling hands on nature's exuberance. Pruning transforms shrubs into topiaries or hedges that outline geometrically shaped beds and walkways.

INFORMAL GARDENS: Because they rely on the asymmetrical arrangement of various plant masses, informal gardens are subtler and more difficult to plan. When pruning plants in informal settings, gardeners enhance their natural forms, rather than carving new shapes. Informality lends itself to curving paths and borders that flow with the terrain.

Some homeowners like to combine formal and informal elements in their landscape. Symmetry and geometry work well near the house, which itself is a series of geometrical forms. Farther away from the house, free-flowing lines and looser edges can take the lead. You can combine formal and informal elements by letting plants grow unrestricted within the confines of formal garden beds.

ELEMENTS OF COMPOSITION

The appearance of most gardens changes season by season and year by year. Some changes are haphazard, due to weather, disease, or prolific plants. But other changes are by design. Understanding the elements of composition empowers you to create a garden that's visually pleasing all year long.

When you look at a garden, your mind perceives it as a series of shapes and patterns. An agreeable garden plan has these shapes and patterns arranged with careful attention to the basic design principles of unity, repetition, diversity, balance, and flow.

Repeating colors and shapes unify this planting. The white flowers in the middle and the tassel form of the goldenrod in back provide diversity and prevent the design from being monotonous.

UNITY: For overall unity, plant scale should be consistent with the kind of garden you're creating. Rock gardens, for example, have low-growing plants that enhance rather than mask the beauty of the stones.

REPETITION: Some repetition of forms and colors is useful to unify space, but too much can be dull unless you also consider the principle of diversity.

DIVERSITY: If, for example, dark red is a unifying theme in your garden, you can avoid monotony by introducing spots of contrasting color, by changing plant sizes and textures, and by using diverse flower forms.

BALANCE: This term refers to the visual weight of different plant combinations in the garden. If a design on one side of a central axis reflects the other side, the balance is symmetrical. If both sides look different, but carry similar visual weight, the balance is asymmetrical. Looking at a balanced design in both individual sections of the garden and the overall property gratifies the mind.

FLOW: Smooth transitions from one area of the garden to the next guarantee the flow of the entire design.

A focal point unifies a garden design and organizes the field of vision. A bench at the end of a flower-lined path can focus or complete a design. You can also create a dramatic focal point by manipulating the scale of your garden plants.

STRATEGIES FOR GROUPING PLANTS

Some gardeners find it tempting to use color as the primary organizing principle when planning perennial gardens. Certainly, it is a major consideration (the following chapter covers color in detail). However, grouping plants by other criteria—such as mass, texture, or lines in the garden—is just as worthy of attention, for these subtleties contribute to the design's overall impact.

Mass refers to a plant's visual weight and bulk. Plant size, leaf color, and texture combine to give the effect of mass. For example, a large, dark colored, bold-textured plant has more mass than a small, light green or bluish perennial with finely textured foliage. The mass of a plant is significant not just in relationship to other plant masses in the design, but also to open space.

When thinking about size, it's important to remember that a perennial may not grow to its expected full height the first year or two in a garden. Once established, the plant will not grow any taller but will continue to grow outward. When you plan a garden, keep in mind the perennial's mature spread—the width it can grow before needing to be divided—so that you allow enough space.

This primarily green scene becomes interesting because of the use of textures. The large coarse leaves in front are softened by the fine textured white flowers to the left.

MASS SIMILAR FLOWERS

Planting in drifts—grouping like flowers or planting several plants of one perennial species together—is a way to create mass. Drifts have more power than single blooms. For a natural effect, mass flowers in asymmetrical drifts flowing in and out of other flower groups. Use odd numbers of plants arranged densely in the middle and sparsely near the edges.

ARTFUL USE OF TEXTURE

Skillfully combining textures enhances a garden's charm. Take both the flowers and the foliage into account. For perennials in particular, foliage is on view far longer than the flowers. To achieve a harmonious yet eye-catching look, combine coarse plants with plants of medium texture. At the same time, group medium-textured plants next to those with fine textures.

LINES IN THE GARDEN

Gardens are composed of many lines. Lines describe the edges of things that pull your eye through a scene. The concept is easier to understand if you think of line as an outline. It's not quite the same thing as shape, which is three-dimensional. Instead, it's the outline of a shape—the edge of the bed, the silhouette of plants and other items in and around a garden.

HORIZONTAL LINES: Horizontal lines run parallel to the ground. They can be above the ground, such as a broad, dense tree canopy or the top of an enclosed arbor, or on the ground. On the ground, garden pathways are the most obvious example of horizontal lines.

Bed lines are an important type of horizontal line. These are the lines you create when shaping planting areas, formed by the separation between lawn and planting area or between paving and planting. They may be formed of stone, brick, plastic, or metal edging, or a simple line cut with a shovel. Regardless of the size of the bed, the flow of its line has an effect on the design of the space.

CURVING LINES: Horizontal lines may be curvilinear—smooth and sinuous with many curves. Use these lines when you want to give the perennial garden a serene look. Sweeping bed lines and meandering paths are characteristic of gardens featuring curvilinear lines.

STRAIGHT LINES: Straight lines with sharp angles and corners form rectilinear patterns. These kinds of lines suggest activity. They are contemporary and formal in feel and speed your eye through the landscape. Straight lines connected to symmetrical curves are called arc-and-tangent.

VERTICAL LINES: Vertical lines keep a garden from becoming boring. As accents, they create a rhythm, moving the eye up and down and through the plants in the garden.

The most apparent vertical lines in a landscape are vines and tree trunks. Other vertical lines are formed by posts, arbors, fences, or walls.

Though they run up and down, vertical lines don't have to be perfectly straight. They may slant or ramble upward, as with a climbing vine. Nor do they have to be tall. A spiky clump of iris foliage contrasts well with flat, horizontal surfaces of a pond, a bed of low-growing trailing ground cover, or paving. For the most punch, set groups of plants or other items with vertical lines in clusters.

The design above makes good use of horizontal and vertical lines. Left: The yellow flowers are a strong vertical line in the garden. Below: The path and the lawn are examples of lines on the ground plane.

PLANTING IN LAYERS TO DEFINE THE GARDEN

Perennials are most often grown with plants of many kinds, usually arranged in first, second, and third tiers. Formal or naturalistic, layers give the garden a relaxed, abundant look, as exemplified by a meadow or woodland.

The first tier serves as the carpet, where low-growing plants cover the ground and sprawlers and lace layers of the bed together. The middle layer of intermediate size plants provide a ladder between the front- and back-tier layers. This middle layer is like the forest understory, knit from compact shrubs and perennials. The third tier creates a canopy, tree-line, or skyline of the tallest plants. It often includes evergreen trees and shrubs that enclose the space like a hedge, rise to the high point in the center of an island, or form a backdrop in the border.

In a large garden, each layer can be full-size. In a smaller garden, you must scale them down; use shrubs to play the role of trees, and narrow, space-saving plants to substitute for plumper ones.

Layers define this planting. The third tier plant to the right of the bench anchors the scene, while the front tier softens the transition between bed and path.

START WITH THE THIRD TIER

This layer establishes the garden line and can create a powerful silhouette, so it's the place to begin.

Skyline plantings integrate the garden with surrounding trees or buildings. They enclose the garden and bring it into balance within the scale of its surroundings. Often called "the bones of a garden," well-chosen backdrop plantings not only provide a supportive framework, they can take a leading role with floral fireworks all their own.

Big plants create a visual stop, framing bed or border by blocking out distractions such as cars and road signs. Traditional garden design relies on shrubs and trees for the backdrop, but many oversize perennials also work well.

Taller plants can occasionally be placed in front of shorter ones. This technique gives the beds a surprisingly different appearance when approached from different angles. It also creates a living veil and adds an intriguing sense of mystery as plants are glimpsed through the structure of another.

In island beds of mixed plantings, the tallest plants need to be toward the center where they don't obscure the shorter plants.

In smaller spaces, a 4-foot wall of false

Three distinct layers: the backbone third tier rises above the house. The middle layer connects the front and back tiers. The first tier carpets the ground.

indigo will provide a natural screen, with dark blue, pealike flowers in early summer. Airy masses of Brazilian verbena weave into a fine scrim, veiling everything that lies behind it in a shimmering haze of purple-blue clusters.

In large yards, tall ornamental grasses—with their bursts of color, great stature, and changing seasonal interests—are natural candidates to provide screening, privacy, and a backdrop for flower beds. Evergreen pampas grass spreads great silken plumes. Some late-blooming goldenrods raise their heads high, while Joe-Pye weed looms taller still, producing a great mist of lavender-purple inflorescence. Giant coneflower makes a majestic backdrop, rising treelike to enclose the yard or garden.

Many backdrop perennials spend spring and summer climbing skyward, reserving their bloom for late summer or autumn. These plants offer flowers or foliage in the fall, when this framework takes the stage itself.

The perennials you choose for the third tier set the tone for the garden, whether casual or formal. Ruffled, irregular layers have an informal effect. A straight line of any single plant, especially one with an architectural shape, suggests a crisp, clean edge. Formal gardens usually are geometrical and can be framed with third-tier plants whose lines are echoed by others in the middle and first tiers.

Whatever the style of your garden, be aware of scale. Overly large plants can dwarf plants in other tiers. The progression of perennials should be gradual.

Maiden grass and Joe-Pye weed are strong backbone plants. The Russian sage, coneflower and shasta daisy could be backbone plants or middle tier plants depending on the scale of the garden.

PLANTING IN LAYERS TO DEFINE THE GARDEN
continued

FIRST AND SECOND TIERS

ECCENTRIC AND ARCHITECTURAL

Chinese rhubarb
Gunnera
Mullein
Purple coneflower
Sea holly

First- and second-layer plants should merge with third-tier plantings, easing the eye groundward. Within a garden, additional layers create an inner topography that plays up shape and texture. Relaxed interior arrangements create a fascinating flow of form as well as color.

Second-tier plantings are an intermediate layer between the first tier and the back border, creating a transition between the backdrop and the border's edge. In larger gardens, there may be two or three intermediate levels. In smaller beds, one layer will suffice.

For an informal setting, you can plant a multiplicity of intermediate layers. You won't need to rank plants so strictly by their size. In formal plantings, the intermediate layer should be uniform. Choose plants of consistent height and similar shape and arrange them in patterns to show the qualities that catch your eye.

Front and mid-border plants often display a charming informality. Edge the front of a bed or border using low-growing plants with foliage texture and color that contrast with the lawn or pathway. Lamb's-ear, with its silver-furred leaves, is a favorite edger. Coral bells is another exquisite choice. First-tier edging plants can form a continuous strip along the garden's front border for a formal effect; however, a combination of low-growing plants is also pleasing. Alternate clusters of different types of plants to create a subtle edge, but one that clearly states: The garden begins here.

THE POWER OF SHAPE

As you think about overall garden design—the interplay between tiers—contrasting shapes have a role. In fact, many garden designers concentrate more on the natural shape of their perennials than on any other feature, even color.

You can get the shape you want, of course, by shearing, but that's repetitive work and stresses the plants. It's far easier to start with shapes bestowed by nature instead of those imposed by human hands.

This garden has three distinct layers, but rather than lining up from front to back, they are mixed together. This gives the garden an added sense of depth and ensures an interesting view.

Spiky and turret-shaped plants punctuate this sloped planting. Mounds and sprawlers balance the bed.

FAN AND FOUNTAIN

Daylily
Fountain grass
Giant feather
    grass
New Zealand
    flax
Yellow flag
Yucca

MOUNDERS AND SPRAWLERS

Baby's breath
Canterbury bells
Catmint
Creeping phlox
Cushion spurge
Wormwood

Though perennials grow in a myriad of forms, it's easy to remember some basic shapes. Plants described as architectural have a framework with definitive lines. Eccentric plants also have a strong framework but grow more freely.

Plants that resemble fans and fountains are similar to each other. However, the foliage of fan-shaped plants tends to be flat whereas that of fountain plants shoots out in different directions.

Turrets, which are reminiscent of castle towers, and slender spikes add vertical interest to the garden by reaching upwards. Mounders, on the other hand, stay low. Sprawlers, which are looser, seem to hug the ground.

There are perennial shapes that play especially well against one another. Fans and fountains, mounds and sprawlers, sturdy towers and slim turrets—all can be endlessly recombined into exciting partnerships.

Pair a fan-shaped iris with foamy baby's breath. Silky Mexican feather grass softens look and line, and structural stonecrop adds strength. Striking plants like rodgersia 'Superba' require equal partners to keep them balanced.

Large-scale plants with different textures and colors—for instance, feathery ferns and ligularia—work well. So will large masses of smaller plants, such as hardy geraniums or astilbes.

Eccentric spires of silvery mullein become magnificent when placed against large and simple maiden grass.

Flower shapes and sizes also contribute to your garden's design statement. Plants may bear multiple or single blooms that may be flat, round, clustered, bell- or cuplike, tiny or large. Foliage is just as diverse.

The beauty of designing with perennials is the freedom to experiment, whether you're seeking serenity in the repetition of similar shapes or excitement in a variety of combinations. Be patient and you will discover just the right combination of design elements that make a garden uniquely yours.

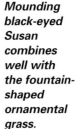

Mounding black-eyed Susan combines well with the fountain-shaped ornamental grass.

SPIKE AND TURRET

Blazing star
Bugbane
Delphinium
Foxglove
Mullein
Torch lily

USING EXTRA-LARGE PERENNIALS

Modern life is full of straight lines and rigid routines, but a garden in which plants dominate and nature rules with its own wild ways is a constant refreshment to the spirit. More and more designers are stressing plant-driven rather than florally driven gardenscapes.

TRY BIG, BOLD PLANTS

In these new style gardens, boldly shaped, oversize plants often play the space-defining role traditionally assigned to hardscaping (paving, walls, trellises, and arbors). But even in the smaller garden, large plants have their place, lending a surprising sense of the dramatic.

In warm climates where a wide range of true tropical plants flourish, it's easy to give any garden a lush, jungle-like appearance. No substitutes are needed; warm climates support the real thing. Gunnera and New Zealand flax grow to amazing proportions where heat and moisture are ample. Drier hot climates nourish a wide range of astonishing desert plants, including dozens of spurges as well as broad-bladed grasses and swirling, sword-leaved yuccas.

Mild-winter areas allow hardy tropicals and large-leaved foliage plants that can handle moderate frost to create the impression of jungle abundance. In recent years, plant explorers have increased our palette with dozens of more cold-hardy perennial forms of former tropical house plants. Many of these new introductions are finding their way into "tropicalismo gardens," which celebrate joyful gigantism. Characterized by a sense of exuberance, this style features sculptural character with spunky style. Ambitious designers mingle large-scale native plants from their own regions with allies and exotics from all over the world, creating a world-mix of plants that thrive together in the garden.

Plants of prehistoric dimension add a tropical appearance to the landscape. Some suggestions: ostrich fern (top) thrives in moist shade in a woodland garden, gunnera (center) produces massive leaves, and Chinese rhubarb (bottom) prefers to grow in a sheltered border.

Cold-winter gardeners can create a surprisingly convincing jungle garden by selecting the largest possible members of common perennial families. An enormous clump of zebra grass (above) boasts splendidly striped foliage.

Long-stalked and bronze-tinged rodgersia (above right) is handsome, but one or two plants are all that is required.

Some hostas reach remarkable proportions, for example, 'Blue Mammoth', Sum and Substance, and this 'August Moon'.

BIG, BOLD & BEAUTIFUL

Cardinal flower
Chinese rhubarb
Goatsbeard
Gunnera
Certain hostas
Joe-Pye weed
Ostrich fern
Pampas grass
Plume poppy
Pokeweed
Rodgersia
Rose mallow
Tatarian aster
Zebra grass

In the home landscape, big, bold exotic plants in pots and oversized ferns worthy of a prehistoric jungle—combined with cottage garden favorites like delphiniums—create a decidedly tropical feel.

PERENNIALS FROM SMALL TO LARGE

Use this chart to help you combine perennials according to size and form. So that you can quickly find a perennial of the size you need at a glance, they are organized in order of height from short to tall. Each perennial listed is accompanied by a sketch of its typical form, approximately to scale. Remember that this chart is a rough guide; the size given and the form shown can vary according to the cultivar selected, as well as region, weather, and horticultural practice.

Creeping phlox (*Phlox subulata*) 3–6"

Kamtschatka stonecrop (*Sedum kamtschaticum*) 4–9"

Dwarf crested iris (*Iris cristata*) 6"

English primrose (*Primula vulgaris*) 6–9"

Allegheny foam flower (*Tiarella cordifolia*) 6–12"

Sweet violet (*Viola odorata*) 8"

Plumbago (*Ceratostigma plumbaginoides*) 8–12"

Barrenwort (*Epimedium × rubrum*) 8–12"

Fringed bleeding heart (*Dicentra eximia*) 9–18"

Basket-of-gold (*Aurinia saxatilis*) 12"

Yellow corydalis (*Corydalis lutea*) 12"

Japanese painted fern (*Athyrium nipponicum* 'Pictum') 12"

Bergenia (*Bergenia cordifolia*) 12"

Pink (*Dianthus*) 12"

Twinspur (*Diascia barberae*) 12"

Lungwort (*Pulmonaria saccharata*) 12"

'Georgia Blue' speedwell (*Veronica peduncularis* 'Georgia Blue') 12"

Dwarf blue fescue (*Festuca glauca*) 12"

Lamb's-ears (*Stachys byzantina*) 12"

Vial's primrose (*Primula vialii*) 12–15"

Columbine (*Aquilegia*) 1–2'

Marsh marigold (*Caltha palustris*) 12–18"

Fleabane (*Erigeron* hybrids) 1–2'

Lenten rose (*Helleborus orientalis*) 12–18"

Patrinia (*Patrinia scabiosifolia*) 12–18"

Japanese blood grass (*Imperata cylindrica* 'Red Baron') 12–18"

Variegated Japanese sedge (*Carex morrowii* 'Variegata') 12–18"

Hardy geranium (*Geranium*) 1–2'

Maidenhair fern (*Adiantum pedatum*) 12–20"

Golden grass (*Hakonechloa macra* 'Aureola') 1–2'

Creeping verbena (*Verbena* hybrids) 12–18"

Spiked speedwell (*Veronica spicata*) 10–36"

Coral bells (*Heuchera* hybrids) 1-2'

Stokes' aster (*Stokesia laevis*) 1–2'

Lady's mantle (*Alchemilla mollis*) 18"

Threadleaf coreopsis (*Coreopsis verticillata*) 18"

Leopard's bane (*Doronicum orientale*) 18–24"

Geum (*Geum*) 18"

Catmint (*Nepeta × faassenii*) 18–24"

Pincushion flower (*Scabiosa caucasica*) 18–24"

Hardy chrysanthemum (*Chrysanthemum/Dendranthema* hybrids) 1–3'

White sage (*Artemisia ludoviciana*) 2'

Sea holly (*Eryngium amethystinum*) 2'

Crimson pincushion (*Knautia macedonica*) 2'

Shasta daisy (*Leucanthemum × superbum*) 2'

Christmas fern (*Polystichum acrostichoides*) 2'

Japanese primrose (*Primula japonica*) 2'

Stonecrop (*Sedum spectabile*) 2'

Blanket flower (*Gaillardia × grandiflora*) 2–3'

Beard-tongue (*Penstemon*) 2–3'

Fern-leaf yarrow (*Achillea filipendulina*) 2–3'

Masterwort (*Astrantia major*) 2–3'

Gooseneck loosestrife (*Lysimachia clethroides*) 2–3'

Hybrid sage (*Salvia × sylvestris*) 2–3'

Toad lily (*Tricyrtis hirta*) 2–3'

Peach-leaf bellflower (*Campanula persicifolia*) 2–3'

Red valerian (*Centranthus ruber*) 2–3'

Crocosmia (*Crocosmia* hybrids) 2–3'

Hay-scented fern (*Dennstaedtia punctilobula*) 2–3'

Tufted hair grass (*Deschampsia caespitosa*) 2–3'

Bleeding heart (*Dicentra spectabilis*) 2–3'

Baby's breath (*Gypsophila paniculata*) 2–3'

Daylily (*Hemerocallis*) 1–3'

Bee balm (*Monarda didyma*) 2–3'

Japanese iris (*Iris ensata*) 2–3'

Balloon flower (*Platycodon grandiflorus*) 2–3'

Variegated Solomon's seal (*Polygonatum odoratum* 'Variegatum') 2–3'

Black-eyed Susan (*Rudbeckia fulgida*) 2–3'

Astilbe (*Astilbe × arendsii*) 2–4'

Hardy aster (*Aster*) 2–4'

Northern sea oats (*Chasmanthium latifolium*) 30"

Male wood fern (*Dryopteris filix-mas*) 2–4'

Purple coneflower (*Echinacea purpurea*) 2–4'

Bearded iris (*Iris* hybrids) 2–4'

Siberian iris (*Iris siberica*) 2–4'

Purple moor grass (*Molinia caerulea* 'Variegata') 2–4'

Oriental poppy (*Papaver orientale*) 2–4'

Garden phlox (*Phlox paniculata*) 2–4'

Obedient plant (*Physostegia virginiana*) 2–4'

Goldenrod (*Solidago* hybrids) 2–4'

Foxglove (*Digitalis purpurea*) 2–5'

Meadow rue (*Thalictrum*) 2–6'

Anise hyssop (*Agastache foeniculum*) 3'

Blue star (*Amsonia tabernaemontana*) 3'

Butterfly weed (*Asclepias tuberosa*) 3'

Blue oat grass (*Helictotrichon sempervirens*) 3'

Frances Williams hosta (*Hosta sieboldiana* 'Frances Williams') 3'

Blazing star (*Liatris spicata*) 3'

Lupine (*Lupinus* Russell hybrids) 3'

Cinnamon fern (*Osmunda cinnamonea*) 3'

Peony (*Paeonia* hybrids) 3'

Mullein (*Verbascum chaixii*) 3'

Japanese anemone (*Anemone × hybrida*) 2–4'

False indigo (*Baptisia australis*) 3–4'

Globe thistle (*Echinops bannaticus*) 3–4'

False sunflower (*Heliopsis helianthoides scabra*) 3–4'

Ligularia (*Ligularia*) 3–4'

Cardinal flower (*Lobelia cardinalis*) 3–4'

Hollyhock mallow (*Malva alcea*) 3–4'

Perennial fountain grass (*Pennisetum alopecuroides*) 3–4'

Russian sage (*Perovskia atriplicifolia*) 3–4'

Rodgersia (*Rodgersia pinnata*) 3–4'

Helen's flower (*Helenium autumnale*) 3–5'

Purple loosestrife (*Lythrum salicaria*) 3–5'

Cushion spurge (*Euphorbia polychroma*) 3–5'

Monkshood (*Aconitum*) 3–6'

Torch lily (*Kniphofia uvaria*) 4'

Ostrich fern (*Matteuccia struthiopteris*) 4'

Feather reed grass (*Calamagrostis × acutiflora* 'Stricta') 4–5'

Tree mallow (*Lavatera thuringiaca*) 4–5'

Silver spike grass (*Spodiopogon sibiricus*) 4–5'

Perennial sunflower (*Helianthus × multiflorus*) 4–6'

Goatsbeard (*Aruncus dioicus*) 4–6'

Bugbane (*Cimicifuga*) 4–6'

Delphinium (*Delphinium elatum*) 4–6'

Pokeweed (*Phytolacca americana*) 4–6'

Joe-Pye weed (*Eupatorium purpureum*) 4–7'

Hollyhock (*Alcea rosea*) 4–8'

Boltonia (*Boltonia asteroides*) 5'

Rose mallow (*Hibiscus moscheutos*) 5'

Switch grass (*Panicum virgatum*) 5'

Giant feather grass (*Stipa gigantea*) 5'

Pampas grass (*Cortaderia selloana*) 5–12'

Yucca (*Yucca filamentosa*) 2–12'

Queen-of-the-prairie (*Filipendula rubra*) 6–8'

Gunnera (*Gunnera manicata*) 6–10'

Chinese rhubarb (*Rheum palmatum*) 6–10'

Plume poppy (*Macleaya cordata*) 8'

Maiden grass (*Miscanthus sinensis*) 8'

New Zealand flax (*Phormium tenax*) 8–10'

PLANTING PLAN FOR AN INFORMAL GARDEN

This garden of perennials contains some all-time favorites as well as a few less widely known whose virtues should be better appreciated. It's an informal garden. Design details include a pleasing blend of shapes, mass, color, and height. Beds or borders should have three distinct layers: a first tier, second or middle tier, and a strong, tall third tier to anchor the bed.

The display will be summer-long, starting in late spring with Siberian iris and concluding in fall with Frikart's aster, showy sedum, sundrops, and perhaps a second flowering of beard-tongue and daylilies.

Dominating the scene in the third tier are colewort, with airy 8-foot flower panicles, and shrubby false indigo. Around them are plants that offer an assortment of leaf shapes, sizes, and textures, and flowers in colors from cool to warm, pale to bright. Good, well-drained soil, sun for most of the day, and routine watering will satisfy this set of plants.

The main plant list contains perennials that will succeed in Zones 5 through 9, given routine watering. Gardeners in dry-summer Zone 10 should plant the alternative selections; gardeners in dry-summer Zone 9 may choose from either list.

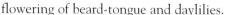

MAINTENANCE DETAILS

Plan on cleaning up the dead foliage and spent flowering stems in this garden once a year. In warmer zones, complete the cleanup in late fall or winter. Where freezing winters are the rule, you can delay the work until early spring, but fall is preferable. A few of the perennials will need further trimming. Where catmint foliage remains alive over winter, cut back the stems by about half before spring growth starts so that plants remain compact.

Among the alternative selections, cut back the artemisia by half, and lightly head back the ground morning glory and fleabane as needed to keep the plants from becoming

Variegated maiden grass (here with Shasta daisy) is another good substitute for colewort. It matches colewort in size and form.

PLANTING PLAN

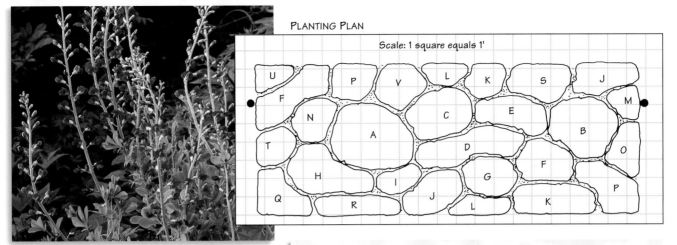

Scale: 1 square equals 1'

Blue false indigo is part of the summer-long display in this informal garden design.

rangy. Apply an all-purpose fertilizer just as growth begins each year.

How often you need to dig up and divide the perennials in this garden depends on the particular perennial, the culture it receives, and your climate (plants in the warmer zones typically need more frequent dividing). Crowded clumps and declining performance indicate that dividing is needed.

In two or three years, you may need to replace the mallow and beard-tongue, which are on the main plant list. Every three or four years, you may need to divide and replant the yarrows, shasta daisy, sage, threadleaf coreopsis, coral bells, Frikart's aster, showy sedum, and sundrops.

The daylilies and Siberian iris can go longer without division. The catmint and cranesbill are less predictable; whenever their performance declines, divide and replant them, or start new plants. Consider as permanent plants: colewort, false indigo, baby's breath, balloon flower, and lady's mantle.

Of the alternative selections, you may need to replace the artemisia and toadflax every four or five years (you can start new plants from cuttings). Dig, divide, and replant the dahlias and the vervain about every three years to keep them from overrunning their neighbors. Divide or replace the ground morning glory and fleabane only when reduced vigor indicates the need. The gaura and lily-of-the-Nile can remain undisturbed.

PLANT LIST

A 1 Colewort (*Crambe cordifolia*)
B 1 Blue false indigo (*Baptisia australis*)
C 1 Baby's breath (*Gypsophila paniculata* 'Bristol Fairy')
D 5 Fern-leaf yarrow (*Achillea filipendulina* 'Coronation Gold')
E 7 Hollyhock mallow (*Malva alcea*)
F 12 Shasta daisy (*Leucanthemum* × *superbum*)
G 1 Balloon flower (*Platycodon grandiflorus*)
H 9 Sage (*Salvia* × *superba*)
I 2 Siberian iris (*Iris siberica* 'Ego')
J 4 Cranesbill (*Geranium endressii* 'Wargrave Pink')
K 5 Showy sedum (*Sedum spathulifolium*)
L 5 Daylily (*Hemerocallis* 'Stella de Oro')
M 2 Daylily (*Hemerocallis* 'Bertie Ferris' or other orange-apricot miniature cultivar)
N 2 Daylily (*Hemerocallis*, tall light yellow selection)
O 2 Catmint (*Nepeta* × *faassenii*)
P 3 Threadleaf coreopsis (*Coreopsis verticillata* 'Moonbeam')
Q 3 Lady's mantle (*Alchemilla mollis*)
R 4 Coral bells (*Heuchera sanguinea*)
S 5 Yarrow (*Achillea* 'Moonshine')
T 3 Beard-tongue (*Penstemon barbatus* 'Prairie Fire')
U 1 Sundrops (*Oenothera fruticosa*)
V 2 Frikart's aster (*Aster frikartii*)

ALTERNATIVE SELECTIONS
A 3 Dahlia, bush type, yellow, bronze, or peach selection
C 1 Artemisia (*Artemisia* 'Powis Castle')
E 3 White gaura (*Gaura lindheimeri*)
G 2 Vervain (*Verbena rigida*)
I 3 Toadflax (*Linaria maroccana*)
J 4 Fleabane (*Erigeron karvinskianus*)
N 2 Lily-of-the-Nile (*Agapanthus orientalis*)
Q 2 Ground morning glory (*Convolvulus mauritanicus*)

Note: The letters match the clump labels on the plan. The numbers represent how many of each plant are needed. If a clump label repeats, divide the plants equally among clumps.

VARIATIONS

This bed was designed to be viewed from all sides. For a narrower planting, cut the depth from 8 feet to 6 feet. Draw a line connecting the dots on the ends of the plan, then omit plants in the smaller portion. This eliminates the sundrops (U), Frikart's aster (V), yarrow (S), daylily (M), four shasta daisies (F) in one plant group, and one plant group each of threadleaf coreopsis (P), 'Stella de Oro' daylily (L), showy sedum (K), and cranesbill (J).

COLOR
IN THE GARDEN

Deep green leaves and a splash of purple keep these yellow and white beds interesting.

The yellow foliage and purple flowers contrast with harmonious results.

Flower and foliage color bring the garden to life, turning the daily greenery of our gardens into a full-color harmony.

Color stimulates our senses, awakens our emotions, and surrounds us with beauty. Color work is an art, not a science, and its vocabulary is simple:

■ A hue is a pure color such as orange or blue. The more saturated it is, the more intense it will appear against a green backdrop. Less saturated colors, such as pastels, recede.

■ A tone is either a shade (darkened) or a tint (lightened) of a pure color. Clean pastel pink, for example, is light and bright; murky red is heavy and dark.

Color charts and wheels can help us understand basic color compatibilities, but there are no hard and fast rules for coloring gardens because tastes are so personal. Some people like things subdued; others delight in the brazen and enjoy a brilliant clash of hues. The garden color that's right for you should gladden your spirit and suit your sensibilities.

Tension exists between
these shades of yellow,
orange, red, and blue. The
combination evokes the
colors of a sunset.

**Yellow and pink
play important
roles in this
composition.
The yellow
dominates
because of its
position in the
foreground
and its
electrifying hue.**

LIGHT AND COLOR

When painting your garden with color,
use your intuition fortified with a few
techniques gleaned from artists. Painters
and photographers know that light has
everything to do with how people perceive
color. All day long and into the night,
the tints and shades of every flower and leaf
shift with the sun, from the slanted light of
morning to the floodlight of noon and the
backlight of evening.

Position also matters; when direct light
strikes an entire plant or a row of plants set
on a bank, it may reveal subtones in the
foliage—often purple or copper or burgundy—
that may remain hidden in massed plantings.
Indirect or filtered light (what gardeners call
high, dappled, or light shade) brings out depths
in soft colors that stronger light may bleach.

is bronze or burgundy, and cooler
and darker when set amid pale blue
forget-me-nots.

Seasonal color alters the garden
constantly, from spring's pastels to summer's
rainbow, autumn's sunset tints, and winter's
green-gray-brown. Develop color themes for
each area in the garden or the garden as a
whole and repeat those same colors through
the seasons.

If you've chosen blue as your color theme,
keep other colors secondary to it. Planting
yellow summer bloomers will change the
dominant color to yellow, and blue will
become secondary. Consult the color chart
(pages 52 and 53) to pick your color themes,
allowing different colors to lead from area to
area or season to season, supported by a
family of secondary colors.

COMPANION PLANTS: COLOR PARTNERS OR COMPETITORS?

Companion plants can be color partners
or competitors, supportive or challenging.
Partners chosen for color balance will create
harmonies. Competitors will create
excitement and drama.

For example, mix dark orange with purple
and deep, singing red and you'll evoke a
sunset. Sherbet orange blended with chalky
yellows and white looks light and cool, fresh
and sparkling.

Clean orange and sea blue are midweight
colors that balance each other, while the
same orange matched with a red of similar
value will edge toward a flamboyant clash
(often quite pleasurably). The same clear red
looks hotter and brighter against foliage that

**Scarlet and
orange-yellow
are harmonious
partners of
equal weight.**

All of the elements in a woodland scene (above left) contribute to the white theme, including the trunks of the birch trees. Sunlight changes the effect of whites (above right), making them appear even whiter.

COOL COLORS:
WHITES & PASTELS

Trendsetting English garden designer Gertrude Jekyll popularized color-theme gardens in the late 19th century. She was the first to suggest grouping plants that bloom at the same time and insisted that no color can be fully appreciated on its own.

Color values are relative, she explained, so any color comes into its own only in relationship to others. A red-themed garden, for instance, would include red's complement, green (its opposite on the color wheel). To continue the theme through the seasons, flowers with red buds, berries, or red-veined petals and plants that offer new red growth or red fall color would also find a place. A white garden could contain plants with white or near-white flowers or silvery leaves or white-variegated foliage.

WORKING WITH WHITE

White as a theme can seem difficult to work with, but it is especially valuable for those who enjoy their gardens in the evenings when dying light makes white blossoms glow. It is challenging to match the whites of various flowers, and some combinations make off-whites look dingy. Temper the brightness of white flowers with textured foliage plants. Be cautious with pure white; it can be glaring and harsh unless mixed with lustrous greens.

Jekyll preferred off-whites—shades she called skim milk, eggshell, or bone, and yellowed tints like butter and cream. Blended with plenty of gray, sage, and olive foliage, these colors weave a sumptuous tapestry.

Jekyll also thought sticking too closely to a theme was silly. If off-whites look best, or pale blue, pastel peach, or shell pink emphasize the cool quality of white, use them! Don't sacrifice effect for strict consistency.

COOL IT DOWN WITH BLUE

Colors on the blue side of the spectrum are considered cool, while those on the red side are hot. A palette of soft

Pastel pink is a cool companion for white (far left). Blue and pink are more cool companions to white (left).

A blue shale path echoes blue bellflowers in this cool-themed garden with yellow yarrow and marguerite and apricot mullein (left).

The many shades of white include phlox (above right) and Lenten rose (right).

blues, yellows, and greens yields a cool, refreshing appearance. Pastel blues and yellows look light and luminous, particularly in the evening. Silvery or blue-gray foliage will emphasize their shimmer, and chartreuse or lime greens will invigorate both blues and purples. Chilly tints of peach with icy apricot, salmon, and chalky yellows with gray and blue foliage make a frosty color scheme.

Matte, muted purple foliage like that of common sage, whose fuzzy texture turns it pewterlike, is likewise cooling. Almost any pastel tint fits comfortably into cool combinations, whereas pastel shades (grayed or French pastels) work best in warmer schemes.

The soft shade of this yellow 'Terracotta' yarrow works well with cool and warm colors. It's a good blender or transition color.

Foliage can be a part of the cool color scheme, too, as blue-leafed cardoon (Cynara cardunculus) demonstrates.

WARM COLORS:
REDS & ORANGES

This design features partners of equal weight; no color dominates.

Cheerful, joyous, ebullient or gaudy, hot colors create instant excitement. Reds, purples, and orange look brash, brazen or brilliant, depending on how they are grouped. Any combination is bound to be memorable, but unless you are aiming for unrestrained riot, be deliberate.

Successful hot combinations have partners of equal weight and value, and significant

Heat up the garden with yellow torch lily (top), orange butterfly weed (above), and red chrysanthemum (bottom).

In planting of monochromatic red, the plants are not the same shade, but are equal in weight.

Orange and blue paired together create tension, which adds excitement and drama.

The darker purple lupines seem to fade into the background when combined with the vibrant pink flowers.

Repeated vignettes carry a color theme throughout the perennial border. The pink in the foreground is repeated in the back; clumps of yellow tie everything together.

assistance from surrounding foliage. Screaming orange demands the support of a dazzling red; soft pink would look insignificant next to it. When the main colors are both saturated, such as plum purple and apple red, dark green foliage will anchor them.

Rich, deep reds and purples can disappear into the background. Lighter reds mixed with shocking pinks and purples make more murky colors sing, bringing them to the forefront, especially with a lift of chartreuse foliage. Darker oranges and smudgy reds become volcanic when partnered with silver, gray, or blue-green foliage. Purple and blue leaves lend weight and depth to bright oranges and fresh greens, high colors that seem to "float" on their own.

DEVELOPING A THEME

In choosing the palette for your garden, consider the overall effect you want to achieve. Solid sheets of unbroken color work well in larger landscapes but seem relentless in smaller gardens, especially when many of the plants are long bloomers.

It's most effective to repeat colorful vignettes—small groups of related-color plants—throughout the garden. Each vignette should have plants for each season—spring, summer, autumn, and even winter. In formal settings, space these color repetitions precisely. Cottage or naturalistic gardens, however, call for informality. Avoid a boring sameness; vary form, height, mass, and texture within each color grouping.

This garden shows off the potential of colorful foliage. Two types of variegated hostas, yellow golden grass, blue hostas, and solid green plants combine well to create a colorful garden.

ADD FOLIAGE COLORS TO THE PALETTE

People often begin gardening because they fall for the flowers. But over time, their appreciation of foliage increases as well.

Green is the most common color in the plant world—the basic black of gardening—and green is often not considered when choosing plants. However, the thousands of shades of green can give the garden body and depth and can be used in the palette just like other colors.

COUNTLESS SHADES OF GREEN

There are hundreds of alternatives to basic green foliage. Strikingly beautiful gardens can be made by combining green foliage with plants that have blue and gold, silver and bronze, or red and purple leaves. Harmonious or contrasting foliage can be combined even more readily than flowers, and it persists far longer. Luminous or softly gilded foliage will brighten a shady corner. Stronger sun brings out hidden undertones in deep-colored foliage and strengthens the flush of fall. Leaves present a remarkable range of shapes and sizes as well as texture and finish.

Perennial foliage offers the opportunity to develop stunning seasonal effects, starting with earliest spring. Peonies produce coppery

Golden creeping Jenny provides an electrifying foil for clumps of burgundy-leaved coral bells, spikes of bulb foliage, and a host of textures.

red new leaves atop black or burgundy stems. Certain hardy geraniums have hot red new leaves, while many spurges are sizzling chartreuse, glowing orange, or frosty purple. In fall, the clear gold of balloon flower foliage, the shocking pink of beard-tongue, and the ember red of plumbago all contribute to the garden's gaiety.

USING VARIEGATION

Variegated foliage lightens the garden tapestry, and strikingly variegated shade plants can illuminate dark spaces.

Choose simple patterns—perhaps an edging of cream or pink or yellow—and large, restful leaves. Powerfully patterned plants can lend focus to a jumble and can elevate a dull planting to high art. But they may also create visual chaos if used too much. If your vignettes have become overly variegated, add plain plants with large, simple leaves.

Variegated leaves tend to scorch in full sun, yet the plants need adequate light to develop their best coloration. The answer is to plant them where they receive indirect, filtered, or diffused light. Morning sun rarely burns foliage, and where high shade is scarce, planting on the north side of tall companions will create pockets of afternoon shade.

The contrast of black mondo grass and silvery white lamb's-ears adds punch to the garden.

Japanese blood grass is as colorful as any flower but has longer-lasting impact. Here, it is combined with 'Rheingold' arborvitae, a shrub, with high-voltage results.

TOP 10 VARIEGATED PERENNIALS

'Benediction' Bethlehem sage
'Hadspen Cream' brunnera
'Ruby Veil' coral bells
'Herman's Pride' dead nettle
'Great Expectations' hosta
Japanese painted fern
'Morning Light' maiden grass
Variegated Solomon seal
Variegated yellow flag iris
'Golden Sword' yucca

Look closely at any old master portrait, like The Clown with the Lute *by Frans Hals, and you'll see many surprising tints.*

subject's eyes, around the mouth, there are smeary greens and pallid grays that mingle with orange or yellow. Up close, the blending colors are not pleasing, but seen as a whole, the composition resolves these smears and bits and globs into an image of potent beauty. Blending colors in the garden allows you to merge stronger colors. With careful placement of plants in blending colors, gardeners can achieve the subtle yet striking results found in portraits of the Old Masters.

WORKING WITH STRONG COLORS

Blending colors come in two large groups that can be loosely described as pale or deep. Use them to merge stronger colors; their blending tones make gentle transitions from one flower or foliage color to the next.

Pale tints lend brilliance and sparkle to deep-toned compositions. Tints of milk, cream, butter, and bone will brighten anything from midnight blue and purple to searing reds and oranges, as well as dainty pastel combinations. In stronger-colored compositions, bright pastels—peach and salmon, canary and chalk yellow, sand and chamois, buff and biscuit—will lighten the heaviness of hot or sullen colors.

Deep shades add depth to colorful but unsaturated combinations that "float" or that seem unpleasantly brash. Murky mixers such as mahogany and port, or tobacco and cordovan are retreating colors, yet these shades add weight to bright combinations. Smudgy shades can intensify contrast, making vivid colors more brilliant and lifting soft ones

MASTERFULLY BLEND COLORS

Bright pastel pinks are blending colors to the reds (below). Deep purple grounds the other colors (center). Variegated foliage is a highlight (right).

When shopping for plants, people often gravitate toward those with clear, bright colors. However, there are myriad subtle, in-between tones that lend a painterly quality to color work.

For example, close inspection of *The Clown with the Lute* portrait (above) reveals a dozen such tints on every inch of canvas. Under the

from obscurity into prominence.

Just as in a portrait, well-chosen intermediate shades mellow the harsh, meld the otherwise incompatible, and create transitions between areas with different color themes. Foliage plants are excellent in this role. Each has its own texture, gloss or matte, which dresses up not only its own appearance but that of its neighbors. Use foliage plants as mixer plants in small amounts, as accents and as echoes. In contrast to plants that carry the main color theme, use mixers sparingly and with an eye to the overall effect of the composition.

FINDING THE RIGHT BLENDERS

Blenders tone down color schemes so that brash colors scintillate rather than shock. To find effective blenders, take flower and foliage samples from each main player in a composition to a good nursery. Use them to find plants that create links between incompatible colors.

Color changers, plants with foliage that alters in different lights, help ease the tensions. For example, blue-green spurges offer tints of copper or mahogany, depending on the light, that will awaken color echoes between hot and cool tones. Purple-leaved perennials, such as loosestrife, appear bronze to almost orange in some lights and smoky purple in others.

To illustrate the concept of proper color blending with flower and foliage, the receding shadows and forward-seeming highlights have been removed from this garden image (top). The shadows represent the retreating colors; the highlights represent the bolder ones. Note how flat and unsatisfying the border appears. With the highlights restored (center), their role in building relief with darker plants becomes more obvious. And finally, with both shadows and highlights added (bottom), the setting has mellowed into a satisfying composition; the shadows and highlights make easy transitions between seemingly incompatible color areas.

THE SPECTRUM OF COLORS

Use this chart like a color wheel. From left to right, the colors go from warm to cool. From top to bottom the colors decrease in intensity, with the top row being the strongest hue and the bottom row the palest tint. The colors across each row are of equal weight.

THE WARM RANGE

Iris
'Distant Fire'

Astilbe
'Bono'

Daylily
'Monte Carlo Red'

Threadleaf coreopsis
'Golden Shower'

Lenten rose

Fringed bleeding heart

Blanket flower
'Burgundy'

Cutleaf coneflower
'Golden Glow'

Iris
'Winemaster'

Garden phlox
'Harmony'

Butterfly weed
'Gay Butterflies'

Basket-of-gold

Daylily
'Chicago Silver'

Purple coneflower

Daylily
'Raging Tiger'

Iris
'Tut's Gold'

Daylily
'Bejeweled'

Yarrow
'Fire King'

Daylily
'Flames of Fortune'

Goldenrod

Iris
'Toastmaster'

Chrysanthemum
'E.M. Robinson'

Daylily
'Top Gun'

Daylily
'Green Glitter'

Helleborus
× *sternii*

Cottage pink

Daylily
'Elmo Jackson'

English primrose

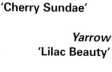
Iris
'Cherry Sundae'

Yarrow
'Lilac Beauty'

Masterwort
(mature blossoms)

Iris
'Luscious Lemon'

Erigeron karvinskianus

Carnation 'Jun'

Iris
'Flaming Victory'

Purple coneflower
'Alba'

THE COOL RANGE

Corsican hellebore
(mature)

*Hungarian
speedwell*

*Siberian iris
'Tropic Night'*

*Fleabane
'Dignity'*

Corsican hellebore
(at prime)

Balloon flower

*Iris sibirica
'Pansy Purple'*

*Iris 'Loganberry
Squeeze'*

Red hot poker

*Frikart's aster
'Monch'*

False indigo
'Purple Smoke'

Oriental poppy

Myrtle
spurge

*Siberian iris
'Harpswell Haze'*

Pincushion flower
'Butterfly Blue'

Carnation

Mediterranean
spurge
'John Tomlinson'
Globe thistle
'Taplow Blue'

Fleabane
'Azure Fairy'

*Geranium
'Birch Double'*

Meadow rue

Douglas iris

Iris
'Inland Passage'

*Geranium
malviflorum*

Yarrow
'Hope'

Iris pallida

Milky bellflower

*Geranium
'Johnson's Blue'*

Masterwort
'Margery Fish'

*Sea holly 'Miss
Willmott's Ghost'*

Catmint
'Six Hills Giant'

*Primula
marginata*

Masterwort

*Boltonia
'Snowbank'*

Iris
'Space Odyssey'

*Anemone
'September Charm'*

PLANTING PLANS FOR A WHITE GARDEN

A garden of white flowers has undeniable romantic appeal. On a sunny day it is refreshing; in cloudy or foggy weather it is soft and luminous. At night it becomes shadowy, ethereal, otherworldly—a setting out of *A Midsummer Night's Dream*.

Many so-called white gardens include flowers of pale cream, ice blue, and blush pink. Except for the blue-flowered Russian sage, this planting scheme favors truly white blossoms, augmented by plants that have gray or silvery white foliage (some of which have insignificant flowers of yellow or blue). For a white-flowered substitute for the Russian sage, choose colewort from the alternative selections; it forms a 6-foot-tall cloud of tiny white flowers.

Although the greatest variety of flowers appears in summer, the plants bloom from spring into fall. During periods with few blooms, the foliage emphasizes the garden's overall white scheme.

All of the plants specified will grow in Zones 7 and 8 and the colder parts of Zone 9. To grow the garden in Zone 6 and colder regions, plant the suggested alternative climbing rose. Substitute lamb's-ears for lavender cotton in regions colder than Zone 5. In Zones 9 or 10, substitute the other alternative selections.

Locate the garden where it will receive six or more hours of sunlight a day during the growing season and water it on a normal schedule. Because the planting includes shrubs, perennials, and annuals, maintenance is varied. The honeysuckle hedge shouldn't need regular trimming—it grows compact and hedgelike without shearing—but occasionally you may need to head back wayward growth. Each year in late winter, assess the other shrubs (roses, summersweet, European cranberrybush) and do whatever pruning is necessary to keep them shapely.

Late winter or early spring is also the time to tidy up the perennials, dividing and replanting, or replacing, any that have declined in vigor. Cut down last year's spent stems of those that die back each fall or winter. Head back by up to half the shrubby perennials, such as 'Powis Castle' artemisia and lavender cotton, to keep plants compact and leafy. When the soil has warmed, set out plants of the one annual—deliciously fragrant flowering tobacco.

To prevent the evergreen candytuft from scorching where winters are cold and snow-free, lightly cover the plants with cut evergreen boughs in late fall.

VARIATIONS

If this double-armed planting takes more space than you have available, consider making a rectangular bed 24 feet long by 8 feet wide. Select one arm of the design and drop the other, continuing the bed line across the paved area to the wall or fence. This reduces the paved seating area to a triangle, leaving enough room for a chair or small bench.

'Snowbank' boltonia has snowy white flowers and sturdy stems.

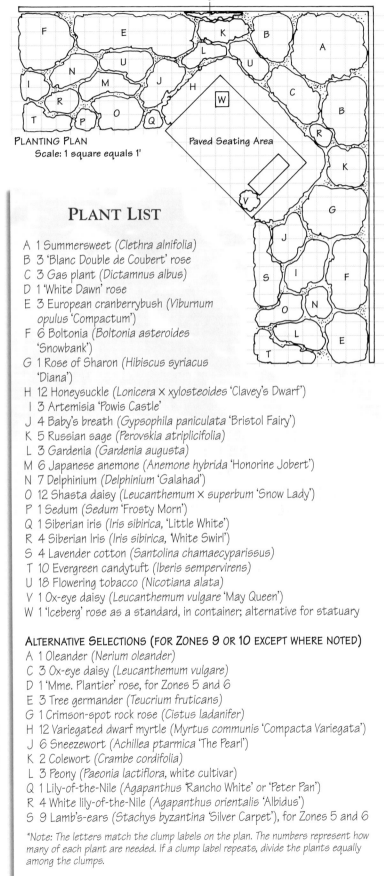

PLANTING PLAN
Scale: 1 square equals 1'

Paved Seating Area

PLANT LIST

A 1 Summersweet *(Clethra alnifolia)*
B 3 'Blanc Double de Coubert' rose
C 3 Gas plant *(Dictamnus albus)*
D 1 'White Dawn' rose
E 3 European cranberrybush *(Viburnum opulus 'Compactum')*
F 6 Boltonia *(Boltonia asteroides 'Snowbank')*
G 1 Rose of Sharon *(Hibiscus syriacus 'Diana')*
H 12 Honeysuckle *(Lonicera × xylosteoides 'Clavey's Dwarf')*
I 3 Artemisia 'Powis Castle'
J 4 Baby's breath *(Gypsophila paniculata 'Bristol Fairy')*
K 5 Russian sage *(Perovskia atriplicifolia)*
L 3 Gardenia *(Gardenia augusta)*
M 6 Japanese anemone *(Anemone hybrida 'Honorine Jobert')*
N 7 Delphinium *(Delphinium 'Galahad')*
O 12 Shasta daisy *(Leucanthemum × superbum 'Snow Lady')*
P 1 Sedum *(Sedum 'Frosty Morn')*
Q 1 Siberian iris *(Iris sibirica, 'Little White')*
R 4 Siberian Iris *(Iris sibirica, 'White Swirl')*
S 4 Lavender cotton *(Santolina chamaecyparissus)*
T 10 Evergreen candytuft *(Iberis sempervirens)*
U 18 Flowering tobacco *(Nicotiana alata)*
V 1 Ox-eye daisy *(Leucanthemum vulgare 'May Queen')*
W 1 'Iceberg' rose as a standard, in container; alternative for statuary

ALTERNATIVE SELECTIONS (FOR ZONES 9 OR 10 EXCEPT WHERE NOTED)
A 1 Oleander *(Nerium oleander)*
C 3 Ox-eye daisy *(Leucanthemum vulgare)*
D 1 'Mme. Plantier' rose, for Zones 5 and 6
E 3 Tree germander *(Teucrium fruticans)*
G 1 Crimson-spot rock rose *(Cistus ladanifer)*
H 12 Variegated dwarf myrtle *(Myrtus communis 'Compacta Variegata')*
J 6 Sneezewort *(Achillea ptarmica 'The Pearl')*
K 2 Colewort *(Crambe cordifolia)*
L 3 Peony *(Paeonia lactiflora, white cultivar)*
Q 1 Lily-of-the-Nile *(Agapanthus 'Rancho White' or 'Peter Pan')*
R 4 White lily-of-the-Nile *(Agapanthus orientalis 'Albidus')*
S 9 Lamb's-ears *(Stachys byzantina 'Silver Carpet')*, for Zones 5 and 6

*Note: The letters match the clump labels on the plan. The numbers represent how many of each plant are needed. If a clump label repeats, divide the plants equally among the clumps.

The silver-gray foliage and lavender flowers of Russian sage and ghostly sea holly add dimension to an all-white garden.

PLANTING PLANS FOR A HOT, BRIGHT GARDEN

As spring turns to summer, hot colors dominate the garden: red, yellow, and orange. Butterfly weed (left) and black-eyed Susan (right) set gardens ablaze.

This bed fairly shouts, "Hey, look at me," though dark glasses might be in order. Red, orange, and yellow jostle for attention, punctuated by patches of vibrant purple. The perennials (and annuals on the alternative list) reach their brassy climax appropriately in summer and, weather permitting, will last into fall. Much of this brightness is provided by those mainstays of summer: members of the daisy family. Aside from the roses, which give color from spring into fall, all the plants are perennials. For a planting scheme that features summer annuals, use the list of alternative selections.

This vibrant garden bed needs as much sun as possible. Bright colors, sunshine, and summer warmth combine to create a scene that radiates. The main plant list is suitable for Zones 4 through 9 and dry-summer Zone 10. The alternative selections are annuals for the same zones, although gazania and blanket flower may not be at their best where the summers are wet.

In Zones 4 through 7, maintenance begins in fall, when you will need to protect the roses from lethal winter temperatures. The two standard tree roses are particularly vulnerable and will need special attention. In all zones, late winter or early spring is the time to prune roses, to remove weak and worn-out wood, and to shape the plants. Perennials should get an annual cleanup. Remove the dead leaves and spent stems in fall or in early spring before growth begins.

PLANTING PLAN

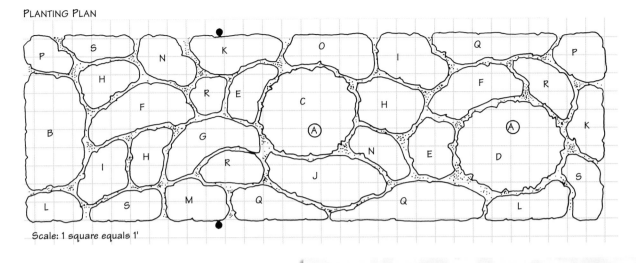

Scale: 1 square equals 1'

In Zones 4 through 7, you will need to replace the beard-tongue and dahlias each year; the other perennials will need dividing and replanting periodically as they become overcrowded.

VARIATIONS

You can cut the length of the bed by one-third by drawing a line between the two dots shown on the plan and eliminating the plants in the smaller portion. Doing so shrinks the number of 'Goldfink' coreopsis required to four, and the alternative purple scarlet sage to eight. To make a better edge at the shortened end of the garden, plant five blanket flowers instead of the butterfly weed, three evening primroses instead of the common yarrow, and four sage plants instead of the beard-tongue. If you are using the alternative list, substitute 12 French marigolds for the African marigolds, two zinnias for the common yarrow, and five gazanias for the beard-tongue.

PLANT LIST

A 2 'Redgold' standard rose (tree)
B 3 'Europeana' rose
C 8 Daylily (Hemerocallis, yellow cultivar)
D 8 Daylily (Hemerocallis, red cultivar)
E 5 Butterfly weed (Asclepias tuberosa)
F 9 Fern-leaf yarrow (Achillea filipendulina 'Coronation Gold')
G 5 Common yarrow (Achillea millefolium 'Fire King')
H 13 Black-eyed Susan (Rudbeckia hirta)
I 4 Golden marguerite (Anthemis tinctoria 'Aureum')
J 5 Lanceleaf coreopsis (Coreopsis lanceolata)
K 7 Lanceleaf coreopsis (Coreopsis lanceolata 'Goldfink')
L 3 Threadleaf coreopsis (Coreopsis verticillata 'Zagreb')
M 3 Mouse ear coreopsis (Coreopsis auriculata 'Nana')
N 4 Helen's flower (Helenium autumnale 'Brilliant')
O 7 Blanket flower (Gaillardia grandiflora 'Baby Cole')
P 3 Sundrops (Oenothera fruticosa)
Q 10 Dahlia, bedding type, preferably red or orange flowers
R 9 Beard-tongue (Penstemon 'Pike's Peak Purple')
S 11 Sage (Salvia × superba)

ALTERNATIVE SELECTIONS
E 13 African marigold (Tagetes erecta, yellow selection)
J 9 Zinnia (Zinnia grandiflora, orange selection)
K 15 Purple scarlet sage (Salvia splendens, purple selection)
L 7 Annual blanket flower (Gaillardia pulchella)
M 8 Gazania, yellow cultivar
N 12 Flowering tobacco (Nicotiana alata, red selection)
O 23 French marigold (Tagetes patula)
P 5 Narrowleaf zinnia (Zinnia angustifolia)
Q 14 Scarlet sage (Salvia splendens, red selection)
S 18 Gazania, orange cultivar

Note: The letters match the clump labels on the plan. The numbers represent how many of each plant are needed. If a clump label repeats, divide the plants equally among the clumps.

For the boldest effect, plant in large clumps. These 'Red Magic' daylilies can be used in spot D on the plan, which calls for eight red daylilies.

PLANTING PLANS FOR A FOLIAGE GARDEN

Even though many of the plants in colorful foliage gardens are gray, the mix of textures and plant shapes is interesting. Lavender provides a stiff upright to mounded habit and fine texture.

This planting scheme gives a different color angle: your chance to say it with foliage. A few of the plants bear flowers, but the floral show is merely a dividend in a planting that is a colorful tapestry of leaves from spring through fall. One green-leaved plant—wall germander—adds an exotic and colorful counterpoint to the reds, yellows, and grays.

With one exception, this planting will thrive in Zones 5 through 9, given well-drained soil and sun for at least six hours each day. The elder needs more winter chill than Zones 8 and 9 can offer. In these zones, choose silverberry from the alternative selections. Gardeners in dry-summer Zone 10 should choose all the alternative selections—the silverberry instead of the elder, the dusty miller instead of the Russian sage, and the kalanchoe instead of the Japanese

The gold-edged leaves of 'Gold Sword' yucca break up the soft rounded forms of gray plants.

PLANT LIST

A 1 Purple smoke tree (Cotinus coggygria 'Royal Purple')
B 1 Vicary golden privet (Ligustrum × vicaryi)
C 1 European red elder (Sambucus racemosa)
D 3 Russian sage (Perovskia atriplicifolia)
E 1 Yucca (Yucca filamentosa 'Gold Sword' or 'Bright Eagle')
F 1 Japanese barberry (Berberis thunbergii 'Atropurpurea')
G 6 English lavender (Lavandula angustifolia)
H 2 Rue (Ruta graveolens 'Jackman's Blue')
I 7 Japanese blood grass (Imperata cylindrica 'Red Baron')
J 9 Lavender cotton (Santolina chamaecyparissus)
K 5 Wall germander (Teucrium chamaedrys)
L 8 Sedum (Sedum spurium 'Dragon's Blood')
M 5 Tricolor sage (Salvia officinalis 'Tricolor')
N 2 Maiden grass (Miscanthus sinensis)
O 4 Catmint (Nepeta × faassenii)
P 1 Spirea (Spiraea japonica 'Limemound')
Q 1 Variegated purple moor grass (Molinia caerulea 'Variegata')

ALTERNATIVE SELECTIONS

C 1 Silverberry (Elaeagnus pungens 'Maculata')
D 3 Dusty miller (Senecio viravira or S. cineraria 'Silver Dust')
F 1 Christmas tree kalanchoe (Kalanchoe laciniata)

Note: The letters match the clump labels on the plan. The numbers represent how many of each plant are needed. If a clump label repeats, divide the plants equally among the clumps.

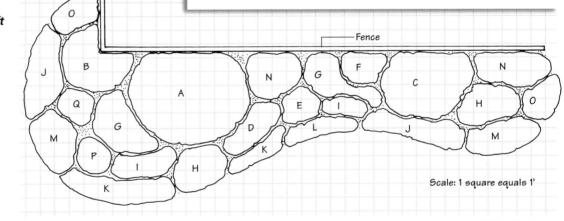

Scale: 1 square equals 1'

PLANTING PLAN

barberry. The alternative selections may also be used in Zone 9.

Once-a-year maintenance should keep this planting presentable. In late winter or early spring, do some general cleanup and pruning. Cut back the Russian sage, catmint, and maiden grass to within a few inches of the ground. Cut back the English lavender and tricolor sage by about half to promote compact growth.

As necessary—perhaps not yearly—cut back the lavender cotton and wall germander to keep them compact. Thin the oldest, most unproductive stems from the spirea; if necessary, prune to shape the vicary golden privet and European red elder. After several years, the sedum may start to become patchy. When this happens, fill in the bare spots with new cuttings, or replant entirely with new cuttings or plants. You can also dig and divide old sedum plants to rejuvenate them. Even a small piece of stem will root and become a new plant.

VARIATIONS

You can easily shrink the size of this bed by a third. Draw a vertical line through the plan, between the Japanese barberry (F) and the European red elder (C) and eliminate all the plants on the right.

If the back of the garden line needs to be straight rather than curved around a corner, extend the existing back line to the edge of the bed, eliminating the catmint planting (O) and one lavender cotton plant (J).

PLANTING PLANS
FOR SPECIAL GARDENS

Perennial gardens delight the senses in so many ways. This chapter features planting plans for several special gardens: a butterfly garden, a fragrant garden, a hummingbird garden, and a rock garden.

In the previous chapters, you learned how to incorporate season of bloom, form, texture, and color into your garden design. Now think about adding the sensory features of these special gardens. The planting plans list the plants and how many are needed (plus alternate plants for different zones), give maintenance information, and include a scaled drawing so you can recreate the garden.

There's more to a rock garden plant than ability to take root in a crevice. Most are also compact in size and grow well in full sun.

BUTTERFLIES

It doesn't take much to draw butterflies to the garden; simply planting some of their favorite perennials brings them in. Choose from among the plants listed for the butterfly garden on page 63, or substitute plants in the Encyclopedia of Plants that attract butterflies. Many types of butterflies will visit your garden if you plant food sources for butterflies in their larval stage and provide water and shelter.

FRAGRANCE

Some perennials perfume the air. Others make good cut flowers so you can enjoy their scent indoors or outside. The plant list for the fragrant garden shown on page 65 offers many favorites. The Encyclopedia of Plants also notes which plants are known for their pleasing fragrance.

HUMMINGBIRDS

Hummingbirds rely on plant nectar as a food source. They are strongly attracted to tubular flowers, and seem especially fond of red and orange flowers. If you plant the hummingbird garden shown on pages 66 and 67, your

garden will surely become a favorite stop on the hummingbird's constant search for nectar.

Be sure to include a bench where you can enjoy the tiny birds, or plant your garden near a window where you can enjoy the hummingbirds without disturbing them.

ROCK GARDENS

Rock gardens are included in this section because they are the place to indulge a love of tiny plants. A well-planted rock garden is a miniature, contained landscape. Rock garden plants can also be fragrant and lovely to look at. If there's a place in your yard for a rock garden, consider the garden shown on pages 68 and 69. The Encyclopedia of Plants lists many creeping plants and crevice dwellers ideal for rock gardens.

Whatever your perennial passion, you'll get plenty of ideas from the following pages.

Purple coneflower attracts butterflies, such as this great spangled frittary. Various birds will feast on its seeds all winter.

Black-eyed Susan and crocosmia are plants that attract butterflies (above). Sweet-smelling roses climb an arbor while lavender lines the path of this fragrant walkway (right).

PLANTING PLANS FOR A BUTTERFLY GARDEN

A sure way to lure butterflies into your garden, no matter where you live, is to plant their favorite flowers.

This butterfly garden brings together 13 plants known for their appeal to various butterflies. The flowering starts in mid- to late spring with catmint. In mid- to late summer, it peaks with the tall Joe-Pye weed, common butterfly bush, and butterfly weed dominating the show. It then continues into fall, until cool weather calls a halt.

MAINTENANCE DETAILS

Establish this bed in full sun, perhaps in a lawn, and give plants routine watering. In Zones 5 through 9, you can use plants in the main list; in dry-summer Zone 10, choose the alternative selections, replacing the Joe-Pye weed with lantana and the spirea with red valerian.

A standard cleanup in late winter or early spring is the major maintenance for the year. Clear out dead leaves, dead plants of last year's flowering tobacco, and spent flowering stems on the perennials. Cut back the butterfly bush to 6 to 12 inches from the ground, and cut back the English lavender, spirea, and catmint by about half. Eventually, you will need to dig up most of the perennials in early spring and divide them to rejuvenate the plantings. First among these, after several years, will be the black-eyed Susan, both forms of coreopsis, and the common yarrow.

VARIATIONS

If you want a smaller, shallower bed, you can cut the planting in half. Divide the plan by drawing a line between the dots, and plant whichever half appeals more to you. To attract a variety of butterflies it's also important to include food plants for their larvae. Dill, fennel, carrot, and parsley are all popular food plants for butterfly species. Wild plants such as nettle, milkweed, clover, and violet are also attractive to butterfly larvae.

PLANT LIST

A 1 Butterfly bush (Buddleia davidii)

B 2 Spotted Joe-Pye weed (Eupatorium maculatum)

C 3 Butterfly weed (Asclepias tuberosa)

D 4 English lavender (Lavandula angustifolia)

E 5 Autumn Joy sedum

F 9 Common yarrow (Achillea millefolium)

G 6 Catmint (Nepeta x faassenii)

H 3 Japanese spirea (Spiraea japonica 'Anthony Waterer')

I 3 Lanceleaf coreopsis (Coreopsis lanceolata)

J 5 Threadleaf coreopsis (Coreopsis verticillata 'Moonbeam')

K 6 Daylily (Hemerocallis, yellow-flowered cultivar)

L 15 Jasmine tobacco (Nicotiana alata)

M 6 Black-eyed Susan (Black-eyed susan fulgida 'Goldsturm')

ALTERNATIVE SELECTIONS

B 2 Lantana (Lantana camara)

H 7 Red valerian (Centranthus ruber 'Albus')

Note: The letters match the clump labels on the plan. The numbers represent how many of each plant are needed. If a clump label repeats, divide the plants among the clumps.

PLANTING PLAN

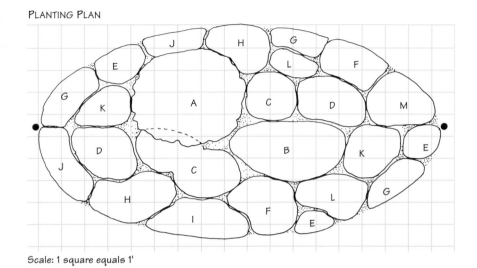

Scale: 1 square equals 1'

Variety is the secret to attracting butterflies. The more flowers you grow, the more butterflies you will see. Shown above: black-eyed Susan and Joe-Pye weed.

This monarch larva is feeding on butterfly weed. To bring butterflies into a garden, provide them with food, water, and shelter throughout their life cycle.

PLANTING PLANS FOR A FRAGRANT GARDEN

A garden without fragrance is like a movie without sound. Dianthus perfumes the entire garden in early summer (below).

Fragrance is the attribute that places many attractive flowers in the "especially beautiful" category. It also elevates more mundane plants to a special status. A pleasing aroma not only enhances the moment, it also calls up memories associated with the particular scent. Few things are more soul-satisfying than having a corner of a garden devoted to olfactory as well as visual pleasure.

Flower and plant aromas are infinitely varied, and scents are dispersed in several directions. Some blossoms release their fragrance into the air, perfuming a garden from a distance. Others reveal their scent only when you put your nose into their petals. Plants with aromatic foliage may not bring their essential oils into effect until you brush against them or bruise their leaves. This garden contains representatives of all three types of fragrant plants.

From the first violets in late winter or early spring to the final roses of fall, this fragrant planting offers flowers and scent almost continually. The peak display will be in early to midsummer, when all but the violets, iris, and peony will be blooming.

MAINTENANCE DETAILS

Give the plants at least six hours of sun each day and routine garden watering. With two exceptions, the plants in the main list will grow in Zones 5 through 9 and dry-summer Zone 10. The apple geranium (in the container) should spend winter protected from frost in Zones 5 through 9, while the peony's need for winter chilling means it won't bloom in Zones 9 and 10. The alternative list gives a peony substitute—the wallflower—for Zones 9 and 10, as well as other notably fragrant options for those two warm zones.

In mid- to late fall in Zones 5 and 6, put the 'Penelope' rose "to bed" for the winter; *Ortho's All About Roses* explains how to

PLANTING PLAN

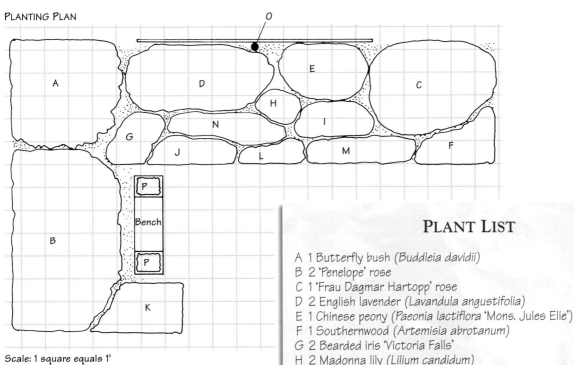

Scale: 1 square equals 1'

PLANT LIST

A 1 Butterfly bush (*Buddleia davidii*)
B 2 'Penelope' rose
C 1 'Frau Dagmar Hartopp' rose
D 2 English lavender (*Lavandula angustifolia*)
E 1 Chinese peony (*Paeonia lactiflora* 'Mons. Jules Elie')
F 1 Southernwood (*Artemisia abrotanum*)
G 2 Bearded iris 'Victoria Falls'
H 2 Madonna lily (*Lilium candidum*)
I 7 Cottage pink (*Dianthus plumarius*)
J 5 Cheddar pink (*Dianthus gratianopolitanus*)
K 8 Sweet violet (*Viola odorata*)
L 5 Common mignonette (*Reseda odorata*)
M 12 Sweet alyssum (*Lobularia maritima*)
N 8 Jasmine tobacco (*Nicotiana alata*)
O 1 Woodbine (*Lonicera periclymenum* 'Serotina')
P 2 Apple geranium (*Pelargonium odoratissimum*) in container

ALTERNATIVE SELECTIONS
A 1 Sweet olive (*Osmanthus fragrans*)
E 2 Wallflower (*Erysimum linifolium* 'Variegatum')
O 1 Star jasmine (*Trachelospermum jasminoides*)
P 2 Gardenia (*Gardenia augusta* 'Veitchii') in container

Note: The letters match the clump labels on the plan. The numbers represent how many of each plant are needed. If a clump label repeats, divide the plants among the clumps.

protect roses. In all zones, yearly garden maintenance starts in late winter or early spring with cleanup and pruning. Clear out dead leaves, spent flower stems, and remains of last year's annuals: Jasmine tobacco, common mignonette, and sweet alyssum. Remove winter protection from the 'Penelope' rose if necessary, then prune all of the roses to shape them. Cut the English lavender and southernwood back halfway, and the butterfly bush to 6 to 12 inches from the ground.

Replant the sweet alyssum and mignonette when you can work the soil; set out new Jasmine tobacco plants when the soil has warmed. Replace plantings of cheddar pink, cottage pink, and wallflower with cuttings or new plants when existing plantings become sparse and rangy. Dig and divide the bearded iris every third or fourth summer. If the bearded iris become too crowded, they will produce fewer flowers.

VARIATIONS

You can alter the shape of this planting (though you'll sacrifice a place to rest and savor the scents) by extending a horizontal line so that it separates the butterfly bush (A) from the 'Penelope' roses (B), then planting just the long rectangle. If you want to retain the L-shape and bench in a shorter plan, you can eliminate the southernwood, the 'Frau Dagmar Hartopp' rose (C), and about one-third of the sweet alyssum (M).

English lavender releases its fragrance when its stems and flowers are crushed.

PLANTING PLANS FOR A HUMMINGBIRD GARDEN

Hummingbirds possess a universal charm. Their iridescent plumage immediately attracts attention and their unique method of flight and overall panache inspire wonder and admiration.

A staple of the hummingbird's diet is flower nectar—nature's sugar solution—which supplies energy for the birds' incessant motion. A sure way to attract hummingbirds, then, is to offer an abundance of their favorite nectar-bearing flowers, ideally in a part of your garden sheltered from the wind.

Brightly colored flowers are a powerful hummingbird attractant. Red and orange shades are the birds' favorite colors, though they give blue and pink a share of attention. Funnel-shaped and tubular blossoms also pique the birds' curiosity, offering the hope of nectar at the base of the flowers.

The plants in this hummingbird garden, therefore, focus on the red sector of the spectrum, from the orange butterfly weed to the red-purple butterfly bush, and include the warm pink shades of summer phlox, coral bells, and foxglove. Flowering starts in spring with coral bells, scarlet trumpet or goldflame

honeysuckle, and foxglove; reaches a peak in summer; then fades in fall with the last blooms of scarlet sage, petunia, flowering tobacco, and beard-tongue.

Several varieties of hummingbirds frequent gardens in the West and Southwest; east of the Plains, only one, the ruby-throated hummingbird, visits during the year's warmer months. The main plant list covers eastern and western gardens in Zones 5 through 9; plants in the alternative list can be used in western Zone 9 and should be used in dry-summer Zone 10.

As soon as the weather permits gardening in late winter or early spring, clean up the planting, removing dead leaves and the spent plants of last year's annuals: jasmine tobacco, petunias, and scarlet sage. Cut back the old flowering stems of the perennials: beard-tongue, foxglove, summer phlox, and bee balm. Prune the butterfly bush to 6 to 12 inches from the ground. Thin and train the scarlet trumpet or goldflame honeysuckle as needed. Head back any wayward growth on the old-fashioned weigela, but wait until after it has flowered to prune it for size.

PLANT LIST

A 1 Scarlet trumpet
    honeysuckle (*Lonicera ×
    brownii* 'Dropmore
    Scarlet')
B 1 Old-fashioned weigela
    (*Weigela florida* 'Bristol
    Ruby')
C 1 Butterfly bush
    (*Buddleia davidii* 'Nanho
    Purple')
D 1 Butterfly weed
    (*Asclepias tuberosa*)
E 13 Beard-tongue
    (*Penstemon barbatus*
    'Prairie Fire')
F 17 Coral bells (*Heuchera
    sanguinea*)
G 3 Torch lily (*Kniphofia
    uvaria*)
H 7 Strawberry foxglove (*Digitalis × mertonensis*)
I 3 Bee balm (*Monarda didyma* 'Cambridge Scarlet')
J 14 Jasmine tobacco (*Nicotiana alata*, red or pink)
K 16 Petunia (*Petunia × hybrida* red selection)
L 4 Summer phlox (*Phlox paniculata*, orange or red
    cultivar, such as 'Orange Perfection')
M 10 Scarlet sage (*Salvia splendens*)

ALTERNATIVE SELECTIONS
A 1 Goldflame honeysuckle (*Lonicera × heckrottii*)
B 1 Butterfly bush (*Buddleia davidii*)
C 1 Autumn sage (*Salvia greggii*)
E 13 Columbine (*Aquilegia*, long-spurred hybrid)
I 1 Scarlet monkeyflower (*Mimulus cardinalis*)
L 5 California fuchsia (*Zauschneria californica*)

*Note: The letters match the clump labels on the plan. The numbers
represent how many of each plant are needed. If a clump label
repeats, divide the plants equally among the
clumps.*

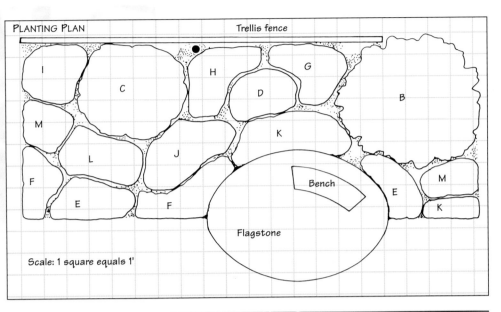

PLANTING PLAN   Trellis fence

Scale: 1 square equals 1'

Flagstone

Bench

*Bee balm
attracts
hummingbirds
and honey bees.
Plant it in moist
soil and wait
for the
hummingbirds
to arrive.*

When the soil warms and frost
danger has passed, set out new
plants of the annuals.

VARIATIONS

The recommended plants play to
the hummingbird's favorite color:
red. If this scheme is too vibrant for
your taste, you can alter it by
choosing alternative colors. Use a
pink-flowered beard-tongue such as
'Prairie Splendor'; a pink-flowered
bee balm, such as 'Croftway Pink';
a white-flowering jasmine tobacco;
pink, blue, or purple selections of
petunia; pink or lavender cultivars
of summer phlox; or violet-flowered
scarlet sage.

*Tubular flowers,
even hooded
ones like this
self heal
(Prunella
vulgaris) are
especially
attractive. This is
a ruby-throated
hummingbird.*

PLANTING PLANS FOR A ROCK GARDEN

Rock gardens embrace plants in a range of textures, from soft creeping plants like thyme and sedum to the tall and spiky yucca. The art lies in skillfully combining textures, colors, and size.

In its most sophisticated form, a rock garden recreates the rock-strewn landscape found above the timberline on a mountain. It is a garden for culturally demanding plants. At its other, most casual, extreme, the rock garden may be a dry-set stone retaining wall embellished with prostrate annuals, perennials, and succulents that find rootholds in the crevices. Many rock-gardening enthusiasts practice an art that lies somewhere between the two extremes, designing gardens that skillfully mingle rocks and small plants in a naturalistic manner.

This rock-garden plan features easy-to-grow shrubs and perennials, all of which are good rock-garden subjects because of their sizes and growth habits. Plants in the main list will thrive in a sunny location in Zones 5 through 8 where summers are humid and in Zones 5 through 9 where summers are fairly dry. Gardeners in dry-summer Zone 10 should substitute plants from the alternative selections; gardeners in dry-summer Zone 9 may use plants from either list. In all zones, give the plants well-drained soil and regular watering. Although the rock-garden plan is shown as a ground-level garden surrounded by pathways, you might want to use the same plan for a raised garden or even for a planting on a gentle slope.

Because you won't be able to find rocks that exactly match the sizes or shapes in the drawings, use the plan as a general guide rather than a blueprint. It is a key to harmonious plant associations and an illustration of natural-appearing rock groupings.

When selecting rocks, choose those native to your area, if possible. Local rocks will look the most natural. Position the rocks as they would appear in nature. A garden of craggy miniature Matterhorns, for example, looks artificial.

Maintaining a rock garden is an ongoing exercise in tidying. There is never a great amount of labor at one time, but neglected edges show up clearly. Begin by removing dead leaves and old flowering stems in late winter or early spring, then assess the condition of the plants. Lightly head back or shear spreading shrubs and perennials overgrowing their bounds. Replace any shorter-lived perennials (such as evergreen candytuft) that remained sparse or patchy after last year's trimming. During the growing season, remove spent flowers as they fade.

VARIATIONS

You can vary the garden's dimensions and size to suit your space and assortment of rocks. All the plants except the conifers and shrubs are

Hen and chicks are ideal for rock gardens. They are almost maintenance-free and thrive in hot, dry conditions. Young plants are easy to divide and use elsewhere.

PLANTING PLAN

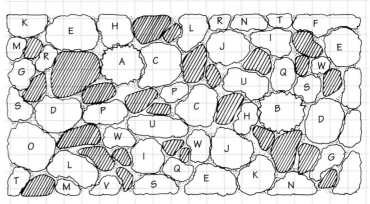

Scale: 1 square equals 1'

low-growing, with the very lowest-profile individuals at the perimeter of the garden. If you alter the size of the plan, use the perimeter plants to finish off the edges.

PLANT LIST

A 1 Dwarf Hinoki false cypress (*Chamaecyparis obtusa* 'Nana')
B 1 Oriental arborvitae (*Platycladus orientalis* 'Minima Glauca')
C 2 Winter heath (*Erica carnea*) or Scotch heather (*Calluna vulgaris*)
D 2 Japanese barberry (*Berberis thunbergii* 'Crimson Pygmy')
E 3 Sun rose (*Helianthemum nummularium*)
F 5 Woolly thyme (*Thymus pseudolanuginosus*)
G 6 Hen and chicks (*Sempervivum tectorum*)
H 3 Ozark Sundrops (*Oenothera missouriensis*)
I 2 Moss pink (*Phlox subulata*)
J 4 Evergreen candytuft (*Iberis sempervirens*)
K 5 Wall rockcress (*Arabis caucasica*)
L 3 Basket-of-gold (*Aurinia saxatilis*)
M 4 Cheddar pink (*Dianthus gratianopolitanus* 'Tiny Rubies')
N 5 Carnation (*Dianthus* 'Bath's Pink')
O 1 Soapwort (*Saponaria officinalis*)
P 3 Japanese blood grass (*Imperata cylindrica* 'Red Baron')
Q 4 Woolly yarrow (*Achillea tomentosa*)
R 5 Sea thrift (*Armeria maritima*)
S 6 Cranesbill (*Geranium cinereum*)
T 5 Sedum (*Sedum spathulifolium*)
U 4 Cranesbill (*Geranium endressii* 'Wargrave Pink')
V 5 Cinquefoil (*Potentilla cinerea*)
W 5 Cottage pink (*Dianthus plumarius*)

ALTERNATIVE SELECTIONS
A 1 Japanese cedar (*Cryptomeria japonica* 'Lobbii' or ' Nana')
C 2 Dwarf jasmine (*Jasminum parkeri*)
D 2 Heavenly bamboo (*Nandina domestica* 'Nana')
I 2 Fan flower (*Scaevola aemula* 'Blue Fans')
V 5 English daisy (*Bellis perennis*)

Note: The letters match the clump labels on the plan. The numbers represent how many of each plant are needed. If a clump label repeats, divide the plants among the clumps.

PREPARING TO PLANT

These beautifully finished perennial beds are a result of careful planning. All garden elements, including paths and irrigation, were considered before planting.

Preparing to plant perennials requires two key elements: knowing the best place to put the garden, and then getting this site ready for the plants. Determining how you want to use perennials helps you discover where they can go to work for you in your yard. Then you can make plant choices to match the design and functional requirements of your particular situation.

Taking the time to plan will result in a garden that is healthier and better looking.

PLANNING

Why and how do you want to use perennials? What short- and long-range goals will these versatile plants help you meet? To answer these questions, begin by visualizing the big picture of your entire landscape.

Walk into your yard and look around. Get a visual image of the existing landscape. Yes, you already know what's there. But take the time to really see your yard. Identify its

The path was laid first, before the ground was cleared and soil was tested and amended.

permanent elements, such as trees, sidewalks, outbuildings, the swimming pool, the water garden, fences, and other components that you plan to keep. Next identify problem areas and any elements you dislike about the landscape, such as patches of bare ground, gaps between existing plants and your lawn, shady spots under trees, wet or dry spots where nothing seems to grow, weedy or unkempt areas, or spots where the landscape seems drab.

Also, note the cause of the problem areas. For example, is an area too wet, dry, or shady? Does the current design no longer suit your tastes? Have you added new structures since the original landscape was established, leaving the area looking fragmented or, perhaps, creating problems by redirecting runoff and forming a wet spot or by deepening shade so nothing will grow?

Finally, think about the future. Do your plans include installing a new structure such as a pool, storage shed, or playhouse that may

not fit in with the current landscape design?

As you examine the big picture, think about where perennials might help. Perennials are better solutions for some problems than for others. They do more than perk up drab areas. For example, they may be the best choice for soggy or dry soil.

EXECUTING THE PLAN

With this big picture in mind, you can hire a professional landscaper to create a design, or you can develop a plan yourself with surprising ease. Here's how: Photograph your current landscape, either in one large panoramic shot or in several smaller shots that you can tape together. These "before" photos help document changes. They'll help especially if you need advice from a professional when selecting plants. You can take the photos with you to the nursery or garden center to help the sales staff better understand your needs.

MAP YOUR LANDSCAPE

Begin your landscape design with a correctly scaled base map.

Make a base map of your current landscape. This is simply a diagram or illustration of your yard; it will help you think through your plant selection and placement options to ensure that your investment of time and money results in success. It also lets you connect your plant selection to the big picture so that the various components of your landscape flow together.

Drawing a base map is generally the first step when renovating an existing landscape or starting one from scratch. When you're only looking for a spot to grow perennials, making a map may seem excessive. But without a plan, you might be tempted to plop plants into the ground without much forethought, perhaps magnifying existing problems or creating new ones. If the plants you choose aren't suited for the location, they can be difficult to maintain and may even die. A haphazardly planned garden could chop up the landscape rather than enhance it by pulling all the elements together.

You don't have to be artistic with your base map; a simple sketch will do. However, you will need accurate dimensions of the bed areas to order the right number of plants, so measure your yard, then draw the base map to scale. It will help to have someone hold one end of a long tape measure while you take measurements.

Transfer these dimensions to graph paper (1 inch equals 10 feet), noting north and south on the drawing and indicating all property lines and angles. Include easement measurements from city records. Then draw in all existing buildings and paved areas, such as driveways, sidewalks, and walkways.

Once you've drawn the base map, sketch in any large permanent plantings or structures, such as trees, hedges, arbors, and shrub beds.

TRYING THINGS OUT

Now you're ready to incorporate your ideas. Lay tracing paper over the base map and sketch out any thoughts you have about locating the perennial garden. For example, if you want to enlarge a bed or replace some lawn with perennials, sketch new borders on the tracing paper to see how your ideas will fit. Where you are using perennials to solve a problem, such as boggy soil, explore different shapes for the bed.

It may take several trial sketches to find one that suits your tastes, so keep experimenting until you're happy with the outcome. Remember, there's no one correct design for a yard. View these sketches as a

If you need help visualizing your landscape in three dimensions, build a tabletop model using household items to represent structures. Delineate ground cover beds and walkways with string.

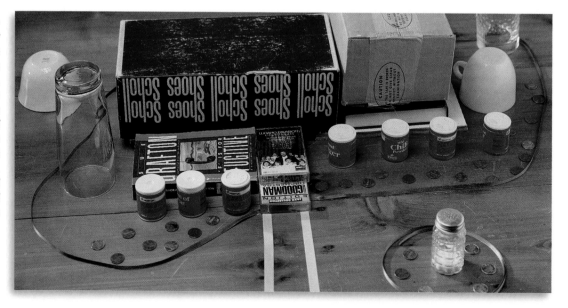

Another way to try out a plan is to "plant" it with items such as trash cans, laundry baskets, empty pots, and hoses. These items can be easily moved around to achieve the desired effect and give you an idea of how the actual plants will fit in the landscape.

chance to brainstorm ideas. Avoid censoring your ideas; one off-the-wall design may lead you to the perfect solution for your landscape.

THREE-DIMENSIONAL PLANS

If you have difficulty visualizing how your plan will translate to the yard, you can bring this two-dimensional image to life by arranging a tabletop model. You'll need at least two colors of string or yarn, tape, and a few handy household items to represent existing structures and plants, such as a magazine or sheet of paper to signify your house, small notepads to denote outbuildings or other structures, and glasses, salt shakers, coins, and similar small objects to represent trees and shrubs. Try to find objects with shapes similar to those of your plants.

Arrange these objects on the table to reflect their existing locations in your landscape. Then mark existing walkways, driveways, shrubs, and other physical boundaries with one color of string or yarn. Tape this string in place so it won't shift as you work.

Next, use the other colored string to outline potential sites for your perennial beds. This is your "play" string; use it to experiment with as many arrangements as you can come up with. As you tinker with it, think about any other elements you may add to your landscape in the future. You may want to use several colors of string to outline all your ideas.

When you are satisfied with the location of the garden, secure the string to the table with

tape. Photograph your tabletop scene to have for future reference.

This tabletop model is only a guide to your landscaping plans, not a blueprint set in stone. It's quite all right to change the design as you begin the actual work.

SETTING PRIORITIES

If you decide to do additional projects while choosing a location for the garden, set priorities for them based on your list of goals and your visual images of the landscape. Renovating a landscape takes time, money, and energy, and it often must be done in stages based on your time and resources.

If, for example, you develop plans that require moving soil to install a drainage system or irrigation lines or to build retaining walls, start with these projects, then put in the garden. By tackling projects in this order, you avoid disturbing the perennials or having to replant them.

List your projects in order of importance, and think again about how perennials fit in. There may be spots where they are part of the overall landscaping plan—perhaps to fill out an existing bed. In other places, perennials may be the focus of your desired changes. Decide where and how you want to use them, and plan your purchases accordingly.

Finally, be sure to file the information— lists, drawings, and photographs—for future reference. Even if you finish the landscape in one season, you won't regret having the information on hand if you decide to make changes later.

MATCH PLANTS TO THE SITE

Match plants to the microclimate of your site. Where the microclimate creates an environment much different from normal, choose plants to take advantage of that difference.

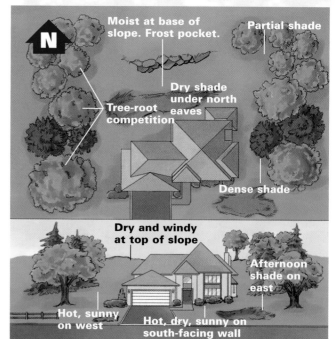

Moist at base of slope. Frost pocket.

Partial shade

Tree-root competition

Dry shade under north eaves

Dense shade

Dry and windy at top of slope

Afternoon shade on east

Hot, sunny on west

Hot, dry, sunny on south-facing wall

Having a base plan will help you decide which plant qualities best meet the needs of your landscape. The next step is to identify the growing conditions in your yard, then find plants that thrive under those conditions.

HARDINESS ZONES

Some plants thrive only in certain climates, while others grow virtually anywhere. For most plants, though, cold temperatures are the limiting environmental factor. Although some plants readily tolerate –20° F, others quickly succumb when the temperature drops to 10° F. So the first thing to look for in a perennial is hardiness.

Plant hardiness zones identify the coldest temperatures expected in a region. The map on page 245 will help you determine the hardiness zone of your locality. Then, as you browse the Encyclopedia of Plants, which starts on page 146, you'll notice that each entry specifies a hardiness zone. Any

perennial with a hardiness rating that matches the climate in your region, or that can take colder weather, should do fine in your yard. For example, if you live in Zone 6, you can grow plants that are hardy in Zones 4 to 6, but not plants hardy only to Zone 7.

MICROCLIMATES

Microclimates put a kink into the broad statement of hardiness. These small areas, where the soil and climate differ from surrounding areas, are often affected by the contour of your terrain. For example, cold air has a tendency to slide down a hill and accumulate at the bottom. So the bottom of a hill and other low-lying areas may be more prone to frost than the rest of your yard. In fact, this area may be cold enough that you need to plant a perennial that is a zone hardier. Water also runs down slopes, and the bases of slopes are usually wet. At the same time, the tops of hills and slopes may be drier than other areas; select drought-tolerant plants for these spots.

Exposures also affect soil and air temperatures. Typically, a southern exposure warms the landscape; areas facing north tend to be colder.

Areas next to the house generally are warmer than

Barrenwort is a good choice for dry shade.

TOP 10 PERENNIALS FOR DRY SOILS

SUN
Butterfly weed
Yarrow
Blanket flower
Creeping verbena
Yucca

SHADE
Barrenwort
Dwarf crested iris
Solomon's seal
Male wood fern
New Zealand flax

outlying areas. Here you might be able to plant a Zone 7 perennial in your Zone 6 landscape. Soil next to a building with a concrete foundation may be more alkaline, too, and runoff from your roof or gutters can keep these areas damp. Also, you should be aware that drying wind tunnels can occur between houses.

You can identify the microclimates in your landscape by observing existing plants. Plants may seem lusher and more productive in some spots, while only certain plants may flourish in others. Discrepancies in plant growth are signs that growing conditions are not the same on every part of a site.

Marsh marigold, horsetail, and yellow flag iris thrive in wet soil. These are planted on the bank of a pond.

TOP 10 PERENNIALS FOR WET SOILS

SUN
Marsh marigold
Rose mallow
Japanese iris
Cardinal flower
Yellow flag iris

SHADE
Maidenhair fern
Variegated Japanese sedge
Ligularia
Japanese primrose
Rodgersia

SOIL TYPES

If your landscape is endowed with rich, fertile soil, nearly any plant will thrive. If, however, your soil is less than ideal, don't despair. There is a perennial for virtually any site.

For example, plants such as phlox, butterfly weed, and salvia require few nutrients and grow in poor soil. For dry sites, seek out drought-tolerant plants, such as ice plant, Solomon's seal, or yarrow. Wet soil is ideal for bog plants such as marsh marigold, Japanese primrose, and many ferns.

Sun and shade also affect your choices. For a wooded area, choose shade-tolerant plants, such as hostas, ferns, and ivy. On sunny sites, your choices are almost limitless. If you share your yard with deer, look for plants that offer some resistance to deer, such as globe thistle, Joe-Pye weed, yucca, and Chinese rhubarb.

SEVERE ENVIRONMENTS

Many perennials are well-adapted to severe climates where few other plants will grow. Near a coastline with salty air and soil and windy skies, select perennials that withstand salinity and drier, breezier conditions. Among these are creeping verbena, New Zealand flax, and wormwood. The quick-reference tables shown at right and opposite offer a sampling of plants for specific sites. The Encyclopedia of Plants details site needs for many other perennials.

The plans that begin on the following page will get you started. These are designs for a small garden, shade garden, water-thrifty garden, and damp-soil garden. Each plan includes a plant list and alternative selections. Whatever your garden conditions, you will find something that suits your needs.

TOP 10 PERENNIALS FOR SEASIDE

SUN
Wormwood
Yarrow
Northern sea oats
Crocosmia
Creeping verbena

SHADE
Japanese anemone
Bergenia
Coral bells
Beard-tongue
New Zealand flax

TOP 10 PERENNIALS FOR CONTAINERS

SUN
Perennial fountain grass
Hardy chrysanthemum
Lamb's-ears
Creeping verbena
Yucca

SHADE
Coral bells
Astilbe
Japanese painted fern
Bergenia
Variegated Japanese sedge

TOP 25 DEER-RESISTANT PERENNIALS

SUN	SHADE
Wormwood	Japanese anemone
Butterfly weed	Goatsbeard
Globe thistle	Astilbe
Spurge	Japanese painted fern
Joe-Pye weed	Bergenia
Oriental poppy	Variegated Japanese sedge
Yarrow	Lenten rose
Monkshood	Bethlehem sage
Black-eyed Susan	Chinese rhubarb
Yucca	Bugbane
Goldenrod	Christmas fern
Blue star	Cinnamon fern
False indigo	

PLANTING PLANS FOR A SMALL-SPACE GARDEN

Many gardeners have limited space, and with many obligations and the fast pace of life, many gardeners have limited time to devote to their hobby. This planting scheme presents an assortment of attractive, easy-to-grow plants that will provide interest throughout the growing season in a space of only 12×5 feet. Children interested in starting a garden may find this a rewarding project. The low-maintenance plants in this design and the small space ensure that most gardeners will find the time and space to create this garden.

MAINTENANCE DETAILS

This garden was designed for full sun in Zones 5 through 9 and dry-summer Zone 10. Four of the five alternative selections are optional choices for gardeners in Zones 9 and 10; the jade plant choice is for Zone 10 only. Because the plants are small and feature small flowers and fine-textured foliage, this planting looks better in a raised bed. Use untreated railroad ties, construction timbers, or two or more courses of brick to make a slightly raised planting that will show off the garden. Plants should have well-drained, reasonably good garden soil and routine garden watering.

PRE-SEASON CLEANUP

Just in advance of the growing season, in late winter or early spring, tidy up the planting. Remove the dead leaves and any spent stems of last year's flowers. Cut back the roses and evergreen candytuft by about half, and trim plants that are encroaching on their neighbors. Head back rangy stems on the dwarf mugo pine to maintain compactness, cutting them back to branching stems or to the base of a year's growth.

During the growing season, groom the planting to keep it neat. In Zones 5, 6, and 7, apply a winter protection of evergreen boughs or salt hay in late fall or as soon as the ground freezes; this will offset the freeze-thaw cycles that can damage raised-bed plantings in cold regions.

PLANT LIST

A 1 Dwarf mugo pine (Pinus mugo var. mugo)
B 5 Miniature hybrid rose, such as 'Popcorn' or 'Rosemarin'
C 10 Evergreen candytuft (Iberis sempervirens 'Autumn Beauty')
D 3 Dalmatian bellflower (Campanula portenschlagiana)
E 3 Wall rockcress (Arabis caucasica)
F 7 Cheddar pink (Dianthus gratianopolitanus 'Tiny Rubies')
G 4 Woolly thyme (Thymus pseudolanuginosus)
H 5 Blue fescue (Festuca glauca)
I 2 Stonecrop (Sedum spathulifolium)
J 2 Mt. Atlas daisy (Anacyclus depressus)
K Pearlwort (Sagina subulata)—1 to 2 flats cut in 2-inch squares; plant 6 inches apart

ALTERNATIVE SELECTIONS

A 1 Variegated jade plant (Crassula Ovata 'Compacta Variegata')
D 2 Serbian bellflower (Campanula poscharskyana)
E 3 Alpine geranium (Erodium reichardii)
H 10 Red star (Rhodohypoxis baurii)
J 2 New Zealand brass buttons (Leptinella squalida)

Note: The letters match the clump labels on the plan. The numbers represent how many of each plant are needed. If a clump label repeats, divide the plants among the clumps.

PLANTING PLAN

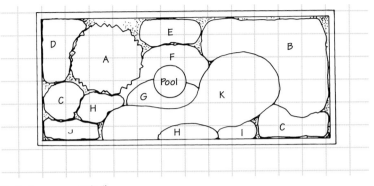

Scale: 1 square equals 1'

VARIATIONS

This planting was designed to be the specified size, but you can vary the color scheme by selecting different cultivars. Instead of the suggested white or pink roses and 'Tiny Rubies' cheddar pink, you could select a crimson variety such as 'Zing Rose' and a red miniature rose, or choose a scarlet selection of hardy carnation, which would contrast brightly with an orange or yellow rose. Reliable carnation varieties include 'Snowfire', 'Cheyenne', 'King of Blacks', and 'Arctic Fire'.

Blue oat grass can be substituted for the blue fescue called for in this planting plan.

Compact Dalmatian bellflower is a good choice for a garden with limited space.

PLANTING PLANS FOR A SHADE GARDEN

Brighten shady spots in your landscape with perennials that thrive in low light. Hostas and ferns are two dependable shade-lovers.

Gardeners often regard a shaded yard as a limitation, knowing that it is a poor location for such favorites as roses, irises, peonies, and a host of seasonal annuals. But all it takes is a changed view to welcome this shade garden of azaleas, hostas, and astilbes.

Shade comes in various forms. Light shade is the brightest; it comes through lattice or an open-canopied tree. At the other extreme is the dense shade found under a heavy foliage canopy. The amount of shade also varies from partial (morning sun, afternoon shade) to day-long. Even day-long shade ranges in degree from the fairly light form cast by shadows of tall trees or buildings to the gloom in a narrow passage between buildings.

The beds in this garden are shaded by the canopies of the dogwoods (or evergreen pears) included in the planting scheme. In an already shady spot, you can omit the trees without affecting the design. The main plant list will serve Zones 5 through 9, though gardeners in Zones 7 and 8 can choose from the broad range of azaleas available in their local nurseries. The alternative selections should be used in Zone 10 and may be considered for Zone 9 gardens. The alternative azaleas, in particular, are more suitable for Zone 9 gardens than the azaleas on the main list. In all areas, the planting requires routine garden watering.

Varied foliage and flower colors make this planting attractive from early spring until frost spells an end to the growing year. Lenten roses and violets usher in the flowering season, followed by azaleas, brunnera, bleeding heart, bloodroot, and foxglove.

In late spring and summer, Serbian bellflower, astilbe, and summersweet provide a burst of color; hostas bloom too, although most are not especially showy. Overhead, the kousa dogwoods spread clouds of color. The season finishes in fall with the Japanese anemone and the colorful foliage of the azalea and dogwood.

The time for maintenance is late winter or early spring, before the year's growth begins in earnest. Clean out the dead leaves and trim the spent flowering stems of last year's perennials. Prune the summersweet

PLANT LIST

A 2 Kousa dogwood (*Cornus kousa*)
B 2 Pink-shell azalea (*Rhododendron vaseyi*)
C 4 Royal azalea (*Rhododendron schlippenbachii*)
D 3 Azalea (*Rhododendron* 'Northern Lights')
E 1 Summersweet (*Clethra alnifolia*)
F 4 Ostrich fern (*Matteuccia struthiopteris*)
G 7 Lenten rose (*Helleborus orientalis*)
H 3 Siebold hosta (*Hosta sieboldiana*)
I 10 Strawberry foxglove (*Digitalis* × *mertonensis*)
J 10 Wavy hosta (*Hosta undulata* 'Mediovariegata')
K 2 Astilbe (*Astilbe* 'Red Sentinel')
L 7 Brunnera (*Brunnera macrophylla*)
M 6 Old-fashioned bleeding heart (*Dicentra spectabilis*)
N 1 'Piedmont Gold' hosta
O 7 Spotted dead nettle (*Lamium maculatum* 'White Nancy')
P 4 Sweet violet (*Viola odorata*)
Q 2 Bigleaf ligularia (*Ligularia dentata* 'Desdemona')
R 8 Serbian bellflower (*Campanula poscharskyana*)
S 2 Bloodroot (*Sanguinaria canadensis*)
T 4 Japanese anemone (*Anemone japonica*)

ALTERNATIVE SELECTIONS

A 2 Evergreen pear (*Pyrus kawakamii*)
B 2 Azalea (*Rhododendron* 'Nova Zembla')
C 4 Azalea (*Rhododendron* 'Chionoipes')
D 3 Azalea (*Rhododendron* 'Sherwood Orchid')
E 1 Bigleaf hydrangea (*Hydrangea macrophylla* 'Tricolor')
F 5 Southern sword fern (*Nephrolepis cordifolia*)
H 3 Kaffir lily (*Schizostylis coccinea*)
J 12 Variegated lilyturf (*Liriope muscari* 'Variegata')
K 3 Japanese anemone (*Anemone japonica*)
M 10 Columbine (*Aquilegia* McKenna Hybrids)
N 3 Common calla lily (*Zantedeschia aethiopica* 'Minor')
Q 2 Ligularia (*Ligularia tussilaginea* 'Aureo-maculata')
S 5 Polyanthus primrose (*Primula* × *polyantha*)

Note: The letters match the clump labels on the plan. The numbers represent how many of each plant are needed. If a clump label repeats, divide the plants among the clumps.

if it is growing out of bounds or, if you are using the alternative list, cut back the hydrangea by at least half. Wait until just after flowering to shape the azaleas. If the Serbian bellflower, Japanese anemone, or brunnera is spreading too far, dig out the excess plants.

VARIATIONS

This shaded garden is planned as a woodland walk, perhaps along a mossy stone path or under a canopy of tall deciduous trees. However, if your space is limited, either portion of the planting can stand by itself.

Columbine is an alternative to old-fashioned bleeding heart. It brightens the shade in spring with its cheery blossoms, and combines well with the textures and colors of the other perennials in this design.

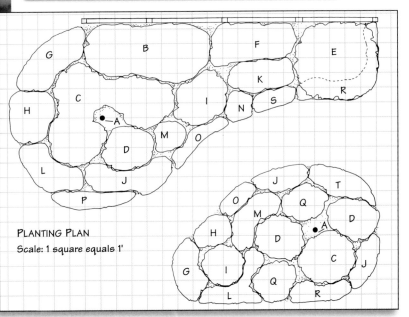

PLANTING PLAN
Scale: 1 square equals 1'

PLANTING PLANS FOR A WATER-THRIFTY GARDEN

'Gold Plate' yarrow and sneezeweed are among the perennials that are tolerant of drought and heat.

Many favorite garden plants need a regular supply of water to look their best. If natural rainfall during the growing season doesn't provide enough, then you must water regularly.

Watering poses a problem if you can't always be there when needed with the hose or if you're trying to conserve water. The solution is to find attractive plants that flourish on limited water.

This planting scheme features an assortment of water-thrifty plants that thrive in Zones 5 through 9; gardeners in dry-summer Zone 10 should use the alternative selections, and gardeners in dry-summer Zone 9 may choose from either list. Most of the color comes from the flowers, but three plants—Japanese barberry, lamb's-ears, and fountain grass—offer colorful foliage rather than showy blossoms. In the main planting, flowers are concentrated in summer and early fall. A garden containing the alternative selections will have a slightly longer flowering period. It will start in spring with the rock rose, bush morning glory, and fleabane and continue well into fall with the Mexican bush sage.

In all areas, establish the bed in well-drained soil where plants will receive full sun.

Although these plants can take some dryness between waterings, just how much water they'll need depends on your climate: temperature, rainfall, wind, and cloud cover. You can be sure, however, that they'll be standing tall when roses, snapdragons, and lawn start to droop.

A basic spring cleaning (in late winter or early spring) gets the garden set for the year. Clear out the dead leaves, and cut down the spent flower stems on the perennials. Cut back the catmint and English lavender by about half, and cut back the Russian sage to about 6 inches. Lightly prune the Japanese barberry as needed to keep it from encroaching on neighboring plants.

VARIATIONS

If space is limited, you can cut the planting in half. Draw a line from the back of the bed to the front between the fern-leaf yarrow (C) and the Japanese barberry (A); plant the half that contains the fern-leaf yarrow, reducing the numbers of cupid's-dart (H) (or the alternative vervain) to three and the lamb's-ears (L) also to three.

PLANT LIST

A 1 Japanese barberry (Berberis thunbergii)
B 2 Russian sage (Perovskia atriplicifolia)
C 6 Fern-leaf yarrow (Achillea filipendulina 'Coronation Gold')
D 3 Fountain grass (Pennisetum alopecuroides)
E 6 Purple coneflower (Echinacea purpurea 'Magnus')
F 6 Black-eyed Susan (Rudbeckia fulgida 'Goldsturm')
G 3 Butterfly weed (Asclepias tuberosa)
H 5 Cupid's dart (Catananche caerulea)
I 2 Cushion spurge (Euphorbia polychroma)
J 3 Blazing star (Liatris spicata 'Kobold')
K 4 Yarrow (Achillea 'Moonshine')
L 6 Lamb's-ears (Stachys byzantina 'Silver Carpet')
M 2 Cinquefoil (Potentilla 'Abbotswood')
N 3 Lanceleaf coreopsis (Coreopsis lanceolata 'Goldfink')
O 4 Catmint (Nepeta × faassenii)

ALTERNATIVE SELECTIONS

A 1 Crimson-spot rock rose (Cistus ladanifer)
B 2 Mexican bush sage (Salvia leucantha)
D 3 Purple fountain grass (Pennisetum setaceum 'Atrosanguineum')
G 3 Gaura (Gaura lindheimeri)
H 2 Vervain (Verbena rigida)
I 2 Sea lavender (Limonium latifolium)
J 1 Bush morning glory (Convolvulus cneorum)
M 4 English lavender (Lavandula angustifolia 'Hidcote')
O 2 Fleabane (Erigeron karvinskianus)

Note: The letters match the clump labels on the plan. The numbers represent how many of each plant are needed. If a clump label repeats, divide the plants among the clumps.

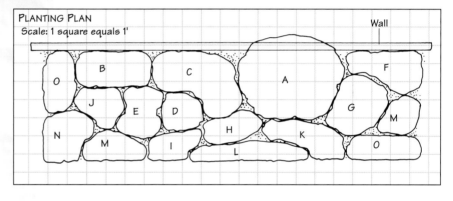

PLANTING PLAN
Scale: 1 square equals 1'
Wall

Purple coneflower is another perennial that survives and even thrives in dry conditions.

Planting Plans for a Damp-Soil Garden

'Golden Queen'
globe flower
thrives in
damp soil.

Most familiar garden plants thrive in well-drained soil; during active growth their roots need abundant air. Poorly drained soil contains little air in its pores so few plants grow in it. However, a few perennials have adapted to stream- and pond-side growing conditions. They are a good choice for low wet spots in a garden.

This planting primarily consists of more attractive moisture-loving plants. Although some grow well in drier situations, most perform best with constantly moist soil.

Flowering begins in early to mid-spring with the sky blue blooms of forget-me-not and lasts into fall with the red and blue cardinal flowers (or the alternative New England aster). Without giving you an eye-jolting blast of mass color, this bed is nonetheless always interesting; its varied foliage textures and colors are punctuated by flowers in yellow, red, pink, purple, and blue. The alternative selections give you the chance to vary the planting palette.

In cool-summer regions, place the bed in full sun; but in warmer areas, locate the garden where it will receive light shade during the hottest part of the day. Because wet sites are found most often in climates with frequent rainfall during the spring and

PLANTING PLAN

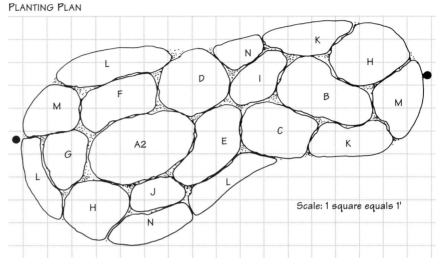

Scale: 1 square equals 1'

summer growing seasons, these plants were chosen for moist-summer Zones 5 through 9.

In late winter or early spring, before the perennials break dormancy, remove dead leaves and spent flowering stems from the previous year. After several years you may need to dig up and divide the bee balm, cardinal flower, and New England aster.

VARIATIONS

This bed was designed to be an irregular island, perhaps surrounded by lawn in the low spot of a garden. However, if you need a bed that will fit against a wall or fence, draw a line between the dots at either end of the plan and plant the larger portion, using just two of the yellow flag iris (B).

PLANT LIST

A 2 Queen-of-the-prairie (Filipendula rubra 'Venusta')
B 4 Yellow flag iris (Iris pseudacorus)
C 1 Narrow-spiked ligularia (Ligularia stenocephala 'The Rocket')
D 1 Ligularia (Ligularia dentata 'Desdemona')
E 3 Yellow flag iris (Iris pseudacorus)
F 3 Cardinal flower (Lobelia cardinalis)
G 2 Columbine meadow rue (Thalictrum aquilegifolium)
H 5 Globe flower (Trollius europaeus 'Superbus')
I 2 Bee balm (Monarda didyma 'Violet Queen')
J 2 Spiderwort (Tradescantia virginiana)
K 8 Variegated purple moor grass (Molinia caerulea 'Variegata')
L 10 True forget-me-not (Myosotis scorpioides)
M 4 Siebold hosta (Hosta sieboldiana)
N 3 Lanceleaf hosta (Hosta 'Lancifolia')

ALTERNATIVE SELECTIONS
A 2 Goatsbeard (Aruncus dioicus)
C 3 New England aster (Aster novae-angliae)
E 2 Purple loosestrife (Lythrum salicaria 'Morden's Pink')
F 2 Cardinal flower (Lobelia × gerardii 'Vedrariensis') for Zones 8 and 9
I 2 Bee balm (Monarda didyma 'Cambridge Scarlet')

Note: The letters match the clump labels on the plan. The numbers represent how many of each plant are needed. If a clump label repeats, divide the plants equally among the clumps.

Cardinal flower is one of the alternative selections for this damp-soil garden.

TAKE CARE OF YOUR BODY

Don't overstress your knees, back, or wrists. Wear knee pads or kneel on a foam pad. Keep your back straight when bending or lifting. Bend at your hips or knees.

After planning comes the work. Before breaking ground, you'll find it helpful to review some techniques for protecting your back, arms, legs, feet, and hands. These suggestions apply whether you're starting fresh or working in a garden that's been there for several years.

First, wear appropriate clothing. Put on long pants to protect your legs from cuts and scrapes as well as from skin irritations. Wear a cap or broad-brimmed hat to protect your face if you're spending a lot of time in the sun. Apply sunscreen, at least SPF 15, even on cloudy days.

Wear heavy shoes or boots, especially when using motorized equipment such as a rototiller or mower or when digging with a shovel. Heavy soles make it easier to push a shovel into the soil, and their thick uppers protect your toes and feet from injury should you slip. Don't disable safety shutoffs, even if they make equipment inconvenient to use.

Gloves are especially important when digging in rough soil or applying fertilizers, pesticides, or mulches that may contain irritating substances.

BEND FROM THE HIPS

When digging, especially if you are breaking new, tough ground, keep your back straight, your shoulders upright, and your knees bent. Don't slump or stoop.

Bending from the waist to weed or plant will strain your back. Instead, bend from the hips (see box below left), squat, or get some knee pads and kneel as you work. Avoid squatting for extended periods of time to avoid muscle pulls and wear and tear on your knees and lower back. Rest on your knees and sit back on your feet if you need a break.

Work the ground when it is moist but not wet; wet soil is heavier and harder to lift than drier soil. Take small scoops with your shovel so you aren't straining to lift a heavy load. As you lift, grip the shovel close to the blade for better leverage. To protect your back and shoulders from injury as you lift the shovel or swing a hoe, do so in one fluid movement rather than in short jerks.

EASY ON THE WRISTS

Digging just a few holes is not extremely taxing. But if you are planting a large area with many holes, the repetitive motion can stress your wrist. A shovel, rather than a trowel, may be easier on them. Or, if the holes are relatively small, use a trenching tool or other small-sized shovel.

If using a trowel, push it deeply in the soil and lift the dirt in an easy motion that does not stress your wrist. Go slowly and try to keep scoops small and light. Digging as

FIND YOUR HIP JOINTS

Few people actually know where their hips are. Try this technique. Put your hands on where you think your hip joints are. Now, are they really on your hips? Or on the outside of your thighs?

To find your hip joints, put your hands in your pockets and lift one leg up. Feel where the joint creases under your hand. That is your hip joint. It is halfway between the bone that sticks out in the front of your hip, and your pubic bone.

Now that you've found them, try bending over from your hip joints. Feel how that keeps your lower back straight and long. This is a much stronger position for your back, whether you are lifting something or just bending over to weed or pick up an object.

though you were scooping with a spoon is particularly hard on wrists. Use the entire forearm in a fluid motion to avoid wrist injury when planting large numbers of perennials. You may also want to wear a brace that keeps the wrist immobile.

Another technique is to grab the trowel handle with your thumb on top and the bowl of the trowel facing you (upper right). Dig by pulling the trowel toward you. This technique works best in well-prepared, friable soil.

If you already have problems with your wrists, try the trowel shown in the photo below right. The grip forces you to keep your wrist straight; the optional brace helps immobilize the wrist even further. You'll find it takes a while to become comfortable using this trowel.

When using clippers or pruners, switch them from hand to hand to avoid repetitive motion injury in your wrist or hands. Buy the best pruners you can afford. High-quality tools will take the brunt of the force, rather than directing it to your hand, arm, and back.

Avoid stress on your wrist: Keep it in the neutral position—in line with the long bones of the arm as if arm and hand were hanging loose at your side.

If you already have problems with your wrists, look for specialized trowels that will help prevent further damage.

PROTECT YOUR FEET

Make soil preparation easier and protect your feet by wearing boots whenever you dig. Choose hard-soled boots that support your ankle and have a low but definite heel so you can set your foot securely on the tread of the shovel.

GREAT GARDENS START WITH GREAT SOIL

When you improve the soil before planting you make a smart investment. It yields a high return in prettier, healthier, sturdier, lower-care perennials.

N ext year's performance is built into this year's perennial roots. Thus, success starts with making the soil around the roots the best it can be.

Perennials grow the fastest, are the sturdiest and healthiest, and bloom the brightest in loose, well-drained, weed-free, fertile loam with a pH of about 6.5. Before planting, figure out which of these characteristics your soil lacks, then fix it.

It's best to work soil in fall. Preparing soil then allows time for the soil-enhancing activity of worms, frost, and rain to supplement your work, amendments to make their changes, and the soil to settle so it is ready for planting. But whatever time of year you work, make sure the soil is friable. Squeeze a handful of soil, then open your hand. The soil should not ooze water or crumble readily when poked.

LOOSE SOIL

Loose soil has lots of pore space for air and water to move through. Think of it this way: In a 2-quart pot of soil, air and water should take up the equivalent of 1 quart of space. In loose soil, perennial roots spread wide and fast. The plants are steadier in wind and less likely to topple over as they reach full height. With their wider spread, the roots have more resources from which to draw water and nutrients.

Many soils need loosening because they're dense or compacted from foot traffic, grading, or seasonal flooding. As an example, just eight passes with a bulldozer during construction or re-landscaping work can reduce air and water space in a soil that had the ideal 50 percent to only 5 to 10 percent. Kids' play can be nearly as hard on the soil.

Perennials grow best in beds with loose soil 18 inches deep, but you need dig only as deep as necessary to loosen the compacted layer. Sometimes only the top few inches of soil may be dense, but it's also common to find

SINGLE-DIGGING

Use a spade or spading fork to loosen the top 8 to 10 inches if the soil is an acceptable loam, drainage is good, and no compacted layer exists within the top 18 inches. Loosen the soil by inserting the fork to its full depth, then pulling back on the handle to lever the tines. You can compost any sod stripped from the area.

DOUBLE-DIGGING

Dig a 9-inch-deep trench across the bed, stockpiling soil on a tarp. With a fork, loosen the trench bottom to 9 inches deep; top with compost. Dig a second trench, tossing its soil into the first. Loosen, add compost, and continue to the end of the bed. Fill the last trench with the set-aside soil. Rake to level the soil; soil will settle but be higher than before. Avoid standing in the trenches.

a compacted layer about 9 inches below the surface under relatively loose soil. This deeper compaction may exist because your proposed garden was farmland or a vegetable garden repeatedly tilled to that depth.

Soil is loose if you can easily dig in it. If you must soak soil before digging or need to use a pickax to make a hole, it needs to be broken up. You can loosen soil by hand or with a tiller.

BY HAND: Use a spade or spading fork (a fork's tines better penetrate dense soil) to cut, lift, or reset soil. Manual loosening works best in small areas; in weedy areas where each square foot of soil must be inspected and cleared of weed roots; in existing beds between established plants and tree roots; and in soil that must be loosened deeper than a tiller's 9- to 10-inch reach.

Single-dig to loosen well-drained loam. Double-dig to break up hardpan (a layer of soil densely packed by machinery or traffic, preventing the free flow of water and air) or to loosen soil 18 inches deep, if necessary. (See the illustrations at left.)

TILLING: As rototillers slice, lift, cut, and drop soil in chunks, they increase the amount of air between clods. But using one is practical only in large gardens free of perennial weeds and tree roots. Tillers are hard to maneuver in small areas; tree roots deflect tines; and perennial weeds multiply when their roots are chopped.

Avoid overtilling or working in wet soil. Soil cut too many times by a tiller or shovel becomes structureless, like sifted flour. Till only enough to turn, not pulverize. Repeated tilling can also cause hardpan; check every few years to see if hardpan is developing at the 8- to 9-inch depth. Shoveling or tilling wet clay soil can churn it into a concretelike slurry. Both conditions make it hard for air and water to move through the soil.

Turning or tilling soil is a good time to add materials to help prevent future compaction. Use porous substances that don't crush easily and have relatively large particles, such as coarse builder's sand, composted pine bark, or commercial additives such as perlite. Before turning or tilling, spread a 2- to 3-inch layer of the material over the area. Then mix it into the entire depth that needs loosening.

Materials that act like magnets to soil particles, such as compost, composted pine bark, and gypsum (calcium sulfate) are even better additives. Grains of clay and sand gradually attach themselves to the additives, so the soil becomes rounded crumbs rather than densely packed layers. Gypsum is most effective in saline soils.

SHEET COMPOSTING: If you are in no rush, sheet composting is a method that

Tillers are useful for loosening topsoil or deeply mixing in amendments. Small-statured gardeners find rear-tine self-propelled tillers easier to operate.

To test structure, put a handful of soil in a sieve. Gently lower the sieve into a bowl of water, then lift it out and look for soil particles left in the water. The better the soil structure, the fewer there will be. In a garden with good soil structure, fewer nutrients will leach away when water passes through the soil.

Grubs, soil bacteria, fungi, and earthworms do a lot of soil work for you. As they move through the soil, they mix amendments and organic mulch into the soil for you.

GREAT GARDENS START WITH GREAT SOIL
continued

gradually loosens soil through the activity of grubs, soil bacteria, fungi, and earthworms. It is especially useful between established plants and around trees roots where you can't till.

Spread a 2- to 3-inch layer of fast-decomposing organic materials such as leaves, shredded newspaper or compost over the soil. Cover it with a 2-inch layer of mulch. Keep the area moist. Soil organisms will mix the layers over one or more seasons.

To speed the process, use a knife attachment for a tractor tiller or a pipe puller to cut slits in the soil 2 feet apart and as deep as the attachment will go before spreading the sheet of organic materials. Under trees, drill 18-inch-deep holes every 2 feet with an auger.

DRAINAGE FOR HEALTHY PLANTS

Drainage describes how water and oxygen move through the soil. Water flows through soil pores, drawing air behind it. Well-drained soil is the ideal combination of water and oxygen. It feels like a moist sponge.

Many plant failures are linked to drainage, and it can be difficult to recognize the connection. Both excessively wet and dry soils inhibit root growth. In wet soil, plants grow poorly, need staking, die back, wilt, and come under attack from insects and diseases. Even though hardy, such plants may die in winter.

Poorly drained soil holds too much water, is soggy, and may smell sour. Coarse-textured

TESTING DRAINAGE

How well do water and air move through your soil? Don't be misled by the type of soil. Even clay can drain well, and sand can drain poorly. To check drainage, first dig an 18-inch-deep test hole. Fill the hole with water and let it drain. This thoroughly wets the soil along the sides of the hole. Fill the hole again.

Next, record the inches of water left in the hole after one day. This information tells you whether you need to raise the bed to improve drainage. For example, if 9 inches of water remain after one day, raising the bed 9 inches is advisable. Finally, note the total time required for the hole to drain.

- If the soil is fast-draining, the hole empties in less than 3½ hours.
- If the soil is well drained, the hole empties in 3½ to 24 hours.
- If the soil is moderately well drained, the hole empties in 24 to 72 hours.
- If the soil is poorly drained, the hole empties in 3½ to 7 days.
- If the soil is very poorly drained, the hole empties after 7 days.

WHAT TO DO WITH THE RESULTS OF THE DRAINAGE TEST

If your soil is...	Then you should...
Fast-draining	Mix a 2- to 3-inch layer of moisture-retentive amendment (compost or clay soil) into the bed. Mulch with materials that break down within a year. Grow drought-tolerant plants. Check soil moisture frequently; water carefully, using drip irrigation systems or soaker hoses.
Well drained	Do nothing special. Grow all types of plants.
Moderately well drained	Grow species suited to moist, well-drained soil. Or raise the bed 1 inch for every inch of water left in the test hole after one day.
Poorly drained	Install drain tile, or raise the bed 1 inch for every inch of water left in the test hole after one day. Grow only species suited to moist soil and imperfect drainage.
Very poorly drained	Install drain tile. Or raise the bed 1 inch for every inch of water left in the test hole after one day. Grow only species suited to wet soil. Water carefully, delaying irrigation until the top few inches of soil have been dry for as many days as the test hole held water.

Grass and weeds grow readily into unprotected beds (a). Standard lawn edging, which extends 4 to 5 inches into the ground, restrains the roots of grass but does not stop deeper-running species such as quackgrass (b). Carpet runner, protective plastic sold in 27-inch-wide rolls, can be used as a deeper barrier (c). Slice it lengthwise to make strips as wide as the rooting depth of nearby weeds (for example, three 9-inch-wide or four 6½-inch-wide strips).

soil, such as sand, generally does not store water. Keeping it moist is a challenge.

Drainage testing is easy and worth the effort—do it before planting to prevent costly problems later. (See the box on page 88.)

PREVENT WEEDS

Weeds are unsightly and compete with perennials for water, light, and nutrients. Any weeds left in a bed after preparing the soil will be back unless you take steps to eradicate them or block their return. Persistent weeds, such as dandelions and perennial grasses, can return from overlooked root remnants and tangle with your perennials. Then you'll have to uproot the perennial to remove the weed.

Before tilling under or removing sod or existing plants for the new bed, identify what else is growing there; then you can take the right steps to prevent weeds.

Cool-season turfgrasses are relatively easy to kill. Till them under, mulch heavily, and wait two to three weeks for remnants to sprout. Then weed out the sprouts or treat them with a nonselective, nonresidual herbicide, such as glyphosate or glufosinate-ammonium. Alternatively, physically remove the lawn by digging it out with a sod lifter.

TOUGHER WEEDS

Perennial weeds, such as thistle, dandelion, bermudagrass, kikuyugrass, quackgrass, and bindweed, are a different case. They require deep, careful digging to remove all running roots, and even then, you will probably miss some. Don't till live perennial weeds; that chops them up and more weeds emerge to slow establishment of the ornamentals.

One control method is to loosen the soil, then dig up the weeds. Wait 60 days to plant the garden, digging or killing any sprouts that

pop up. This method works only during the growing season.

Another strategy involves treating the actively growing weeds with herbicide, waiting for top growth to die, mowing the dead vegetation short, and reapplying weed killer as needed over a 60-day period.

After the waiting period, till or turn the area to break up the dead roots. Because this brings up seeds of annual weeds, keep the turned soil moist for a few weeks to let the seeds sprout. Kill the seedlings with herbicide or a shallow hoeing.

Use an herbicide absorbed through the plant's leaves, such as glyphosate, 2-4D, or glufosinate-ammonium; check the label to see if the herbicide has residual activity. Some root-absorbed herbicides could remain in soil and stunt or damage new perennials.

ANNUAL WEEDS

Where annual weeds, such as crabgrass and purslane, dominate, turn the soil or apply

Building a raised bed with straight sides maximizes the drainage area. Simply hilling up the soil improves drainage only at the center of the hill, not at the sides, which are barely above the original grade.

GREAT GARDENS START WITH GREAT SOIL
continued

Amendments for fertility and structure:

Greensand, a rock powder, provides potassium and some phosphorus.

Cottonseed meal supplies nitrogen and some phosphorus and potassium.

Steamed bonemeal supplies phosphorus and a small amount of nitrogen.

Dried poultry manure provides nitrogen, phosphorus, and potassium.

herbicide. Later, till in the dead residue. Mulch or mix a pre-emergent weed killer, such as trifluralin (Treflan), into the top inch of soil to prevent reinfestation.

KEEP OUT NEW WEEDS

After cleaning up the bed, the last step is to note nearby sources of weeds and prevent them from reinvading. If weedy neighbors spread by below-ground runners, install a vertical root barrier that is as deep as the roots run around the bed. To bar weeds that creep on the surface (for example, ground ivy), periodically remove or kill them at the garden's edge. Control weeds that spread by seed, such as many annuals and some perennials (violets and dandelions) by mowing closely to prevent seed set.

SOIL FERTILITY

A bed that is loose, well-drained, and weed free is almost ready. But before you plant, make some simple observations about fertility and add fertilizer accordingly.

Fertility is a measure of the type and amount of nutrients plants can obtain from the soil. The main source of nutrients is mineral matter—the sand, silt, and clay that make up a soil. Water in the soil gradually breaks down the minerals and becomes nutrient-rich. The plants absorb and use this water. Because clay has tiny particles and a porous structure, more water infiltrates clay particles than sand, so it is more fertile than sand.

Another source of nutrients is humus—decomposing organic matter that gives soil a dark color.

A rough gauge of fertility can be gained from looking at the grass and weeds growing in the future garden spot and the soil's color. If the bed is dark clay that supported lush growth in the recent past, treat it as a naturally fertile soil that doesn't need heavy or special fertilization. Add a soil test to your list of tasks to do eventually. But if the soil is sandy and light in color, and plants did not grow well, mix in ½ pound of 10-10-10 fertilizer, then make it a priority to get the soil tested by a lab before the growing season is too far gone.

No matter the soil type, you can mix in up to ½ pound of 10-10-10 fertilizer or ¼ pound of 20-20-20 per 100 square feet of bed as you prepare the garden. Rake it lightly into the top few inches of the soil. The granules will dissolve and spread down, ensuring equal amounts of nitrogen, phosphorus, and potassium the first season.

IMPROVE SOIL STRUCTURE

Any soil can be made loose, well-drained, and weed free. However, for the best combination of these traits, plus fertility and moisture retention, the ideal is loam. Loam is a mix of the materials that contribute to soil texture: sand, silt, and clay. It, too, is a texture, which is a description of the relative amounts of sand, silt, and clay in a soil.

Loam is considered ideal because it has enough clay particles to be fertile and large sand particles to drain quickly and warm up early in spring. When topsoil is needed to build up existing soil, it's best to use a loam.

Your soil may have an imbalance of sand, silt, or clay, which can cause problems. For example, excess clay makes for a sticky soil that water and nutrients are slow to move through. Sandy soil retains less moisture and fewer nutrients than clay or loamy soils. In such situations, gardeners often focus on changing their soil's texture. But improving the structure (the way individual soil particles bind together) is a more practical way to improve plant growth, and structure is easier to change than texture.

Well-structured soil is composed of small granules, which it easily crumbles into when squeezed. It holds water, air, and nutrients better than poorly structured soil, which collapses into disconnected grains when wet.

To improve soil structure, add organic matter at every opportunity. Microorganisms feed on the organic matter and produce a "glue" that coats mineral particles and causes them to stick together in moisture-, air-, and nutrient-retaining granules. Till or turn organic matter into the soil as you prepare the bed or add it by sheet composting. Aim for a 2- to 3-inch layer of moistened peat moss or compost, or a 3- to 4-inch layer of chopped tree leaves.

MAINTAINING GOOD SOIL

Routinely loosen soil by cultivating with a hoe, minitiller, or fork. This is especially important in soils with a high percentage of silt because these tend to "cap"—the surface layer becomes dense and nearly impervious to air and water.

ACID, NEUTRAL, AND ALKALINE SOIL—PERENNIALS FOR EVERY pH

Most perennials grow well if the soil pH is between 6 and 7, but some prefer more acid, others more alkaline conditions. Here are representatives of the various groups:

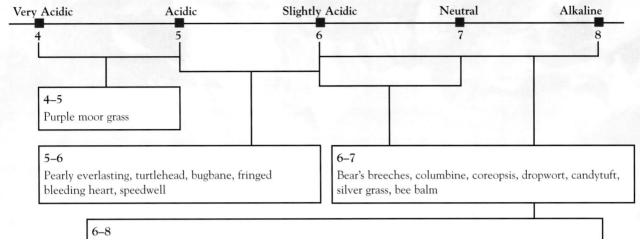

Very Acidic	Acidic	Slightly Acidic	Neutral	Alkaline
4	5	6	7	8

4–5
Purple moor grass

5–6
Pearly everlasting, turtlehead, bugbane, fringed bleeding heart, speedwell

6–7
Bear's breeches, columbine, coreopsis, dropwort, candytuft, silver grass, bee balm

6–8
Baneberry, anemone, aster, astilbe, bellflower, clematis, pinks, delphinium, hibiscus, blanket flower, false sunflower, purple bush clover, sundrops, fleece flower, buttercup, salvia, pincushion flower

CHANGING SOIL pH

A soil pH between 5.5 and 6.5 is considered ideal because that's the range in which the most nutrients are available without harming plants. To measure pH, have soil tested through the county extension office. Lower pH with sulfur (ground soil sulfur, iron sulfate, or flowers of sulfur); raise it with lime (agricultural or dolomitic limestone). Thoroughly mix these materials into the top 6 to 8 inches of soil in the fall before planting. The change will last a season or longer. Retest soil before adding sulfur or lime again.

If Soil Is...	Add...per 100 square feet
Clay	
To lower pH 1 point	2 pounds of soil sulfur or 7½ pounds of iron sulfate
To raise pH 1 point	10½ pounds of limestone
Sandy	
To lower pH 1 point	1 pound of soil sulfur or 3 pounds of iron sulfate
To raise pH 1 point	2¾ pounds of limestone
Loam	
To lower pH 1 point	1½ pounds of soil sulfur or 5 pounds of iron sulfate
To raise pH 1 point	7½ pounds of limestone

Keep the organic content high by using a 1- to 3-inch blanket of organic mulch and natural forms of fertilizers such as manure. These encourage worms and soil microorganisms. Add amendments (the same you used when preparing the bed) in small amounts every time you rearrange, add, or divide plants in the bed.

SOIL TEXTURE

Total depth: 3"
Clay: ½" or more, making it 16% of total. Clay settles in several days to a week.
Silt: 1", 33% of total. Silt settles in 10 to 180 minutes.
Sand: 1½", 50% of total. Sand settles in 10 minutes.
Conclusion: Sandy soil

Put 1 cup of soil and 1 tablespoon of dishwasher detergent in a quart jar. Fill jar with water; cap and shake. Particles settle in this order: sand, then silt, organic matter, and clay. The depth of each layer gives clues as to soil type. Measure the total depth of the soil that settles out; then measure each layer. Divide layer depths by total depth.

■ **Loam:** 40% sand, 40% silt, 20% clay.

■ **Sandy soil:** 50% or more sand. May dry out and nutrients leach rapidly. Monitor watering; use degradable mulch; apply fertilizer frequently, lightly.

■ **Clay soil:** more than 25% clay. Tends to pack down. Add organic matter; use degradable mulch; avoid walking on bed.

■ **Silt soil:** more than 40% silt. Tends to pack down, excluding air and causing water to bead up and run off. Add organic matter; use degradable mulch; avoid walking on bed.

CHOOSING & GROWING PERENNIALS

Find a nursery that carries a wide selection of plants. Container-grown plants (inset) have adapted to confined quarters, and their roots may be growing in circles.

You've worked hard to lay the groundwork. Now you're ready for the fun—choosing perennials that will enhance your surroundings with stunning flowers and foliage.

Before you head to a garden center or browse through catalogs, do a little more homework. Know the cold-hardiness for your region (see the USDA map on page 247). Also, review the growing conditions in your yard—areas may vary. Is the soil well- or poorly drained? Fertile or lean? Does it steadily retain moisture or dry out between waterings? Will your perennials get full sun or part shade? Do some spots get more wind than others?

When matched to a compatible site, your perennials will be full, bloom readily, and stand a better chance of fending off insects and disease. Take notes to have handy while mulling over plant choices and shopping. Then peruse the Encyclopedia of Plants starting on page 146 to find plants that will please you and will happily— and healthfully—grow in your yard.

SHOPPING FOR PLANTS

Finally, think about where you'll find plants. The Yellow Pages can direct you to local garden centers. Mail-order sources can be

reached by phone or the Internet. Local newspapers' gardening sections may announce plant swaps. Here's an overview of each plant source and its pros and cons.

GARDEN CENTERS

Buying at garden centers lets you carry out your purchases and plant them right away. Experts there can help you fine-tune your shopping list and answer questions about plants in stock you may not have researched. The perennials may carry a guarantee, and the garden center's location may make replacement convenient.

In general, plants at garden centers are available in 4-inch pots or gallon containers. Some nurseries offer smaller or larger sizes.

Garden centers tend to stock only several hundred of the tens of thousands of perennial species and varieties. If that is your only source, you may need to make substitutions for the original choices on your list.

MAIL ORDER

Mail order lets you shop without pulling out of the driveway. But the real enticement is being able to track down specific varieties not available at local garden centers, as well as having a choice of size and price.

To find mail-order resources, consult references, such as *The Andersen Horticultural*

Perennials come in many sizes. Here's an assortment: (A) cell pack (B) 3-inch pot (C) 4-inch pot (D) 6-inch pot (E) 8-inch or 1-gallon pot (F) 5-gallon tub (G) rooted cutting (H) division (I) field-grown clump.

Library's Source List of Plants & Seeds. Or put the Internet to work. Enter a specific plant name in a search engine. You'll turn up dozens of online catalogs offering that plant.

With mail-order sources, you won't be able to inspect plants close up. A catalog might indicate plant size, but quality may be unknown. It's wise to limit your first order until you're acquainted with the quality and size of plants sent by a particular retailer.

Mail-order selections usually arrive potted or bare-root (dormant, with roots protected in a moist medium). It's also possible to find perennials as first-year seedlings packed in plastic cells, typically six to a pack.

Perennials in six-packs cost much less than container-grown plants. If you buy plants this small, however, you may have to wait an extra year for a strong garden display.

Try to plant your order as soon as possible. However, if you must wait a few days, keep the plants moist and cool. Do not store them longer than a week.

GROWING PLANTS FROM SEED

Starting plants from seed appeals to many people. Seed costs less than plants, and it's fascinating to watch plants develop. However, do think about expenses beyond seed packets, including seed-starting potting medium, containers, and grow-lights and the electricity to run them. And you'll need to invest time tending seedlings and waiting until they reach blooming size (typically one to three years).

Opting to grow perennials from seed widens the selection you can grow. Some hybrid perennial varieties are sterile and can't be grown from seed. Others won't come

true—the seedlings do not carry the parent plant's traits. You can obtain offsprings of these varieties only as divisions or cuttings.

PERENNIALS FROM FRIENDS

You can find perennials to divide in friends' gardens and at community or garden club

Buy the healthiest-looking plants the garden center has to offer. Look for specimens that are not yet in bloom and make sure the pot has a plant marker so that you remember the exact cultivar you bought.

SOURCES FOR PLANTS
continued

The aster (center) is an ideal transplant. Its roots just fill the soil mix. The variegated obedient plant (left) is pot-bound. With all its root growth massed at the bottom of the pot, it may establish slowly. The coral bells (right) is poorly rooted. Its root ball is likely to crumble during planting, which will damage the roots.

plant exchanges. Such divisions are often far larger specimens than nurseries offer. You may have the opportunity to talk to the gardener who grew the plant about how large it will be and how it will perform in your environment.

Another plus: Divisions are almost always field grown—taken from outdoor beds. They're in tune with the prevailing weather in your area, whereas plants grown in greenhouses or in other states may require hardening off before planting (see page 95).

Selection at exchanges is limited. Many of the plants spread aggressively; they are available because the original plant needs curtailment or frequent division. Long-lived, clump-forming species, such as peonies and false indigo, are shared less often.

Bear in mind that problems may move with a plant. Professionally grown plants are cleaner because growers have more options available to them to keep plants free of insects and diseases. In the case of soil-dwelling problems, such as crown rot, verticillium wilt, and nematodes, pros can fumigate potting soil, a tactic not usually practical in a home garden.

Even the best garden-grown specimens host some pests. It's prudent to rinse soil off a division before taking it home and to keep that plant under a watchful eye in your garden.

SELECTION TIPS

With so many plants available, how can you choose confidently? Judge the plant not just by flowers, but by its leaves, roots, and eyes.

LEAVES: These should be uniformly green, unblemished, and at least as large as your references indicate—all signs of good nutrition and low stress. Such plants will move smoothly into a garden. Avoid plants with limp leaves or dried, brown leaf edges.

ROOTS: Gently slide the plant partway out of its pot to check root condition. Roots should be firm, like fresh, crisp vegetables. They should just fill the pot, binding the soil mix together but not circling the sides and bottom in a dense pot-bound layer.

Pot-bound plants do not transplant well because their root tips are massed at the bottom. That means the plant has fewer points to grow out of the potting soil and into the garden soil.

Also watch for loose soil mix shifting away from the root mass when you tip the pot. Such a plant is too small for its pot and price tag, and its root ends are likely to shear off at planting. The broken roots will be prone to fungal infection and will need time for healing before new growth can commence.

EYES: An eye on a perennial is a bud on the roots that's ready to grow into a shoot. Each eye may produce a single stem or a cluster of leaves and a flowering stalk. The number of eyes is directly related to the plant's health and how much energy it stored during the previous growing season. The more eyes, the bigger and more quickly the plant will grow.

SIZE: Perennials spend much of their first season establishing roots in a bed and show little increase in size. If the plant is one that establishes quickly, it can double or triple in size the second season. Perennials bought in small pots often do that. And because their roots grow quickly out of the potting soil into the bed, they can match or surpass their larger counterparts in a year.

HOW MANY TO BUY?

The number of plants that will fit into your garden depends on the garden's square footage (sq. ft.) and how far apart the plants should be from each other. Because perennial gardens are generally filled with plants having varying spacing requirements, you may find it helpful to measure the area allotted for each clump individually. The chart lists three common-size gardens and eight plant spacings. To determine the number for your garden, follow this formula:

number of plants = area of planting space ÷ spacing^2

Spacing (inches)	30 sq. ft.	100 sq. ft.	170 sq. ft.
4	270	900	1530
6	120	400	680
8	68	225	383
10	44	144	245
12	30	100	170
15	19	64	109
18	14	45	76
24	8	25	43

PLANTING THE PERENNIAL BED

Well-planted perennials thrive. These have room to grow; they're not planted too low or too high in the ground, and each one has a watering crater.

Perennials may be planted any time of year, but they make the strongest start if planted when the air is cool and the soil warm and moist. Cool air retards top growth while moist, warm soil stimulates rooting, allowing plants to establish wide, drought-resistant, stem-stabilizing bases.

The best times to plant are midspring when weeping cherries, forsythia, and Dutch hyacinths are in full bloom, and early autumn before leaf fall when 'Autumn Joy' sedum and perennial fountain grass have passed from flower to seed.

Overcast and drizzly days are ideal for planting. Avoid the middle of a hot day—when water from leaves is lost more quickly than it can be replaced. Even if no permanent damage is done, recovering from wilt consumes energy that the plant could have used to push roots into the new site.

If you must plant in the hot sun, erect shade screens. Plant into moist, friable soil and water each plant immediately afterward.

HARDENING OFF PERENNIALS

When northerners vacation in the Tropics or lowlanders visit high altitudes, they must gradually acclimate to intense sun or thinner air. Plants are no different. Perennials grown in a greenhouse without wind, wide temperature swings, or direct sun need hardening off—time and stimulus to toughen cell walls and readjust fluid levels so they don't break, dry up, or burn outdoors.

Not every perennial requires hardening. Transplants between outdoor beds don't usually need it. Because garden soil will insulate new bare-root perennials, they can

be planted right away, even if 32° F weather is likely. Leaves on the transplant and shoots from the bare roots are tough from the start.

Perennials that have been in a dark package in the mail and those sold from inside a greenhouse in early spring are not ready to be planted. When buying perennials from an outdoor sales area, ask whether they have been hardened off or simply moved out each day from indoors.

If the plants need hardening off, place them in a spot protected from the wind and out of the midday sun for a day. At night, cover them against rapid cooling or move them into a protected area—near the house or in a shed, for example. The next day, give the plants an additional hour of late-morning or midafternoon sun. Protect them again at night. Increase the light and expose them to wind over two more days before planting.

PLANT SPACING IS KEY

Before digging, set the perennials in the bed or mark the bed where each plant will grow; adjust spacing based on mature widths. This is also your chance to adjust the arrangement so that the bed looks aesthetically pleasing from the beginning.

It may seem as though your new perennials are too far apart. But resist the urge to plant them closer. Otherwise, you'll be forced to thin or divide the plants after only a year. Avoid filling between perennials with annuals; this not only reduces the water and nutrients available to each plant, but also discourages their root growth. Because perennial tops usually grow only as wide as their roots spread the preceding year,

PLANTING THE PERENNIAL BED
continued

Match the digging tool to the pot: a trowel for a 3-inch pot, a small spade for a 4-inch container, and a standard spade, square or round point, to plant large clumps and 8-inch or larger pots.

temporary fillers may actually preserve gaps and delay the garden's maturity.

To minimize the bare look, you can move all plants in a drift (a grouping of one kind of perennial) fractionally closer together. This tactic widens the spaces between drifts. Such spacing creates an attractive outline of each plant grouping. It also gives you room to work in the garden without stepping on and compressing soil above new roots.

Some gardeners lay out the garden bed by setting out potted plants. Others place a stake or marker where each perennial will grow. Some even use markers of varied colors and heights to match the expected show. You might draw lines and even a planting key with bonemeal or flour to outline locations of plant groups. Each technique gives you the chance to visualize the garden and make changes before planting.

THE RIGHT PLANTING TOOLS

When you're ready to plant, select the best tool. Match the size of the tool—trowel, spade, or shovel—to the size of the holes needed. A trowel is best for cell packs up to 4-inch pots. Use a shovel or spade for small bare-root plants. Once you spread the roots wide for planting, they will probably need a bigger hole than you first thought.

DON'T PLANT TOO DEEP

Most roots grow horizontally or at a gentle downward angle, so it's better to dig wide rather than straight-down holes. If you disturb the soil beneath the plant too much, the plant may struggle or die as it sinks with the settling subsoil.

If you loosened the whole bed during soil preparation, simply dig holes as wide as the pots (or root spread of bare-root perennials). But if you didn't work the bed because the soil was loose enough to begin with, or you plan to loosen it gradually by sheet composting, dig slope-sided holes twice as wide as the root balls or the roots when spread out. Slope-sided holes yield more rooting area than those with straight sides.

Plant perennials to grow at the same level as they were in the pot or field. With few exceptions, setting perennials too deep invites stem-rot and crown-rot problems. Planting

Most root growth occurs in oxygen-rich surface layers. It's a better use of your time and energy to dig wide, slope-sided planting holes than straight-sided holes.

too high (so that the root ball's shoulders are above ground) is also a problem and likely to retard growth. Upper roots grow the most after planting; if they're set high, dry air will check their growth.

To calculate the proper planting depth for potted perennials, set a still-potted plant into a hole. Check whether it is too high or low. Adjust the hole as needed. If you must return soil to the hole, tamp it well to prevent settling.

Determining the proper planting depth for bare-root perennials requires garden savvy. If the plant tag doesn't have specific directions, look at the color of shoots (eyes) and stems, if any, on the root mass. White or pink shoots and eyes were below ground before and should be covered to about an inch deep again. Where an eye shows green, it was receiving sunlight and should be just above the ground. Stain on stems likely marks the ground level. If there are no visible eyes or stem stains to offer clues, position the root mass so it's barely covered to about 1 inch below ground.

ROOTS ARE FRAGILE

Handle root balls carefully as you remove the pot. Don't lift a plant out of the pot by pulling on its stems. Instead, invert the pot, support the soil on your spread fingers or hands, and lift the pot off the root ball.

When a plant will not slide out easily, rap the inverted pot sharply on its rim while supporting the weight of the soil. Or, if a container is flexible, roll it on a hard surface to separate root mass from pot. Or cut off the pot.

If you happen to buy a pot-bound plant, it will require some tough love at planting time. In other words, you'll have to injure the plant to promote the best root growth. Otherwise, the roots will probably grow only from the bottom of the root ball. So be assertive. Slice off the bottom layer of roots and score the sides vertically in several places. After taking time to repair its injuries, the plant will

develop new roots at each point where the roots were severed.

Another technique for handling pot-bound plants is to butterfly the roots. Slice once or twice vertically into the root mass from the bottom halfway to the top. Spread the two halves over a mound of soil in the planting hole. (See page 98.)

Bare roots are deceptively brittle and dead-looking. Having been packed for cold storage or shipping, they lie flat. Soak the roots in water for an hour or two. This replaces water lost in shipping and makes the roots more

HANDLE WITH CARE

Some perennials transplant without a hitch, others bear a bit of watching after a move to prevent wilting or blowing over in the wind. Still others sulk, even after being moved with the greatest care. Here are some examples from each group. For the rest, look to the Encyclopedia of Plants.

EASY: Daylily, hostas, lady's mantle, daisy, coreopsis, Siberian iris, ornamental grasses

AVERAGE: (watch for wilt or wind damage) Astilbe, turtlehead, bearded iris, obedient plant

HARD: Yellow corydalis, monkshood, Japanese anemone, gas plant, false indigo, blue flax, ornamental mullein

Dig a planting hole at least as wide as the spread-out roots of your bare-root perennial. Soak bare-root perennials in a bucket of water to moisten any dry roots.

PLANTING THE PERENNIAL BED
continued

When unpotting a perennial, spread your fingers around the stems to support the soil's weight. Invert the pot and lift it off with your other hand.

Check the depth as you plant. The top of the root ball should be level with the soil's surface.

When roots are badly pot-bound, butterfly the roots. Slice up into the root ball from the bottom and spread the roots wide across mounded soil.

Plant bare-root perennials with their eyes barely covered or within an inch of the surface. Make a mound of soil in the hole and spread the bare roots over it.

flexible. Dig a hole at least as wide as the fully spread roots and half as deep as it is wide. Form a sloping mound in the center of the hole, high enough to bring the eyes or stems to just at or below ground level. Now splay the roots over this mound. They should be spread wide when planted so the plant will be stable in the future and draw water and nutrients from the widest area.

With the plant in the hole or on the mound, begin filling the hole. Tamp to displace air pockets but not so hard as to overly compress the soil. Fill the hole halfway, pat the soil with your hands, water to allow air pockets to settle, and finish filling.

Use excavated soil to fill in around new plants. Avoid using special soil as backfill, a practice that has been proven to discourage the wide rooting of healthy perennials.

Plants will root best if both the original root ball and the earth around it stay moist throughout the first growing season. Build a watering crater to trap and hold rain and irrigation water until they soak into that vital area. About 2 to 3 inches of soil beyond the root ball or farthest spread root, scrape excess or leftover excavated soil into a circular levee about 1 inch high, around the entire perennial.

Now water, filling the crater. Repair any washouts. Whenever you water, the crater will trap a full ration for the roots below.

KEEP ROOTS MOIST

While perennials become established, irrigate with a watering can or a hose-end shower wand. Both devices let you target individual plants; the craters prevent wasteful runoff to unplanted areas. Desirable perennials grow, whereas areas between perennials stay dry enough to discourage weeds.

New perennials dry out more quickly than established plants. That's because their potted root balls are artificially narrow and have been pampered in terms of watering and fertilizer. Their roots can't sustain their oversize tops with normal irrigation. Water carefully until you see vigorous new growth, a sign that roots are growing out.

NO FERTILIZER NEEDED

Don't rush to fertilize new perennials. In preparing the bed, you ensured the plants have all needed nutrients. However, if you didn't follow those steps and plants need to be fed, avoid using a fertilizer containing water-soluble nitrogen until the plant begins strong new growth. Use slow-release fertilizer instead. Also avoid applying excess nitrogen. It can soften roots and make them more susceptible to soil-borne diseases.

A new plant may need more than water, sun, and nutrients. Beneficial microorganisms, such as fungi and bacteria, regularly attach themselves to roots. They give roots an increased water-collecting area in exchange for carbohydrates. The plant becomes established quicker. Light-colored soil or soil so compacted before preparation that it was airless may lack beneficial microorganisms. In this case, use products that contain mycorrhiza to raise the level of the microorganisms living in the soil.

APPLY A BLANKET OF MULCH

All plantings profit from mulch, which is any material that covers the ground, conserving moisture, moderating soil temperature, and suppressing weeds by shading out weed seeds.

Apply a blanket of mulch to cover the whole bed, including watering craters, but leave a bare ring an inch or two out from the crown of each perennial. Mulch resting against perennial stems can trap heat and moisture there, and rot the stems.

Spread woody mulch, such as bark or composted ground wood, 1 to 2 inches deep. Spread leafy mulches and hulls, such as shredded leaves, pine straw, cocoa hulls, and peanut shells, 2 to 3 inches deep.

ANTICIPATE THE LEANERS

Moist, secure, and blanketed, most perennials need no more special attention. A few may, however, benefit from staking. For example, a spring-planted bearded iris may bloom before its roots spread far enough to anchor the heavy blossom. If the plant topples, it can uproot itself. Spring-planted peony, delphinium, blazing star, cardinal flower, and beard-tongue may also have trouble supporting their first flowers. Any large-flowered species is at risk if forced into early bloom—which many garden centers do to stimulate early sales.

To prevent toppling, place a stake next to each main stem, driving it into the undisturbed soil below the plant. Tie the stems to the stakes as they grow.

Directing water into the craters around new perennials ensures that irrigation water won't run away from the roots until it has had a chance to soak in.

Spread mulch up to and over the rim of the watering crater, but avoid letting it rest against the plant stems.

If you must plant in the hot sun, shade the plants during the hottest part of the day for a week or two. This shade is dark cloth attached to stakes.

WATERING NEW PERENNIALS

1ST DAY Plant and water the perennials.
IN 2 DAYS Three days after planting, check soil moisture; water again if it's drying down. Fill watering crater. If water soaks in immediately, fill crater again until the water soaks in gradually.
IN 3 MORE DAYS Check soil moisture and water if soil is drying down.
IN 4 MORE DAYS Check and water as needed.
IN 5 MORE DAYS Check and water as needed.
IN 6 MORE DAYS Check and water as needed.
IN 7 MORE DAYS Twenty-eight days after planting, the perennials are on schedule for weekly water checks, the same as the rest of the garden.

WATERING

Rotary and oscillating sprinklers are good for covering large areas and rinsing off dusty foliage

Watering cans and shower wands are efficient for filling watering craters of new plantings quickly.

Drip irrigation systems and weeper hoses conserve water while wetting the soil and keeping foliage dry.

Professional growers put only experienced employees in charge of watering, people who know how much water plants need, how to measure it, and when to adjust amounts and techniques. Here are the secrets to watering plants like a professional.

HOW MUCH TO WATER?

Perennials need an average of 1 to 2 inches of water per week. How do you know if you apply that much?

To measure the output of a sprinkler, let it fill a rain gauge to the 1-inch mark, or use a straight-sided container, such as a tuna can. Filling it may take 15 minutes to six hours, depending on water pressure, hose length, sprinkler type, size of area, wind, and evaporation rate.

To measure the output of a drip or weeper line, check the soil 1 foot from an emitter or the far end of the hose. One inch of water wets clay soil 3 to 4 inches deep and sandy soil 18 inches deep. Dig down that far with a trowel. If the soil feels cool or moist, it has received 1 inch of water. It will take several hours to apply 1 inch of water through a drip system or weeper hose.

UNDERSTAND THE SITE

Every site has unique wet and dry areas. A bed catching overthrow from a neighbor's sprinklers won't need as much water as beds under rain-blocking eaves or next to brick walls, which wick away moisture. Check all beds regularly until you know which are the first and last to dry out. Use those as indicator beds to determine when it is time to water.

Several conditions affect how often you water and the technique you use. The illustration on page 101 demonstrates how water needs can vary across a landscape.

RAIN: Monitor weather reports or check the rain gauge, then water each week to make up the difference. In large beds, use several rain gauges to ensure that all plantings receive an inch of water.

SOIL TYPE: One inch of water may keep clay moist for more than a week, but excessively drained sandy soils may need frequent light waterings totaling more than 1 inch per week.

SOIL CONDITION: Infiltration rate—how quickly moisture seeps into soil pores—may be slow on compacted soil and on slopes. Some silty soils repel water if they're dry. Compensate by watering slowly, or water in spurts, stopping when water begins to run off, restarting after it soaks in. Use a mulch; it collects water, preventing runoff.

PLANTS: Some perennials sulk if denied water for a day; others like it dry. Most fall in between. For easy maintenance, group perennials by their particular watering needs.

CRITICAL WATERING TIMES

Plants are needier at some times than others, especially when growing rapidly. Species that can normally shrug off weeks of summer drought may suffer from dry down in early spring and be weak all season.

It's important to water in fall, when perennials aren't growing many leaves but are adding roots at a rapid rate. Moisture in fall can greatly improve the next year's show.

New plants dry out more quickly than perennials with wide, established root systems. Regularly check newly planted perennials during the first season, with watering can in hand.

Water in the early morning for the best results. At first light, the air is calm and plants take up water rapidly so there's little waste. The foliage dries quickly as the air warms and breezes stir. This thwarts leaf diseases that thrive on damp leaves and high humidity.

There are exceptions to morning irrigation. In hot, dry regions where water is scarce, nighttime irrigation cuts losses to evaporation. Risk of infection is not significant, because humidity-loving leaf diseases are suppressed by the very dry air.

Some plants, especially recent transplants, may need midday watering to cool the air and prevent wilt. You might water at every opportunity if you're helping certain plants recover from stress, such as heavy insect infestation or hailstorm damage.

In the final analysis, when the soil is dry and plants need water, turn on the sprinklers, regardless of the hour.

Those who base watering on rainfall and soil moisture know that it may not be needed every week. In some regions, it may be necessary only four or five times a year. Where perennial gardens are extensive, watering may take hours and run around the clock. The infrequency of such evening and nighttime shifts makes them no more risky than late-night rains.

WAYS TO WATER

Choose the watering system—overhead or direct-to-soil, automatic or manual—suited to the site and your needs.

Overhead systems cleanse foliage, keeping dust-related problems and mite damage low. Their output is easily measured, and the systems are readily available in many forms. But your plants are at increased risk of leaf diseases, runoff on windy and hilly sites, and battered foliage if plants grow across a spray path.

Direct-to-soil watering conserves water and keeps foliage dry, but you may have difficulty measuring amounts applied or remembering to be vigilant with drip lines and weepers. In such invisible flows, clogs can go unnoticed until plants downstream wilt.

An automatic system frees you from wrestling with hoses. But it may lull you into checking soil moisture less often. Overwatering and dry corners may go unnoticed.

A manual system with overhead and direct-to-soil elements plus semiautomatic extras may be best for perennials. Most botanical gardens employ these hybrid systems in perennial areas.

SPECIAL CASES

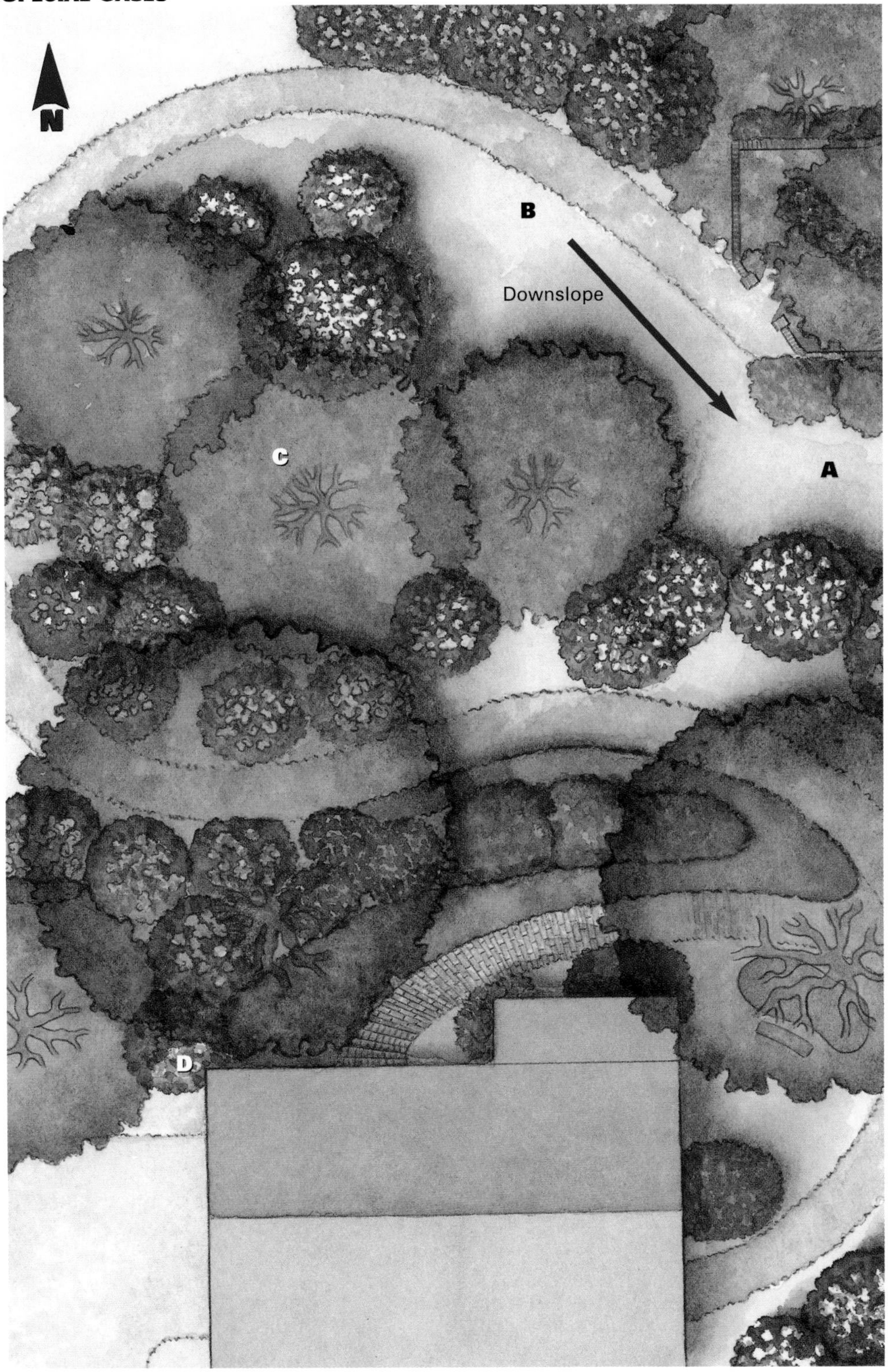

N

Downslope

B

C

A

D

A–Low area: Don't overwater; runoff from higher areas keeps it wet.
B–Severe slope: Water slowly or in short frequent spurts to avoid runoff. If the slope faces south, sun dries soil; check moisture often.
C–Under trees: Check soil moisture often; tree roots quickly take up excess water.
D–Wind tunnel: Use drip system or hand water to ensure all plants receive water because wind distorts sprinkler pattern.

FERTILIZING

Fertilizing promotes healthy growth and large flowers.

Just as you can't rely solely on rainfall for the best perennial show, you can't expect nature to supply all the nutrients perennials require. Gardeners' standards

FERTILIZERS FOR ACID-LOVING PLANTS

Fertilizers for acid-loving plants contain sulfur and certain nutrients, such as iron, that wouldn't normally be available in alkaline soils. The sulfur produces weak sulfuric acid, which helps dissolve nutrients from soils normally too alkaline to release them. Use these products if you want to grow an acid-loving perennial such as gas plant in alkaline soil.

are higher than nature's. They want larger flowers, fuller foliage, and greater stature than can be had without help. Processes such as weeding, deadheading, cutting flowers, and removing plant debris disrupt the natural recycling of nutrients. And since most garden perennials are exotic species (not native in an area), soils probably lack minerals they need. You're going to have to fertilize.

WHAT FERTILIZERS DO

Some people believe that fertilizers feed plants and stimulate plant growth. Not true. Plants create their own food through photosynthesis—by making sugars and starches (necessary fuel) from carbon dioxide and water, using the energy of sunlight. Growth and flowering are controlled by temperature, sunlight, water, and internally produced hormones.

Fertilizers simply provide essential elements. These elements allow plants to create enzymes, fuel photosynthesis, and do other things in the way that vitamins help humans build strong bones and have a healthy glow.

Generally, to ensure essential elements are available, fertilize when perennials first start growing each year and again when flower buds begin to form. Ideally, you would fertilize each plant on its own schedule, because each species starts to grow and flower at different times—cool-season perennials first, later-emerging species weeks or months later. However, most gardens contain dozens of species, and most gardeners have dozens of other priorities. So the best compromise is to fertilize to meet average growth and blooming peaks.

FERTILIZER SCHEDULE

Roots have no teeth and so can't chew fertilizer pellets or bits of rock phosphate. The

EXCEPTIONS TO THE RULES

Some perennial species grow best in lean soil, which is low in nitrogen. Others are heavy feeders and require more than average amounts of nitrogen. The following are among the most common perennials with differing needs:

HEAVY FEEDERS

- Astilbe
- Clematis
- Delphinium
- Peony

Pale older leaves (lower ones), smaller-than-normal leaves, and thin stems indicate nitrogen need.

LIGHT FEEDERS

- Artemisia
- Barrenwort
- Mullein

Weak stems, reduced flowering, and rank growth may indicate too much nitrogen has been applied near the plants.

WHEN TO FERTILIZE AND AMOUNTS TO APPLY

The type of fertilizer you use will govern when and how often you need to fertilize as well as how much to apply.

Fertilizer Type	Example	Total amount* needed per growing season		When to Apply
		100 sq. ft.	10 sq. ft.	
Quick-release powders (The nitrogen dissolves in water and is immediately available.)	15-30-15 Miracle-Gro All Purpose or any soluble fertilizer that starts with 15% nitrogen (first number).	2⅔ cups or 1⅓ lb.	4½ tbsp.	In midspring, when large trumpet daffodils bloom, apply 1½ tbsp. per 10 square feet of garden dissolved in water according to label directions. Apply 1 tbsp. per 10 square feet every two weeks until you've supplied the full amount (by midsummer).
	10-52-10 Miracle-Gro Bloom Booster or any high-phosphorus (middle number) soluble fertilizer	2⅔ cups or 1⅓ lbs.	2 tsp.	Can be used in place of 15-30-15; apply when flower buds are forming.
	30-10-10 Miracid or any soluble fertilizer with 30% nitrogen	1⅓ cups	2 tbsp.	Starting in midspring as large trumpet daffodils bloom, apply ½ tbsp. per 10 square feet of garden every two weeks until you've supplied the full amount.
Standard granular (Nitrogen dissolves quickly and is available to plants soon after fertilizer is applied)	12-12-12 lawn and garden fertilizer or other granular fertilizers with 10 to 14% nitrogen	3 cups or 1⅔ lbs.	5–6 tbsp.	Scratch half the recommended amount into the soil's surface in spring once most of the plants have started to grow. Repeat in late spring when Siberian irises are in full bloom.
	5-10-5 garden fertilizer or other fertilizer containing 5% nitrogen	7 cups or 4 lbs.	¾ cup	Scratch half the recommended amount into the soil's surface in spring once most of the plants have started to grow. Repeat in late spring when Siberian irises are in full bloom.
Slow-release materials, granular and natural organic products (Nitrogen available only when soil is warm and moist; lasts for two to three months)	14-14-14 Osmocote or other sulfur-coated urea product with 14% nitrogen	2½ cups or 1⁴⁄₁₀ lbs.	4 tbsp.	Scratch the entire amount into the soil's surface in early spring as bulb foliage emerges.
	5-5-5 all purpose or other product with 4 to 6% nitrogen	10⅔ cups or 4 lbs.	1 heaping cup	Scratch the entire amount into the soil surface in early spring as bulb foliage emerges. Repeat in autumn when tree leaves begin to fall.

Use these amounts in the absence of soil test results. They will provide nitrogen at the rate of 2 pounds of nitrogen per 1,000 square feet per year. Some perennials may need more or less than that per year (see the Encyclopedia of Plants for species noted as heavy or light feeders). A soil test will tell you which fertilizer formula is best to provide the appropriate amounts of phosphorus and potassium for your garden. (Tbsp. stands for tablespoon, lb. for pound.)

only nutrient a root can use is one dissolved in water. Fertilizers applied in solution, such as Miracle-Gro, are immediately usable. But they will leach out of the root zone as rain and irrigation water move through soil. So it's best to use such products biweekly or monthly in small doses from the time your plants begin to grow until their foliage matures.

Many standard granular fertilizers also dissolve readily, although at a slower pace than soluble fertilizers. The garden may need two or three applications of these fertilizers in a season.

Slow-release fertilizers supply elements over a long period. These materials include sulfur- and polymer-coated urea products, such as Osmocote, and organic materials, such as manure or fish meal. With slow-release fertilizers, you can apply all or most of the season's ration in one application in late

FERTILIZING
continued

fall or midspring, one to three months before plants will use it.

A hybrid schedule suits many plants and gardeners. A slow-release product may be applied once a year and supplemented with faster-acting, more concentrated water-soluble products as foliage color and other plant responses dictate.

CHOOSING A FERTILIZER

The major nutrients provided by most fertilizers are nitrogen (N), phosphorus (P), and potassium (K). Phosphorus and potassium are minerals; nitrogen comes from decomposing organic matter and from the atmosphere through rainwater.

A soil test will tell you the nutrients available in your soil and recommend amounts of supplemental fertilizer needed. For instance, soil test results may advise you to use a high-phosphorus fertilizer such as 5-10-5 (5 percent nitrogen, 10 percent phosphorus, 5 percent potassium). Check local government directory listings for a county or state extension service office near you. Without soil test results to guide your choice of fertilizers, choose one that provides balanced amounts of nitrogen, phosphorus, and potassium, such as 14-14-14 or 10-10-10.

CALCULATING AMOUNT

How much fertilizer to apply is based on perennials' use of nitrogen. Nitrogen is a double-edged sword. It is essential to all plant parts in all growth phases, but too much can promote growth of foliage at the expense of flowering. The resulting excessively succulent tissue is susceptible to insects and disease. You should calculate fertilizers to provide enough but not too much nitrogen.

The average perennial fares well if its bed is fertilized so that 1 pound of actual nitrogen is spread over about 500 square feet. A bag of 10-10-10 contains 10 percent nitrogen, so 10 pounds of that fertilizer is the right amount to work into 500 square feet of bed. Here's how it's figured: 10 percent multiplied by 10 pounds equals 1 pound of nitrogen. Calculations for other fertilizers and smaller areas are provided in the chart on page 103.

APPLYING FERTILIZERS

Because fertilizer must dissolve to be of use to plants, mix it in water (water-soluble types) or spread it on bare soil and scratch it in (granular and slow-release products).

A good time to spread fertilizer is just before you plan to weed a perennial bed because weeding will help mix the fertilizer into the top inch or two of soil. Scatter granules as evenly as possible across an area. Avoid depositing any on the foliage, where it may cause a contact burn.

Water immediately after fertilizing. This dissolves some of the fertilizer and washes any granules or dust off foliage.

You can opt to use a combination of fertilizers, such as blood meal to supply nitrogen, steamed bonemeal for phosphorus, and greensand for potassium. (Apply these products long before plants need them, because all are slow-acting.) Or you might want to supplement an all-purpose fertilizer with superphosphate (phosphorus) or muriate of potash (potassium).

When combining materials, apply each one in a separate pass. Because of their differing sizes and weights, mixing materials and applying them together can result in an uneven application of one product or another.

WHAT NUTRIENT DEFICIENCIES LOOK LIKE

Deficiency	Symptom
Nitrogen	Small leaves, short thin growth; leaves turn uniformly yellow, starting at the bottom of the plant; they may take on a reddish hue in severe cases; leaves drop
Phosphorus	Bronze to red to purplish coloration to dull green leaves; shoots short and thin
Potassium	Margins or outer edges of older leaves yellow along their margins and eventually die; potassium deficiencies are rare
Magnesium	Areas between veins of older (lower) leaves turn yellow and die
Boron	Young terminal foliage becomes distorted or thickens or both; foliage may develop yellow spots; terminal buds cease growth; stems may branch but these new stems are also affected
Sulfur	Uniform yellowing of new and young foliage
Iron	Areas between veins of young leaves turn yellow followed by bleaching of the entire leaf to cream or white
Copper	White mottling on and death of newer foliage; leaves may be small, linear, and distorted; shoots die back
Manganese	Yellow foliage
Molybdenum	Leaves do not fully expand; color may be bluish green
Zinc	Small narrow leaves in a rosette-like whirl

PATROL FOR PESTS

Your garden will be free of serious pest problems if you site plants well and keep up on day-to-day chores, including patrolling for pests. Check the color and growth of your plants regularly, and look for early signs of trouble. Inspect new plants weekly during their first season; check older plants about once a month.

You may not know what to expect from a new perennial. After buying an unfamiliar plant, search for a healthy established example in a nearby garden to learn what is normal. A public botanical garden is ideal for finding such plants, but if you don't have access to one, you may find good examples in your neighbor's yards, a local park, or in a display garden at a nursery.

Keep an eye on this healthy specimen to gauge whether any changes in your plant—leaf color and size, growth rate, blemishes—are normal. Subtle changes may indicate a problem is developing.

For example, the comparison plant is bright green but the leaves on your perennial are olive-green, or your plant has stopped growing while the other continues to add leaves. These are early warning signals.

If your plant is struggling or developing problems, check how its growing conditions differ from those of the healthy plant. Is it in more sun or more shade? Wetter or drier soil? A windy site or a protected one? Give your plant the same environment and care as the healthy one.

BE ALERT

When patrolling for pests, look closely at the youngest and oldest foliage for signs of insect feeding or disease. Soft new growth is the first to be attacked by some insects and diseases. Other pests thrive among the dense, dark lower and inner leaves.

A check of leaf undersides may reveal insects or their eggs. This is also the place to find readily identifiable disease symptoms. Also look for signs of damage or infection in the roots of an ailing plant and at the base of faltering shoots.

WHERE TO GO FOR HELP

Turn to the chapter on Troubleshooting, starting on page 124. It will help you diagnose problems that develop in your perennial garden and to deal with them. You will also find information in this book's Encyclopedia of Plants, *The Ortho Home Gardener's Problem Solver,* or other references such as *Diseases and Pests of Ornamental Plants,* by P. P. Pirone.

Learn all you can about a problem before reaching for a remedy. References can help you determine how serious a problem is, whether it's likely to get worse or spread to other plants, and when to take action.

Lacebugs and spider mites are just a few of the insect pests that feed on the undersides of leaves.

Inspect new plants regularly and established plants once a month. Particularly pay attention to leaf undersides, foliage near the ground, and tip growth to catch early signs of trouble.

WEEDING AND MULCHING

Weeds such as quackgrass are trouble for perennial gardeners. They spread on running roots, can live many years, and grow back quickly from tiny pieces of root.

Identify your weeds so you will know how they spread. Then locate and block the source. Weeds most commonly spread by running roots, seeds, or both.

Perennials are healthier in a weed-free bed because they have less competition for water and nutrients. Eliminating weeds also opens space between plants, which improves air circulation, helps control fungi, and cuts down on places where pests hide.

For best weed control, plant into a clean bed. Keep it clean with regular pulling or hoeing and apply mulch or use preemergence herbicide to suppress weed seedlings.

BIWEEKLY OR MONTHLY WEEDING

Effective weeding begins with a simple, practical definition of weed: any plant growing where you don't want it.

Weed every two weeks during a bed's first season. Weed thoroughly, then renew the mulch or preemergent wherever you disturbed the soil. In time, fewer new seedlings will sprout in each two-week interval, and weeding once a month will suffice in the second and subsequent years.

Avoid weeding more frequently; pulling out weeds brings subsurface, dormant weed seeds

into the light. If you weed every time you pass a bed, you may be tempted to shake the soil from the weed's roots, scattering more seeds. Unless you cover or treat all disrupted and dropped soil, weeds will sprout before your next serious weeding session.

KNOW THE ENEMY

Knowledge is power. Know weeds by name, root type, and life cycle—annual, biennial, or perennial—to help keep them at bay. (Learn about specific weeds and how to eliminate or reduce their sources on pages 140 and 141.) Hoe, pull, kill, or smother weeds before they set seed.

HOEING AND PULLING

Hoeing works best when the hoe is sharp, the soil slightly dry, and the seedlings uniformly small. Use a short-handled hoe so that you can get in close to the plants and maintain control of the blade, minimizing nicks to perennial stems.

Pulling, which is time-consuming, is best for removing an occasional overlooked weed and older seedlings that are not easily hoed, killed, or smothered. It's most effective in loose soil, where a tug yields all or most of the roots. Keep beds loose with regular additions of organic matter. Or have a garden fork handy to insert deeply into the ground and loosen the soil as you pull.

Although many gardeners like to weed when soil is softened by rain, doing so may be more frustrating than productive. Weeding always leaves some weeds only partly dislodged. If soil is moist when you work, these weeds are more apt to recover than when soil and air are dry. Any dredged-up weed seeds have a better chance to germinate. You're also more likely to compact the soil. Working when plant foliage is wet can spread plant diseases among the perennials. Also, post-rain weeding removes moisture from a bed. The weeds are full of water that might have been absorbed by the bed's rightful tenants.

KILLING ANNUAL OR BIENNIAL WEEDS

Herbicide is one way to kill annual and biennial weeds. Select a herbicide such as

Take care with herbicides. Use a barrier, such as a piece of cardboard, to protect desirable plants from splashes, drips, or drifting spray.

Spot treat by painting herbicides on weed foliage. Be sure the product dries before allowing adjacent perennials to touch treated weeds.

This large can keeps herbicide spray contained, protecting nearby perennials. Spray through a hole in the can's bottom.

glyphosate that leaves no residue in the soil after being absorbed through the leaves. Apply herbicide carefully, only on calm days. Always shield desirable perennials from overspray or herbicide dripping off taller plants.

You can also kill weeds by smothering—that is, by blocking light and physically preventing the weeds from finding their way to the sun's rays. Smother very small seedlings under 2 inches of mulch. You may have to flatten older weeds under newspaper weighted with 2 inches or more of mulch. The newspaper eventually decomposes.

SUPPRESS NEW SEEDLINGS

After removing annual and biennial weeds, suppress new seedlings by applying a preemergence weed killer or putting down a blanket of mulch. You can spread a preemergence herbicide, such as trifluralin or corn gluten meal, on bare soil. Scratch it lightly into the top inch to kill weed seeds as they sprout. Preemergents should not normally affect established perennials.

Use preemergents only as directed on the package label and only in places and seasons when weeds have been a problem. In dry years and in some types of soil, they have the potential to reach levels harmful to sensitive perennials.

Two inches of mulch also stops many weed seeds from sprouting. The layer denies them light or keeps them so far under cover that the seedlings exhaust their reserves and die before reaching light. Where it is 2 inches

deep, mulch may be 100 percent effective. But where it must taper off near crowns of perennials, it is less so. If mulch is your weed prevention strategy, be vigilant about weeding under the skirts of perennials.

Whether you choose to apply preemergence herbicide or mulch, time it for your weeds' life cycle. Warm-season species, such as crabgrass and purslane, germinate in mid- to late spring. You can prevent them by having the herbicide or mulch in place by midspring.

Cool-season weeds, such as chickweed and tall rocket, germinate in fall, late winter, or very early spring, then grow so rapidly that they'll often be in bloom by your first midspring visit to the bed. Where cool-season weeds are common, apply preemergence herbicide or mulch at fall cleanup.

Weeding tools should suit you and the weed. Long handles spare knees, but short handles are easier to control near plant crowns. Keep hoes sharp to undercut weeds. Use forks to loosen soil as you search for roots. Dandelion diggers are good for tap-rooted weeds, triangular blades for deep roots.

WEEDING AND MULCHING
continued

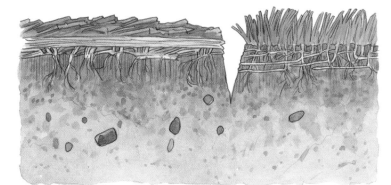

Smothering is usually effective if the weeds are covered during at least two months of their most active growing season. If you smother weeds in May, the garden will be ready to plant in September (and vice versa).

WEEDS: CLUMPER OR RUNNER?

Some perennial weeds form clumps. Others have running roots at, near, or far below the soil surface. (This trait is identified for each perennial weed on pages 140 and 141.) As you encounter new weeds, including once-desirable perennials that proved to be weedy, check the roots to know what you're up against.

CLUMPERS: Clump-forming perennials, such as dandelions or plantains, may have a root that can generate a new top; their clumping nature keeps them stationary. Remove as much of their root as possible.

Use a garden fork to loosen deeply next to the weed, then pull.

Alternatively, treat clump-formers or any perennial weed with glyphosate or a similar product. Work when the weed's foliage is lush so it absorbs a large dose.

After pulling or killing the weed, monitor for resurgence from surviving root tissue. It's not unusual to pull or treat a well-established perennial weed three or four times before its reserves are exhausted. Always mulch an area bared by weed removal; that bare soil is likely to be full of seeds from the removed plant.

Preemergence weed killer spread evenly on the soil surface kills weed seeds as they sprout. Used as directed, it is not usually harmful to plants.

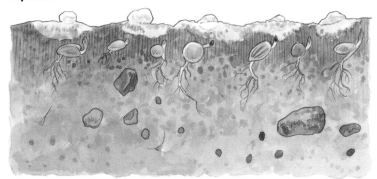

RUNNING ROOTS: Perennial weeds with running roots include grasses, mint, and artemisia. Loosen the soil with a garden fork everywhere you see sprouts of these plants. Then remove them, beginning at the center of the colony and working out to the newest shoots. This may be the only way to find and remove runners that have not yet sent shoots to the surface. Where the runners infiltrate desirable perennials' crowns, loosen the soil and pursue them into that stronghold, even if this means lifting the perennial.

Killing running-root perennials can be tedious. Sprouts often surface within the crowns of desirable perennials where weed killer cannot be applied. Then you must dig up the perennial to remove the weed's roots. Also, whether you dig up the weeds or apply herbicides, you must check the area every few days for new shoots that emerge. Several follow-up treatments may be required, and any long delay between checks gives weeds time to regenerate and prolongs the battle.

The hardest perennial weeds to eliminate are ones with running roots that go deep and wide, such as quackgrass and bindweed. If you see such a plant in an area before planting, allow extra time between preparation and planting—even several seasons—to be sure the bed is clean. If such weeds are established in a bed or have invaded it from surrounding areas, your only options are repeated digging, or killing with herbicide and follow-ups every few days. Even these tough weeds will shrink and die in a season or two if you are faithful to a follow-up schedule.

MULCH AS WEED CONTROL

Mulching a weed-free bed not only keeps the bed clean, it has other benefits. It prevents rapid heating or cooling of the soil, thereby allowing steady root growth. It reduces water loss to evaporation. If an organic material is used as mulch, its particles become soil-enriching humus as they decompose. In addition, a well-chosen mulch with a color and texture complementary to the perennials can make the whole bed more attractive.

Many materials can be used as mulch. Select one that is the color and texture you prefer, is readily available, and fits your garden budget. Also consider scent—some people like the odor of ground fir bark or cocoa hulls; others don't.

The best perennial mulches are organic materials that will decompose between 12 and 18 months after application. Once broken

Until the perennial expands to cover the area around its crown, weed seeds are likely to sprout in this no-mulch area. Be sure to weed under the skirts of perennials until they have filled out.

For weeds with running roots, loosen the soil; slice through the densest part of the colony with a spade; lift a section at a time to establish root depth. Holding the most thickly rooted section, loosen under the roots to 'chase' every runner out.

MUCH MISUNDERSTANDING ABOUT MULCH

MYTH 1: *Rake away mulch in spring to allow soil to warm up.*

This is a misconception based on English practice. In cool, mild climates and areas far enough north that spring sun is at a low angle, removing the mulch may hasten warming. But in most of the United States, soil temperatures rise rapidly in spring, even under mulch.

MYTH 2: *Don't mulch in fall until the soil freezes.*

No need to wait. Apply mulch anytime existing material is too thin to suppress weed germination. If you mulch heavily to protect crowns during winter, do so after freezing temperatures have stopped growth. Where voles are a problem, do wait until the soil freezes stops them from taking up residence in the mulch and feeding on plant crowns over winter.

MYTH 3: *Salt-marsh hay is the best mulch for perennials.*

Every region has a traditional, preferred, or most readily available mulch. Salt-marsh hay is no better than any of a dozen other regional mulches. Gardening books written by Northeastern gardeners in the mid-1900s popularized salt-marsh hay, and its reputation lives on.

MYTH 4: *Oak leaf and pine needle mulches are so acidic they kill plants.*

Stop worrying. Almost all organic mulches affect soil pH as they break down. Oak and pine foliage are two that produce a slightly acid reaction. They are not useful where soil is already very acid and you wish to raise the pH, but in slightly acid to very alkaline soils they are excellent mulches. The notion that pine needles kill plants may be related to the barren earth often found under pines. This absence of vegetation usually has more to do with the lack of water under a pine than the soil pH, which may be alkaline despite decades of needle fall. Oak leaves contain tannic acid, which is said to leach into standing water. Plant failure probably occurs because of poor drainage rather than low pH.

MYTH 5: *Mulch must be worked into the soil as it breaks down.*

Unnecessary. Once mulch is decomposed enough that it is no longer recognizable, allow it to mix into the soil during weeding or other garden work, but don't make a special effort to incorporate it. Soil organisms, such as earthworms, will do that for you with far greater effect and less trauma to plant roots.

MYTH 6: *If mulch is added every year, the soil level in a bed increases rapidly.*

Two to 3 inches of mulch decompose to roughly ¼ inch of compost, which degrades further into humus and water-soluble nutrients. Plants take up the nutrients to incorporate into their tissues. You remove the remains of last year's mulch every time you remove plant matter in weeding, dividing, or general cleaning up. New mulch usually adds only enough material to replace what's lost in this cycle.

MYTH 7: *Mulch attracts termites.*

Not true. There is no evidence that termites are attracted to mulched areas. Mulch does contribute to cool, moist, rich soil, which will sustain more life of all kinds than dry, worn-out soil. Such variety and quantity of creatures is a sign of fertile soil and is usually self-regulating in that predator organisms in the soil will act to keep any pest populations in check.

MYTH 8: *Weed barrier cloth hidden under bark is an excellent mulch for perennials.*

Plastic and woven "weed barriers" do not effectively curb weeds. Weeds can grow in decaying mulch on top of the barriers. Barrier cloths do not allow clumps of perennials to increase in size, cost more than mulch alone, and reduce the amount of oxygen in the soil, which lowers soil fertility. Plastic mulches stop air movement into the soil; weed barrier cloth, while air-permeable, reduces the activity of worms tunneling between the soil's surface and the subsoil, which indirectly decreases soil oxygen.

WEEDING AND MULCHING
continued

CHOOSE A MULCH

Mulch	Properties*	Other notes
Shredded, chipped, or processed bark	Brown; darkness varies; smallest particle size tends to be darkest, but widely variable so look before you buy if color matters. Coarse to fine in texture, widely variable. Uses nitrogen as it decomposes and could intercept fertilizer applied to plants; little effect on pH.	All bark and wood products may bring slime mold with them; it is rarely harmful but is unsightly. Use products with small chunks. Large chunks get in the way whenever you need to disturb the soil, are slow to decompose, and attract slugs.
Chipped wood	Gray-white to light brown; often fades to much paler color. Medium texture. Uses lots of nitrogen as it decomposes; little effect on pH.	Not recommended. May consist of recycled wood colored with vegetable dye, which leaches. Wood containing copper or arsenic, such as pressure-treated lumber, may have herbicidal properties.
Sawdust	Yellow to white; fine texture. Uses lots of nitrogen as it decomposes; little effect on pH.	Cultivate regularly; otherwise fungal strands can web particles together and block water absorption.
Hulls: cocoa bean, pecan, buckwheat, peanut	Color and texture vary. Often supply nutrients as they decompose. Less likely to tie up nitrogen than wood products; neutral to acidifying effect on pH.	Availability varies.
Residue: spent hop, ground corncob	Color and texture vary. May supply nutrients as it decomposes; neutral to acidifying effect on soil pH.	Acquaint yourself with the odor of these mulches before selecting one.
Yard waste, compost, spent mushroom compost	Very dark brown to black-brown; fine texture. May supply nutrients. Neutral to acidifying effect on pH.	Test pH and soluble salts. Extremely alkaline compost with high-soluble salts is common and may stunt perennial growth. Check cleanliness by sifting for pieces of weed roots; then fill a pot with compost, moisten it, and watch for weed seedlings.
Leaves: deciduous tree leaves or pine needles	Color varies from light brown to yellow; texture varies. Supply nutrients as they decompose; neutral to acidifying effect on pH.	May include tree and weed seeds. Appearance is best if shredded; large, slow-decaying leaves such as sycamore, oak, and Norway maple can mat unless shredded. Pine needles can be slippery underfoot.
Stones	Color and texture vary. Rarely supply nutrients. Limestone increases pH.	Not recommended among perennials since they get in the way whenever you need to disturb the soil.
Chicken grit	Gray color; fine texture. No nutrient value. Little effect on pH.	For perennials intolerant of moist soil pressing against foliage or crown, or for windy and rooftop beds where lighter mulches may blow away.
Turface	Gray-brown color; medium texture. No effect on nutrients or pH.	For perennials intolerant of moist soil against foliage or crown and windy and rooftop beds where lighter mulches may blow away.
Shredded paper	Color varies; medium texture. Little effect on nutrients. No effect on pH.	Low cost. Avoid use of glossy paper, which may contain toxic inks. Often unattractive and should be covered by a more attractive mulch.
Grass clippings	Pale green to straw color; fine texture. High in nitrogen. Little effect on pH.	Low cost. Apply cool and fresh from mower bag. Must renew more often than most. May contain weed seeds. Don't use clippings sprayed with weed killer within two weeks of mowing
Cones, spruce or pine	Color varies; texture coarse. Insignificant effect on nutrients or pH.	Economical way to recycle materials. Low cost where conifers are abundant.
Spent soilless potting mix from patio containers	Dark brown; fine texture. No effect on nutrient levels. Acidifying effect on pH.	May promote weed growth.
Coffee grounds, egg shells, other food-preparation castoffs	Color and texture vary. May supply nutrients. Some materials are acidifying, others mildly alkaline.	Economical way to recycle materials. Ask at coffee shops and office building coffee stations about obtaining coffee grounds.

Dark brown to black-brown colors work well with the widest range of perennial foliage and flowers; fine-textured mulches with a smooth appearance are the most complementary. For overly acidic or alkaline soil, avoid mulches that raise or lower pH.

These perennials were planted at the same time but mulched with different materials to demonstrate how a mulch can affect the growth rate. Those grown in high-carbon wood mulch (top of the photo) are smaller than those grown in leaf mold (bottom).

Fine shredded bark

Coarse shredded bark

Cocoa hulls

Processing residue

Compost

Leaf mold

Pine straw

down into earthy-scented, unrecognizable dark crumbs, they can be allowed to mix into the soil during the normal course of garden activities.

Mulches that decompose more rapidly, such as grass clippings, must be renewed as the mulch layer becomes thin and weed seeds begin to sprout. Those that decompose more slowly or not at all—rocks, large wood chunks, or the chips of decay-resistant bark, such as eucalyptus or cypress—may cause extra work for the gardener when dividing perennials, fertilizing, or weeding. That is, those mulches must be moved out of the way and put back later so that they do not mix with the soil as you work.

Do not overmulch. One to 2 inches of wood chips, bark, or stony material is sufficient. Materials that are quicker to break down, such as leaves, cocoa hulls, or compost, can be applied 2 to 3 inches thick.

If piled too deeply initially, grass clippings will rot to a slimy mess, then dry to a water-shedding, cardboard-like mat. Spread clippings no more than 2 inches deep at a time; they'll dry without matting. Once dry, you can put another layer on top of the first.

GROOMING PERENNIALS

Removing faded flowers is called deadheading. It keeps a garden neat, stimulates additional blooms, and can help prevent some diseases. Deadheading also cuts down on "volunteer" perennials that may become weeds.

Grooming is a constant chore, but the more often performed, the lighter the task. Daily or weekly, removing spent flowers and damaged or browning foliage keeps the garden pleasantly tidy and the gardener aware of its state and subtle changes. This chore also eliminates old tissue where some diseases can establish a foothold on otherwise healthy plants. In addition, it manipulates nature's floral insurance policy. On the stems or crowns of most perennials are buds that can but don't always develop into flowers or flower stalks. Grooming stimulates these buds and ensures plentiful blooms.

Use scissors, clippers, shears or trimmers to remove spent blooms. Just aim to send all or most of a plant's ripening seedpods to the ground. Hedge shears, string trimmers, and even mowers are all effective grooming tools. Some quick-cut tools may leave a plant with more rough edges than pruners or scissors, but new growth soon covers up the cuts.

There are two main grooming practices—in addition to generally picking up—and each has its own purposes.

DEADHEADING—removing flowers as they fade but before seeds begin to ripen—stimulates long and repeated bloom in many perennials. Deadheading signals waiting flower buds to grow.

A perennial might double or triple its bloom time when deadheaded. But even if plants don't respond with more flowers, deadheading is worthwhile. Removing spent petals and stems gives a garden a fresh look. It eliminates old tissues where diseases can gain a foothold on otherwise healthy plants. However, there are times when deadheading is not desirable. For example, when a plant has attractive seed pods or the seeds attract songbirds to your garden, you may not mind the browning blossoms.

How you deadhead a perennial depends on how its flowers grow. The photos on page 113 show the six main blooming patterns for plants. Turn to page 115 for directions for deadheading each of them.

As autumn draws near, you'll need to groom more often to keep up with the fading plants. Trim back plants that have become droopy. But allow upright grasses and statuesque perennials to remain in place so you can see which ones hold their dramatic effect into the winter season.

CUTTING BACK—lopping off both leaf and flower—stimulates production of new stems and leaves. It removes much or all of a plant's foliage in one step. Cut back when a perennial's flower production has fallen off for the season. As each stalk blooms out, cut it to the ground or to a point where new growth is evident.

Fast-growing, early-blooming perennials that become ragged or brown by July are candidates for cutting back hard. That means to prune them all the way back to the ground. Keep the plants well watered until new growth has developed. A large perennial clump can be cut back hard in sections (left) to reduce the size of the temporary hole this leaves in a garden—the east half of the clump might be cut first, followed by the west half seven to 10 days later.

Veronica—standard spike

Blazing star—top-down spike

Coreopsis—ascending bloom

Anemone—descending bloom

Daylily—tip cluster

Bellflower—multicluster

By knowing how the flower blooms, you will be able to deadhead most effectively. Some plants open from top to bottom, others from bottom to top. See the charts on page 114 and 115 for more detailed information about deadheading perennials.

Cutting back hard takes all the stalks at once, removing most or all of the plant's foliage in one day. This is done most often to perennials that grow quickly, bloom before summer's heat, or tend to cease vegetative growth once seeds begin to ripen.

It eliminates tired foliage and encourages the plant to replace it with fresh green leaves, which makes the whole plant look better.

Cutting back hard is a shock to a plant, so take care which perennials you do this to.

Spare newly planted or stressed perennials. For instance, though the Encyclopedia of Plants lists coreopsis as a candidate for cutting back hard, stick with simple deadheading if your plant suffered deer browsing or you transplanted it this season.

Pamper cut-back perennials to support new growth. Give them plentiful water after cutting. Once new growth appears, sidedress the plants with 1 to 2 tablespoons of a balanced liquid fertilizer, such as 20-20-20 dissolved in water.

Perennials with branched flower stalks: Remove single blooms as they fade. New flowers develop farther up the stalk on thin stems. Cut back the entire stalk when these stems are too lanky.

GROOMING PERENNIALS
continued

DEADHEADING GUIDELINES FOR LONG-BLOOMING PERENNIALS

Deadheading nets a higher return from some perennials than others. The following are among those that yield the most—blooming especially long or well—after being deadheaded or cut back.

Plant Name	When to Deadhead	Notes
Anise hyssop	Late summer	Cut when flower stalk that has already bloomed is longer than the part with developing flower buds. For later blooms and stronger stems, deadhead earlier and lower on plant.
Bee balm	Midsummer	Remove flowers as they age. Youngest have petals at center, top of disk; oldest flowers, around outer edge of disk.
Bellflower	Early to midsummer	Clip individual flowers plus stems as they fade, then remove entire spike or cluster when last buds have opened.
Blanket flower	Mid- to late summer	Remove whole flower and its stem. Cut back entire stalk when flower stems become too thin and flowers too small.
Blue flax	Early to midsummer	Clip flower stalk to above a leaf when length of stalk that has already bloomed exceeds portion still developing flower buds (produced at tips above seedpods).
Checkerbloom	Mid- to late summer	New flowers are produced at tip of stalk. Remove entire spike when more than half its length has bloomed.
Coral bells	Early to midsummer	Cut off entire flowering stalk at its base when more of its length has bloomed than is developing bloom.
Daisy	Mid- to late summer	Remove whole flower and its stem as center of flower disk turns gold. Cut back entire stalk when flower stems become too thin and flowers too small.
Delphinium	Mid- to late summer	For sturdiest stems on second bloom, cut spike to just above a healthy leaf. Cut entire flower stalk down to basal foliage when flower production slows.
Globe thistle	Mid- to late summer	Remove whole flower and its stem. Cut flower stalk to ground when bud production on that stalk slows.
Jacob's ladder	Late spring to early summer	Cut when each stalk reaches point where more than half its length has already bloomed. Cut entire stalk to ground when its flower production slows.
Lanceleaf coreopsis	Early to late summer	Remove whole flower and its stem. Cut back entire stalk when flower stems become too thin and flowers too small.
Many-flowered sunflower	Midsummer to fall	Remove whole flower and its stem. Cut flower stalk to the ground when bud production on that stalk slows.
Obedient plant	Late summer to fall	Cut to just above a healthy leaf when the flower spike has finished blooming along more than half its length.
Perennial bachelor's button	Late spring to early summer	Remove each faded flower and its stem, cutting to just above a healthy leaf. Cut entire flower stalk when flower production slows.
Perennial salvia	Early to midsummer	As flower stalks begin to lean away from vertical, cut all to just above main mass of foliage. New flowering shoots may develop from base of plant or along stems.
Pincushion flower	Mid- to late summer	Remove whole flower and its stem. Cut back entire stalk when flower stems become too thin and flowers too small.
Purple coneflower	Midsummer to fall	Remove whole flower and its stem. Cut back entire stalk when flower stems become too thin and flowers too small.
Speedwell	Mid- to late summer	Cut to just above a healthy leaf when the flower spike has finished blooming along more than half its length.
Tall phlox	Late summer to fall	Remove individual flowers from cluster, or cut whole cluster when there are more faded outer flowers than central buds.
Yarrow	Mid- to late summer	Remove individual flower and its stem when central floret opens. Cut to just above a sturdy side shoot.

WHERE TO CUT

Study the flower structure from the bottom of the stem to the tip of the petals to recognize the order in which buds open. Then remove spent flowers and clip stems to promote the buds that will develop into the largest flowers with the thickest stems. Here are the most common types of flower stem arrangements showing the order in which flowers will form and bloom:

A. First flowers to open
B. Buds that will open later
C. Where new flowers emerge after deadheading

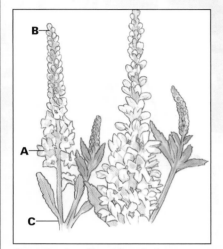

Standard spike: *The tip keeps growing as lower flowers open. Nip individual faded flowers from base of the spike. Eventually, cut off spike when bloomed-out section is longer than portion with buds. Cut lower on the stalk, just above a node, where a leaf joins a stem. Several small stalks develop to replace the one cut. Thin to a single spike if desired.*

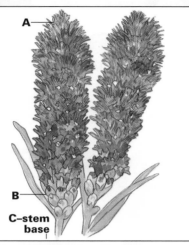

Top-down spike: *Tip flowers open first and bloom proceeds downward. Clip off top of spike as upper flowers fade, or cut entire spike anytime after flower buds on the bottom half open. Additional flower stalks usually develop from leafy part of remaining stem if you cut off the first spike before the lowest buds open.*

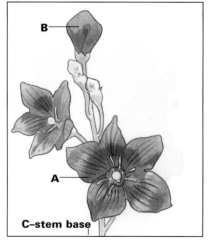

Tip clusters and heads: *Flowers clustered on a single leafless or nearly leafless stem open one by one. Remove each blossom as it fades or the whole stalk as the last flower finishes blooming. Any subsequent bloom will sprout from the base of the plant. For heads, where blossoms are tightly packed, remove the whole stalk after the last flower fades.*

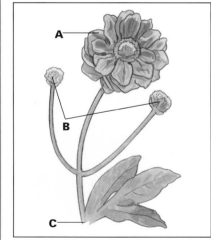

Branched flower stems, descending bloom: *The central, tallest flower opens first. Remove each flower and its stalk as it fades, cutting just above a side branch that has yet to bloom.*

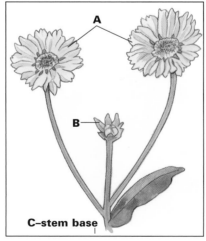

Branched flower stems, ascending bloom: *Lower flower buds open first. Remove each flower as it fades and clip to main stalk. Cut back main stalk completely when it's ungainly.*

Multicluster flowers: *Open flowers appear all along the stalk, but the flowers in each cluster bloom one by one. Cut the whole stalk down to leafy growth when the last flower blooms.*

DIVIDING

Even with all the cutting you do to groom perennials, they'll still produce energy to store for the next year. This season's nine-stem bee balm may debut next spring with 25 stems. The following year the number may run to three figures. Fast-spreading species like this bee balm, obedient plant, and some artemisias, will overrun less aggressive neighbors. Periodically divide these overachievers to reduce the size.

Slower growing perennials need division, too. Unchecked growth takes a toll on a perennial's appearance. In clump-forming species, such as coral bells and daylilies, many stems growing where once there was just one means there's more competition for nutrients, water, and light. Leaves and flowers become smaller. The plant doesn't rebound as fast from problems or cutting back.

Diseases and insects thrive amid weakened tissues and find shelter in crowded stems. Pests, such as powdery mildew on phlox and four-lined plant bug on pincushion flower, multiply in these conditions.

The longer a perennial grows without division, the more likely it is to succumb to pest problems. Some perennials get into trouble quickly and should be divided every two to three years. Others can stay in place for five to six years with little or no loss in health or looks. A few need division so rarely that they are considered permanent plants.

Some gardeners divide a plant right after it has impressed them with its mature beauty, figuring it's all downhill after the peak. Others know that a plant will gradually decline in vigor or bloom count; they wait to divide until these effects are noticeable.

TIMING

Divide perennials in spring or fall, when plants reestablish most quickly. Cool air and warm soil result in more root than shoot growth, so transplants can really dig in. Rain is more reliable in spring and fall and there's less evaporation, which ensures that the reduced root system can meet the plants' needs for water. Soil stays more evenly moist and thus more conducive to root growth, with less follow-up watering to do.

Divide spring-blooming perennials in fall and fall bloomers in spring. This provides the longest possible time for a plant to reestablish between division and its next bloom cycle. When it blooms, its roots will be wider and heavier, and thus, the plant will be sturdier.

Sometimes you can't choose the time for dividing. For example, you may need to

Eyes: *Multiple eyes or buds form each year at the base of the previous season's stems or on rhizomes or tubers. Each bud will be a new stem and eventually form its own set of roots. Slice cleanly anywhere between the eyes to produce divisions with their own eyes and roots. Even the smallest of these divisions will grow, but those with three to seven eyes are best for replanting.*

Forked taproot: *Some perennials form one or a few main roots that grow vertical taproots. If a taproot forks below the soil surface to form multiple crowns, that root can be split lengthwise to yield pieces that each have a crown, a portion of taproot, and branching roots or root buds.*

Offsets: *Some perennials expand by forming offsets—or daughter plants—connected "at the hip" to the mother plant. Snap or slice through these connections to obtain pieces with three to seven eyes.*

Runners: *A perennial's roots may run at or below the soil surface and produce new plants at a distance from the mother plant. Or its stems may grow along the surface, forming daughter plants. Each can be cut away to become an independent plant.*

Taproot, single crown: *Not all taproots form multiple crowns. To obtain divisions from single-crown taproots, slice off eyes with some root attached or cut off pencil-thick side roots. Plant them at an angle just below grade.*

renovate a bed that contains both spring-blooming species and fall bloomers. Go ahead and divide; then give the plants a little extra aftercare. Stake any divisions that will bloom shortly after being replanted. If it's spring, refrain from cutting plants back hard because that reduces leaf surface and energy levels before roots can rebuild starch reserves. If you're dividing in summer, give extra attention to follow-up watering, and set up screens to block drying winds and midday sun for a week or two.

LIFT OUT PLANTS, CUT ROOTS

To divide, use a garden fork to loosen soil all around the plant. Put your fork under the plant and work the handle like a lever. Many perennials will pop right out; others will need further digging.

Try to get as much root as possible, but don't hesitate to cut roots. When a perennial needs dividing most, it's not unusual to reduce its root mass and stem count by three-fourths.

If you are unfamiliar with the perennial, shake or rinse most of the soil off the roots so you can see its configuration. You may grow thousands of perennial species in your life but you need to know only about five rooting patterns (see page 116). Once the pattern is evident, how to proceed should be apparent.

KEEP YOUNG PLANT PARTS

The youngest parts of a plant, usually the outside edges of a clump, are the healthiest and most vigorous. They have had the least exposure to pests, and they've received the best nutrition—from nutrients outside the main root ball in soil not yet exhausted by older plant parts.

Keep these youngest pieces. Discard the central, older parts. Clip off frayed and injured roots. Remove all weed roots that have infiltrated the perennial's root ball.

Before replanting divisions, renew the soil to replace nutrients and organic matter. If the perennials you lifted fill a wheelbarrow, mix at least one wheelbarrowful of compost or peat-topsoil mix into that spot before replanting. This prevents transplants from settling into unsightly depressions and also rebuilds the soil's nutrient bank. Divisions that sink below grade are less likely to benefit from airflow around stems and more likely to suffer from excess or standing water.

EXPERIENCE ELIMINATES STEPS IN DIVIDING

Once you know what type of roots there are on a given species, it's possible to skip steps in dividing. The following procedure lets you obtain divisions or reduce a perennial's size without disturbing the entire clump. Always add compost or peat-topsoil mix around the mother clump in a volume equal to the roots and soil removed.

One or more pie-shaped wedges can be removed from a plant that forms offsets, such as hosta. Slice to or beyond the plant's center so that you remove not only outer growth but part of the central, older portion.

When perennials produce shoots from shallow runners or stems that recline and develop their own roots, you can cut new shoots from the parent plant and transplant them to a new location.

Where new shoots arise from deeper-running roots, it's possible to loosen and excavate next to the mother plant, then reach below to snap off or cut away a section of root and shoot.

STAKING

Stake plants before they flop. These grow-through supports were placed over this globe thistle in early May (left). Within three weeks, the plant hides the supports (right). The globe thistle's size requires three grow-throughs. Interlocking them improves stability.

Grow-through stakes can be gridded or open, like tomato cages. Place them over the perennial. Guide stems through the supports as they grow. Open stakes provide unobtrusive support for plants that flare out from a narrow base. Individual braces support single stems.

Most garden perennials are not the same as their wild counterparts. They've been improved by breeding. However, the improvements often include larger, taller, heavier flowers that can't stand up to the elements without help.

Sometimes the garden setting creates the need for staking plants that are otherwise sturdy. You'll have to stake in windy locations and where the soil is too lean or too rich for the plant. Staking will correct plants that lean toward the light where sunlight is strongly one-directional, such as on the east or west side of a building.

Tall, large-flowered species, such as delphinium, peony, and foxglove, usually require staking. Others tend to flop only in certain circumstances, such as yarrow in a rich soil.

Predicting the fall may take a season's experience with a plant to learn whether it will need staking or will stand on its own.

Stake a plant in spring while it is still short. Stakes, cages, and other props might look awkward when first placed. If they do draw the eye, don't be concerned. Perennials grow so quickly from midspring to early summer that they rapidly cloak the stakes with foliage.

Don't bother to stake after the plant has fallen. Once a perennial has flopped over or been beaten down by rain or wind, cut the

flowers and enjoy them in a vase. Even if the fall didn't break the stems or crease them so they can no longer conduct water to the flowers, nothing looks less natural than a plant lassoed to a stake.

Place single-stake props at graceful angles rather than straight up and down so that stems appear to spray naturally up and out from a single point (the plant's crown). It can be instructive to place the stakes first and be happy with their arrangement before tying in any stems. Green stakes often but not always blend best. Many gardeners keep several different colors of stakes at hand.

SUPPORT, DON'T STRANGLE

Pictured on this page and opposite are many types of stakes and supports for perennials. Note that all allow the stem to move. Even stems that grow through a support grid can sway. Motion is important in plant growth. Cell walls become stronger when the stems are occasionally rocked by wind. When you tie a stem to a stake, tie the twine in a figure eight. That tethers the plant but doesn't prevent motion.

Tight ties can also cut off the vital flow of water; a constricted stem may die before being able to bloom. Use wide, straplike ties rather than thin, stringy material to tie stems; the latter is likely to pinch or snap the stem it binds. Use the soft, natural-colored hemp or green Velcro straps sold at garden centers. Avoid wire, coated-wire twist ties, and fishing line. Don't be stingy—use several ties per stem to distribute the weight.

Tree trimmings are an abundant source of stakes called pea shrub stakes. In early spring, insert the cut ends into the ground around the crown of the perennial, twiggy fingers up.

For single-stemmed perennials, use an individual brace, attaching it to the plant with a loose figure-8. For a more natural look, place it at an angle to the plant.

Grow-through supports work for multistemmed perennials. They come in various sizes and grids, or make your own from bamboo and string.

Drive several stakes into the ground around large clumps of multistemmed perennials. With twine, connect the stakes in a grid over the perennial.

Use interlocking plant stakes for propping up floppy but lightweight flower stems.

NO-STAKE SUPPORT

One alternative to using stakes is to grow unsteady plants next to sturdy ones. The stems of one can lean on the other in an effect called weaving. The look may be a little unusual, but it's often breathtaking.

Another option to staking is to pinch plants, which promotes shorter stems and a bushier habit less likely to tumble.

The term pinch might mislead you— it can mean nipping off soft stem tips between thumb and forefinger, but more often it means cutting back stems with sharp shears. Many gardeners are familiar with pinching in relation to chrysanthemums but haven't realized how many other perennials can be clipped back several times between early May and their bloom time to achieve the same effect. The Encyclopedia of Plants notes whether a perennial is pinchable.

GOOD COMPANIONS FOR WEAVING

■ Aster and feather reed grass
■ Blazing star and false sunflower
■ Delphinium and hollyhock
■ Jupiter's beard, masterwort, salvia, and bugbane
■ Meadow rue and maiden grass
■ Monkshood and goatsbeard
■ Tall perennial geraniums and false indigo

Pinch stems one or more times in spring to early summer. Pinched plants are sturdier and shorter, so staking is less necessary. Be aware that pinching delays flowering.

Stake a perennial if it has heavy flowers (left), has fragile stems and is in a windy site (center), or grows where light is so strongly one-sided that its flowering stems reach for the sun (right).

SEASONAL CHORES

When seasons change, perennial gardens change. Perennial gardeners learn to take a few extra steps to see the plants safely through the off-season and give them the best start every spring.

END-OF-SEASON PRUNING

In autumn, when nighttime temperatures drop to near or below freezing and leaves begin to fall from deciduous trees and shrubs, pull out the pruners and shears. Cut back herbaceous perennials that are going dormant and falling down, such as peony and bleeding heart. Shear them to just above ground level.

Removing all of a herbaceous plant's foliage in fall will not harm the plant, even if it is still green when you begin work. Buds for next year are already set at the base of the stems or just below ground level. Cutting removes some of the clutter from a garden, making other fall tasks easier to complete.

Pass by perennials such as lavender, sage, Russian sage, and thyme that set next year's growth buds above ground on woody branches. Woody perennials winter best if left intact until early spring. Plants that are not woody but have attractive evergreen foliage, such as Lenten rose and coral bells, can also be left intact over winter.

Hold off cutting perennials with persistent herbaceous stems—black-eyed Susan, 'Autumn Joy' sedum, and ornamental grasses that are not usually knocked down by snow. Now step back to think about how the scene will look from fall until spring. Cut back the plants that do not aesthetically enhance the cold-weather landscape.

Rake or bundle your cuttings. Put them on a compost pile or shred them and use them as mulch.

Cut back hostas, daylilies and other herbaceous perennials that form buds at or below the ground (left). Wait until spring to cut back woody perennials such as Russian sage that set buds on woody branches (right).

FALL CLEANUP

PREVENT DISEASE AND PESTS: Be thorough in cutting and cleaning up plants that had significant disease or insect problems or are highly susceptible to pests. Take precautions when disposing of the waste. Don't shred these plants for mulch; their foliage, stems, and leaf litter may hold fungus spores, bacteria resting bodies, or insect eggs and should be removed from the area.

One way to dispose of infected or suspect debris is to compost it in a pile kept hot by regular turning. The heat of active decomposition kills most diseases and insects. You can also bury the debris at least 18 inches deep or burn it if local regulations allow.

APPLY SLOW-RELEASE FERTILIZER: After cutting and raking away debris, save time on next year's work by applying a slow-release fertilizer such as 8-6-8 bulb food or 6-2-0 Milorganite. Spread ¼ to ½ cup for every 10 square feet. This material will become mixed into the soil and covered during the next steps in fall cleanup. It will degrade gradually so that by spring its nutrients will be available to perennials during their first flush of growth.

WEED THOROUGHLY: Remove all weeds that were hiding under the skirts of perennials. Loosen and remove persistent perennial weeds, lifting perennials from the bed if necessary to trace and eliminate all weed roots.

If the bed is encircled by a root barrier, check for and grub out running weeds that may have slipped under, over, or in between sections of edging. Repair and re-anchor edging as necessary.

DIVIDE, PLANT, ADD BULBS: Divide spring-blooming perennials that need renewal or restraint. It's also a good time to dig out and discard perennials that have not performed up to expectations, and replace them with species better suited to the site and your needs. While you're making design changes, consider adding spring-blooming hardy bulbs around and even beneath late-emerging species, such as hibiscus and Japanese anemone.

RENEW MULCH: Now add mulch around the crowns and between perennials, bringing this blanket up to the desired depth: 1 to 2 inches of woody material or bark, 2 to 3 inches of leafy matter, pods, or hulls.

Use the abundance of tree leaves, which can be shredded or used whole, as mulch. Avoid using black walnut leaves, which break down into compounds that can stunt or kill some perennials. Mix large, decay-resistant leaves, such as sycamore, oak, and Norway maple, with smaller leaves to prevent formation of dense mats. Or mow or shred such leaves before applying.

PROTECT A SPECIAL FEW: Every perennial gardener sooner or later tries to push the hardiness of a plant. If you're growing a few marginally hardy perennials—species not known to be reliably hardy in your hardiness zone—applying 12 to 18 inches of loose, airy mulch over the crown and root zone may give the plants enough protection to survive the winter. A mound of straw covered with evergreen boughs held down by a length of wire-mesh fencing works well.

This protection also may prevent damage to perennials that are planted very late—less than three to four weeks before frost is likely to enter the soil. Water the plants well, being sure to moisten the soil all around the root ball, before applying the mulch.

Finally, clean up your tools and put away the wheelbarrow and hoses for the winter. It's going to be a wonderful, easy spring because your perennial garden is so well prepared.

Gardens can look attractive all year. Cut back selectively to create a winterscape of plants with sturdy stems and attractive forms.

SPRING START-UP

When the foliage of the earliest bulbs emerges in your yard, cut down and dispose of the perennial stems you left standing for winter interest. Remove any protective mulches from marginally hardy and late-planted perennials, and check the beds for crusted or matted mulch that may slow perennial reemergence. You don't have to remove the mulch; just break up the mats.

Give summer-blooming woody perennials a haircut to promote dense growth. Cut the stems of lavender, Russian sage, thyme, Montauk daisy, and artemisia so that only a few healthy buds remain at the base of each branch. Although it seems drastic, this cutting promotes dense growth very quickly.

You may choose to cut back some evergreen foliage now. Taking away Lenten rose's winter-tattered leaves can make its early-spring show that much prettier, and cutting away old coral bells foliage showcases emerging greenery.

Fertilize perennials as they emerge in spring, if you didn't give them a helping of slow-release fertilizer in fall.

Weed thoroughly; there are always a few weeds that escaped notice in fall, usually under or behind those perennials you left standing for winter interest. Top mulch as necessary to deny weed seeds a place in the sun. Then sit back and enjoy the show.

SPARE THE BUDS

Cut back hard woody perennials like lavender in early spring. Remove spent foliage and trim remaining stems nearly to the ground (see plants at the sides of the photo).

Within three weeks, the plants will be growing strong and be cleaner and neater-looking, unlike the untrimmed lavender in the center of the photo.

MAKING MORE: BASIC PLANT PROPAGATION

Most perennials can be grown from seed. Just like annuals, new plantings of perennials need to be kept moist and warm. When the seedlings emerge, move the tray into the light. As they grow, transplant the seedlings into larger pots.

Most perennials can be grown from seed. The process is generally the same as starting the seed of annual flowers or vegetables.

Fill clean, freely draining pots with moistened seed-starting soil mix. Read seed packets for special instructions about planting depth, chilling or heat required. Unless the instructions advise otherwise, distribute seeds evenly on the soil mix and cover them to three times their depth. Keep the soil mix moist and at 70° F until seedlings begin to emerge. Then move the tray or pot to a sunny window or place it on a shelf with fluorescent lights close overhead.

If instructions say the seed requires light to germinate, don't bury the seed. Scatter it on the soil surface, and cover the pot or tray with glass or clear plastic to prevent drying. Remove the cover as soon as seeds sprout.

Seed packets often list days to germination. Many perennials, such as balloon flower, shasta daisy, and basket-of-gold, germinate in just 7 to 10 days. Others are slower; astilbe may take 6 to 8 weeks to sprout.

SPECIAL HANDLING

Species with hard seed coats, such as lupine, germinate more quickly if soaked in lukewarm water for 24 hours or scraped vigorously between sheets of sandpaper before sowing.

Some seeds require stratification—a period of cold, moist storage—in place of a winter's rest. Gas plant is one. It requires moisture and cold (40° F or less) for two to three months. Mix such seeds with slightly moistened peat in a closed plastic bag and refrigerate before

planting. Other seeds need cool temperatures to sprout. For example, coral bells and candytuft seed packets will instruct you to give the seeds two to three weeks at 55° F.

Perennial seed can be sown directly outdoors. Late summer or fall is a good time for this, accommodating quick-sprouting seeds as well as those that require winter cold.

CARE FOR SEEDLINGS

Whether planted indoors or out, in pots or flats, seedlings should be kept evenly moist. Adequate air circulation is important to control a seedling's worst enemy—the fungal disease called damping-off. Clean pots, sterile soil mix, and good air circulation, which you can achieve by spacing pots several inches apart or installing a small oscillating fan, are ways to avert this problem.

When the seedlings develop two or three true leaves, transplant them into 4-inch pots. Feed weekly with regular fertilizer at half strength. Prevent legginess by maintaining high light intensity. Pinch growing tips occasionally to promote bushiness.

Harden off the perennial when its roots fill its 4-inch container, then plant it in the garden. If you choose to transplant it to another pot, move it just one pot size at a time—from a 4-inch to a 5- or 6-inch container, and so on. Let the roots be your guide for how often to transplant: Some perennials may take two years to fill a gallon pot.

PERENNIALS FROM CUTTINGS

Growing from cuttings is a way to make more of perennials that don't come true from seed, are difficult to divide, or are slow to increase to a clump size that invites division.

To take a cutting, choose a healthy, vigorously growing shoot without flower buds that is firm—if bent, it would snap. Snip a 4- to 6-inch section of this shoot, remove its lowest leaves and stick it, cut side down, into moist, sandy soil. Push it deeply enough into the soil to bury the nodes or joints stripped bare of leaves. If the stem is not firm enough to push into the soil without bending, make a hole with a clean stick, pencil, chopsticks or other object, then insert the cutting and firm the soil around it. Maintain polarity on the cutting—the end that was uppermost on the plant must remain upright or the cutting won't root.

There are two types of cuttings: tip cuttings, which include an intact tip, and stem cuttings, which may or may not have a tip.

A 12-inch shoot might yield one tip cutting plus two 4-inch-long stem cuttings. Some perennial species root best from tip cuttings. Others, such as bleeding heart and aster have tips that are never quite firm enough to make good cuttings, so you will be discarding the tip and using a stem cutting from nearer the base of a shoot.

You don't need to use a rooting hormone as most perennials root readily without it. If you choose to use hormone, dip the lower end of the cutting into the hormone before sticking it into the soil mix.

Protect cuttings from drying out during the time it takes them to form roots. Keep them carefully watered so the soil stays moist, but never wet enough to encourage rot. Grow them where they are shaded from the midday sun. One simple system is to stick cuttings in a pot, insert several stakes just taller than the cuttings, then enclose the cuttings with a clear plastic bag. Use a rubber band to secure the bag around the pot rim. The plastic maintains moisture around the cutting; the stakes keep the plastic and condensation off of the cuttings, avoiding rot. A bagged cutting usually needs no watering. Most cuttings root within a month.

Wilting or dead leaves on a cutting indicate the cutting did not take. New growth—emergence of additional leaves—is a sign that roots have formed.

TIMING

Many perennials that bloom in mid- and late summer produce shoots good for cutting by late spring or early summer. Variegated obedient plant, hardy hibiscus, and Russian sage are in this category and are good candidates for cuttings because of slow growth or difficulty of division. Species that bloom early in the year often produce the best stem cuttings after the plant has bloomed from new shoots that develop in summer. Rooted cuttings can be transplanted into the garden as any other potted plant once their roots have filled their pots.

To take a stem cutting, choose a healthy shoot without flower buds. The stem should be firm—one that, if bent, would snap. Cut a 4-inch piece.

Remove lower leaves from the stem cutting. Dip the stem into rooting hormone, making sure all sides of the stem are dusted with hormone. Then make a hole in the soil with a clean pencil and insert the stem.

Keep the cutting moist. Place a small plastic bag over the top. Small stakes pushed into the soil will keep the bag from collapsing on the cutting.

Most perennials root within one month. New leaves are a good sign that the cutting has rooted. Tug gently. If there is some resistance, use a spoon to gently lift the cutting out. If it has developed roots, transplant it to a larger pot. If it doesn't have roots yet, put it back in the soil.

TROUBLESHOOTING

Close inspection can reveal insects before they become a problem.

Most perennials are low-maintenance plants with few insect or disease problems, especially if the plants are well-sited and well-tended. But exceptions to the rule abound, as with all plants. Some perennials are highly susceptible to specific insects or diseases; others occasionally suffer from pests. And in some years, if conditions are right, a perennial that has never been been affected by any pest could come under an attack.

The pests that trouble perennials are as diverse as the plants themselves. Among them are insects such as aphids, mites, caterpillars, and scales; diseases such as powdery mildew, wilts, blights, rusts, molds, and anthracnose; and animals such as rabbits, deer, and moles. Slugs and other pests that thrive in the thick, moist mulch under a perennial can be especially serious.

Often, the problems you see in perennial gardens may resemble those of pests but are actually have what are called abiotic, or non-living, causes. For example, you might think the garden has a disease when what you see are symptoms of nutritional imbalances, poor drainage, and wind or sun scorch. Physical damage from hail looks like slug damage.

Routinely patrolling your garden for problems, as described on page 105, is the first step in making a diagnosis and is key to keeping pests from getting out of hand. Once you discover a problem, it's important to learn its cause. Only then can you select a solution that is sure to work.

HOW TO OBSERVE

Diagnosing plant problems requires careful observation of the perennial and its environment. The key to accurate diagnosis is knowing how to look for clues and what types of clues to look for. The checklist on pages 126 and 127 gives a step-by-step procedure and will help you develop a case history, eliminate unlikely explanations for the problem, and find the real cause.

Begin your observations by examining the garden from a distance. Are several plants affected or only one?

When several plants in one area are showing symptoms of distress, take a look at growing conditions, especially soil problems. Look for patterns and relationships among all the plants. Are the affected plants randomly distributed in the garden? Or do they follow a regular pattern, for example, an entire corner of the garden or a straight line through it?

SYMPTOMS ON ONE PLANT

If only one plant has symptoms, note its general condition. Is the entire plant affected or only a few stems, branches, or leaves? If the entire plant shows symptoms, the cause is often found on the plant's roots or in the soil.

Check the soil. Dig up small plants or carefully dig a hole beside large perennials to examine roots. Investigate drainage. If you weren't involved in preparing the soil for the garden, probe the soil with an auger to determine its depth and type. Also test its pH.

Where the problem is confined to one part of a plant, take a closer look at the part that shows symptoms. Discolored or mottled leaves may indicate an insect or disease problem, a need for fertilizer or better drainage. The color and pattern of the discoloration will help you identify the problem. A 5- to 15-power hand lens lets you see symptoms not visible to the naked eye.

You may have to dig into a plant to find the cause of a problem. If a stem has a hole in it, cut through it to see what's there. Borers sometimes tunnel into stems. Look at the core of a wilted stem. If it has turned black, the plant may have a vascular disease.

When checking sick plants, be aware of changes in the environment. As trees grow, yards become progressively shadier. Full-sun perennials that have thrived for several years may now be suffering from lack of light.

If the initial inspection does not reveal an obvious reason for the symptoms, developing a case history may lead you to a less conspicuous cause of the problem. For help, run through the questions in the "Checklist for Diagnosis" on the following pages.

Carry your investigation as far as you need to. Digging into the plant or cutting through stems may offer important clues.

CHECKLIST FOR DIAGNOSIS

This checklist will help you sort out whether a problem results from a pest or from something else going on in the plant's environment. Use it in conjunction with the profiles of the typical troublemakers found in perennial gardens that follow on pages 132 through 145.

Because leaves and flowers are the easiest to examine, begin your examination with them (unless it is apparent that the problem is elsewhere). Then move down the plant to its stems and crown and finally to the roots. Also keep in mind the plant's growing conditions, recent weather and garden activities around the plant.

WHAT TO LOOK FOR

KIND OF PLANT
■ What type of plant is it?
■ Does it prefer moist or dry conditions? Have you given it those conditions?
■ Is the perennial hardy in your region?
■ Does the plant grow best in acid or alkaline soil? What is your soil pH?

AGE
■ Is the plant young and tender, or is it old and in a state of decline? Plants with tender foliage and old declining plants are more susceptible to pests; however, the younger ones are better able to shrug off problems.

SIZE
■ Is the plant abnormally small?
■ Was the perennial recently transplanted? Has it had time to become established, or are its roots still in the original rootball?
■ How much has an established perennial clump expanded in the last few years? Is the center of the perennial declining so that the plant is ready to be divided and renewed?
■ Is the clump much smaller this year than in previous years?

SYMPTOMS
■ When were the symptoms first noticed?
■ Have symptoms been developing for a long time, or did they appear suddenly?
■ Have you seen the same problem on the same plants in past years?
■ Where are the symptoms: on the leaves, flowers, stems, or the whole plant?
■ Do you see abnormal growth, discoloration, or injuries anywhere on the plant?
■ Do you see insects or evidence of their past activity, such as holes, droppings, sap, or sawdustlike material, on or around the plant?
■ Does the plant have an odd color?

■ Is the growth stunted, puckered, or twisted? Is it wilted?
■ Are the leaves abnormal in size, color, shape, or texture?
■ Is the plant shedding leaves?
■ Do you see holes or ragged margins on the affected plant parts?
■ Does it look like something has tunneled through a leaf or turned the leaf into a "windowpane"?
■ Does a powdery material coat leaves?
■ Are there spots on the leaves or blooms? What size, color, and shape are they? Are they papery or succulent?
■ Are all the leaves or flowers affected, or only those on a few stems?
■ Do the stems appear to have a wound?
■ If only a few stems are affected, cut one of them off. Split it down the center. Do you see a dark stripe or insect larvae inside?

PLANT CONDITION
■ Is the entire plant affected or only parts of the plant? Are symptoms found on only one side of the plant or throughout the plant?
■ If only one side or part of a plant shows distress, which side or which part is it? Is that the sunny side of the plant or do prevailing winds come from that direction?
■ If the entire plant is affected, what do the roots look like? Are they white or light-colored and healthy looking, or are they discolored or distorted?
■ How do the roots smell? A strong foul odor is an indication of rotting roots.

LOCATION OF PROPERTY
■ Is the property near a large body of fresh or salt water? How high is the water table? Does it affect soil drainage? Does seaspray blow onto the garden?
■ Is the property located downwind from a factory, or is it in a large polluted urban area?
■ Is the property part of new housing that was built on landfill or compacted soil?

LOCATION OF PLANT
■ Is the location sunny or shady? Has it always been?
■ Is the plant growing next to the house or an outbuilding? Are the walls light in color so that they reflect light? Is the light intense enough to support plant growth?
■ Is the structure made of brick? Mortar can raise the pH of soil around the foundation.
■ How windy is the location?
■ How close is the garden to a road? Are de-icers such as salt used on the road in winter?

■ Is the garden on or near a slope? It's difficult to keep plants on the top and sides of a slope moist enough, while the base of a slope may be overly wet.

RELATIONSHIP TO OTHER PLANTS
■ Are there large shade trees overhead?
■ Are nearby plants also affected? Are they the same species?
■ How close are other affected plants?

WEATHER
■ Have weather conditions been unusual (especially cold, hot, dry, wet, windy, snowy, and so on) recently or in the past few years?

MICROCLIMATES
■ What is the climate in the immediate vicinity of the plant?
■ Do eaves or other structures block rainfall or irrigation water from reaching plants growing underneath them?
■ How much light is the plant receiving? Is it the optimum amount for the plant?

SOIL CONDITIONS
■ What kind of soil is the plant growing in?
■ How deep is the soil? Does a layer of rock or hardpan lie beneath the topsoil?
■ Is the soil hard and compacted? Does it appear crumbly in spring when it is moist and then harden or crack in dry weather?
■ What is its pH? Is it what the plant needs?
■ Does the soil drain well? Does water stand on its surface after rain or irrigation? Does the soil have a sour smell?
■ Within the past several years has there been construction that disturbed the soil in the garden, such as laying an electrical line to a deck or installing irrigation lines?
■ What type of mulch do you use and was it obtained from a reputable dealer?
■ Are weeds or grass growing around the base of the plant? How thickly?
■ Did you use weed barrier cloth?

RECENT CARE
■ How long has it been since you fertilized and watered the garden?
■ Have you applied fungicides or insecticides to this or nearby plants recently? Was the treatment for this problem or another one?
■ Is the plant listed on the product label?
■ Was the pesticide applied according to label directions?
■ Did it rain soon after you made the application, washing off the spray?
■ Did you spray on a windy day?
■ Have you or a nearby neighbor recently used weed killers or weed-and-feed fertilizers?
■ Does your lawn spreader throw lawn care products into the garden?

PUTTING IT ALL TOGETHER

Once you have put together a case history for your ailing perennial, read the rest of this chapter for more clues to the diagnosis. The pests profiled in the chapter are organized into categories containing a dozen or more insects or diseases that cause similar damage. It covers all the main troublemakers you'll see in a garden.

Just as there are far more perennials any one of us can ever grow, there are more pest species than gardeners need to know. By learning pests by category, you can quickly learn to recognize and deal with problems. Check the photographs and descriptions of symptoms associated with each group of pests.

Also look up the plant in the Encyclopedia of Perennials. The entries identify the most common pests and diseases that affect a plant and offer some suggestions for control. You'll find more complete information about pests through your local cooperative extension office. Or check out references such as *Ortho's Home Gardener's Problem Solver*.

Use references to evaluate damage levels and potential spread, too. The references can help you determine how serious a problem is, whether it's likely to get worse, whether it may spread to other plants, and when you should take action.

Check flowers as well as foliage when diagnosing problems.

CONTROLLING PESTS

Hitting aphids on plants with a sharp blast of water controls the insects. The blast rips off their mouthparts as it knocks them off the plants. Even if they crawl back on the plant, the aphids can't feed.

In your pest patrol, be on the lookout for predator insects such as ladybug larvae (top) and green lacewings (below). These help keep pest populations under control.

Some pest problems are mainly cosmetic—unsightly but not serious. You can let such problems run their course. If symptoms worsen or the pest population continues to build, you may decide that it's worth the time or expense to take action.

Other pests are life-threatening—they can kill plants—and you should deal with them decisively and quickly. Rarely is it possible to eliminate all such pests from a garden. Instead, the key to success is to manage them.

One way to do that is with integrated pest management (IPM). This approach coordinates cultural, mechanical, biological, and chemical control methods. Control measures range from simple methods such as picking bugs off the plants to more involved methods such as changing the way you care for the garden, to spraying pesticides.

Determining when to act decisively against a pest by spraying pesticides and when it's best to handpick the insects, use cultural controls or apply biological controls, takes time and education. Learn which pests can be problems for your perennials, the type and extent of damage that's possible, the point at which natural controls quit working, and what

methods are available for managing the pests. Be aware that when using an IPM approach, you must accept some damage to your garden.

Also keep in mind that most pest control measures require repetition. If the instructions for using a particular pesticide or other control call for you to repeat the process three times in three weeks, do it to kill successive generations or residual organisms. If you don't, the pest may rebound and you'll be back to square one.

INTEGRATED PEST MANAGEMENT

With IPM, instead of reaching for a pesticide the moment you see a problem, you first examine the circumstances, then select the most appropriate control. For example, a few beetles feeding on a few plants may be nothing to get excited about. But the situation depends on the type of beetle, how quickly it reproduces, and how much damage you can tolerate. There are five main steps to IPM that will help you sort out when to act.
■ Plant your garden with insect- and disease-resistant perennials, especially if your region is prone to certain pests or diseases.

■ Take time to learn about any potential problems the plant may face. Your county extension agent or local nursery staff can tell you what insects and diseases affect perennials in your area and the levels of damage the plants tolerate. These professionals can also point out the kind of damage a pest causes and its seriousness.

Because tolerance to pests varies among perennial species and cultivars, ask a professional about just how much damage is possible. Besides knowing what the plant can take, you also need to decide how much damage to the plant you can tolerate.

■ Patrol consistently for pests. Watch for problems and identify the cause of any that arise (disease, insect, animal, or environmental). Estimate the scope of the problem and look for the presence of natural predators that may help control pests for you.

Keep a record of when a pest appears in your garden on your calendar or in a garden journal. Many pests are seasonal, and once you associate them with calendar dates, you can practice prevention rather than post-damage revenge.

For example, if Japanese beetles started feeding on your plants in early July one year, they are likely to do so in future years. Covering the beetles' favored plants in late June with lightweight floating row cover fabric allows you to see and kill beetles before they can damage foliage.

Knowing when certain pests usually appear can also help in handling exceptions. For instance, aphids and other sucking insects proliferate when plants are growing most actively and producing abundant soft, moist tissue. It's unusual to see aphids in August, so part of developing a case history for aphids in August would be to determine what is different this year, whether it's the weather or the way you've cared for the garden.

■ Choose a control. When pest populations are low, a cultural control, such as increasing watering frequency, may be all that is necessary. If cultural controls do not work, or if the problem is out of hand, turn to pesticides, either biological or chemical,

depending on the problem. A combination of control measures, from changing cultural practices to applying pesticides to using alternative methods, helps avoid pesticide resistance while controlling predator populations.

■ Analyze the effectiveness of your chosen control method. Check the results during your next regular pest patrol. If a control worked, it will be apparent and you can relax a bit. If it didn't, you will know to try another approach.

Seek advice from professionals whenever you are in doubt about what to do.

COMPARING PEST CONTROLS

Every pest control method has advantages and disadvantages. Even pesticides considered organic or risk-free can have negative consequences. Gardeners should acquaint themselves with the possible side effects of their chosen pesticides, no matter what the type. Here is a comparison of a home remedy and a commercial product for three major pesticide categories.

Pesticide	Effectiveness	Considerations
INSECTICIDE		
Carbaryl (Sevin)	Kills a wide range of pests; residual lasts 7 days or longer	May damage leaves; sticks well. Odor offensive to some. Use caution when handling, mixing, and applying.
Capsaicin (4 tbsp. hot pepper sauce per quart of water)	Controls many soft-bodied insects; little residual	Material often at hand. Test before use; may burn foliage. Irritates eyes and skin.
FUNGICIDE		
Chlorothalonil	Prevents some fungal diseases; 7–14 day residual	Rarely damages plant. Sticks well. Odor offensive to some. Use caution when handling. Toxic to fish.
Baking soda (1 tbsp. soda + 1 tsp. vegetable oil in 2 quarts water)	Prevents some fungal diseases; lasts until washed off	May burn foliage; test before use. Must be reapplied in wet weather.
MOLLUSCICIDE		
Metaldehyde	Kills any slug that eats it; effective for 14 days; less in rainy weather	Use caution when handling. Toxic to pets and birds.
Ammonia (1 cup in 3 cups water)	Kills slugs on contact; no residual	May burn foliage; rinse after application. Effective only on contact so must be applied when slugs are active (at night or cloudy days). Does not affect slugs it doesn't reach. May irritate eyes, skin, lungs.

CONTROLLING PESTS
continued

IPM ARSENAL

CULTURAL CONTROLS: One of the best defenses against pests is healthy plants, which is more of a prevention than a cure. Proper cultural practices, such as fertilizing and watering in a timely manner, can stop pests from doing major damage to perennials.

MECHANICAL CONTROLS: Pruning to improve air circulation cuts down on many diseases and insect pests. Dividing over-crowded plants also helps keep pests and diseases from developing.

Handpick larger pests such as slugs, snails, and caterpillars. Mulch to prevent water splashing on leaves, which can help reduce some diseases. Set out traps to snare insects, such as moths, worms, and beetles. The traps are baited with natural chemical messengers, which are based on insect pheromones. Be aware, however, that they can attract pests to an area. Rather than being a control, they let you know when it's time to take action against arriving pests.

MANY WAYS TO CONTROL A PEST

There are always options in pest control. Here are all the basic categories of control, from the narrowest in impact—those most likely to affect only the pest—to the broadest—those more likely to affect plants and organisms beyond the targeted pest. With integrated pest management, the option that is effective but narrowest in scope is chosen first, and many different methods of control are used in one garden.

Method	Use when	Comments
Psychological control: Adjust your tolerance level and accept some damage.	Damage is cosmetic in nature or not likely to spread beyond the plant involved.	Continue to patrol in case other problems come up.
Biological control: Encourage or even add natural predators and pathogens such as lady beetles against aphids or scale, predatory nematodes against vine weevil grubs, or the bacteria Bt (*Bacillus thuringiensis*) against caterpillars.	You wish to have seven-day-a-week, 24-hour-a-day assistance in preventing pests from reaching damaging numbers.	Not usually effective in clearing up pest problems that have already reached damaging levels.
Mechanical control: Handpick insects, install screen barriers or fencing, or use any method that physically removes or bars the pest.	Pests are relatively large and few in number. Prevention rather than cure.	More and more often used in botanical gardens and large nurseries when chemical controls such as repellents prove ineffective. Such large-scale professional use is creating demand for and appearance of products such as handheld suction devices to remove insects and inexpensive plastic fencing to exclude deer.
Cultural control: Change the type of soil, amount of sun, availability or method of applying water, or other maintenance procedure to increase plant health and natural resistance. Replace plants with varieties resistant to the existing pests.	Cost of mechanical controls is prohibitive, and you don't want to apply chemical controls, such as near an area where you are trying to attract butterflies or birds.	Always look for resistant varieties when selecting perennials. Restrictions on use of pesticides in public areas have increased the demand for and development of resistant varieties.
Chemical control: Use chemical solutions and powders to repel or kill pests. This category covers all pesticides, including those found in kitchen cleaning products, mineral powders, oils, and toxins derived from plants, synthesized versions of plant products, and petroleum-based pesticides.	A pest problem is already too large or extensive to address by other methods. Use where applying a spray or dust to reach pests on plants that are too tall or numerous for mechanical control to work. Also effective on a large population of one plant species, where a balanced mix of natural predators will not develop effective biological control.	Spraying and dusting chemicals can be less precise than other types of control. Consider the impact of the chemical on the user, neighboring plants, animals, and beneficial insects. Protect sensitive organisms in the area. Do not equate potential harm with origin of the chemical being applied; pepper spray in the eyes may be as damaging as an oil-based chemical in the lungs.

Sometimes you also have to be ruthless and remove affected plants. It's always better to toss a few diseased perennials than to let the disease spread through the bed. Replace them with varieties that are resistant to the pest.

PREDATORS: Many predator insects exist naturally in gardens. They are also available for sale from mail-order companies for you to release in your landscape. Among the best predators are parasitic wasps, ladybugs (or lady beetles), lacewings, predator mites, and parasitic nematodes.

Aphytis melinus and *Metaphycus helvolus* are tiny parasitic wasps that control scale insects. They lay eggs on the scale; the larvae hatch and feed on the scale, killing it. *Trichogramma* wasps do the same to caterpillars. Ladybugs attack and kill a wide range of insect pests, including spider mites, small worms, aphids, and other soft-bodied insects. Lacewings feed on many of the same insect pests. Predatory mites kill the spider mites that attack plants. Parasitic nematodes such as *Steinernema* control ground-living insect pests, including cutworms, grubs, and weevils.

If you decide to use predators, remember that they are living organisms. You can't simply store them in the garage and pull them out when you have problems. For them to be effective, you must provide the right environmental conditions, both in storage and in the landscape when you apply them. Your supplier should be able to advise you about the conditions that predatory organisms require to be most effective.

BIOLOGICAL PESTICIDES: Organic insecticides such as Bt, or *Bacillus thuringiensis*, and neem act against specific pests. For example, one form of the bacteria

Bt kills caterpillars by attacking the lining of their stomachs. Organic insecticides usually leave the beneficial insect population intact.

Insecticidal soap reduces populations of soft-bodied insects, such as aphids and mites. Pyrethrin, rotenone, and neem are pesticides that come from plants. Like all pesticides, they can be toxic to humans and other vertebrates and to beneficial insects.

Homemade pesticides, such as garlic sprays, act more as repellents and, as such, can keep some pests out of your perennial beds. Dormant and horticultural oil sprays smother pests such as mites.

INORGANIC PESTICIDES: Chemical controls are faster-acting and more effective than biological controls. Select materials labeled for your specific pest or disease and follow all label directions.

PESTICIDES ACT IN THREE WAYS:

■ **SYSTEMICALLY**—they are absorbed by the plant and kill pests that feed on plant tissue and sap.

■ **BY CONTACT**—they kill pests they touch.

■ **BY LEAVING A RESIDUE ON THE PLANT'S SURFACE**—they kill insects as they eat foliage and blooms.

Pesticides can kill friendly organisms that might help you battle the pests. Before spraying, check the predator population in your landscape.

The best thing to remember about pest control is that well-sited, weed-free, well-watered and properly fertilized perennials are likely to be pest free. If you find pest problems developing in a bed, don't step up pest control measures until it's certain that plant selection, watering, weeding and fertilization are all appropriate.

Many products, both synthetic and biological, are available for controlling pests. Match the product to the pest and the situation. Handle all pesticides with care and follow all label directions.

INSECTS, MITES, AND MOLLUSKS

Plant bugs, like most sucking insects, concentrate on soft new foliage and do the most damage to the small young leaves.

Soft-bodied, slow-moving aphids cluster on stem tips, flower buds, and the undersides of young foliage. Aphid feeding can siphon off so much water that flower buds abort and new leaves are stunted or cupped.

Spittlebugs suck juices from stems. Look for them on the stems below growth that is distorted.

Foliage attacked by whiteflies may look similar to that damaged by mites. Surfaces under the feeding site may be shiny or sticky from insect droppings. Check the undersides of the leaf; whitefly nymphs shed exoskeletons there. Look for adults flying from the plant when disturbed.

Mites are too small to be seen by the naked eye, but the distinctive pale, stippled appearance of the foliage will alert you to check for these eight-legged spider relatives. Look at the undersides of leaves with a magnifier.

Small creatures can wreak havoc on a garden. These tips will help you protect your perennials from an array of insects and other crawling pests.

SUCKING INSECTS: These include aphids, plant bugs, mites, spittlebugs, thrips, and leafhoppers, all of which suck nutrient-rich liquid from plant cells. Sucking insects cause little noticeable damage unless the population reaches a certain size. Then you may start to see disfigured plants with pockmarks or pale spots drained of nutrients. These pests prefer young foliage, and their feeding frequently causes the new growth to be stunted, puckered, or twisted. The plant may shed heavily damaged foliage.

■ **CONTROL STRATEGIES:** Identify which pest is the problem. If it is mites, begin spraying with miticides, such as fenbutatin-oxide (Orthenex), when damage first becomes noticeable. Insecticidal soap, acephate (Orthene), and carbaryl (Sevin) are effective against many sucking insects. Summer-weight horticultural oil, hot-pepper spray, and some insecticidal soaps kill both insects and mites (check the label). Follow label directions.

Dislodge mites, aphids, or nonflying stages of whiteflies and leafhoppers. Hose off foliage, both upper and lower surfaces. Repeat every few days until new damage ceases.

Lacewings, lady beetles, predatory mites, dragonflies, birds, and other "beneficials" keep pest numbers below harmful levels. To promote them, target sprays only to specific pests; grow a variety of flowering plants as pollen and shelter sites. Or purchase natural predators and introduce them into the garden.

When leaf edges are paler than veins or the leaf appears to be lightly browned, flip the leaf to look for leafhoppers. They drain much sap from a leaf and also inject a toxin that can cause a pale or toasted color on leaf edges.

Clean up well in fall. To remove eggs and overwintering pests on persistent perennial stalks, eliminate plant debris around infested plants. Compost, burn, or remove this debris.

LEAF- AND FLOWER-CHEWING INSECTS: Sawflies, beetles, earwigs, caterpillars, and leaf miners are among these pests. Some of them eat the leaf but avoid the veins. Others tunnel into and eat only the tissue sandwiched between upper and lower leaf surfaces. Many eat the entire leaf or petal. Insects in this group are recognized by the plant they feed on as well as the pattern of their damage—how, when, and which plant parts they eat.

Plants that lose less than 20 percent of their foliage to chewing insects often don't show significant loss of vigor or bloom. In fact, chewing-insect damage often does not even draw attention until it has become severe. At that point it's usually too late to control the pests because their feeding is finished or near an end for the season. Bide your time and plan to fend off the attack next year. Make a note of the date when you first noticed the damage, then subtract two to three weeks. That's when you need to start checking the plants.

■ **CONTROL STRATEGIES:** Destroy the insects as they feed. Sheltered feeders (leaf miners and caterpillars that roll or tie leaves together) are protected from most insecticides but can be controlled by removing and destroying all affected foliage.

To kill sheltered feeders with an insecticide, select a product with systemic action, such as acephate (Orthene). Plants absorb systemic insecticides and incorporate them in their tissues. The insect ingests the poison as it feeds.

Chewing insects that feed openly (beetles, earwigs, sawflies, and some caterpillars) can be plucked off by hand and destroyed or sprayed with a contact insecticide. These kill by directly contacting the insect. Use carbaryl (Sevin), malathion, or insecticidal soap. Young caterpillars can be killed if leaves they eat are dusted with a stomach poison such as Bt, or *Bacillus thuringiensis*, a bacteria affecting moth and butterfly larvae. Stomach poisons temporarily coat the outside of a plant and the insect ingests them as it feeds.

Destroy the insects as they lay eggs, or destroy the eggs. Most sawfly, leaf miner, and caterpillar eggs are deposited on the plant two to three weeks before damage reaches noticeable levels.

Check your notes on when damage first appeared in previous years. Then, two to three weeks before that date, apply a contact insecticide to kill egg-laying adults. Or wait

Flowers that open with brown streaks and distortions are probably infested with thrips. The insects are 1/20 inch long and might be visible at the base of petals.

Sawflies (caterpillarlike larvae of nonstinging wasps) blend with the leaves they eat and clean up the evidence of their presence by shaving leaf edges until they have devoured everything but the leaf stalk. Watch for this damage only on plants susceptible to sawfly damage.

Many beetles eat foliage and flower petals. Most chew holes all the way through a leaf, but some, such as Japanese beetles, are skeletonizers. They cut away a leaf's surface, then eat the tissue beneath, leaving a thin skin between the intact veins. They gradually turn a leaf into a lacy skeleton. Japanese beetles are active during the day.

Leaf miners lay eggs on the host plant's foliage. The eggs hatch and the larvae chew into the leaf and feed there, each one creating a serpentine tunnel within the leaf. Tissue around the "mine" eventually turns brown. A hole at the widest end of the mine indicates the larva has finished feeding and exited.

INSECTS, MITES, AND MOLLUSKS
continued

until after eggs are laid; then spray summer-weight horticultural oil to suffocate the larvae. Or protect susceptible plants with floating row cover fabric for a week to 10 days.

Clean the garden in fall. To eliminate overwintering eggs or larvae or to expose them to predators and weather, remove and destroy all leaf litter, stems, and mulch from around infested plants. Cultivate the soil lightly and leave it unmulched over winter; frost and predators will kill the larvae.

STEMCUTTERS AND BORERS: Cutworms are caterpillars that chew stalks at their base, cutting off stems near the ground. This can kill seedlings. Larger plants may not be killed, but the injury increases disease risk.

Stalk borers chew into the stem some distance above ground or tunnel down from the tip and feed at the stem's center.

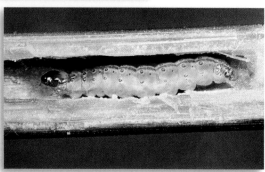

Cutworms are moth larvae that hide in the soil or mulch during the day, then coil around and bite off small stems at night or cut holes in leaves.

European corn borers sometimes drill into the stems of perennial bachelor's button, delphinium, or aster.

Earwigs are sometimes beneficial, preying on other insect larvae, slugs, and snails. But other times they attack plants. Earwigs' nighttime feeding resembles beetle damage, except earwigs often target flower petals. Suspect earwigs if the damage happens overnight and appears first on flower petals. Confirm it by checking the plants by flashlight at night.

Everything above the feeding site is usually killed. Although this may affect only several inches of the stem tip, it may also disfigure the plant, often just before it flowers.

To recognize damage by stemcutters, look for seedlings and small stems cut off at the soil line and left lying where they fell. If you cultivate 2 inches deep near the damage, you are likely to unearth rubbery, coiled gray-brown caterpillars—cutworms.

Wilted stem tips are a sign of borers. Cut the damaged stem below the wilted section and split the stem lengthwise to find the grublike moth larva inside.

■ **CONTROL STRATEGIES:** For stalk borers, apply a systemic insecticide such as acephate (Orthene). For cutworms, apply carbaryl (Sevin) to the bases of susceptible plants.

Cutworms live in the soil over winter. Cultivate the soil where cutworm damage was heavy, and do not apply new mulch so that birds, other predators, and weather can reach the cutworms. Stalk borers overwinter in perennial stalks, so cut and dispose of or destroy stems of plants with borer damage.

To keep cutworms away from seedlings, circle each seedling with a 3-inch-high cardboard tube to form a collar. Press it into the soil, leaving 2 inches above ground.

Newly hatched stem borers and eggs can be dislodged from perennials with frequent forceful cool-water drenches over several weeks, beginning when lilacs bloom.

ROOT-FEEDING PESTS: They include weevils (a type of beetle), root aphids, root mealybugs, and nematodes (soil-dwelling, near-microscopic relatives of parasitic roundworms). Perennial roots attacked by these pests are unable to draw sufficient water and nutrients from the soil and may not be able to support or anchor the plant. Plants that wilt before others and show reduced growth may be suffering root damage. To diagnose the problem, dig up suspect plants and examine the roots.

Root weevils feed from fall to spring. Get suspicious if perennial clumps shrink in size over winter, the foliage of evergreen perennials dries out in early spring, or established perennial crowns peel away from their roots.

An absence of new, crisp, light-colored tips on roots and the presence of small white grubs (⅓ inch) on or near the root mass in fall or spring indicates a root weevil infestation. From midsummer into fall, you can identify adult weevil feeding by notched edges on the foliage of the troubled plant or on neighboring plants.

Small grayish-white insects in clusters on the roots may be root aphids or root mealybugs. Roots stunted and disfigured by nodules indicate nematodes. Some feed in foliage, creating brown areas between main veins. Foliar nematode damage begins with the lowest leaves and spreads upward in hot, damp weather.

■ **CONTROL STRATEGIES:** Adult weevils feed on foliage at night from midsummer through fall. Destroy them by spraying the foliage with a systemic insecticide such as acephate beginning in midsummer; follow label directions. Alternatively, go out at night at frequent intervals, beginning in midsummer, and spread a light-colored drop cloth under the infested plant(s). Shake the plants to dislodge the wingless, night-feeding weevils, then gather in the cloth and destroy the weevils you find there. Continue until you no longer shake off any weevils.

Kill weevil grubs in late summer or fall by drenching the soil under infested plants with acephate or another systemic insecticide.

For root aphids or mealybugs, dip infested root balls into a bucket of water containing carbaryl. Follow the label directions to make the solution.

Remove and burn plants with nematode-infested roots. Replace soil that was in contact with the roots of those plants. Replant the spot with a different species. Whenever possible, select replacement varieties that are nematode-resistant, which should be identified in catalogs with an "N" resistance code.

Remove and burn nematode-infested leaves regularly. Also destroy foliage one or two leaves above such damage.

Encourage or introduce natural predators such as beneficial nematodes to attack all root pests. You can purchase them from some mail-order garden suppliers.

SLUGS AND SNAILS: They are mollusks that rasp holes in foliage. Small plants may be destroyed by their feeding. Larger, more established plants are usually only disfigured.

These pests are most common in shady areas; they are active at night. Inspect damaged plants by flashlight. Slugs are legless, elongated, soft-bodied, and gray, black, or brown. Their eyes sit on stalks protruding from their heads. They range from ⅛ inch to several inches long. Snails carry a shell over their body but have the same stalked eyes. Silvery slime trails may be visible near the damage.

■ **CONTROL STRATEGIES:** Use bait or granules containing metaldehyde or methiocarb. Scatter the pesticide around damaged plants and in nearby shaded, moist areas where the pests may hide during the day. Repeat this process following label directions until the amount of new damage

Some caterpillars feed in the open, trimming leaf edges evenly or cutting rounded, irregular holes into the leaf. Other caterpillars create shelters in which to feed by folding a leaf to make a pocket or pulling two leaves around themselves and gluing them together with silk.

Slugs and snails use their tongue to grate holes in leaves, usually between the veins and within the leaf blade rather than at the margin.

Clumps of perennials that shrink in size over winter, have desiccated foliage, or peel away from the ground for lack of new roots may be infested with root weevils.

Distorted, stunted roots with unnatural nodules are typical of nematode infestation. Roots may be discolored in advanced cases.

is reduced or eliminated. Do not use these products around pets or small children.

Provide objects under which slugs and snails can hide from the sun, such as hollowed-out fruit rinds, moist sections of cardboard, or slug traps. Check traps daily in late afternoon and destroy the pests.

Where slug and snail damage was heavy the previous year, rake away all mulch and debris in early spring and dispose of it off-site or in a hot compost pile. This removes many overwintering slugs, snails, and eggs. Do not mulch the area until spring rains have tapered off or summer heat has begun. During this time, set out traps to catch any survivors.

DISEASES

Protect your plants from debilitating diseases. Learn to recognize the symptoms and practice prevention. **LEAF SPOT, RUST, AND SCORCH:** These are some of the most common fungal and bacterial infections that disfigure perennials. Spots are distinct when they first appear but may merge over time to form large, irregular dead areas. Rusts are fungal spots that are reddish-brown and raised. Scorch appears as dead leaf margins.

Although spots, rusty marks, and burnt leaf edges may occur without any connection to disease, it's wise to investigate further when they appear. Read more about the affected plant so you can rule out causes such as genetics; some plant species develop natural spots or streaks as leaves age. Also take a critical look at the environment and the plant's recent care; leaves can scorch or discolor under adverse conditions, such as heat, drought, and overfertilization.

In addition, it's important to know whether you face a disease or insect because control strategies aimed at one will usually have no effect on the other. To distinguish between the two, look closely at spots and dead leaf margins. A hand lens helps. If a blemish is caused by disease, leaf tissue is generally intact while an insect's chewing creates a hole or scrape marks. However, the center of older diseased spots may dry up and fall out.

Dead areas caused by disease often have concentric rings or expand in bands that are pale green where the infection is still spreading; yellow in tissue that has been infected a bit longer; and brown or black at the points that were first infected.

Advanced stages of an infection are often very distinctive, with marks caused by a particular disease having a certain shape, margin, or color. Reference books often describe only these advanced symptoms. Once you know to watch for a problem, you should be able to catch it earlier—when infected areas simply appear paler than surrounding tissue or look water-soaked. These early signs are more visible if you hold the leaf up and look through it toward a light source.

Infection often starts on lower, older foliage and in the interior of the plant—wherever there is less light or air movement or more moisture and stress. Later, it spreads higher on the plant as spores from the first spots are spread upward by splashing water.

■ **CONTROL STRATEGIES:** Even when many leaves are disfigured, most perennials can still produce enough energy to address day-to-day needs and come back bigger the next season. Your main concern should be arresting the infection's spread so it will not recur.

Remove debris around infected and susceptible plants. Check often for infected leaves and remove them immediately. Cut down and remove herbaceous stems at the end of the season. Burn potentially infectious material or throw it away. Dispose of it in a compost pile only if you regularly turn the pile to keep it heated to 140° F. Wash your hands and tools after working with infected plants. Often, this is the only control needed to keep these diseases in check.

Select plants carefully. If you learn that a perennial you have or plan to buy is susceptible to these diseases, consider alternative species or try to purchase disease-resistant varieties.

Manage susceptible plants to reduce infection. Grow plants in the recommended amount of sun, keep them well-watered, provide a well-drained bed, and don't over- or underfertilize. Thin out the plants every year, spacing clumps farther apart and watering only in the morning. These tactics make the area unfriendly to fungi because drying air circulates freely between widely spaced stems and wet foliage dries quickest at midday.

Apply preventive fungicides to particularly susceptible plants. Fungicides protect uninfected tissue and may reduce the contagiousness of existing infection. They cannot repair damaged areas.

Begin spraying several weeks before your pest patrol experience tells you that symptoms

Leaf spot on bellflower may signal botrytis, an aggravating fungal infection because it infects and kills barely developed flower buds in early spring.

Concentric rings typically mark alternaria leaf spot, right. *The darker outer area is active infection; the brown is dead and dying tissue. All leaf spots may coalesce into large areas,* center. *Mildew,* above, *is rarely life-threatening but often disfiguring. Although you may not see the telltale "dust" until late summer, control is by prevention earlier in the season.*

fungicide applications are generally necessary, at intervals stipulated on the fungicide label.

Use two or more fungicides. Alternate their use during a season and from year to year to reduce the chance that the fungus or bacteria will become resistant to these products. When alternating fungicides, make the first few applications with one product, then switch to one based on a different active ingredient. For instance, alternate between a sulfur-based fungicide and one containing captan, chlorothalonil (Daconil), copper, ferbam, horticultural oil, sodium bicarbonate (as in baking soda solutions), or triforine. Read the product package to be sure it is labeled for the particular problem and the plant.

MILDEW: Powdery and downy mildews are fungal diseases of leaves, flowers, and stems. They are named for the white or fuzzy appearance they give to foliage when the infection reaches an advanced stage. Mildews are not usually life-threatening, especially to established perennials, but they can be unsightly.

Mildew proliferates where relative humidity is high. It does not develop in high heat, direct sunlight, or on continuously wet leaf surfaces. Monitor susceptible plants for this disease in spring and again in late summer when the day's warmth fades rapidly in the evening and relative humidity is high.

The characteristic powder or fuzz that may appear on the top or bottom of a leaf, stem, or flower is the final stage of the disease. However, foliage is sometimes infected so rapidly when conditions are right that leaves yellow, curl, and die before the telltale mildew can form. Plant parts that are mildewed or yellowed and curled can't be saved, although the plant may generate new foliage if you take action to arrest the infection.

It's more effective to watch for the early signs of infection. At that first stage, a leaf or stem develops pale blotches—areas where developing fungi are destroying the green chlorophyll within the tissues.

Infection is most likely to start on the youngest foliage during the spring infection cycle and on lower, inner, or shaded foliage later in the year.

■ **CONTROL STRATEGIES:** Clean up. Remove all plant debris from around infected and susceptible plants as you do for leaf spot.

Select and tend plants carefully. Where environmental conditions are right for the development of mildew, be sure to select mildew-resistant species and varieties. (See Encyclopedia of Plants.) Manage susceptible plants to reduce infection, as explained for leaf spot, rust, and scorch.

Apply preventive fungicides, as with leaf spots, rust, and scorch.

CANKERS: Cankers are infections of the stem and are often caused by the same disease organisms responsible for leaf spot. But the damage caused may be far greater than that caused by leaf spot because the canker may spread down into the roots to kill the plant or sideways to kill the whole stem.

Root and crown rot are most often connected with poorly drained soil. If you suspect it, look for soft, rotted black or brown sections at the base of the plant's stems or on the roots.

DISEASES
continued

Look for sunken or discolored spots on stalks or elongated wounds like parted lips on the stems of woody evergreens.

■ **CONTROL STRATEGIES:** Clean up well where cankers are seen. Prune to remove the infected parts. Dip pruning tools in bleach to disinfect. Control leaf spot and other leaf diseases on the plant, to reduce the sources of infection.

ROOT AND CROWN ROT: Root and crown rot are infections of the root and the dormant buds and stem bases of the perennial crown. They are often secondary infections, invading a plant after it has been damaged by excess or insufficient watering, freezing, or excessive fertilizer.

These diseases are most often connected with poorly drained soil. In such areas, look for stunted plants, aborted flower buds, dead leaf tips, or foliage that wilts, then turns yellow or red and dies. If you suspect root and crown rot, examine those plants for soft, rotted black or brown sections at the base of their stems or on their roots. Rotted sections may have a foul odor. The outer covering of a root that's rotted may easily slide off its stringy core.

Symptoms may suddenly appear on the first warm spring days. That's when fungi that invaded roots or buds damaged by freezing, standing water, or drought during the winter begin to proliferate. Sometimes, though, the infection may not be noticeable until winter is long past. This can happen when growing conditions are perfect for that plant during the season after the damage. As much as 20 percent of a root system may be infected, yet there may be no symptoms because the remainder of the plant is able to overgrow the weak parts. Unfortunately, such a plant may collapse quickly as soon as heat, drought, or other stresses appear.

■ **CONTROL STRATEGIES:** Improve growing conditions to support the plant and suppress the diseases. Let the soil dry out between waterings and improve drainage. Make sure plants are growing in the correct amount of light. Don't overfertilize. Avoid overcrowding plants. Ensure strong root systems by dividing perennials regularly.

Root and crown rot diseases don't thrive in biologically active soil. Where you have seen or suspected crown or root rot, mix compost or mycorrhizal innoculants such as MycoRise, MycorTree, or Plant Success into the soil. Then replant the space.

Handle infected plants carefully. Always discard old, weak parts when dividing perennials. If a weak plant shows signs of root or crown rot, dig it up. If it's heavily infected, discard it and the soil around its roots. For those with less rot, cut out diseased portions. Dip the remaining healthy divisions in fungicide. Replant them where the growing conditions are better. Disinfect tools used around the plants with bleach.

BLIGHTS AND WILTS: Blights and wilts are fungal and bacterial infections that enter plants through injuries, roots, or pores on leaves. They then proliferate and clog the water-conducting system.

Investigate stems or plants that wilt suddenly and do not recover after watering. Look for physical damage to stem bases, drainage problems, or root-grazing insects, any of which can cause similar symptoms. If you don't find any of these other causes, suspect wilt or blight. To further differentiate wilts and blights from other problems, cut off a wilted and a healthy stem. Wilts and blights may discolor tissues inside the stem, which you can see by comparing the ends of these cut stems.

Early symptoms of wilt and blight are subtle. Leaves may yellow, or they may wilt and die. Individual leaves, the foliage on one side of the plant, or just the older, lower leaves

Stem canker infections can be more serious problems than leaf infections. A canker may spread on the stem or into the roots to kill whole stems or plants.

may be affected. Usually these leaves remain attached to the plant even after dying. Keep an eye on related plants near a perennial that dies of wilt. The disease may spread to them.

■ **CONTROL STRATEGIES:** Clean up around infected and susceptible plants. Immediately remove infected plants and the soil around their roots. Burn or throw out this infectious material. Dispose of it in a compost pile only if you turn the compost regularly to keep it heated to 140° F. Wash your hands and dip tools in bleach or rubbing alcohol after working with infected plants.

Select and tend plants carefully. If you learn that a particular perennial you plan to buy is prone to blight or wilt, or if an existing perennial exhibits susceptibility, consider alternative species or disease-resistant varieties. Wilt- and blight-resistant plants may be identified by a "V" or "F" in catalogs, for resistance to two of the most common wilt pathogens, verticillium and fusarium.

Keep susceptible plants strong to reduce risk of infection. Divide plants regularly and discard the oldest, weakest parts. Locate plants where they receive the right amount of sun. Keep them watered, improve drainage in the bed, and avoid over- or underfertilizing.

A well-sited, well-tended perennial resists infection better than a plant weakened by adverse conditions.

VIRUSES: Mosaic, ring spot, and other viruses weaken plants. They are most often spread by insects such as leafhoppers, beetles, and aphids. The insects feed on infected plants, then move to healthy plants where their feeding injects the virus.

Reduced growth may be the first symptom of a virus, followed by stunting, irregular growth, and discoloration of leaves and flowers. Flowers may have light or dark streaks in them. Blooming may decrease or stop. Leaves may be curled or have cupped edges, blotches, streaks, or patterns of yellow or white. The discolored tissues often do not die and may be mistaken for variegation.

■ **CONTROL STRATEGIES:** Select plants carefully. Reject plants with viral symptoms.

If you know a species is susceptible to a particular virus, select a variety that has proven to be resistant. For instance, a "T" in some catalog descriptions and on plant tags means the variety is resistant to tobacco mosaic virus.

Remove infected plants immediately. Viruses are not transmitted through soil, so soil removal is not necessary. Control the carriers of the virus. Insects are most often the vectors that carry viruses between plants; the most likely culprits are leafhoppers and beetles, which move freely among plants. Aphids are also known to ingest a virus from one plant then inject it into another. Keep leaf-sucking and leaf-chewing insect populations under control to reduce the spread of viruses. (See control strategies under the various insect groups.)

Insects may transmit viruses to perennials from nearby related weeds, so keep weeds under control as well.

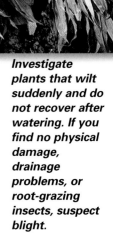

Investigate plants that wilt suddenly and do not recover after watering. If you find no physical damage, drainage problems, or root-grazing insects, suspect blight.

Viruses weaken plants. The first symptom may be reduced growth, followed by stunting, irregular growth, and discoloration of leaves and flowers. Viruses are most often spread by insects such as leafhoppers, beetles, and aphids.

WEEDS: A ROGUE'S GALLERY

Cool-season annuals such as tall rocket germinate in late fall or late winter, robbing perennials of nutrients and space.

Purslane fools us by waiting to sprout until we think the spring weeding is done.

Burdock's large leaves are impressive.

Here are some of the most common and worst weeds of perennial beds. Each weed pictured here represents a group of weeds with the same life cycle—annual, biennial, or perennial—and manner of spread. Effective ways to eradicate the weeds in each group are given. If a weed you seek isn't listed specifically, simply find the group into which it fits to learn some appropriate control tactics.

COOL-SEASON ANNUALS

REPRESENTATIVE: Tall rocket or wild mustard. Seeds germinate in cool weather, late fall, or late winter. Plants are usually large enough to be in flower by the time gardeners begin weeding beds in spring. That means the weeds use up nutrients that could have fueled the perennial bed's resurgence, slow down emerging perennials with their shade, and add another crop of weed seeds to the soil.
CONTROL: Weed thoroughly in fall and apply a seed-smothering mulch or preemergence herbicide to all bare ground. Follow up in early spring as daffodil foliage emerges—remove any cool-season weeds that sprouted in the shallow mulch next to perennial crowns.
OTHER WEEDS IN THIS GROUP: Creeping speedwell, henbit, mouse-ear chickweed, annual bluegrass.

WARM-SEASON ANNUALS

REPRESENTATIVE: Purslane. Seedlings are an indicator of warm soil. They germinate in mid- to late spring as soil temperatures reach 60° F. A sun lover, purslane is most prevalent at the front of a border and between stepping-stones. Because detached, rootless bits of its succulent stems can survive even high heat and generate new roots, it should not be hoed but pulled.
CONTROL: Mulch all bare spaces or apply a preemergence herbicide by midspring. Follow up in early summer and remove any plants that prevailed before they begin to flower. If you fail to take steps early,

use mulch to smother the seedlings while they are still tiny.
OTHER WEEDS IN THIS GROUP: Crabgrass, knotweed, ragweed, redroot pigweed, spurge, wild buckwheat, annual wild morning glory (also called bindweed or hedge bindweed).

BIENNIALS

REPRESENTATIVE: Burdock. This is an impressive weed. Its large, felty leaves can dwarf even the largest hosta. Like most biennials, it is a low rosette of foliage with a taproot in its first year. In its second year, it forms a tall flowering stalk. The flowers are unremarkable, but its grape-sized, super-sticky burrs are unmistakable.
CONTROL: Pull, cut, or apply a nonspecific systemic herbicide such as glyphosate before these weeds flower and set seed. Then keep the area well mulched to prevent existing seed in the soil from sprouting.
OTHER WEEDS IN THIS GROUP: Bull thistle, motherwort, mullein, Queen Anne's lace.

CLUMP-FORMING PERENNIALS

REPRESENTATIVE: Dandelion. This and other clump-forming weeds have one quality that works in the gardener's favor—they stay in one place rather than reaching out with their roots to form colonies. Because dandelion roots are deep, the soil has to be loosened deeply to remove the whole root, or weed killer may have to be applied repeatedly to exhaust the supply of starch stored in the root.
CONTROL: Patrol for and pull or kill these weeds at least once a year before they come into flower. If you can't remove them, at least keep the flowers cut off so new seed isn't formed. After pulling the weeds, maintain a thick mulch or apply a preemergence herbicide to prevent germination of the many seeds deposited in the area. Some clump-forming weeds have shallow, fibrous root systems and are relatively easy to pull. Others are harder to pull, such as dandelion, some tree seedlings with taproots, and plants that grow from bulbs, such as wild garlic. Overcoming taprooted and bulbous members of this group also requires follow-up because they can regenerate from bits of root or bulb left behind.
OTHER WEEDS IN THIS GROUP: Fleabane, pokeweed, violets.

SHALLOW-ROOTED RUNNING PERENNIALS

REPRESENTATIVE: Ground ivy. This plant snakes through lawns, rooting where its stems contact bare soil. In gardens, freed from a mower's restraint, it explodes to become a dense mat, weaving its way 18 inches up into stems of other plants. Its shallow roots are easily pried loose, but it must also be banned from adjacent lawns or it will reinvade. The broad-leaf weed killer Trimec kills it; be sure to overseed and thicken the lawn with better care, or ground ivy seed will return.

CONTROL: Many weeds in this group are like ground ivy—they are easily pulled, apparently with all roots intact. Look closely, though, to see whether pieces of the running roots have broken loose to sprout again. Loosen the soil throughout the area before pulling; apply mulch or preemergence herbicide to prevent recolonization by seed; revisit the area within two weeks to remove sprouted root pieces. Weed barriers are not effective against most of these weeds, which can creep over barriers in just a fraction of an inch of mulch or leaves.

OTHER WEEDS IN THIS GROUP: Catnip, dead nettle, enchanter's nightshade, poison ivy, sour sorrel, violets.

DEEP-ROOTED RUNNING PERENNIALS

REPRESENTATIVE: Canada thistle. Roots run deep and are brittle. Like some of the other worst weeds in this category, they can persist and resprout for as long as two years, despite frequent pulling or spraying with herbicide

CONTROL: You must be more persistent than these plants to beat their extensive root systems. Pulling, cutting, and herbicide applications put a drain on the roots' starch reserves, but with each day in the sun, new shoots replenish those roots. Loosen the soil well and remove all the foliage and as much root as possible. Then return every four to seven days through at least a full season to pull, cut, or apply a systemic herbicide such as glyphosate to the new sprouts. Don't attack just a few times and then turn away for the rest of the season; survivors will surface, grow, and regain all lost ground. Fall is a time plants move food reserves into their roots. A final glyphosate spray in fall is especially effective.

OTHER WEEDS IN THIS GROUP: Bindweed, field horsetail, milkweed, fleeceflower, quackgrass.

Dandelion's deep root draws nutrients that have leached below many plants' reach, so view pulled dandelions as salvaged nutrients— dry them out and compost them.

If you remove ground ivy from a bed but allow it to remain in an adjacent lawn, it will reinvade.

When poison ivy first begins to creep into a bed, it is easy to pull. Cover your skin before touching it. Wash thoroughly afterward.

Canada thistle roots break easily when pulled. They store a lot of starch and can resprout from even the tiniest pieces.

Although it's not native, quackgrass is so fast-spreading and adaptable that it has become a weed almost everywhere in eastern North America.

Bindweed has an extensive root system. Sprouts may surface from root remnants after two years of hard weeding.

Field horsetail or scouring rush fools gardeners. Loosen an area well so that you remove the horizontal running roots as well as the easily pulled vertical pieces.

FOUR-LEGGED PESTS

Groundhogs often knock down large plants to reach the flower buds and succulent tips they prefer.

This section will help you identify furry or feathered culprits and choose a control strategy when plant damage is serious enough to warrant your intervention.

RABBITS: They nibble foliage and neatly snip off individual stems and leaves of many perennials. Damage is often heaviest early in the year. Favorite plants include aster, balloon flower, bellflowers, hosta, pincushion flower, pinks, and purple coneflower.

■ **CONTROL STRATEGIES:** For small plants, exclude the rabbits from the garden or plant by spreading floating row cover—lightweight material that allows light and water to pass through—over it. Keep plants covered until they are well-established and can tolerate some browsing. Fence whole beds or cage large plants individually. Use wire with ½-inch mesh, such as rabbit hutch wire. Make fences 18 to 24 inches tall. (Dark green or black fencing is nearly invisible at a distance for whole-bed fencing. Cages around individual plants are visible in spring when the plants most need protection, but are usually hidden by plant growth within weeks.) Where rabbits are numerous, they may resort to digging; bend the wire to make an 8-inch L at the bottom of the fence. Bury the L under mulch, facing out (see the illustration on page 135).

Capture and relocate the rabbits. Use fresh greens to bait traps, and set them early in the season when other food is scarce. Check local ordinances regulating relocation.

Repellents such as distasteful sprays or scented items may be temporarily effective. Individual rabbits differ in reaction, so change products often, from thiram-based spray to hot pepper wax or blood meal, for example.

Set up scarecrows, such as toy animals with large eyes, near favored plants; move them often. Motion-activated electronic devices startle pests with water sprays or sound.

GROUNDHOGS, GOPHERS, AND PRAIRIE DOGS: These vegetarians are great diggers; groundhogs (or woodchucks) climb as well. Groundhogs prefer shoots, flower buds, and fruit. Prairie dogs and gophers eat roots. This group has diverse tastes, including bellflower, checkerbloom, daylily, delphinium, and phlox.

■ **CONTROL STRATEGIES:** Capture and relocate; use tactics similar to those used for

Rabbits often work from the bottom toward the top of a plant and may prefer one side of a plant or garden that is closer to shelter. They may leave behind clusters of dark brown pellets.

Emerging perennials, like this hosta, are particularly vulnerable. Rabbits bite cleanly through stems and leaf stalks.

To thwart digging, form an 8-inch L at the base of a rabbit fence. Cover it with soil or mulch.

rabbits, such as laying row cover fabric over young plants, or fencing the garden with 1-inch mesh wire (chicken wire). Fence over the beds and all around them. Or make fences 36 inches tall, leaving the top 12 inches unsupported so that an animal climbing the fence will fall outward when reaching that section. These pests are quick to dig, so continue the fence underground with an additional L that extends 12 to 24 inches down and 12 inches outward.

■ **OTHER STRATEGIES:** Use repellents or set up scarecrows, as for rabbits.

SQUIRRELS, GROUND SQUIRRELS, AND CHIPMUNKS: These pests cause damage by digging up recently planted perennials. They don't usually eat perennials but may do so if their population is high and other food sources are scarce.

■ **CONTROL STRATEGIES:** Capture and relocate or destroy the pests. Peanut butter is a reliable bait. Check local ordinances regulating relocation or destruction.

Discourage digging. These critters are most likely to dig where soil has been loosened, such as around new plantings. Cover a freshly planted area with row cover for a few days, weighting the edges of the cloth with logs or planks. To end digging, lay pieces of ½-inch mesh wire fencing on the soil around threatened plants.

Use repellents. Hot pepper wax or blood meal sprayed or spread on the soil may be temporarily effective.

Encourage predators. Cats, hawks, and owls suppress rodents in general.

VOLES: Voles, or "meadow mice," can be especially destructive in winter, devouring bulbs, tubers, and perennial crowns.

Look for clean 1-inch entrance holes, darting motion in beds, and neatly clipped stems or shaved crowns. In cold regions, voles may eat the crowns of lawn grass under cover of snow. When melting snow reveals shallow

furrows cut through a lawn, it's a sure sign that voles have struck.

■ **CONTROL STRATEGIES:** Set out mousetraps baited with peanut butter in early spring before the vole population grows.

Set traps near entry holes. Cover each trap with an inverted shoebox cut out on one side so that the area is dark but open to the voles. Check traps at least once a day. Encourage predators, as you would in handling squirrels.

BIRDS: Occasionally birds are destructive by feeding on or uprooting seedlings or damaging foliage in pursuit of pests.

■ **CONTROL STRATEGIES:** Protect young or special plants. Cover plants with bird netting or row cover, or set up scarecrows.

DEER, ELK, AND MOOSE: They prefer but do not limit their feeding to young growth and flower buds. In winter, they may paw up and crop perennial crowns.

■ **CONTROL STRATEGIES:** Exclude grazers. Install electric fencing or barriers at least 8 feet tall for deer. Dark plastic mesh fencing is effective and reasonably priced.

Set up motion-sensitive scarecrows. These startle intruders with water sprays or sound and are effective from spring to fall if repositioned frequently.

Even if you select "deer-resistant" species, the deer may sample or trample them. Fence them until the plants are well-established and able to tolerate occasional abuse.

Deer eat many perennials and have become so accustomed to people that they cause problems even in city gardens. Fences remain the gardener's best defense against deer.

Each deer herd may have unique tastes, but hostas are so popular that they're dubbed deer candy.

PROBLEMS IN THE ENVIRONMENT

Scorch on fern

It's often difficult to tell from the symptoms whether a plant has a disease, needs fertilizer, or is suffering from a lack of light. The symptoms are just too similar. That's where developing a case history is especially helpful. By taking into account recent weather and changes in growing conditions and the site, you are able to consider all the possible causes of a problem. The following are among the most common environmental problems affecting perennials.

INSUFFICIENT SUNLIGHT: Symptoms of a perennial receiving less sunlight than it requires include stunted growth, small leaves on lanky or stretched-looking stems, and little-to-no flowers. You may see all symptoms or just one or two.

The remedy is to increase the amount of light the plant receives. If it's a neighboring perennial that's blocking the sun, just enlarging the open space around the plant may give the boost of sunlight the plant needs to prosper. More often, the remedy is to cut back overhanging branches shading the garden, or to move struggling plants to a sunnier spot. Though transplanting is always a risk, continuing shade could mean loss of the plant. Make changes gradually or early in the season to avoid sunburning the perennials.

SUNSCALD: Symptoms of sunscald, also called sunburn, include faded and bleached splotches on leaves. The entire leaf may be affected or only part of it,

and the blotches may dry and become brittle.

Plants sunscald when the light exposure is suddenly increased and temperatures are warm. Dry soil exacerbate the likelihood of it occurring. For example, expect sunscald when tree branches sheltering a shade garden are removed in midsummer, exposing the perennials to full sun, or hot sunny days follow a period of cool, cloudy, rainy weather.

To prevent sunscald, temporarily shade the plants with some sort of loose cover. Be sure to provide plants with plenty of water during periods of hot, dry, sunny weather.

SCORCH: When plants scorch, their leaves turn crisp and brown, especially along their edges. Low humidity and high wind on warm days causes excessive loss of water from leaves. The soil may be moist, but roots are unable to supply water to foliage as fast as the leaves transpire it. Scorch is also common when the perennial's root system is unusually small. Fertilizer burn, when excess fertilizer has been applied, causes similar symptoms.

Protect plants from scorch by shielding them from wind. A windbreak or solid fence should help. Sprinkle plants with water during the heat of the day to cool them and raise humidity.

POOR DRAINAGE: Plants lack vigor and wilt even though they have plenty of moisture. Their leaves may be pale green to yellowish in color. Poorly drained soils contain little oxygen. Because of the lack of oxygen, the perennials' small fibrous feeder roots decay. It's this loss of roots that causes the wilt and eventually kills the plant.

Sunscald

Transplant shock

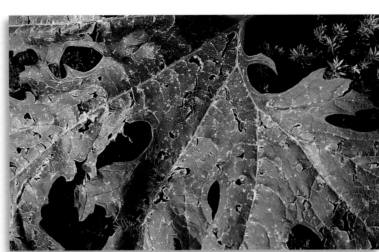

Hail damage

Distortion from 2,4-D misuse

Prepare soil well before planting to avoid drainage problems. If it will take major work to improve drainage, such as by installing drain tiles, grow perennials that are adapted to wet soil or build raised beds.

PESTICIDE DAMAGE: One of the most common pesticides to damage plants is 2,4-D, an herbicide based on plant hormones. The leaves of affected plants will be small and distorted. Damaged leaves won't return to normal, but the plant can outgrow damage.

If you use pesticides correctly, you shouldn't have to worry about them damaging your perennials. Read the label and follow all label directions. Avoid applying materials when it is windy or when temperatures are predicted to be above 90° F. Use a separate sprayer for applying herbicides. To keep lawn chemicals out of your garden, make sure the spreader is in good order. Use a drop spreader near the garden. If all you have is a rotary spreader, take care to stay as far from the bed as it flings materials. If you use a lawn service, be sure to communicate your expectations as to how they should work around your garden.

HAIL: Small to pea-size hail will knock holes in perennial leaves that look like slug, snail, or cutworm damage. Generally, hail damage occurs on just one side of a plant, the side the hail came from. Also, it often rips leaves as well as makes holes in them.

Dried leaf margins from too long an interval between waterings

ENCYCLOPEDIA OF PLANTS

This section features more than 190 of the finest perennials you can grow. Check here to learn about each plant's preferred growing conditions, how to place it for best effect, special needs, and tips for day-to-day care. Plants are listed in alphabetical order by scientific name.

The encyclopedia includes several woody plants, such as clematis. These are shrubs and vines that are particularly well-adapted to growing in perennial gardens and providing a good backdrop or accent to perennials. When planning your garden design, you may want to consider using them.

KEY TO THE ENTRIES

SCIENTIFIC NAME: A plant's Latin name is universally accepted. It is comprised of a genus name and a specific epithet. Together they are a species name. The genus is capitalized, while the specific epithet is not. Both names are in italics. For example, the scientific name for the familiar hollyhock is *Alcea rosea.*

Although sometimes complicated, scientific names have a purpose: Using them will help avoid any cases of mistaken identity, such as when you're searching nursery catalogs, garden centers, or reference books for specific plants.

COMMON NAME: As in the case of hollyhock cited above, this term refers to the everyday name for a plant. Be aware that one plant may have many common names, and that one common name may apply to several plants. To avoid confusion when discussing perennials with gardeners in other areas, use the scientific name as well as the common name or descriptions of the leaf and flower to ensure you are talking about the same plant.

ORNAMENTAL FEATURES: This entry designates why the plant is grown and its peak time. Bloom time may vary with the weather by as much as a week or two from year to year. Spring may commence six weeks earlier and be more prolonged in southern areas. In northern regions, it may begin later and pass more quickly. Fall begins about the same time all over the continent, but ends earlier in northern areas than in southern ones.

■ **EARLY SPRING:** From the bloom of snowdrops and witch hazels until forsythia blooms (roughly March 1–April 15).

■ **MIDSPRING:** From forsythia's peak bloom until flowering dogwood begins to show significant color (roughly April 15–May 15).

■ **LATE SPRING:** From peak flowering dogwood season until peony is in full bloom (roughly May 15–June 15).

■ **EARLY SUMMER:** From the first big display of large-flowered clematis and Hybrid Tea roses until Shasta daisies come into peak bloom (roughly June 15–July 15).

■ **MIDSUMMER:** From the time Shasta daisies peak and blue or pink hydrangeas are in full bloom until rose of Sharon comes into peak bloom (roughly July 15–August 8).

■ **LATE SUMMER:** From the first show of field goldenrod until roadside purple asters bloom (roughly August 8–September 1).

■ **FALL:** From the full bloom of 'Autumn Joy' sedum until burning bushes turn red and silver maple leaves turn color (roughly September 1–late October).

HARDINESS: This term tells you whether a plant will survive winter in your region. The range of hardiness zones listed is only a rough gauge of a plant's ability to withstand summer heat. It does not give information about other stresses in your region, such as drought and pests. The USDA Plant Hardiness Map is on page 245.

SIZE: The dimensions of the plant are presented as height first, then width.

LIGHT REQUIRED: This information says how much sun a plant needs each day to stay in good health, develop to expectation, and bloom well. Measure the amount of sun only during the actual growing season.

■ **FULL SUN:** Six or more hours of direct sun.

■ **HALF SUN:** Four to six hours of direct sun.

■ **SHADE:** Two to four hours of direct sun.

■ **DENSE SHADE:** Up to two hours of sun.

SOIL AND DRAINAGE: It's noted here whether a plant grows best in a certain type of soil or responds better where water drains more slowly or more quickly through soil.

MOISTURE: Some perennials grow best if the soil around their roots is allowed to dry down between waterings. Others are healthiest if the soil is constantly moist. Specific water needs are listed for each plant.

■ **CONTINUOUSLY MOIST:** Water whenever necessary to keep the soil around a plant from drying out. (It should never be soggy.)

■ **AVERAGE WATER:** Water as soon as the soil 2 to 3 inches below the surface is dry.

■ **ALLOW TO DRY DOWN:** Water after the soil has been dry 2 to 3 inches below the surface for one or more days.

■ **TOLERATES DROUGHT:** Once established, a plant can survive long periods without rain or supplemental water.

■ **TOLERATES SOGGY SOIL:** A plant can grow even if the soil is waterlogged at times.

DESCRIPTION AND USES: This section tells you what a plant looks like, how it grows, and what to plant near it. Shape is the form of a plant in the garden (carpet-forming, mounded, vase, or columnar). Uses describes how a perennial complements other plants in the garden. Information includes whether a plant stays in one place (forms a clump), travels (spreading), or travels a lot (invasive).

Growth rate means how long a perennial takes to reach full size.

■ **SLOW:** Width or number of stems may increase only 10 to 25 percent in a year.

■ **MODERATE:** In a year, the plant grows 25 to 50 percent in spread or number of stems.

■ **FAST:** In a season or less, the plant doubles in spread or number of stems

■ **VERY FAST:** The plant more than doubles in spread or number of stems in a season or less.

CARE: This information explains specialized maintenance that deviates from standard care, such as insects and diseases to watch for, specific needs for fertilizer, deadheading, staking, pinching, or cutting back.

RECOMMENDED PLANTS AND RELATED SPECIES: Described in this section are outstanding cultivars (horticulturally propagated plants different from the species) and related species. If none are listed, the main entry is the best or only example available. A cultivar name is capitalized and set off by single quotation marks.

NOTES: This highlights important information that does not fit in other categories, such as whether the plant is poisonous or attracts birds and butterflies.

Picture yourself in the heart of a colorful setting where nature and dwelling harmoniously coexist. This encyclopedia will help you find the perennials for your dream garden.

ACANTHUS SPINOSUS

Spiny bear's breeches

Spiny bear's breeches

- White flowers with dusky maroon jackets, late spring (South) or early summer (North)
- Zones 5–10; will not survive in Zone 5 if drainage is poor
- 3 to 4 feet × 3 feet
- Full to half sun; midday shade in hot regions
- Well-drained, slightly acid to neutral soil

DESCRIPTION AND USES:

This plant is like a living sculpture. In fact, its sturdy 4-foot spires of white flowers and huge, dark, glossy leaves served as models for the carving adorning classical Corinthian columns.

Leaves are spined and thistlelike but not really dangerous. Avoid hiding this big plant at the back of the border; set it in the middle or even the front if your design can accommodate it.

This plant grows slowly at first, then picks up speed to a moderate pace. It has the potential to form a large colony. Spiny bear's breeches is evergreen in warm regions.

The plant combines well with cushion spurge and pearly everlasting. It blooms at the same time as daylily, meadowsweet, and balloon flower.

CARE: In warmer areas, provide some shade during the heat of the day; it may bloom less than in cooler regions. Spiny bear's breeches is generally pest-free, but slugs and snails may be a problem.

New plants can be obtained by digging near the crown in spring, cutting off pencil-thin roots several inches long, and planting them vertically just below soil level, with the cut end up.

Deadheading is optional; the plant will not bloom a second time, and flowering stalks can be attractive after bloom. Cut plants back in late fall (cold areas) or early spring (warmer ones).

NOTES: Spiny bear's breeches tolerates drought, heat, and humidity. It stays evergreen in warm regions.

Pink common yarrow in foreground and yellow fernleaf yarrow in back

ACHILLEA

Yarrow

- Yellow, white, red, or pink depending on species, late spring to midsummer
- Zones 3–9
- 18 to 60 inches × 36 inches
- Full sun
- Well-drained soil; soil type and pH adaptable
- Average water

DESCRIPTION AND USES:

Yarrow is easily recognized for its ferny foliage and distinctive flat-topped flower clusters. Some species are mounded in leaf, columnar in bloom; others form mats. Eighteen- to 24-inch varieties are as tall as wide; taller varieties are wider than tall. The growth rate is fast. Yarrow combines well with false indigo, bellflower, crocosmia, iris, delphinium, coneflower, and daylily.

CARE: Fertilize at half the average rate. Cut stems to the ground after the bloom season ends to encourage new basal foliage. Cut plants back in early spring or late fall. Yarrow is mostly pest-free. Powdery mildew and stem and root rots may occur in wet or very dry soil. The plant resists rabbits and deer.

RECOMMENDED PLANTS AND RELATED SPECIES:

Common yarrow (A. *millefolium*) is a low-growing, rapidly spreading perennial. 'Appleblossom', with peach to lilac-pink flowers, is 2 to 3 feet tall. 'Paprika' is an intense red with yellow centers on 2-foot stems. Fernleaf yarrow (A. *filipendulina*) reaches 3 to 5 feet in bloom. 'Coronation Gold', a hybrid yarrow, is one of the best for drying, with 5-inch-wide golden yellow flowers on sturdy, 2- to 3- foot tall stems; the foliage is gray green. Another hybrid, 'Moonshine', has brilliant yellow flowers and 1-foot-tall silvery foliage that is covered with soft hairs. This plant performs best in dry regions.

ACONITUM CARMICHAELII

Monkshood

- Blue flowers, late summer or fall
- Zones 3–8 (mulch deeply in Zones 3 and 4)
- 2 to 4 feet × 1 foot
- Full sun to part shade
- Well-drained, organic-matter-enriched clay soil
- Continuously moist

DESCRIPTION AND USES: These plants earned their name from the cowl shape of their blooms. All are upright, clump-forming perennials. Plants grow slowly at first then speed up once established. They are good companions for goatsbeard and fragrant bugbane.

CARE: Monkshood does not do well in heat or where nighttime temperatures are above 70° F; provide midday shade. Apply 50 percent more fertilizer than average. Wilting in early spring is a sign of crown rot. Improve winter drainage. Check for bacterial leaf spot and mildew in midspring; remove infected leaves and apply fungicide. Cyclamen mite may be a problem. Monkshood resists rabbits and deer. Deadheading prolongs bloom in areas with extended fall. Cut back to the ground in late fall. Remove and destroy prunings to halt disease.

RECOMMENDED PLANTS AND RELATED SPECIES: Azure monkshood (A. *carmichelii*) is 3 feet tall and sturdy enough not to need staking. 'Arendsii' has large blue flowers in fall. 'Bicolor' monkshood (A. × *cammarum*) has white hoods with a blue border and grows 3 to 4 feet tall in Zones 3-7. 'Ivorine', the earliest to flower, has creamy white flowers on compact plants and grows 2 to 3 feet tall.

NOTES: The plant is poisonous.

'Bicolor' monkshood

ACTAEA RUBRA

Red baneberry

- Bottlebrush white flowers in late spring
- Zones 4–7
- 24 to 36 inches × 24 inches
- Half sun to dense shade
- Well-drained, organic soil
- Continuously moist to average water

DESCRIPTION AND USES: Red baneberry is a large, slow-growing shrubby perennial for shady yards. Its bottlebrush flowers and berries are held above foliage. Good companions include Jacob's ladder, heart-leaf brunnera, and lungwort.

CARE: Red baneberry has no special fertilizer needs and is basically pest-free. Cut it to the ground in late fall after frost kills the top. For more plants, sow fresh seed directly outdoors in early fall after soaking berries to remove pulp from seed. The plant needs several weeks of 70° F temperatures, then several months at or below 40° F, and a gradual warm-up in spring for complete germination.

NOTES: Plants are poisonous. The toxin is concentrated in the berries and root.

Red baneberry

Kiwi

ACTINIDIA KOLOMITKA

Kiwi

- Bright green leaves splashed with pink and white
- Zones 4–9
- 20 feet
- Full sun to shade
- Well-drained fertile soil
- Continuously moist

DESCRIPTION AND USES:
Kiwi makes a colorful perennial garden backdrop. Its large leaves open purple then mature to green marked with vivid pink and white variegation. The coloration is strongest in direct sunlight. It fades in heat and with excess fertilizer or shade. Male vines have the brightest colors, and mature plants tend to be more colorful than young vines.

Look for small white blooms in early summer. They're not showy, but they are fragrant. Female vines produce edible berries that attract birds in fall. Most of the vines that are sold are male, and you must grow both a male and a female vine to have fruit.

Train kiwi to cover an arch or arbor as an entrance to your garden. Its foliage offers a splash of color during a perennial garden's typical down periods. The foliage is beautiful when matched with purple and rust tones, such as brick. Try combining kiwi with purple-leaved plants, such as purpleleaf sand cherry or 'Forest Pansy' redbud. Or consider painting its supporting structure purple.

CARE: Kiwi tolerates both sun and shade but needs sun for the best color. It performs best in half sun and with moderate moisture and good soil drainage. Plants have few pest problems. Prune them continually to keep them in bounds.

In areas colder than Zone 6, kiwi dies down to the ground each winter.

ADIANTUM PEDATUM

Maidenhair fern

- Delicate, lacy, light green fronds
- Zones 3–8
- 10 to 24 inches × 18 inches
- Shade to half sun
- Neutral to limy soil enriched with organic matter
- Continuously moist

DESCRIPTION AND USES:
One of the most beautiful and refined ferns, maidenhair fronds have an unusual "five-finger" pattern on shiny black stems. This elegant fern is gorgeous in moist woodland gardens and as a filler in bouquets. It looks magnificent when paired with Solomon's seal or hosta.

CARE: Grow ferns 18 inches apart in filtered light. Add agricultural lime to acid soils according to soil test results. Keep soil moist during dry summer months.

RECOMMENDED PLANTS AND RELATED SPECIES: 'Japonicum' fronds emerge pinkish bronze. 'Miss Sharples' has chartreuse new growth and larger leaflets. Evergreen maidenhair (*A. venustum*) grows 12 inches tall with pale green fronds on purplish black stems. Fronds have a blue tint in summer and turn yellow-brown in autumn. Southern maidenhair fern (*A. capillus-veneris*) glistens in shade (Zones 7–10).

Maidenhair fern

AGASTACHE FOENICULUM

Anise hyssop

- Dense spikes of blue flowers, midsummer to autumn
- Zones 5–10; less hardy with poor drainage
- 20 to 30 inches × 30 inches
- Full sun to half sun
- Well-drained, slightly alkaline soil
- Average water

DESCRIPTION AND USES:
Columnar in shape and 30 inches tall, anise hyssop is an erect anise-scented perennial. This plant spreads, increasing in size at a moderate to fast pace.

It complements the shapes and textures of peony, black-eyed Susan, phlox, and meadow rue. And it blooms at the same time as late-season daylilies, bee balm, and purple coneflower.

CARE: Anise hyssop requires no special fertilizer treatments and has few pest or disease problems. It may suffer from powdery mildew in hot, dry years. Improve air movement by thinning out shoots. Cut back plants to the ground in late fall. The plant reseeds readily. It is rabbit- and deer-resistant.

RECOMMENDED PLANTS AND RELATED SPECIES: 'Blue Fortune' grows 4 feet or taller and 2 feet wide. Its blue-purple blooms last from June until September. 'Firebird' has interesting salmon to pink flowers; it may be hardy only to Zone 6.

Anise hyssop

ALCEA ROSEA

Hollyhock

- Towering flower spikes, early to midsummer
- Zones 3–7
- 4 to 8 feet × 2 feet
- Full sun
- Rich, well-drained soil
- Continuously moist

DESCRIPTION AND USES:
Short-lived and often considered a biennial, hollyhock is a must for the the cottage garden and back of the border. Great for vertical effect or a living screen, the plant is prized for its old-fashioned charm.

Combine hollyhock with old-fashioned, daisylike sun lovers, such as Helen's flower, black-eyed Susan, or purple coneflower.

CARE: Hollyhock grows easily from seed. Space transplants or seeds 12 inches apart. The plant is vulnerable to slugs, leaf miners, Japanese beetles, and hollyhock rust. Remove diseased foliage as soon as it appears; if necessary, spray with fungicide to control rust. Select newer cultivars, which are less susceptible to hollyhock rust. Although short-lived, hollyhock self-seeds, ensuring its continued presence.

RECOMMENDED PLANTS AND RELATED SPECIES:
Chater's Double Group has double flowers in maroon, red, rose, white, or yellow. 'Nigra' is a single; it is called "black" hollyhock because of its wine-purple blooms. 'Indian Spring' is a single, available in white, yellow, rose, and pink, and grows 7 to 8 feet tall.

Hollyhock

ALCHEMILLA MOLLIS

Lady's mantle

- Airy sprays of yellow-green flowers, late spring to early summer, beautiful foliage
- Zones 4–7
- 1 foot × 2 to 3 feet
- Half sun to shade
- Well-drained, moisture-retentive soil
- Continuously moist to average water

DESCRIPTION AND USES: Tiny chartreuse flowers arch from foot-tall mounds of marvelous, gray-green leaves that resemble a woman's cloak. The downy foliage is a main attraction, with each leaf emerging like pleated velvet and fanning into a circle. Flower stems hover 3 to 6 inches above the leaves.

This clump-former grows at a moderate rate. Its foliage combines well with fringed bleeding heart and toad lily. It blooms at the same time as bellflowers and Oriental poppies.

CARE: Lady's mantle has no special fertilizer needs. Strip off old foliage in early spring, but don't cut plants back hard, because new growth buds form above ground on the semiwoody crown. You can mow to clean up plants in spring; set the mower at 4 inches. Lady's mantel rarely needs division. Deadhead to prevent reseeding. Plants tolerate light foot traffic.

Plants are basically pest free, but spider mites can be a problem, and plant bug may disfigure foliage. In hot and humid summers, lady's mantle is prone to leaf diseases.

RECOMMENDED PLANTS AND RELATED SPECIES: Dwarf lady's mantle (*A. alpina*) is only 6 inches tall. The underside of each deeply lobed leaf has fine hairs, which create a silky, silvery outline.

Lady's mantle

AMSONIA TABERNAEMONTANA

Blue star

- Clusters of blue, starlike flowers, spring
- Zones 3–9
- 1 to 3 feet × 3 feet
- Partial shade or full sun
- Average garden soil
- Average water

DESCRIPTION AND USES: Resembling a 2-foot-tall willow tree, native blue star is long-lived and maintenance-free. Effective in masses, the soft, willowlike texture contrasts with other garden plants. Never invasive, this plant grows slowly and looks beautiful when paired with bergenia or cushion spurge, and it makes a lovely companion for peonies.

CARE: Set nursery plants 12 inches apart. Division is seldom necessary; pests and diseases are not a problem. Shear after flowering, no more than one-third to one-half, so that plants won't grow too tall.

RECOMMENDED PLANTS AND RELATED SPECIES: Arkansas amsonia (*A. hubrectii*) has lacy foliage, steel blue flowers, and brilliant yellow fall foliage color. It is one of the best perennials for reliable autumn color.

NOTES: The milky sap may cause burning or itching on contact.

Blue star

Arkansas amsonia

ANAPHALIS TRIPLINERVIS

Three-veined everlasting

- White blooms, midsummer to late summer
- Zones 3–8
- 12 to 18 inches × 12 to 24 inches
- Full to half sun
- Well-drained, sandy soil
- Requires evenly moist soil

DESCRIPTION AND USES:
Clusters of white pearls on this mounded-shape plant open to yellow-centered buttons with crisp petals. A spreading perennial, three-veined everlasting grows fast. Combine with bear's breeches, speedwell, threadleaf coreopsis, and 'Husker Red' penstemon.

CARE: Three-veined everlasting does not grow well where summers are very hot and humid. It tolerates various soil conditions and excess moisture better than most gray-leaved plants, though it may develop rust.

Apply fertilizer at half the average rate to avoid rank, weak growth. Clean up plants in early spring. Divide them every four to five years; they are easy to move.

Everlasting is basically pest-free but may host larvae of the American Painted Lady butterfly during spring and early summer. Protect new plantings from these leaf-eating caterpillars, but tolerate them on established plants; the caterpillars finish feeding in time for plants to recover and bloom. Plants are deer- and rabbit-resistant.

RECOMMENDED PLANTS AND RELATED SPECIES: 'Summer Snow' is a dwarf that is good for edging. Pearly everlasting (A. margaritacea) is native to dry meadows and slopes. It is more drought-tolerant and should be considered for such situations. It is less able than the other species to tolerate heavy or wet soils. Pearly everlasting is taller (up to 36 inches), later-blooming by two weeks, and less likely to need staking; it has narrower leaves than three-veined everlasting. Japanese pearly everlasting (A. margaritacea var. yedoensis) has larger flowers than the species and may be hardy to Zone 3 with good snow cover.

'Summer Snow' three-veined everlasting

ANEMONE X HYBRIDA

Japanese anemone

- White, pink, or mauve flowers, late summer to fall
- Zones 5–8
- 2 to 3 feet × 1 to 2 feet
- Sun to shade
- Moist but well-drained loam
- Average water to continuously moist

DESCRIPTION AND USES:
Excellent for the middle of the border, anemones bear clusters of flowers on plants that reach 3 feet in bloom. The silky sheen of the 2- to 3-inch blossoms perks up late-summer gardens for weeks; the buds resemble soft pink or white pearls.

For most of the summer, plants hug the ground. Plants are slow to establish and bloom. Once settled in, some varieties grow at a moderate pace; others spread quickly.

In shade, Japanese anemone complements turtlehead and Japanese wax bell; in half sun, purple bush clover and culver's root.

CARE: Avoid sites that are hot or have strong winds, wet soil, or drought. Plants may topple in light, dry soil; use grow-through supports. Some varieties have stouter stems that rarely require support.

Anemones spread by rhizomes and can form large, dense colonies. Plants rarely set viable seed. Cut them back in late fall. Heavy mulch or reliable snow cover increases hardiness to Zone 4.

Japanese anemones have few problems. Nematode infestation and pock-marked foliage from four-lined plant bug feeding can occur. Plants are rabbit-resistant.

RECOMMENDED PLANTS AND RELATED SPECIES: 'September Charm' has single pink flowers, and 'Honorine Jobert' has pure white single flowers, grows 3 to 4 feet tall, and is sun- and drought-tolerant. Flowers are smaller than those on other varieties. 'Queen Charlotte' has semidouble pale mauve flowers, and grows 3 feet tall. 'Whirlwind' has semidouble large white flowers and grows 3 to 5 feet.

Japanese anemone

ANTHEMIS TINCTORIA

Golden marguerite

Golden marguerite

- Yellow daisies, early to midsummer
- Zones 3–7
- 2 to 3 feet × 2 feet
- Full to half sun
- Well-drained soil; tolerates alkaline soil
- Average water

DESCRIPTION AND USES: These masses of bright yellow daisies are very fast-growing and spread by ground-level offsets and seed. The fragrant, finely divided deep green foliage and upright habit combine well with heart-leaf brunnera, daylily, and fountain grass.

CARE: Basically pest-free, the plant may develop powdery mildew and can itself become a pest by self-sowing. Deadhead to prolong bloom and prevent seed set. Cut plants back after the bloom fades to promote new basal growth. Apply fertilizer at half the average rate to avoid soft, floppy growth. Stake with crutches or grow-through supports. The plant is easy to grow from seed or division. Divide plants every two to three years before the oldest, central portion of the clump dies out; offsets are easy to move.

RECOMMENDED PLANTS AND RELATED SPECIES: 'Moonlight', 2 feet tall, has pale yellow flowers. 'Kelwayi', which grows 3 feet tall, has more finely cut foliage and brighter yellow flowers. 'E.C. Buxton' has lemon-yellow flowers and finely cut foliage.

NOTES: The plant tolerates drought and heat.

AQUILEGIA X HYBRIDA

Hybrid columbine

- Yellow, salmon, red, blue, and white blooms, midspring
- Zones 3–9
- 1 to 3 feet in bloom × 1 foot
- Half to full sun; midday shade prolongs bloom period

McKana hybrids columbine

Canadian columbine

- Well-drained, sandy loam; prefers neutral to slightly acid soil
- Average water

DESCRIPTION AND USES: Columbine's nicely textured foliage is topped by sturdy, upright, branched flower stalks, which double or triple the height of the plant. Blooms may be single- or multicolored. Clump-forming, plants grow fast. Combine them with foam flower and woodland phlox, hydrangeas, or white wood aster. The foliage is a good foil for toad lily and tovara.

CARE: Fertilize columbines more frequently than average perennials. Deadhead to prolong bloom. As flower buds swell, check leaves for leaf-miner damage, which appears as light-colored squiggles on the leaf; if severely affected by leaf miner, cut plants to the ground. Clean up dead foliage in late fall.

Plants are relatively short-lived, and dividing is usually not necessary. They will self-sow.

Columbine tolerates alkaline soil. Red-flowered types with hanging blooms generally require wetter soil and are intolerant of drought. Plants grow readily from seed, which requires a period of dry, warm storage (such as on the plant) before it will germinate.

Columbine sawfly can defoliate plants in early summer. Look for wormlike pale green larvae on leaves at bloom time. Occasional problems include powdery mildew, leaf spots, aphids, columbine stalk borer, and, where soil is wet in winter or drainage is poor, crown rot. Although columbine may develop problems, it proves a beautiful plant and worthy of a place in your garden.

RECOMMENDED PLANTS AND RELATED SPECIES: Blue-flowered columbines descend from the western or Rocky Mountain columbine (*A. caerulea*), and prefer more sun and cooler summers. They also tolerate drier soil. Species columbine, particularly the bicolored red and yellow Canadian columbine (*A. canadensis*), may be resistant to leaf miner.

NOTES: The plant attracts hummingbirds.

ARABIS CAUCASICA

Wall rockcress

- White flowers, early spring
- Zones 4–7
- 8 to 12 inches × 18 inches
- Half to full sun
- Well-drained loam and neutral or slightly alkaline pH
- Average water

DESCRIPTION AND USES:
This mat-forming grayish evergreen spreads by rooting where its stems contact moist soil. It forms colonies at a moderate to fast rate—a well-sited 6-inch-wide plant may be 18 inches wide at the end of a season.

Wall rockcress, which can be used as a ground cover, is attractive with columbine, masterwort, and lungwort. Pair with other evergreen perennials, such as coral bells.
CARE: Apply fertilizer at half the average rate. Do not cut plants back in fall; they are evergreen. Trim plants as desired in early spring or after bloom. Deadhead by shearing to promote density. Divide after flowering. Wall rockcress does not grow well where summers are hot and humid, and tends to develop crown and stem rot.

Powdery mildew, rust, and aphids sometimes pose problems, as does club root. Look for deformed, shortened roots on plants that do not thrive or that decline. Destroy infected plants. Do not plant other members of the mustard family where club root has been a problem.
RECOMMENDED PLANTS AND RELATED SPECIES: 'Flore Pleno' (*Arabis alpina* subsp. *caucasica*) has double flowers, is later to bloom than the species, and tends to stay in bloom longer.

'Flore Pleno' wall rockcress

ARMERIA MARITIMA

Sea thrift

- Pink or creamy white flowers, midspring
- Zones 4–8
- 6 inches × 12 inches
- Full sun; in areas with very hot, humid summers, afternoon shade is recommended
- Must have well-drained soil; prefers sandy soil with neutral to slightly alkaline pH
- Average water

DESCRIPTION AND USES:
Lollipop clusters of blooms top evergreen, grassy tufts, which resemble clean, deep green cushions. Flower stalks double the height of this clump-forming plant; its growth rate is moderate.

Sea thrift complements the gray-green foliage of Cupid's dart and the swordlike spears of iris or blackberry lily. It blooms at the same time as catmint.
CARE: This plant is suited to windy sites. It cannot tolerate wet soil in winter. Apply fertilizer at half the average rate. Heavy fertilization causes the center of the clump to blacken and die.

Deadheading keeps young plants blooming through the summer; older clumps will sporadically rebloom. Do not cut plants back in fall; they are evergreen. Propagate sea thrift by division, cuttings, or seed. Cuttings root readily. Seed grows easily.

Sea thrift is basically pest-free.
RECOMMENDED PLANTS AND RELATED SPECIES: 'Ruby Glow' flowers are nearly red. Those of 'Düsseldorf Pride' are deep rose, but this variety may not be as cold-hardy as the species. Protect it with an airy, deep mulch in areas colder than Zone 5.

Pinkball thrift (*A. pseudarmeria*), with white to rose-colored flowers, is taller than sea thrift by several inches. Its larger flower heads are ideal for cut flowers and drying. This species is hardy in Zones 6–8. 'Bevan's Variety' Pyrenees thrift (*A. juniperifolia*) is a 4-inch dwarf. Its pink flowers are nearly stemless.
NOTES: Sea thrift tolerates salt spray and reblooms in cool climates if deadheaded.

'Dusseldorf Pride' sea thrift

ARTEMISIA

Artemisias

- Silvery gray-green foliage
- Zones 4–9
- 1 to 6 feet × 1½ to 4 feet
- Full sun
- Any well-drained soil; neutral to slightly alkaline pH
- Average water

DESCRIPTION AND USES: Most artemisias have magnificent silvery pubescent foliage that complements most other plants in the perennial garden. Their inconspicuous whitish flowers appear in late summer.

For the most part, artemisias are well-behaved, although some, like white sage, spread aggressively through the perennial garden. Use spreaders only where you can control their growth.

Artemisias make a fine backdrop for blue and purple flowers, such as speedwell, blue columbine, and perennial salvia, and for purple-foliage plants. The subtle colors of artemisias' foliage tone down harsh red and orange flowers.

CARE: Apply fertilizer at half the average rate. Artemisias may need staking in rich soils; use a grow-through stake. Plants that fall over can be sheared back by one-third to one-half.

Deadheading is not necessary; spent flowers are not conspicuous, and self-sowing is not a problem. Divide plants every three years, discarding the oldest, central portion. Reduce plant spread as desired in spring.

Stem cuttings taken in midsummer root readily. Seed requires dry, warm storage for several months before it will germinate. Do not cut plants back in fall. Because they are woody perennials, wait until spring, then prune off any dead stems.

Artemisias don't flourish where summers are humid. Stem and root rots can be a problem if the summer is hot and humid or drainage poor.

Painted Lady butterfly caterpillars may feed on artemisias. Leaf rust sometimes occurs. Plants are deer- and rabbit-resistant.

Where artemisias have become a weed themselves, dig out the invasive roots to control them.

RECOMMENDED PLANTS AND RELATED SPECIES: White sage (*A. ludoviciana*) is often confused with dusty miller, but its crushed leaves have a distinct scent. Taller than wide (2 to 3 feet × 2 feet), the plant gives the overall impression of vertical lines. It spreads by shallow rhizomes and grows at a very fast rate.

'Silver King', which is 3 feet tall and deep silver, and 'Silver Queen', which is 2½ feet tall and silver-gray with jagged edged leaves, are almost identical and can be mislabeled. Both are aggressive spreaders. 'Valerie Finnis' grows 18 inches tall and is less aggressive.

Silvermound artemisia (*A. schmidtiana*) is a 1-to 2-foot mound of silky, finely cut foliage. It performs best in cool areas and in soil that is not too fertile. Not aggressive, it flops in mid- or late summer where hot and humid.

'Powis Castle', a hybrid, is very finely textured, 3 to 4 feet tall, and hardy to Zone 6.

'Lambrook Silver' wormwood (*A. absinthium*), with filigreed leaves, is more silvery than most. It grows 2½ feet tall.

Beach wormwood (*A. stelleriana*) tolerates salt spray and water. The foliage is exceptionally furry and more coarsely textured than that of other artemisias. It grows 1 to 2 feet by 2 to 3 feet in Zones 3 to 8. 'Silver Brocade' is an excellent, low-growing specimen, only 6 to 8 inches tall. It is less adapted to the hot, humid Southeast region but does well in containers there.

'Guizho white mugwort (*A. lactiflora*), found in Zones 3 to 8, differs from the rest by having dark green foliage. Long-lasting sprays of white flowers rise 4 to 6 feet over a low mound of leaves. Plants are slow to recover when moved.

White sage

ARUNCUS DIOICUS

Goatsbeard

- Off-white plumes, late spring to early summer
- Half sun to dense shade; tolerates full sun if shaded during the hottest part of day
- Zones 3–7
- 4 to 6 feet × 6 feet
- Any well-drained soil
- Needs consistent moisture

DESCRIPTION AND USES: This perennial has airy off-white plumes and can be mistaken for a small shrub. Its growth rate is slow to moderate.

Combine this upright, medium-textured plant with mounded perennials, such as geranium or bleeding heart.

Play its light green foliage off of darker green turtlehead or blue-green hostas. Use its sturdy stems to support a blue-bush clematis or other clematis that can be cut back hard every spring.

CARE: The plant is basically pest-free. Leaf spot, rust, or leaf scorch may develop, usually where the site is too dry or hot. It resists deer and rabbit damage. The dense root system requires a saw for dividing, though division is rarely needed.

Goatsbeard may self-sow but not to a troublesome degree.

Do not deadhead until you see whether you like the seed heads, which can provide winter interest.

RECOMMENDED PLANTS AND RELATED SPECIES: The cultivar 'Kneiffii' is 3 feet tall in bloom; half the height is flower stalk. Its foliage is finely cut and lacy. Dwarf goatsbeard (*A. aethusifolius*) is just 12 inches tall in bloom, a mound of finely cut foliage and dainty white spike flowers. In bloom two weeks earlier than the species, dwarf goatsbeard is a good edging plant.

Goatsbeard

ASCLEPIAS TUBEROSA

Butterfly weed

- Bright orange flowers, midsummer
- Zones 4–9
- 2 to 3 feet × 2 feet
- Full sun
- Requires excellent drainage, especially during winter months
- Average water; allow to dry down

DESCRIPTION AND USES: A native prairie plant, butterfly weed is highly ornamental, blooms in vibrant colors, and tolerates seaside conditions. It is a must for butterfly gardens. And it is a good choice for meadow gardens because it can compete with grasses.

The bright orange flowers appear as flaring clusters made up of ¼-inch-across individual flowers. These flowers grab onto the legs of visiting butterflies. As the butterfly struggles to pull free, it dusts itself with pollen.

This coarse-textured, vase-shaped perennial is sturdy, clump-forming,

long-lived, and slow-growing. Combine it with finer-textured mounded plants, such as catmint, blue oat grass, fountain grass, or threadleaf coreopsis. For contrast, plant it with gray-leaved globe thistle or ornamental mullein.

CARE: Grow butterfly weed in sandy soil, although it does tolerate clay soil. Fertilize at half the average rate. Deadheading promotes rebloom several weeks later. Cut plants back in late fall. They are slow to emerge in spring. Mark their spot to avoid damage.

The taproot may be intimidating, but the plant is simple to divide. Cut through the top of the root to obtain several eyes and a large slice of the root. You can also make cuttings from pencil-thick roots.

Butterfly weed needs heat to prosper and bloom well; it is not suited to cool summer climates or poor drainage in winter.

Plants are pest-free.

They may suffer from aphid infestation; if so, check drainage. Monarch butterflies feed on this plant, so you may want to tolerate some leaf damage.

RECOMMENDED PLANTS AND RELATED SPECIES: Gay Butterflies Group is a seed mixture that offers orange, yellow, and red flowers on 2- to 3-foot-tall plants. 'High Yellow' has bright yellow flowers. For moist sites, there's swamp milkweed (*A. incarnata*), which has fragrant mauve flowers.

'Gay Butterflies' butterfly weed

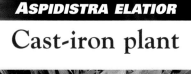

ASPIDISTRA ELATIOR

Cast-iron plant

Cast-iron plant

- Grown for evergreen foliage
- Zones 8–10
- 2 feet × 2 feet
- Shade to dense shade
- Prefers rich, well-drained soil
- Allow to dry down

DESCRIPTION AND USES: This tough plant requires little attention to thrive. Its large, broad, dark green leaves grow in patches.

Large, well-established plants occasionally produce purplish brown flowers that develop inconspicuously among leaves or underground. Leaves grow on stout stems and have prominent veins.

Cast-iron plant make a good underplanting for azaleas and camellias.

CARE: Cast-iron plant tolerates deep shade better than many other plants. It endures poor soil, drought, and neglect but prefers rich, porous soil. Water it when the soil is fairly dry. Remove dead or bleached leaves. Fertilize moderately to enhance leaf growth. Propagate by division. Space plants 2 feet apart.

RECOMMENDED PLANTS AND RELATED SPECIES: 'Variegata' has dark green leaves with alternating white stripes. 'Milky Way' has white-speckled foliage.

ASTER NOVAE-ANGLIAE

New England aster

- Flowers of white and shades of violet, pink, and near-blues, late summer and fall
- Zones 4–8
- 6 feet × 3 feet
- Full to half sun
- Most garden soils
- Continuously moist to average water

DESCRIPTION AND USES: Consider this perennial as an excellent autumn alternative to chrysanthemums. It may be a mounded dwarf 18 to 24 inches tall and wide or a columnar giant up to 6 feet tall and half as wide. With fast to very fast growth rate, it spreads by shallow rhizomes.

Combine asters with ornamental grasses, sedum, or Joe-Pye weed. Plant them with crocus and other early bulbs. Grow dwarf asters with blazing star or daylilies.

CARE: Deadhead plants to prolong bloom. You may need to stake tall varieties or plants growing in half sun where light is strongly one-directional. Stake individual stems, use grow-through supports, or pinch plants monthly from midspring to early summer for short, dense plants.

Cut plants back in late fall. If seeds are intended as winter forage for birds, wait until early spring to clean up the planting.

Asters are easy to grow from seed. Some varieties self-sow. Divide plants every two to three years in spring to control spread and renew plant vigor. Discard the oldest, central section. Replant small, five- to seven-eye divisions for strongest stems and best disease resistance.

Protect asters from rabbits, deer, and woodchucks. Powdery mildew and rust can be problems; water to keep soil moist and foliage dry. Wilt can infect older plantings; grow new plants from tip cuttings in a bed that hasn't recently hosted an aster family member. Plants attract Japanese beetles and sometimes stalk borers.

RECOMMENDED PLANTS AND RELATED SPECIES: 'Alma Potschke', red-violet blooms, 3 to 4 feet; 'Purple Dome', 1½ to 2 feet. New York aster (*A. novi-belgii*) has slightly larger flowers. Gardeners in coldest regions should not select late-blooming varieties, which may not flower before frost.

'Alert' New York aster

'Alma Potschke' New England aster

ASTILBE X ARENDSII

Astilbe

- White, pink, red, or mauve flowers, early to midsummer
- Zones 4–8
- 2 to 4 feet × 2 feet
- Half sun to shade; tolerates sun if soil is constantly moist
- Rich loam with organic matter; neutral to acid pH
- Continuously moist to wet soil

DESCRIPTION AND USES: Easy-to-grow astilbe brightens a shade garden. The feathery blooms are superb for the woodland border or massed as a ground cover. The flower cluster may be a tight, upright spike; a compact steeple; or a loose, drooping plume. Foliage forms a bronze to green ferny mound. Astilbe pairs with coarse-textured and upright plants. Hosta, lungwort, rodgersia, Japanese wax bell, toad lily, turtlehead, and meadow rue are good companions.
CARE: If moisture needs are met, astilbe tolerates many soil types and a wide soil pH range. Provide 50 percent more fertilizer than for average perennials. Early-blooming varieties will rebloom if deadheaded. Cut back in early spring or late fall. They rarely need division, but to obtain more plants, divide in spring or fall. Use a sharp tool to cut the woody crown into sections with several eyes each. Watch for wilting afterwards. Astilbe is vulnerable to powdery mildew, leaf scorch, rust, Japanese beetles, spider mites, and root weevils.
RECOMMENDED PLANTS AND RELATED SPECIES: 'Bridal Veil' is 2 to 3 feet tall with pinkish white flowers. Early-flowering 'Fanal' grows 2 feet tall and has dark red flowers above bronze leaves. 'Granat' is a midseason bloomer with carmine-red flowers. 'Rheinland' (A. *japonica*) has clear pink flowers on 2-foot plants. Chinese astilbe (A. *chinensis*) is a late-summer bloomer; it tolerates drier conditions. 'Pumila' grows 8-plus inches and has mauve-pink blossoms. 'Sprite' star astilbe (A. *simplicifolia*) has open plumes of pink and grows up to 12 inches.

Chinese astilbe

'Granat' astilbe

ASTRANTIA MAJOR

Masterwort

- White, pink, and rose flowers, late spring to early summer
- Zones 4–7
- 1½ to 3 feet × 1½ feet
- Half to full sun; increase water in full sun
- Rich, well-drained loam with plenty of organic matter
- Average water to continuously moist

DESCRIPTION AND USES:
A charming cottage garden flower, masterwort grows 2 to 3 feet tall in cool climates but struggles in the South. White, rose, and pink flowers can all occur in the same planting over the years. The flowers are domed clusters on wiry, branched stems. Plants form a dense, slowly spreading clump (rhizomes).

Masterwort is dynamite with pink astilbes and hosta, Siberian iris, white gaura, and perennial flax.
CARE: Plants do not tolerate drought or hot summer nights. Supply 50 percent more fertilizer than for average perennials. Deadhead for prolonged and repeat bloom. If not deadheaded, masterwort will self-sow but not to nuisance levels. Cut back foliage in late fall or early spring to avoid leaf spot. Plants rarely need division. They are pest-free, but protect them from rabbits and woodchucks.
RECOMMENDED PLANTS AND RELATED SPECIES: 'Alba' produces 2-foot white flowers. 'Lars' is a vigorous variety with dark red flowers; 'Primadonna' (A. *major*) has purple blooms on 30-inch-tall plants.

Masterwort

Japanese painted fern

ATHYRIUM NIPPONICUM VAR. PICTUM

Japanese painted fern

- Silvery purple fronds
- Zones 3–8
- 18 inches × 15 inches
- Full shade
- Well-drained humus-rich soil
- Continuously moist

DESCRIPTION AND USES: This most colorful of garden ferns pairs well with primrose or dwarf astilbe.

CARE: The plant thrives in full shade but develops its best color in filtered light. Plant 1 foot apart for colorful ground cover, 2 feet apart for accent.

RECOMMENDED PLANTS AND RELATED SPECIES: Graceful lady fern (*A. filix-femina*) is vigorous and up to 3 feet tall but looks lacy and delicate. It is tolerant of dry soil and easy to grow.

AURINIA SAXATILIS

Basket-of-gold

- Brilliant yellow blossoms, spring
- Zones 3–7
- 9 to 12 inches × 18 inches
- Full sun
- Well-drained soil
- Allow to dry down

DESCRIPTION AND USES:
Tiny yellow flowers completely cover these bushy plants with gray-green foliage.

Basket-of-gold struggles in hot, humid areas and is often short-lived. It is useful in front of borders or in rock gardens and is especially attractive spilling over rock walls. The plant pairs well with 'Homestead Purple' verbena and 'Louisiana' woodland phlox.

CARE: Plant basket-of-gold in a sunny area with excellent drainage about 8 to 12 inches apart. Cut it back after flowering. Water only in drought and don't fertilize. Division in the fall is the easiest method of propagation.

RECOMMENDED PLANTS AND RELATED SPECIES: 'Citrina' is 10 to 15 inches tall with lemon yellow flowers. 'Dudley Nevill' grows to 10 inches tall and has buff-colored flowers; there is also a variegated version called 'Dudley Nevill Variegated'. 'Tom Thumb' is only 3 to 6 inches tall but a vigorous selection.

Basket-of-gold

BAPTISIA AUSTRALIS

Blue false indigo

- Blue, purple, white, or yellow flowers, midspring
- Zones 4–9
- 3 to 4 feet × 4 feet
- Full to half sun
- Deep, well-drained soil with plentiful organic matter
- Average water

DESCRIPTION AND USES:
Count on this easy-to-grow, long-lived North American native. Its attractive flowers on tall spikes give way to decorative seedpods.

Blue false indigo is useful as the backbone of a garden. The slow-growing, clump-forming, shrublike plant tends to have bare ankles. It pairs well with sword-leaf inula, perennial geranium, hardy ageratum, and black-eyed Susan. Blue-black pea pods persist through winter. Winter stems complement ornamental grasses and gray-foliaged perennials, such as Russian sage.

CARE: Space plants 3 feet apart in well-drained, neutral, or acid soil of average fertility. Water in dry weather until plants are established. In shade, use grow-through supports. Cut back plants in late fall or early spring. Plants are generally pest-free.
RECOMMENDED PLANTS AND RELATED SPECIES: 'Purple Smoke' (3 to 4 feet tall) has charcoal-green stems and pale lilac flowers; it grows in Zones 3–8. White wild indigo (*B. alba*) grows 2 to 3 feet tall and has a 3-foot spread.

Blue false indigo

BELAMCANDA CHINENSIS

Blackberry lily

- Miniature orange or yellow-orange flowers, midsummer
- Zones 5–10
- 18 to 24 inches in leaf, 30 to 40 inches in bloom × 18 inches
- Full to half sun
- Well-drained, sandy soil
- Average water

DESCRIPTION AND USES: This undemanding native of China and Japan is valued for its imposing flat fans of foliage and crimson-speckled blossoms. The flower buds open in succession, each bloom lasting a day. When the fruit pods split open in fall, they reveal clusters of shiny black berries.

Swordlike foliage and tall flower stalks set off this fast-growing plant. Combine it with ornamental grasses, cushion spurge, blanket flower, or globe thistle.
CARE: This plant is not a good candidate for areas with cool, moist summers or wet soil in winter. Deadhead as tip cluster. The plant self-sows and is short-lived. Renew the planting by division in spring every two to three years.

Blackberry lily is susceptible to iris borer and iris soft rot. Check for leaf damage in spring; remove and destroy all foliage and stems in fall.
RECOMMENDED PLANTS AND RELATED SPECIES: 'Freckle Face' is a short version with pale orange blossoms. 'Hello Yellow' is unspotted. Candy lily (× *Pardancanda norrisii*), is 2 to 3 feet tall with violet, cream, orange-red, salmon, or yellow blooms.

Blackberry lily

BERGENIA CORDIFOLIA

Heart-leaf bergenia

- Unusual foliage makes a wonderful textural statement
- Zones 4–8

Heart-leaf bergenia

- 12 inches × 12 inches
- Full sun in northern regions, half sun or afternoon shade in southern ones
- Rich, well-drained soil
- Continuously moist

DESCRIPTION AND USES:

Admired more for its bold-textured clumps of cabbagelike leaves than for its pink flowers, bergenia brings architectural beauty to gardens. The 12-inch-long, round to heart-shaped leaves have a leathery texture and gleam like polished wood.

Evergreen in most climates and semievergreen in the coldest ones, the leaves often take on magnificent reddish hues in fall and winter unless temperatures are harsh. Irregular flower clusters are held above the leaves on thick stalks. Plants spread slowly by rhizomes and pair nicely with bleeding heart or ferns.

CARE: Bergenia performs well in almost any rich, moist, well-drained soil. Plants don't do well in areas with excessive heat or drought. In cold regions, protect them from bitter winds.

Space plants 12 to 18 inches apart. Divide them if they become crowded. To control spread, limit water and fertilizer. Slugs can be a problem.

RECOMMENDED PLANTS AND RELATED SPECIES: 'Perfect' has round leaves and deep pink flowers on 18-inch stems. It is hardier than the species to Zone 3. Hybrids: 'Bressingham White' starts out pink and gradually turns pure white. It is a late bloomer. 'Bressingham Ruby' has bright pink flowers and a maroon hue to the underside of leaves, and outstanding fall and winter color. 'Evening Glow' has reddish purple flowers and maroon leaves in winter. 'Silver Light' has white flowers flushed pink.

BIGNONIA CAPREOLATA

Cross vine

- Red-orange flowers, spring into summer
- Zones 6–9
- 10 to 20 feet per year, height depends on structure
- Full sun to shade
- Soil with plenty of organic matter
- Allow to dry down

DESCRIPTION AND USES:

From late spring well into summer, this Southerner provides a massive, long-season display of fragrant red-orange blooms. They look great against brick or tan walls, and their color complements strong purples. The species is fragrant, though most cultivars lack scent.

Cross vine

Cross vine's tubular blossoms attract hummingbirds. Its shiny, dark green leaves turn reddish purple in the South but in colder climates tend to brown by the end of winter. Plants grow quickly.

Train cross vine on a sturdy arbor to shade your garden. Pair it with other spring bloomers.

CARE: Cross vine tolerates heavy shade but blooms best in full sun. Protect the leaves from winter winds. Its tendrils wrap around other plants, and onto netting and chain link. The adhesive discs at the tips of the tendrils allow the plant to climb tree trunks and masonry surfaces. You will want to prune it to control its size and to protect structures. Cross vine is rarely troubled by pests.

RECOMMENDED PLANTS AND RELATED SPECIES:
'Atrosanguinea' has reddish purple flowers. 'Tangerine Beauty' is clear orange. 'Velcyll' is orange on the outside and yellow on the inside. It is hardier than 'Tangerine Beauty'.

BOLTONIA ASTEROIDES

Boltonia

- Profuse white and pink daisylike flowers, fall
- Zones 4–9
- 5 feet × 3 feet
- Full sun to half shade
- Any garden soil
- Average water

DESCRIPTION AND USES: With its frothy stand of yellow-centered late-season, 1-inch-wide daisies, boltonia could be mistaken for an aster. However, it grows better in hot-summer regions than aster. It's a good partner for other late-bloomers, such as Russian sage, Japanese anemone, and ornamental grasses.

CARE: Boltonia thrives in any soil but performs best in well-drained soil of average fertility. Space plants 18 inches apart.

Plants seldom need staking despite boltonia's impressive 4- or 5-foot height. In hot regions, plants do better if they are planted in some shade, but staking may then be required. Or cut plants back to 12 inches in late spring to shorten plants and make them more bushy. Divide plants every three or four years. Boltonia resists mildew.

RECOMMENDED PLANTS AND RELATED SPECIES: 'Pink Beauty' sports lavender-pink blossoms with silver-blue foliage.

'Snowbank' has extra-sturdy stems, snowy white flowers, and blue-green leaves.

'Snowbank' boltonia

BRUNNERA MACROPHYLLA

Heart-leaf brunnera

- An airy froth of sky blue flowers, early to midspring
- Zones 3–8
- 18 inches in bloom × 24 inches
- Shade to dense shade
- Moist, well-drained soil
- Average water to continuously moist

DESCRIPTION AND USES: In springtime, a cloud of tiny blue flowers hovers above brunnera's low mound of heart-shaped leaves. The dark green, coarse-textured foliage is a good partner for blue-green, lacy, ferny, and upright plants, such as fringed bleeding heart, fragrant bugbane, astilbe, perennial flax, and Jacob's ladder.

CARE: Heart-leaf brunnera scorches in hot, sunny sites; variegated cultivars are especially prone to this. Plants tolerate full sun only where summers are cool and moisture steady. Cut spent blooms back to the leaves. Deadheading prevents self-sowing, especially for variegated cultivars, which produce green seedlings that crowd out the parent. Dig out excess plants and seedlings annually; don't leave their roots. Divide plants as needed every four to five years. Brunnera is basically pest-free and slug-resistant.

RECOMMENDED PLANTS AND RELATED SPECIES: 'Langtrees' is variegated with splashes of silver. 'Jack Frost' is silver with darker veins.

Heart-leaf brunnera

CALAMAGROSTIS X ACUTIFLORA

Feather reed grass

- Strong vertical effect
- Zones 4–9
- 3 to 6 feet × 2 feet
- Full sun
- Ordinary or moist soil
- Average water

DESCRIPTION AND USES: Stiffly upright, this cool-season clump grass changes alluringly through the season. Spring brings a fountain of light green leaves, which by early summer is topped with tall, feathery, pink inflorescences. These change to light purple in early summer then ripen into golden wheatlike sheaves by midsummer. The seed heads remain attractive into fall. Feather reed grass is a good companion for black-eyed Susan or sedum for beauty that lasts well into winter.

CARE: This is one of the few grasses that will thrive in wet clay. Space plants 2 feet apart. Divide crowded clumps in spring after new growth begins. Cut plants back in late winter or spring. Plants tolerate seaside conditions.

RECOMMENDED PLANTS AND RELATED SPECIES: 'Stricta' is 3 to 4 feet tall. 'Karl Foerster', 5 to 6 feet, blooms 2 weeks later. In Zone 5, 'Overdam' has variegated, white-striped foliage and grows 2 to 3 feet.

'Karl Foerster' feather reed grass

CALOCHORTUS

Mariposa lily

'Golden Orb' mariposa lily

- Flowers in many colors and shapes, summer
- Zones 5–10
- 2 to 3 feet × 2 to 3 feet
- Full sun or part shade
- Well-drained, neutral to slightly acid sandy loam
- Allow to dry down

DESCRIPTION AND USES: A native wildflower across western North America, mariposa has blooms that are erect and cup-shaped, spreading and star-shaped, or nodding. The plant has slender, grasslike foliage.

CARE: Mariposa lily grows from a bulb, and requires well-drained soil and ample air circulation. Plant bulbs 3 to 5 inches deep in the garden or 2 to 4 inches deep in containers (five or six bulbs per 6-inch pot). Protect bulbs from alternate freezing and thawing by mulching the bed over winter. Deadhead as flowers fade.

Plants require a long dormant period of dry soil after flowering. (In native sites, mariposa lily receives no moisture during summer.) In rainy areas, lift and store the bulbs in dry packing material.

Or grow bulbs in a container with drainage holes in the bottom. Lift containers from the bed, allow them to dry, and store indoors over winter.

Containers also protect mariposa lilies from gophers, squirrels, rabbits, field mice, and birds. Birds, snails, and slugs may also be problems.

RECOMMENDED PLANTS AND RELATED SPECIES: Species hardy in Zones 4–5 include Gunnison's mariposa (*C. gunnisonii*), which flowers in colors ranging from white to magenta, and green-banded mariposa (*C. macrocarpus*).

In Zones 6–10, try butterfly mariposa (*C. venustus*), which comes in many beautiful colors. It is more tolerant of heavy soils than other *Calochortus* species. Also for Zones 6–10, fairy lantern (*C. albus*) has nodding white flowers and tolerates more water in summer and shade than most species.

CALTHA PALUSTRIS

Marsh marigold

- Bright yellow spring blossoms
- Zones 5–7 (Zone 6 east of the Rocky Mountains)
- 15 inches × 15 inches
- Full sun or partial shade
- Wet soil
- Continuously moist

DESCRIPTION AND USES:
Marsh marigold is a wetland native that forms attractive, foot-tall clumps of rounded, kidney-shaped leaves (which get smaller as they progress up the stem) topped with 1- to 2-inch yellow flowers. Marsh marigold often goes dormant after it blooms.

This plant is ideal for low-lying spots where water stands, for the edge of streams, and around water gardens. Combine it with water iris, Siberian iris, and other perennials that like wet feet.
CARE: Plant marsh marigold in full sun or partial shade. Space plants 18 inches apart in wet soil or submerge their crowns in up to 1-inch-deep water. If plants become crowded, divide them during their summer dormancy.
RECOMMENDED PLANTS AND RELATED SPECIES: 'Flore Pleno' is an outstanding double form with 2-inch-wide yellow flowers.

'Alba' has brilliant white single blooms that contrast strikingly with the shiny foliage; however, it is much more difficult to obtain. (Some sources list it as *C. palustris alba*.)

Marsh marigold

CAMPANULA

Bellflower

- Violet, blue-violet, or white bells, late spring to midsummer
- Zones 3–8
- 9 inches to 3 feet × 15 inches
- Full to half sun
- Well-drained soil
- Average water to continuously moist

DESCRIPTION AND USES:
Bellflowers are among the finest of perennials. They vary from short, diminutive ground-huggers to tall upright plants. All have bell-shaped flowers, which turn up or down.
CARE: Bellflowers grow in a wide range of soil pH. They do not tolerate drought, full shade, hot summer nights, or wet soil. Plants may self-sow. Named varieties often come true from seed.

Deadhead to prolong bloom and promote repeat bloom. Divide plants in fall or spring every three to five years or when clumps begin to open in center; they are easy to move. Stake taller varieties. Do not cut back in late fall or early spring, unless slugs and snails are a problem. Plants attract rabbits and woodchucks.
RECOMMENDED PLANTS AND RELATED SPECIES: Peach-leaf bellflower (*C. persicifolia*) has white, pink, or violet out-turned bells on wiry stems above fine foliage. It is a vigorous spreader and less heat-tolerant than others. Clustered bellflower (*C. glomerata*) has white or violet flowers in early summer; it is 12 to 36 inches tall. Cut it back hard after bloom. Milky bellflower (*C. lactiflora*) has violet, pink, or white blooms on 3-foot stems in midsummer. Use grow through supports. Carpathian bellflower (*C. carpatica*) is a 9- to 12-inch-tall mound; it blooms in late spring to early summer.

Peach-leaf bellflower

CAREX

Sedge

- Handsome foliage
- Zones 5–9
- 1 to 2 feet × 1 to 2 feet

'Bowles Golden' tufted sedge

- Shade in hot areas; sun in areas with cool summers
- Moist, well-drained soil
- Allow to dry down

DESCRIPTION AND USES: The colorful foliage is evergreen in hot regions, semievergreen in colder ones. It grows in clumps and has a low, arching form. This compact grass look-alike is an excellent choice for shady borders, and in Southern gardens will supply year-round beauty and interest. It is pretty as an accent, in masses, or as an edging. Dense growth continues to become denser with time.

CARE: Plant in full or partial shade in hot areas, sun in cold areas. It prefers a moist, well-drained soil. Space 18 inches apart. Don't overwater. Cut back the previous year's foliage in spring.

RECOMMENDED PLANTS AND RELATED SPECIES: Variegated Japanese sedge (*Carex morrowii* '*Variegata*') has silvery variegated foliage. Handsome 'Bowles Golden' tufted sedge (*C. elata*) is 24 inches tall with bright golden yellow leaves that have thin green margins. 'Aurea' has green leaves with a yellow margin. The yellow color fades as summer temperatures rise.

CATANANCHE CAERULEA

Cupid's dart

Cupid's dart

- Light blue flowers, summer to early fall
- Zones 4–7
- 24 inches in bloom × 12 inches
- Full sun
- Well-drained, sandy soil
- Average water, allow to dry down between watering

DESCRIPTION AND USES: Cupid's dart has papery blue flowers with a dark eye on wiry stems. Its rosette of narrow gray-green foliage hugs the ground; in bloom, the flower stems rise to 24 inches. Plants grow quickly in clumps.

Because it is a delicate "see-through" plant with leafless flower stems above low foliage, it is pretty backed by nonaggressive plants that have greater substance. Or plant it with controlled spreaders with gray-green foliage, such as sedum, butterfly weed, lamb's-ears, gas plant, artemisia, perennial salvia, or dwarf blue fescue.

CARE: Cupid's dart grows well in windy sites. It is heat- and drought-tolerant but does not grow well in wet soil or high heat and high humidity in summer. Plants are short-lived, though fundamentally pest-free.

Deadhead cupid's dart to prolong bloom. It does not need to be cut down in late fall or early spring, because stems and foliage decompose rapidly over winter. Divide plants every two to three years.

RECOMMENDED PLANTS AND RELATED SPECIES: For white flowers, grow the variety 'Alba'.

NOTES: The scientific name stems from the Greek word for powerful incentive. This and the common name refer to the use of the flowers in love potions.

CENTAUREA MONTANA

Perennial bachelor's button

- Blue-violet blooms, midspring
- Zones 3–8
- 12 to 18 inches × 24 inches
- Full to half sun
- Any well-drained soil
- Average water, tolerates drought

DESCRIPTION AND USES:
The mounded, gray-green plants are 12 to 15 inches tall and topped by flowers on leafy 18-inch stems. Blooms are 2 inches across with wispy frills radiating from a darker center. Plants rebloom in midsummer if cut back.

A fast-growing clump-former, perennial bachelor's button increases by offsets and self-sows readily. Its downy foliage fills in around later-emerging, taller and narrower plants, such as balloon flower, Russian sage, checkerbloom, and butterfly weed. The blue flowers combine well with candytuft, and Oriental poppy.

CARE: Plants tolerate wind, heat, drought, and high-pH soil but not wet soil, especially in winter. Cut them back hard after spring bloom to promote lush new foliage and to prevent self-sowing, which is especially common in cool climates. Cut-back plants may bloom a second time in summer You might want to allow some seedlings to grow to renew the planting

Divide perennial bachelor's button every two to three years; they are easy to move. If plants are grown where they receive shade or if days are hot in spring, the flowering stems will stretch and require staking. Support them with short crutches.

Plants are basically pest-free but occasionally attacked by stalk borer. They will grow from bits of root, so be sure to remove all the root of unwanted seedlings. There is no need to cut back in late fall or early spring; foliage self-destructs neatly over winter.

RECOMMENDED PLANTS AND RELATED SPECIES: 'Alba' has white flowers. 'Rosea' and 'Carnea' are pink. 'Grandiflora' has larger blooms. Persian cornflower (*C. dealbata*) is a 24- to 36-inch pink-flowering relative that blooms several weeks later than perennial bachelor's button. Growing conditions and care are the same.

Perennial bachelor's button

CENTRANTHUS RUBER

Red valerian

- Iridescent reddish-pink blooms, summer
- Zones 5–8 (Zone 4 with protection)
- 24 inches × 24 inches
- Full sun
- Well-drained, neutral to alkaline soil
- Tolerates drought

DESCRIPTION AND USES: This old-fashioned, bushy plant grows to 2 feet in mild climates but can't take the combined heat and humidity of the Deep South.

Easy-to-grow red valerian is one of the longest-blooming perennials. Its numerous flowers are especially beautiful combined with white sage or lamb's-ears. It performs well in stone walls.

CARE: Plant red valerian 12 to 15 inches apart in full sun in well-drained, neutral to alkaline soil. Deadhead to promote repeat blooming. Pests are never a problem, but plants can be short-lived. They have problems with heat. Divide plants in spring or fall.

RECOMMENDED PLANTS AND RELATED SPECIES: 'Albus' is an excellent variety that produces ivory-white flowers. 'Coccineus' has deep rose-red blossoms.

NOTES: Red valerian is also known as Jupiter's beard.

Red valerian

CERATOSTIGMA PLUMBAGINOIDES

Plumbago

- Intense blue flowers, late summer to fall
- Zones 5–9
- 8 inches × 15 inches
- Full sun to partial shade
- Well-drained soil
- Average water

DESCRIPTION AND USES:
This low-slung perennial spreads by underground stems and is perfect for rocky areas. It has masses of gentian blue flowers from summer to late fall, plus red-tinged leaves that turn bronze in autumn for long-lasting seasonal color.

Use plumbago to underplant spring-blooming bulbs, to act as a ground cover in sunny spots, or to ramble over rocks.

CARE: Plumbago thrives in well-drained, good-quality soil but will tolerate a wide range of soil types, from clay to sand. It does poorly in wet soil, but plants spread rapidly in light sandy soil.

Space plants 12 inches apart. In areas where their tops aren't killed by cold, cut them back hard in early spring. Divide in early spring if clumps die out in center.

Plants are late to emerge in spring.

RECOMMENDED PLANTS AND RELATED SPECIES: Blue leadwort (*C. griffithii*) is similarly handsome with deep blue flowers red-margined evergreen foliage. In fall the leaves take on red and yellow hues. It is hardy in Zones 6–8.

Plumbago

CHAMAEMELUM NOBILE

Chamomile

- White flowers, midsummer
- Zones 4–10
- 4 to 12 inches × 15 inches
- Full sun
- Well-drained, sandy soil
- Allow to dry down; tolerates drought

DESCRIPTION AND USES: This apple-scented perennial herb has lacy, finely divided leaves and small, daisylike flowers. It grows in a flat mat against the soil and tolerates foot traffic well, releasing a lovely aroma when crushed underfoot.

You don't have to relegate chamomile just to your herb garden. It is a wonderful lawn alternative when mowed. Or grow it between stepping-stones and pavers or in bulb beds. Its lacy foliage is a good foil for coarser-textured perennials.

CARE: A sunny location with well-drained, slightly acid, sandy soil suits chamomile best. However, the plants also tolerate heavy soil.

Space plants 12 inches apart. Trim or mow them in spring after they flower to a height of 3 to 4 inches, particularly if you use chamomile as a lawn alternative. Propagate chamomile from seed, cuttings, or division in early spring.

RECOMMENDED PLANTS AND RELATED SPECIES: 'Flore Pleno' is a double-flowered form.

Chamomile

CHASMANTHIUM LATIFOLIUM

Northern sea oats

- Ornamental grass grown for light-green blades
- Zones 4–8
- 30 inches to 48 inches in bloom × 18 inches
- Sun or partial shade
- Rich, well-drained soil
- Allow to dry down

DESCRIPTION AND USES:
Northern sea oats is one of the best grasses for partial shade. Its flower stems arch from bamboolike clumps. The flowers are lovely in dried arrangements and as a focal point or ground cover in the garden.
CARE: Plant in sun or partial shade in rich, well-drained soil. Space 24 inches apart. This grass may self-seed and become a problem in the perennial garden.
NOTES: Plants turn bronze in autumn.

Northern sea oats

CHELONE OBLIQUA

Rose turtlehead

- Deep rose-purple flowers, late summer to fall
- Zones 4–9
- 2 to 3 feet × 1 foot
- Dense shade to full sun
- Any moist, neutral to acid soil
- Average water to soggy soil

DESCRIPTION AND USES: This perennial gets its name from its flowers, which resemble the heads of snapping turtles. It is a sturdy, vertical or columnar plant with medium-textured, deep green foliage. It spreads by shallow rhizomes at a moderate rate, forming wide, dense colonies.

Grow rose turtlehead with mounded plants, finer- or coarser-textured plants, and species with rounded flowers: aster, black-eyed Susan, globe flower, meadow rue, queen-of-the-prairie, rodgersia, buttercup, Himalayan fleece flower, sedum, Japanese wax bell, daylily, dropwort, and maiden grass.

CARE: Plants tolerate heavy clay and alkaline soils. Where summers are very hot or in full sun, constant moisture is essential.

Apply 50 percent more fertilizer than for average perennials. To keep turtlehead in check near less aggressive plants, reduce the colony in spring each year.

Plants can be pinched several times between midspring and midsummer to reduce height at flowering. Deadheading is not needed.

Cut back plants in late fall or early spring. Divide them every four to five years or topdress in late fall with 1 to 2 inches of compost to rejuvenate the clump. After moving the plants, pamper them. Seed germinates erratically unless first exposed to high heat in moist soil.

Turtlehead is pest-free but powdery mildew may occur, particularly where soil is dry.

RECOMMENDED PLANTS AND RELATED SPECIES: 'Bethelii' is more floriferous, deep rose-pink-flowered. 'Alba' is white-flowered and slow growing. White turtlehead (*C. glabra*) is similar but has white flowers with a red tinge. Pink turtlehead (*C. lyonii*) is similar to rose turtlehead but has paler rose flowers. 'Hot Lips' has somewhat brighter and darker blooms.

Rose turtlehead

CIMICIFUGA RAMOSA

Fragrant bugbane

Fragrant bugbane

- White spikes in midsummer
- Zones 3–8 (may need protection in Zone 3)
- 3 feet in leaf, 6 feet in bloom × 2 to 3 feet
- Half sun to dense shade
- Moist acid soil with plentiful organic matter
- Continuously moist to soggy

DESCRIPTION AND USES: Fragrant bugbane forms neat 3-foot-tall mounds of coarsely divided foliage. Elegant spikes of white flowers on sturdy stalks double the plant's height. Plants are tallest where soil is continuously moist or wet. Some cultivars have maroon leaves.

Bugbane is a clump-former with slow to moderate growth. It is attractive with other coarse, mounded plants such as hosta, rodgersia, and heart-leaf brunnera.

It blooms with toad lily, azure monkshood, and purple bush clover.
CARE: Fragrant bugbane prefers acid soil but tolerates neutral to slightly alkaline pH. It does not do well in heat and drought. Avoid planting it in full sun unless soil is constantly moist. Apply 50 percent more fertilizer than the average. You may need to stake plants where light is strongly one-directional. Use individual braces. Cut down plants in late fall or early spring. Deadheading is not necessary; plants rarely need division. They are basically pest-free.
RECOMMENDED PLANTS AND RELATED SPECIES: Black snake root (*C. racemosa*) has white spires in midsummer that reach 4 to 8 feet. Kamchatka bugbane (*C. simplex*) is studded with pearly white buds that tease from July until mid- to late fall, finally opening to ivory bottlebrushes after first frost. Plants form clumps or spread slowly by rhizomes. They grow 3 to 5 feet tall.
NOTES: Some sources list cimicifuga under the botanical name *Actea*.

CONVALLARIA MAJALIS

Lily-of-the-Valley

Lily-of-the-valley

- Bell-shaped white or pink flowers, spring
- Zones 3–8
- 6 inches × 6 inches
- Shade to dense shade
- Average water to continuously moist

DESCRIPTION AND USES: In spring, this dense, fragrant perennial has stalks of sweet-scented, bell-shaped flowers with scalloped edges. Most lilies-of-the-valleys have single, snow-white flowers, but there are some cultivars with double flowers and some with pink blooms. Some varieties have variegated leaves. Use lily-of-the-valley in shady areas under trees and shrubs.
CARE: Lily-of-the-valley thrives and spreads rapidly in moist soil. In dry soil, it survives quite well but does not spread. Heat also slows the spread of the plants.

Space plants 6 to 12 inches apart. Water them well throughout the year. Fertilize in fall after the first frost. In colder regions, protect plants from severe winter weather by covering beds with mulch in fall. Propagate lily-of-the-valley by division in fall.
NOTE: Fruit is poisonous.

CLEMATIS HYBRIDS

Clematis

- Stunning displays of large colorful flowers, late spring to summer
- Zones 3–8
- 5 to 8 feet a year
- Shade
- Well-drained soil
- Allow to dry down

'Nelly Moser' (above)
Jackman clematis (right)

DESCRIPTION AND USES: These big-blossomed beauties always draw raves. Unfortunately, clematis have an unwarranted reputation for being finicky and a challenge to prune.

Because large-flowered hybrid clematis are generally restrained in habit and lightweight, they are good choices to interweave through a perennial garden. Let them grow over the perennials, shrubs, small trees, and other vines. When the companion finishes its show, the clematis will continue.

CARE: Clematis grows best with cool roots and leaves exposed to the sun. Plant vines so their roots are shaded; then train the stem to grow into the light—for example, on the north side of a shrub, tree, or tree stump. Or plant a vine behind a trellis and let it grow through the supports. It will eventually shade its own roots. Heavy mulching with bark or wood chips also helps keep the roots cool.

Dig the planting hole deep enough to bury 2 or 3 inches of the stem. The stem will send out its own roots, increasing the odds of plant survival. If the plant wilts soon after planting, the plant will probably resprout from the base because of these extra roots. Keep new plantings moist but not flooded.

Good drainage and moderate moisture are important to clematis. Additional balanced fertilizer each spring will help maintain or increase plant vigor.

Clematis grows well on netting, chain link, and light trellises. Choose an attractive structure because the vines are deciduous and do not hide supports in the winter.

Prune clematis to control growth, to encourage flowering, and to remove dead stems. The key to pruning them is determining whether your clematis bloom on last year's or this year's wood, or both.

Clematis fall into three groups when it comes to pruning. Group I clematis include spring-flowering evergreen and early to midseason flowering species. These bloom on last year's wood. Prune them after their flowers fade, but no later than in July.

Group II clematis bloom on last year's wood but also have a second flush of flowers on the current year's growth. Remove all dead and weak stems in late winter or early spring; cut remaining stems back to a pair of strong buds. Pinching stems occasionally stimulates branching.

Group III clematis are later-flowering, blooming on this season's growth. Without pruning, this group rapidly becomes overgrown. Prune in late winter or early spring, cutting plants to 1 foot above the ground for the first two or three years after planting, and to 2 feet for older plants.

Clematis is basically pest-free, but a disease called clematis wilt can be a problem.

RECOMMENDED PLANTS AND RELATED SPECIES:
There are dozens of cultivars; here is a small sampling: 'Nelly Moser' has pinkish flowers with dark pink stripes; those of 'Miss Bateman' are creamy white with reddish centers. Other flower colors: 'Candida', white with yellow centers; 'Ville de Lyon', red; 'Madame le Coultre', white; 'Mrs. Cholmondeley', bluish-

'Earnest Markham'

Solitary clematis

Tube clematis

purple. Jackman clematis (C. × *jackmanii*) blooms in early summer and sporadically throughout summer; it has violet-purple flowers. 'Comtesse de Bouchaud' blooms silvery rose all summer. 'Niobe' has deep ruby flowers with yellow centers from late spring into summer.

Two shrubby clematis: Solitary clematis (C. *integrifolia*) is 1½ to 3 feet tall. The early to midsummer blooms are dark blue nodding bells. Tube clematis (C. *heracleifolia*) is a late summer bloomer with clusters of blue flowers along the stem. It is 2 to 3 feet tall.

Coreopsis

- Yellow daisylike flowers, early to midsummer
- Zones 4–9
- 1 to 3 feet × 1½ feet
- Full sun to part shade
- Well-drained, neutral to slightly acid sandy soil
- Average water

DESCRIPTION AND USES: The yellow to golden to brassy-yellow daisies of coreopsis light up perennial gardens. Some cultivars are short and mounded; others are loosely columnar. Plants grow quickly. They combine well with perennial salvia, ornamental mullein, and speedwell, or with ornamental grasses.

CARE: Coreopsis tolerates drought and alkaline soil but does not do well in wet soil in winter. Cut plants back hard after the first flowering to stimulate further bloom.

Deadhead to prolong bloom and prevent self-sowing; coreopsis has branched flower stems. Plants may need staking, especially in rich, moist soil. Use small crutch supports. Apply fertilizer at half the average rate to avoid soft, floppy growth. In late fall or early spring, cut plants back to the ground.

Divide plants every two to three years to maintain vigor. They spread by offsets and are easy to move.

Coreopsis is basically pest-free. Four-lined plant bug can disfigure foliage just before bloom. Powdery mildew or rust may develop, especially if the plants are in shade.

RECOMMENDED PLANTS AND RELATED SPECIES: Lanceleaf coreopsis (C. lanceolata) grows 2 feet tall and has 2½ inch-wide daisies on long, slender stalks. 'Moonbeam' threadleaf coreopsis (C. verticillata) is a standout. Its dainty, pale yellow flowers appear from summer to frost on 10- to 12-inch tall mounds of fine texture. Two new cultivars—'Sweet Dreams', pink with a dark center, and 'Limerock Ruby' with maroon flowers—are available.

Goldfink' lanceleaf coreopsis (top)
'Golden Showers' threadleaf coreopsis (above)

Pampas grass

- Majestic feathery plumes, late summer through winter
- Zones 6–9
- 5 to 12 feet × 5 feet
- Full sun
- Well-drained average soil
- Continuously moist

DESCRIPTION AND USES: Pampas grass is a dramatic accent that looks best as a focal point. Female plants have the showiest plumes. Flower color varies from silver to creamy white. Standing 5 to 12 feet tall with a spread of 5 or 6 feet, pampas grass is the largest and showiest of the grasses.

CARE: Plant pampas grass in full sun in moist, well-drained soil. Water and fertilize regularly. Before new growth begins in spring, cut back and remove dead material collected near base. In cold areas, grow pampas grass in a container and bring it inside in winter.

RECOMMENDED PLANTS AND RELATED SPECIES: 'Andes Silver' is 6 to 7 feet tall with large silvery flower plumes. 'Pumila' is a dwarf with creamy white flowers on 3- to 4-foot stalks. It is very floriferous. 'Patagonia' is 5 to 6 feet tall with striking silver plumes and bluish, gray-green foliage.

Pampas grass

CORYDALIS LUTEA

Yellow corydalis

- Butter-yellow flowers, midspring to midsummer
- Zones 5–8
- 12 inches × 18 inches
- Half sun to dense shade
- Moist, well-drained alkaline soil with plentiful organic matter
- Average water to continuously moist

DESCRIPTION AND USES: Yellow corydalis is one of the best shade plants. The blooms are tiny but appear in eye-catching clusters. Leaves look like those of bleeding heart. Plants grow quickly and spread by reseeding.

Grow corydalis with hostas, particularly gold-variegated cultivars, and yellow-flowered forms of barrenwort, heart-leaf brunnera, or Solomon's seal.

CARE: Corydalis takes sun if soil is cool and constantly moist, but foliage and flower colors fade.

It doesn't do well in heat.

There is no need to deadhead corydalis; it would be quite a chore to do since the plants bear many flowers so freely over a long period. Plants self-sow, but the seedlings are easily weeded out if you desire.

It's hard to find corydalis at garden centers. Plants don't shift well from seed flats to pots. Their delicate stems are easily broken in handling, so the plants don't attract buyers. Packaged seed is difficult to germinate. To obtain corydalis, collect fresh seed from an established planting. Fresh seed germinates readily the following spring if sown immediately after collection. Or get seedlings from friends.

Corydalis rarely needs division; it is difficult to move except as seedling and reestablishes slowly. Plants are basically pest-free.

RECOMMENDED PLANTS AND RELATED SPECIES: Blue corydalis (*C. flexuosa*) has smoky-blue flowers and blue-green foliage. It is striking in cool, rich, shaded areas. Unlike yellow corydalis, it goes dormant in summer. 'Blue Panda' has sky-blue flowers.

Yellow corydalis with fringed bleeding heart.

CRINUM

Milk-and-wine lilies

- Large flowers in spring, summer, or fall
- Zones 8–10
- 24 to 48 inches × 5 inches
- Sun to part shade
- Rich soil
- Continuously moist

DESCRIPTION AND USES: Milk-and-wine lilies have large, fragrant, white, pink, reddish, or bicolor lily-shaped flowers. They add a lush, tropical look to perennial gardens.

CARE: This tough plant is a bulb. To grow it, keep soil moist and well fertilized in the early part of the growing season. Divide plants by removing the offsets from the main bulb. Left undisturbed, swamp lily often forms large clumps. In areas colder than Zone 8, treat milk-and-wine lilies as a tender plant. Lift bulbs and store them indoors over winter. Replant them outside the next spring when the weather settles. Plants are basically pest-free.

RECOMMENDED PLANTS AND RELATED SPECIES: Deep sea lily (*C. bulbispermum*) has pink flowers or red flowers with white insides in Zones 6–10. Powell milk-and-wine lily (*C. × powellii*) has rose-pink flowers. 'Album' is white.

NOTES: It tolerates salt spray.

Powell milk-and-wine lilies

CROCOSMIA X CROCOSMIIFLORA

Crocosmia

'Lucifer' crocosmia

'Venus' crocosmia

■ Red-orange or yellow flowers, midsummer
■ Zones 5–9
■ 18 to 36 inches × 12 inches
■ Full to half sun
■ Well-drained, rich, moist soil; blooms best in clay soil
■ Continuously moist

DESCRIPTION AND USES:

Crocosmia lights up a midsummer border with glowing, funnel-shaped flowers that line the arching tip of each stem. Its flaring, swordlike foliage grows in a vase-shaped clump. Plants spread at a moderate pace by short rhizomes from gladiolalike corms.

Combine crocosmia with coreopsis or black-eyed Susan. Pearly everlasting, cool yellow-green patrinia, or white sage make the blue-green crocosmia jump out in contrast. Try a deep violet-blue delphinium for an arresting sight or ornamental grasses to tone it down.

CARE: Clip off the entire flowering stem when the last bud opens and finishes bloom. Divide plants in spring every three years. Plants may require staking in part shade; use individual braces.

Crocosmia does not tolerate wet soil, poor drainage, or drought. It is sometimes listed as hardy only to Zone 6, but winter losses in Zone 5 probably result from poor drainage or age of the plants rather than hardiness. Older plants with larger roots are hardier. Cover new plants with a thick mulch for the first few winters until the plants are full size.

Slugs and snails may be a problem. Spider mites can be a nightmare; if damage to foliage is extensive, bloom will be reduced.

RECOMMENDED PLANTS AND RELATED SPECIES:

'Vulcan' is deep red-orange and hardier than some varieties. 'Lucifer' is bright red. 'Jenny Bloom' is a yellow-flowered variety. 'Venus' has yellowish pink blooms and grows 18 to 24 inches tall. 'Emily McKensie' has dark orange blossoms.

DELOSPERMA

Ice plants

■ Yellow to deep purple blooms, winter and summer
■ Zones 6–10

Purple ice plant

■ 3 to 4 inches × 24 inches
■ Sun to half shade
■ Well-drained soil
■ Allow to dry down; tolerates drought

DESCRIPTION AND USES:

Ice plants grow close to the ground and provide a quick, thick cover. Their succulent green leaves may vary in shade, depending on the species or variety. Plants have daisylike flowers in colors ranging from yellow to deep purple to red. Plants may bloom in winter and again in summer, often producing flowers sporadically.

CARE: Ice plants love hot, dry, sunny locations. They do well in almost any well-drained soil and require little watering. Ground cover beds of ice plant may require occasional thinning.

Propagate plants from cuttings or division. Space them 4 to 6 inches apart.

RECOMMENDED PLANTS AND RELATED SPECIES:

Hardy ice plant (*D. nubigena*) has 1-inch-wide yellow flowers and emerald green foliage that turns red in fall. It grows to 1 inch tall and 3 feet wide. It is the hardiest species to Zone 5. Purple ice plant (*D. cooperi*) has 2-inch purple blooms on 6-inch-tall plants. It is hardy only to Zone 7. 'Starburst' has magenta flowers with bright white centers and yellow stamens. Its foliage is olive-green with a silvery sheen.

DELPHINIUM ELATUM

Delphinium

- Blue, violet, pink, white, or two-toned flowers, early to midsummer
- Zones 3–7
- 18 inches in leaf, 3 to 6 feet in bloom × 3 feet wide
- Full to half sun
- Moist, rich, well-drained soil
- Average water to continuously moist

DESCRIPTION AND USES: Tall wands of summer flowers top the 18-inch mound of delphinium foliage in spring. Plants develop into a column 3 to 6 feet tall when in blooms.

Combine delphinium with later-blooming tall plants: perennial sunflower, Joe-Pye weed, anise hyssop, fragrant bugbane, ornamental grasses, ironweed, or culver's root. In bloom, delphinium complements queen-of-the-meadow and meadow rue.

CARE: Delphinium does not tolerate wind, heat, drought, or poorly drained soil. It must have shade at midday. Apply 50 percent more fertilizer than the average.

Deadhead plants to prolong flowering; they are a standard spike. Remove the entire flowering stalk, cutting it just above a large leaf low on that stem. New flowering shoots will develop from the stem. After the second bloom, cut the flower stems back to the basal leaves. Water and fertilize, then wait for new basal shoots to emerge and old foliage to wither. Then remove the old stalks.

Thin the shoots on established plants in early spring; allow just five to seven shoots per clump. Stake stems individually, tying them in at 12-inch intervals. Divide delphiniums every three years in early fall; they have offsets. Grow the new plant in beds that have not held delphiniums for several years.

Delphinium grows from seed or stem cuttings taken in spring and rooted in water. Cut plants down in late fall and remove all foliage to reduce pest problems. Leaf spot, powdery mildew, and stem and crown rot can pose problems, as can slugs, snails, and stalk borer. Remove and destroy all discolored foliage and flowers. Do not crowd plants. Apply preventive fungicide.

RECOMMENDED PLANTS AND RELATED SPECIES: Cultivars include Pacific Hybrids, which boast showy spikes of clear, brightly colored double flowers. Plants in the Magic Fountain Series are 2½- to 3-foot-tall bushy plants and come in a range of colors, many with dark centers. They are hardier than taller types. The Belladonna Group has loose, multiple flower stalks and performs better in hot areas than other delphiniums. Each of these hybrid groups has numerous cultivars.

'Blue Fountains' delphinium

Look for fish-shaped flower buds to identify delphinium.

DENDRANTHEMA X GRANDIFLORUM

Chrysanthemum

- All colors except blue, mid- to late summer and fall
- Zones 5–9

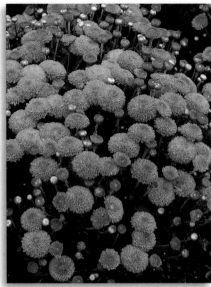

Chrysanthemum

- 12 to 48 inches × 12 to 48 inches
- Full to half sun
- Moist, rich, well-drained soil
- Average water

DESCRIPTION AND USES:
Chrysanthemums come in a variety of growth habits, colors, and flower forms. Plants bloom in mid- to late summer and fall, depending on the variety and your maintenance practices. They combine well with vertical plants, such as purple coneflower, crocosmia, gas plant, ironweed, and ornamental grasses.

CARE: Plant mums four to six weeks before the first expected freeze in your area. They do not tolerate wet soil but will grow well in windy locations if they have plenty of moisture. Apply 50 percent more fertilizer than for average perennials. Pinch several times between midspring and midsummer for bushy, short, later-blooming plants. Northern gardeners should stop pinching by mid-July; southern gardeners, by early August. Unpinched plants may need staking. In Zones 5–6, wait until early spring to cut back plants Or cut them down in fall and cover roots with an airy mulch over winter. Drainage affects hardiness. Mums planted in poorly drained soil or late in the season are less likely to survive winter in Zones 5–6.

Divide plants every two years in spring to keep clumps vigorous; they have offsets. Replant divisions in a different location to prevent pest buildup.

Aphids, Japanese beetles, mites, slugs, snails, and nematodes can be problems. Leaf spot, mildew, and rust infect older, crowded clumps. Rabbits, deer, and woodchucks graze on the flower buds.

RECOMMENDED PLANTS AND RELATED SPECIES: Montauk daisy (*Nipponanthemum nipponicum*) is a semievergreen woody perennial that grows 2 to 3 feet tall with white daisies in fall. It tolerates wind and salt in Zones 5–9; do not pinch in Zones 5–6.

Hay-scented fern

DENNSTAEDTIA PUNCTILOBULA

Hay-scented fern

- Grown for yellow-green fronds
- Zones 3–8 (Zone 7 east of the Rocky Mountains)
- 2 to 3 feet × 4 feet
- Shade to dense shade
- Rich, well-drained, acid soil
- Continuously moist

DESCRIPTION AND USES: The dried or crushed yellow-green fronds of this North American native fern smell like crushed hay, which is the source of the name. The beautiful, hairy, arching fronds have a lacy texture and grow 2 to 3 feet tall.

This easy-to-grow fern tolerates a wide range of conditions. Use it to provide ground cover in a shady border. It is a beautiful backdrop for Japanese anemone or bugbane. In autumn the fronds turn a soft shade of yellow.

CARE: Hay-scented fern grows best in partial to deep shade in rich, moist, well-drained, acid soil but will tolerate open sun and a wide range of soil conditions. Once established, plants can survive in fairly dry soil.

Plant them 3 feet apart. Hay-scented fern may become too invasive for the small garden, but it is attractive and care-free in large gardens where it has room to roam. It spreads by rhizomes. Slugs and snails may be a problem.

DESCHAMPSIA CAESPITOSA

Tufted hair grass

- An ornamental with fine, thin blades and creamy plumes in late summer
- Zones 4–8
- 3 feet × 3 feet
- Sun to half sun
- Damp soil
- Average water

DESCRIPTION AND USES: This graceful grass of glistening, silver-tinged purple spikelets sprouts long-lasting, frothy flowers in late summer. It is an excellent choice for the seaside garden. This fine-textured grass provides year-round interest and is especially attractive with hostas or ferns. In mild-winter areas, leaves turn bronzy yellow and stay evergreen.
CARE: Space plants 18 inches apart. They grow best in partial shade in damp soil but adjust to varied situations. However, tufted hair grass does not perform well in hot, humid conditions. Where soil is dry, work in organic matter before planting.

Remove the previous year's leaves before new growth begins in spring. In areas with mild winter, plants are evergreen.
RECOMMENDED PLANTS AND RELATED SPECIES: 'Bronze Veil' ('Bronzeschleier') grows 2 to 3 feet tall with bronze-yellow tinted flowers and a high heat tolerance. 'Golden Pendant' ('Goldgehänge') has handsome dark green leaves and spikelets that age to a rich golden yellow.

Tufted hair grass

DIASCIA

Twinspur

- Smothered in pink blooms, spring, early summer, and fall
- Zones 8–9
- 10 inches × 12 inches
- Sun or shade
- Rich, well-drained soil
- Continuously moist

DESCRIPTION AND USES: Diminutive flowers (1 inch or less) bloom in showy clusters on low clumps. It puts on a wonderful show early in the summer then again in fall. Diascia is perennial in warm climates but can be grown as an annual in Zones 7 and colder. It can be challenging to grow, but it is worth the effort. Where plants are winter hardy, the plant cascades over rock walls. It makes a good container plant in cold climates.
CARE: Grow twinspur in sun or partial shade in rich, moist, well-drained soil, 15 inches apart. Water to keep moist, but guard against overwatering. Twinspur does not do well in either heat or humidity.

Don't divide twinspur. Take cuttings to ensure survival. In the South, plant in the fall and enjoy the flowers in the spring.
RECOMMENDED PLANTS AND RELATED SPECIES: 'Ruby Field' barber's twinspur (*D. barberae*), the most popular hybrid, is 10 to 12 inches tall with rose-colored flowers. 'Langthorn Lavender' (*D. lilacina*) has lilac-colored flowers on 12-inch-tall stems. 'Blackthorn Apricot' has apricot-colored flowers on 12-inch plants. Rigid twinspur (*D. rigescens*), a robust species, is 1 to 2 feet tall, with 6- to 8-inch-long trusses of spurred, rosy pink flowers.

Barber's twinspur

DIANTHUS

Pinks

'Constance Finnis' allwood pink

'Doris' allwood pink

'Delicado' carnation

'Lemsii' pink

- Colorful carnations in late spring to early summer
- Zones 4–8
- 2 to 15 inches × 2 to 15 inches, depending on species
- Half to full sun
- Sandy soil with excellent drainage
- Average water; allow to dry down between waterings

DESCRIPTION AND USES: Pinks are an old-fashioned favorite, ideal for the cottage garden, the rock garden, or border front. Taller varieties are superb for cutting. Pinks have small, frilly, fragrant blossoms in all colors and combinations except blue. This group includes plants from tiny creepers to 2-foot-tall cut flowers. Flowers may be single, semidouble, or double. The plant forms a mound of grassy foliage.

Combine pinks' grassy silvery, blue-green foliage with coarser front-of-the-border plants, such as geranium, white sage, coral bells, dwarf bearded iris, ornamental mullein, and perennial salvia. Pinks bloom at the same time as perennial bachelor's button, 'May Queen' daisy, and gas plant.

CARE: Pinks do not tolerate wet soil or pH below 6. They take heat and drought, but not heat and high humidity. Fertilize and water plants well throughout the growing season for repeat bloom in fall or late summer where nights are cool. Deadhead to prolong bloom; flowers are on branched stems. Divide plants every two to three years; they have offsets.

Pinks attract rabbits. Leaf spot can be a problem where soil is moist, humidity high, and air circulation poor. To propagate, pull off stem sections, each with a bit of woody basal tissue intact (stem cuttings with a "heel"), and root these in early fall. Cut back foliage in early spring, leaving intact the leafy base of woody stems.

RECOMMENDED PLANTS AND RELATED SPECIES: Allwood pinks (*D. allwoodii*) are 1- to 1½-foot tall plants with gray-green foliage. 'Doris' is salmon-pink with a darker pink center. 'Ian' is rich red with black-red petal edge; it may be hardy only to Zone 5.

Cottage pink (*D. plumarius*) is more cold-hardy (Zone 3) and blooms in yellow, white, and pink. 'Mountain Mist' is rose-pink, mat-forming, and more tolerant of heat and humidity than many others. Cheddar pink (*D. gratianopolitanus*) and maiden pink (*D. deltoides*) are also more tolerant of summer heat and humidity. They are shorter, mat-forming plants. Cheddar pink cultivars: 'Bath's Pink' is pale pink. 'Tiny Rubies' has double, deep pink blooms. Maiden pink cultivars: 'Red Maiden' is red-violet. 'Brilliant' is nearly red (Zone 3).

Carnations (*D. caryophyllus*) bloom in white, pink, red, purple, yellow, and apricot on erect 1- to 2- foot stems in Zones 8–10.

Sweet William (*D. barbatus*) is a biennial or short-lived perennial with flat-topped flower clusters on 12- to 24-inch stems. It forms loose mats of deep green foliage. Colors range from white to pink to dark red; some are bicolor.

'Firewitch' Cheddar pink

DICENTRA SPECTABILIS

Bleeding heart

- **Large pink or white hearts, mid- to late spring**
- **Zones 3–8**
- **18 to 30 inches × 36 inches**
- **Sun to shade**
- **Well-drained, sandy soil with plentiful organic matter**
- **Average water to continuously moist**

DESCRIPTION AND USES: Long-lived bleeding heart is a clump-forming, slow-growing perennial with deep roots. Its distinctive, large pink or white hearts dangle from arching stems. Pair its coarse, smoky-green leaves with coral bells, foam flower, monkshood, turtlehead, dropwort, astilbe, and hostas. Plants bloom with woodland phlox and heart-leaf brunnera. Pair them with toad lily to hide the vacancy if bleeding heart goes dormant.
CARE: Bleeding heart does not tolerate wet soil. If grown in full sun, dry soil, or high heat, plants go dormant, leaving a large gap in the border. Apply 50 percent more fertilizer than average.

No need to cut plants back in fall or early spring. Stems are self-cleaning. Self-sowing is minimal.

Bleeding heart will not flower again without winter cold. Plants rarely need division. Moving them may break brittle roots; plants reestablish slowly.

Plants are pest-free. They are resistant to rabbits, woodchucks, and deer.

RECOMMENDED PLANTS AND RELATED SPECIES: 'Pantaloons' is white. Fringed bleeding hearts (*D. eximia* and *D. formosa*) are later blooming 18-inch-tall relatives with finely divided blue-green leaves. They usually do not go dormant and will repeat bloom if deadheaded. Their flowers are not heart-shaped. They prefer acid to neutral soil.

'Luxuriant' has dark pink to cherry-red flowers. 'Snowflakes' is a dwarf white. 'Adrian Bloom' is rose-red and larger-flowered in Zones 3–9.

Bleeding heart

DICTAMNUS ALBUS

Gas plant

- **Starry white or pale rose flowers on tall spikes, midspring**
- **Zones 3–9**
- **2 to 4 feet × 2 to 4 feet**
- **Full sun to shade**
- **Rich, well-drained soil**
- **Tolerates drought**

DESCRIPTION AND USES:
Gas plant is an impressive sight in bloom or later when its ripe brown seedpods open to form a wand of nut-brown stars. Its starry white or pale rose flowers open on tall spikes over shining, dark foliage. Flowers and foliage have a sharp lemon fragrance, which is pleasant to some, disturbing to others. Plants are clump-forming and slow to grow.

Try gas plant with peony; they are good partners in overall appearance, bloom, and longevity. Gas plant's foliage color and texture contrast nicely with Siberian and Japanese irises, yellow or pink threadleaf coreopsis, globe thistle, and daylily.

CARE: Gas plant does not tolerate poor drainage, or hot nights (over 80° F). Give it 50 percent more fertilizer than for average perennials. Stems falling over mean the plant needs water.

Cut plants back in the spring. Flowers are a standard spike for deadheading. Or leave flowers stalks in place for winter interest.

Plants rarely need division; they have a taproot. Move or divide them in spring or early fall as necessary, or leave in place for a lifetime (it's not true that the plant will die if disturbed). Gas plant can be propagated by root cuttings. Seed is difficult to germinate and may take two full years of freeze-thaw cycles before it does. Plants are basically pest-free. If you see leaf-chewing damage, look closely before taking action; gas plant is a host to larvae of black swallowtail and giant swallowtail butterflies.

RECOMMENDED PLANTS AND RELATED SPECIES: The enchanting flowers of purple gas plant (*D. albus* var. *purpureus*) are mauve-purple with darker veins.

NOTES: Use care in working around the plant on hot days; oil from the leaves on the skin reacts after exposure to sunlight to cause a burnlike rash.

Gas plant

DIGITALIS PURPUREA

Foxglove

- Pink, purple, red, white, and yellow flowers, late spring to early summer
- Zones 4–9
- 4 feet × 3 feet
- Shade
- Moist, acid, well-drained soil
- Average water

DESCRIPTION AND USES: This is a charming, statuesque plant with colorful, bell-shaped flowers for woodland gardens. It is perfect for informal gardens, where foxglove can self-sow at abandon. Or grow it for cut flowers. Actually a biennial, this species self-sows so well you can count on its perennial presence.
CARE: Plant it in partial to deep shade in moist, rich, acid, well-drained soil. Sow seeds outdoors without covering them in late spring or early summer for blooms the following year, or set out plants 18 to 24 inches apart in the fall.

RECOMMENDED PLANTS AND RELATED SPECIES: Plants in the Excelsior Group are 5 feet tall with tightly packed flowers in pastel pink, rose, white, and yellow. 'Foxy' blooms the first year from seed. Treat it as an annual; let it reseed. Alba (*D. purpurea albiflora*) has white blooms. Common foxglove (*D. grandiflora*) is a true perennial, 2 to 3 feet tall with yellow flowers. Strawberry foxglove (*D. × mertonensis*), also a perennial, has 5- to 7-foot-tall spires of coppery rose flowers.
NOTE: Leaves are poisonous.

'White Excelsior' foxglove

DORONICUM ORIENTALE

Leopard's bane

- Cheerful yellow flowers, late spring
- Zones 4–7
- 20 inches × 12 inches
- Half sun to shade
- Rich, moist soil high in organic matter
- Continuously moist

DESCRIPTION AND USES: A rare daisy for shade, leopard's bane has clusters of yellow flowers covering its mound of heart-shaped, dark green leaves. Interplant it with ferns, which will cover up bare spots when leopard's bane goes dormant in summer.
CARE: Although leopard's bane doesn't tolerate heat and it goes dormant in summer after it blooms, plants are easy to grow. Give it light to medium shade in rich, moist soil high in organic matter. Space plants 12 to 15 inches apart. Mulch to conserve soil moisture; water during dry weather.

RECOMMENDED PLANTS AND RELATED SPECIES: 'Finesse' has semidouble, yellow-orange flowers on 15-inch stems. 'Magnificum' forms neat, 15-inch mounds with bright yellow flowers on 2½-foot-tall stems. 'Miss Mason' ('Madame Mason') is 1 to 2 feet tall with canary yellow daisy flowers and more persistent foliage than the species.

'Magnificum' leopard's bane

DRYOPTERIS FILIX-MAS

Male wood fern

- Tall erect fronds with deeply divided leaflets
- Zones 4–8
- 3 to 4 feet × 3 feet
- Shade or half sun
- Neutral to acid, fertile soil
- Tolerates drought

DESCRIPTION AND USES:
Sturdy and masculine compared to the delicate lady fern, this plant grows to 4 feet tall. The adaptable male wood fern is a favorite for the shady woodland setting where it has room to show off.

Plants form substantial clumps. They are attractive in the garden border in combination with toad lily or bleeding heart.

CARE: Plant male wood fern in shade or filtered sun in neutral to acid, fertile soil, spacing them 2 feet apart. Replenish organic matter. Divide larger clumps regularly. If new plants are not divided, the symmetry of the fern may be lost, and it will become a large clump, which many consider attractive. Fronds persist into winter.

RECOMMENDED PLANTS AND RELATED SPECIES:
'Crispa' is a dwarf form with crested fronds. 'Cristata' has divided and crested frond tips. 'Linearis' bears fronds with slender, linear divisions. Autumn fern (*D. erythrosora*) is a colorful evergreen with coppery red new growth that holds its color until mature then changes to a deep glossy green (hardy in Zones 5–9).

NOTES: The plant tolerates drying and poor soil.

Male wood fern

ECHINACEA PURPUREA

Purple coneflower

- Purple or white flowers, early to midsummer
- Zones 3–8
- 2 to 4 feet × 2 feet
- Full to half sun
- Well-drained soil
- Average water

DESCRIPTION AND USES:
Purple coneflower has daisylike petals that circle central cones with an intriguing rusty hue. The petals curl back from the cone as the flowers age. Plants are columnar, coarse-textured, clump-forming, and fast-growing.

The shape and texture of purple coneflower work well with spiny bear's breeches, ornamental grasses, Russian sage, queen-of-the-meadow, blazing star, artemisia, obedient plant, culver's root, checkerbloom, sedum, and others.

CARE: Plants tolerate heat, wind, humidity, drought, and shade, and are basically pest-free. Older, crowded clumps may develop stem dieback, a viral infection; if so, be sure to remove the plants.

Coneflower self-sows; seedlings are variable in height, color, and flower size. Cut back plants in late fall or early spring. Deadhead to prolong bloom into fall; they have branched flower stems.

Divide plants every four to five years in fall or spring to maintain vigor. They have offsets and are easy to move. Staking is unnecessary.

RECOMMENDED PLANTS AND RELATED SPECIES: 'Magnus' has larger, darker pink flowers with a less pronounced central cone. Its petals do not droop with maturity. 'Robert Bloom', 2 to 3 feet tall, has very large, dark pink petals; the cone has a pronounced rusty hue.

'White Lustre' and 'White Swan' have ivory flowers with a sweet, light scent. They are half the height of the species and slow growing.

Pale coneflower (*E. angustifolia*) is 2 to 3 feet tall. Its late-spring to early-summer flowers are paler pink than those of purple coneflower. In Zone 4, the flower stalks are less leafy and more flexible.

Purple coneflower with Russian sage

ECHINOPS RITRO

Globe thistle

- Pale blue flowers, midsummer
- Zones 3–8
- 2 to 4 feet × 2 feet
- Full to half sun
- Well-drained soil
- Average water

DESCRIPTION AND USES:
Spheres of steely blue buds in early summer open to pale blue flowers in midsummer. Plants form a strong, coarse column. They are fast growing and clump forming.

The coarse gray-green foliage and unique spherical flowers are attractive with ornamental grasses, crocosmia, speedwell, obedient plant, checkerbloom, daylily, daisy, and perennial and false sunflowers.

CARE: Flowers fade to pale blue in hot weather. Plants take drought, heat, and shade. Apply fertilizer at half the average rate for perennials.

Deadhead to prolong bloom. Cut plants back by one-third to one-half to lateral flower buds. When new basal leaves start to develop and all flowering is finished, remove the spent flowering stems. Plants will rebloom in fall in cool, moist seasons. Do not deadhead all flowers if attracting birds is desired. Plants readily self-sow.

Globe thistle needs dividing infrequently. Divide plants in spring; they have offsets. Staking is unnecessary. But in shade and rich soil, grow-through supports can help. Clean up the spent plants in early spring.

Globe thistle is basically pest-free but occasionally has problems with stalk borer. Painted Lady caterpillars may knit shoot tips together but will be gone in time for the plant to grow new foliage and bloom.

RECOMMENDED PLANTS AND RELATED SPECIES: 'Taplow Blue' has large, steel-blue flowers; 'Veitch's Blue' is darker blue. Russian globe thistle (*E. exaltatus*) is taller, to 8 feet, with silvery white flowers.

NOTES: The plant attracts birds and butterfly larvae.

'Veitch's Blue' globe thistle

EPIMEDIUM

Barrenwort

- Dainty pink flowers in early spring, evergreen foliage
- Zones 4–9
- 6 to 15 inches × 12 inches
- Shade to dense shade
- Well-drained soil with plentiful organic matter
- Average water

DESCRIPTION AND USES: The flowers of barrenwort are delicately winged and dangle on wiry stems, usually too low to the ground or close in among the foliage to be seen by the casual observer. New leaves start out bronze, expand to green, and show bronze in fall and winter. Plants spread at a slow to moderate pace. This evergreen complements winter-interest shade plants, such as coral bells and foam flower. The subtle two-tone foliage echoes pink-flowered bleeding heart, hybrid lobelia, fringe cups, lungwort, and perennial geranium. It looks elegant with large blue-leaved hostas.

CARE: Barrenwort tolerates drought, dense shade, and competition from tree roots. It is basically pest-free, but root weevils are sometimes a problem. Plants are resistant to rabbits and browsing deer. Cut down the previous year's foliage in late fall or late winter so that next year's flowers are more visible. There is no need to deadhead.

Division is rarely required. Plants have offsets and are easy to move.

RECOMMENDED PLANTS AND RELATED SPECIES: Longspur barrenwort (*E. grandiflorum*) has the largest flowers. Those of 'Rose Queen' are crimson. 'White Queen' blooms silver-white. 'Pierre's Purple' is taller with large purple blooms. Foliage of red barrenwort (*E. × rubrum*) has rosy undertones and margins. Watch for new species being introduced from China and Korea. Some are taller (*E. davidii* and *E. × omeiense*) or have showier flowers (*E. brachyrrhizum*).

Foliage of red barrenwort (above)
Closeup of red barrenwort flowers (right)

ERIGERON

Fleabane

- Wide range of colors, midsummer to fall
- Zones 4–9 (Zones 4–7 east of the Rockies)
- 24 inches × 24 inches
- Full sun
- Sandy, well-drained soil
- Average water

DESCRIPTION AND USES: This dainty yet bushy North American native looks like aster but is even easier to grow. And it blooms earlier. Fleabane is a care-free plant for the front or middle of a sunny border. Plant in drifts of three or more for season-long color.

CARE: Plant 12 to 18 inches apart. Cut back after flowering to reduce weediness and rejuvenate the foliage. Taller varieties may require staking. Divide every three years.

RECOMMENDED PLANTS AND RELATED SPECIES: Daisy fleabane (*E. speciosus*) 'Azure Fairy' is 30 inches tall with semidouble lavender-blue flowers. (Some nurseries sell this as 'Azure Beauty', but that is a different plant.) 'Rosa Triumph' is 24 inches tall, with large, clear pink, double flowers; 'Dimity' is a dwarf, 12 inches tall, with pink blooms. 'Foerster's Darling' ('Foerster's Liebling') is 16 inches tall and has semidouble deep pink flowers. *E. karvinskianus* is a dwarf trailing plant, that bears lovely masses of white to pink flowers all summer. It is hardy in Zones 8–9 but reseeds freely in colder zones.

E. karvinskianus

ERYNGIUM AMETHYSTINUM

Sea holly

- Profuse, steely blue flowers, midsummer
- Zones 2–8
- 2 feet × 2 feet
- Full sun
- Well-drained soil
- Allow to dry down

DESCRIPTION AND USES: Stiff and prickly, this easy-care plant creates a striking effect in a garden. Its handsome form provides interesting contrast in the second tier of a border, combined with wormwood or yellow yarrows.

CARE: Plant sea holly in full sun in well-drained soil. Dry, sandy soils are ideal.

Sow seeds in spring or set out nursery plants 15 to 18 inches apart. The plant's taproot makes it difficult to move or divide. Plants seldom need staking.

Tolerance to salt spray makes sea holly a good candidate for a seaside garden. Plants are extremely cold-tolerant.

RECOMMENDED PLANTS AND RELATED SPECIES: 'Blue Star' alpine sea holly (*E. alpinum*) grows 2 to 3 feet tall. It has large lavender-blue flowers that resemble fireworks (Zones 4–8). 'Blue Cap' flat sea holly (*E. planum*), also called 'Blaukappe', blooms all summer with intense blue flowers. *E. × oliverianum* is 3 feet tall with pale blue flowers and deeply cut foliage.

Sea holly

EUPATORIUM COELESTINUM

Hardy ageratum

'Album' hardy ageratum

Joe-Pye weed

- Powder blue flowers, late summer to fall
- Zones 4–10
- 2 to 3 feet × 3 feet
- Full sun to shade
- Well-drained soil with plentiful organic matter
- Average water to continuously moist

DESCRIPTION AND USES:
Eupatoriums are prized for their late-season blooms. Hardy ageratum's blue flowers open from late summer into fall. Plants grow in mounds and may be much wider than tall. They spread by shallow stolons below the soil surface. Growth is fast.

Hardy ageratum complements plants with vertical lines, such as obedient plant, speedwell, and culver's root.

CARE: Dig out excess plants and seedlings yearly to keep eupatoriums in check. Do not leave roots of significant size in place if trying to eliminate them. Deadhead to reduce self-seeding. Divide plants every four to five years; they have offsets and are easy to move. Staking is unnecessary; pinch plants back if they become floppy. Eupatoriums are basically pest-free. Powdery mildew can be a problem.

RECOMMENDED PLANTS AND RELATED SPECIES: 'Album', has white flowers. Joe-Pye weed (*E. purpureum*) and spotted Joe-Pye weed (*E. maculatum*) have mauve flowers. They grow 7 feet tall by late summer. Plant them in full- to half-sun and moist to wet soil. Stake them in shade and high heat. Plants attract butterflies. 'Gateway' has bronze stems and huge, light-colored blooms; it is 5 feet. 'Atropurpureum' has reddish-purple stems. Joe-Pye weeds are hardy to Zone 3.

EUPHORBIA POLYCHROMA

Cushion spurge

Cushion spurge

- Chartreuse bracts, early to midspring
- Zones 3–7
- 12 to 20 inches × 24 inches
- Full to half sun
- Well-drained soil
- Average water

DESCRIPTION AND USES:
Cushion spurge has clusters of tiny flowers backed by showy, long-lasting chartreuse bracts atop each stem. It is a strongly mounded plant, clump-forming with a slow to moderate growth rate.

Pair cushion spurge with the bright pinks, red-violets, and purples of early tulips, creeping phlox, dwarf bearded iris, and beard-tongue. Plants complement peony foliage. Their stems hide the foliage of fading spring bulbs.

CARE: Where summers are very hot, plant cushion spurge in half sun and divide it more frequently. Cushion spurge is tolerant of heat, wind, and alkaline soil. It does not grow well in high humidity or in wet or poorly drained soil.

You can propagate cushion spurge by tip cuttings taken in late spring or early summer. When cutting, take care to rinse the milky sap from your skin; it can cause a burnlike rash. Deadhead cushion spurge to avoid self-sowing. Divide plants every five to six years to reduce crowding; they have offsets.

Cushion spurge is basically pest-free. It is resistant to rabbits, woodchucks, and deer. Its sap repels moles and voles.

RECOMMENDED PLANTS AND RELATED SPECIES: 'Emerald Jade' grows 12 inches tall and has reliable fall color. 'Purpurea' has a purple cast to the foliage.

Griffith's spurge (*E. griffithii*) is strongly columnar and 30 inches tall. It can sometimes be invasive (Zones 4–8). Flowers of 'Fireglow', flowers resemble glowing, then fading embers. 'Dixter' flowers are red fading to orange, and its foliage has purple undertones; this plant is a less vigorous spreader than 'Fireglow'.

FESTUCA GLAUCA

Dwarf blue fescue

- Ornamental grass with silvery-blue foliage
- Zones 4–8
- 6 to 10 inches × 6 to 10 inches
- Full sun to shade
- Well-drained soil
- Tolerates drought

DESCRIPTION AND USES: This is an attractive grass with slender blades. A lovely, small plant, it offers good contrast in rock gardens or when paired with hardy geraniums or threadleaf coreopsis.

CARE: Plant 8 inches apart. Divide plants every other year and remove flowers to prolong the plant's life.

RECOMMENDED PLANTS AND RELATED SPECIES: 'Elijah Blue' is an excellent form with 8- to 12-inch powdery blue leaves. Hard-to-find 'Solling' is a nonflowering form, 6 to 10 inches tall with beautiful silver-gray foliage.

'Elijah Blue' dwarf blue fescue

FILIPENDULA VULGARIS

Dropwort

- Creamy white flowers, late spring to early summer
- Zones 3–8
- 12 to 18 inches in leaf, 36 inches in bloom × 18 to 24 inches
- Sun to shade
- Most garden soils with plentiful organic matter; prefers neutral to alkaline pH
- Continuously moist to soggy

DESCRIPTION AND USES: The pinkish flower buds of dropwort open to creamy white flowers. They are densely clustered at the tips of tall, nearly leafless stems. The flower stalks rise 3 feet above the mounded foliage. Plants form clumps and grow at a moderate rate.

CARE: Dropwort tolerates heat, if given partial shade and constant moisture, and dry soil where air is cool. It also takes high humidity, wind, and alkaline soil. Plants are basically pest-free, but they may develop leaf spot or powdery mildew in dry soil.

Cut back plants in early spring. Deadhead to prolong bloom, keep the clump neat, and reduce self-sowing; plants have a branched flower stem.

Divide them every five to six years in spring or fall; they have offsets and are easy to move.

Use grow-through support or crutches if needed.

RECOMMENDED PLANTS AND RELATED SPECIES: 'Flore Pleno' has double flowers. 'Kahome' is a dwarf hybrid with pink blooms. Queen-of-the-prairie (*F. rubra*) is 3 to 7 feet tall with coarse foliage and pink cotton-candy blooms in early to midsummer. It forms dense colonies in moist to soggy soil and full to half sun. The plant may require staking in hot summers or dry soil. It is not invasive. 'Venusta' has deeper pink flowers. Clouds of white flowers hover over meadowsweet (*F. ulmaria*) in early summer; it forms dense colonies in moist to soggy soils. Plants are shade-tolerant and 3 to 5 feet tall.

Queen-of-the-prairie

Dropwort

GAILLARDIA X GRANDIFLORA

Blanket flower

- Yellow daisies, early summer to early fall
- Zones 3–10
- 24 inches × 24 inches
- Full sun
- Well-drained soil; prefers sandy soil with plentiful organic matter

Blanket flower

- Average water to continuously moist

DESCRIPTION AND USES:
Blanket flowers are loosely upright to sprawling perennials with coarse blue-gray foliage at the base of the plant. They have large daisies with yellow-marked red petals and scented, warm red-brown centers.

Plants are clump-forming, spreading by short, running roots, and have a very fast growth rate. Blanket flower blends well with yarrow, crocosmia, daylily, patrinia, threadleaf coreopsis, blackberry lily, and ornamental grasses.

CARE: Poorly drained soil is detrimental to plants. Stake tall cultivars or allow them to sprawl; their flowering stems will turn upright. Use grow-through supports or crutches.

Blanket flower blooms continuously into fall, even without deadheading. But seed heads detract from the flowers and make the plant look ragged. So deadhead for neatness; plants have branched

flower stems. Allow some seed to set to promote self-sown replacements of this short-lived perennial.

Divide plants every two to three years in spring; they have offsets and are easy to move. You can propagate them by root cuttings in spring or grow them from seed.

There's no need to cut back blanket flower in late fall or early spring; its stems decompose quickly over winter. To protect the crown in winter in areas with heavy snows, use an airy mulch of twigs.

Blanket flower is pest-free, but it may develop crown rot where soil is wet, particularly in winter.

RECOMMENDED PLANTS AND RELATED SPECIES: 'Goblin' is 9 to 15 inches tall, with mostly red petals tipped with yellow. 'Baby Cole' has a wide red zone on its petals; it grows less than 12 inches tall. 'Burgundy' is a full-sized variety with red petals.

Most named cultivars cannot be grown from seed; the seedlings may vary in height and flower color.

GALIUM ODORATUM

Sweet woodruff

- Tiny white flowers, midspring
- Zones 4–8 (except desert)
- 6 to 12 inches × 6 to 12 inches

Sweet woodruff

- Half sun to dense shade
- Good garden soil, slightly acid
- Average water to continuously moist

DESCRIPTION AND USES:
When sweet woodruff's bright green

leaves are crushed, they emit a fragrance similar to freshly mown hay. The narrow, rough-edged leaves are arranged in whorls along the stem. The leaves are evergreen and change from bright green in summer to light brown in winter. Tiny star-shaped white or yellow flowers appear in clusters.

Use sweet woodruff as an underplanting for thick shrubs; in any shaded spot; or interspersed with lilies and other perennials.

CARE: Space sweet woodruff plants 12 inches apart. They grow best in any good-quality, slightly acid soil in part sun or shade. Where summers are cool, sweet woodruff tolerates sun. Sweet woodruff can be invasive. Plants spread by underground runners, and once established, they spread quickly. Pull runners that creep outside the boundaries you've allotted for them. Propagate sweet woodruff by seed or by division.

GAURA LINDHEIMERI

White gaura

- White flowers, midsummer into fall
- Zones 5–9
- 3 to 5 feet × 3 feet
- Full to half sun
- Well-drained soil with plentiful organic matter
- Allow to dry down

'Siskiyou Pink' white gaura

DESCRIPTION AND USES:
Gaura's dainty flowers dance on wiry stems. Buds are pink, and flowers are white, turning pink with age. Plants continuously produce new flowers without deadheading. In areas with warm springs, plants bloom early. They form an airy column 3 to 5 feet tall, sometimes taller in warm areas. They are clump-forming and fast growing.

Gaura complements spring-blooming perennials with clean, dark green or blue-green foliage, such as blue false indigo, gas plant, peony, blue oat grass, beard-tongue, and soapwort. Its blooms look pretty with balloon flower and tall phlox.

CARE: Gaura tolerates drought, heat, humidity, and wind but not wet soil. Its blooms may fall off in midsummer if nights are hot. Shear plants before they bloom to control height and produce a fuller clump with more flowers. Deadhead occasionally to keep new flower stalks developing (multicluster).

Plants are basically pest-free. Cut them to the ground in late fall or early spring. Or leave them up over winter to reseed; gaura tends to be short-lived. Plants may be divided every two to three years (offsets).

RECOMMENDED PLANTS AND RELATED SPECIES: 'Pink Cloud' has pale pink flowers. 'Crimson Butterfly' has reddish foliage and stems; it grows 1½ to 2 feet. 'Whirling Butterflies' is white; it reaches 1½ to 2 feet; 'Siskiyou Pink' is deep pink and 18 to 24 inches.

GELSEMIUM SEMPERVIRENS

Carolina jessamine

- Yellow flowers, late winter to early spring
- Zones 6–9
- Climbs 10 to 20 feet
- Full to half sun
- Average soil
- Allow to dry down

DESCRIPTION AND USES:
This stellar evergreen vine has shiny, dark leaves that turn purplish in winter. In particularly cold winters, plants are deciduous. The fragrant yellow flower clusters appear in late winter to early spring and sporadically through the spring.

Carolina jessamine has twining stems. Train it on a trellis within the garden for a colorful vertical spring accent. Grow it on an arbor entrance to the garden. Or use it on slopes and walls, climbing posts, or mailboxes in hot settings.

CARE: Plants do fine in average soil and hot sun. They tolerate partial shade but bloom better in full sun. Space them 3 feet apart. Prune after flowering to encourage branching and control growth. If allowed, Carolina jessamine can become a tangled mess.

NOTES: Plants, including flower nectar, are toxic when ingested.

Carolina jessamine

GERANIUM SANGUINEUM

Bloody cranesbill

- Red-violet, pink or white flowers, mid- to late spring
- Zones 3–8
- 1 to 1½ feet × 2 feet
- Half sun
- Well-drained soil
- Average water to continuously moist

DESCRIPTION AND USES:

Bloody geranium is great for care-free color in the front border or as a blooming ground cover. Smaller gardens are best. It is a long-lived, clump-forming perennial; 1-inch-wide blooms stud the plant from mid- to late spring and sporadically all summer. The growth rate is moderate to fast. Pair it with vase-shaped and columnar plants with blooms in yellow or cool colors.

CARE: Grow in full sun or light shade, spacing plants 15 inches apart. Avoid poorly drained or wet soil.

Deadheading is not necessary, but shear plants after they bloom for fresh foliage and to reduce self-sowing. In early spring cut back hard if desired or if plants had leaf spot the previous year. Divide plants every five to six years to renew vigor; they have running roots and are easy to move.

Bloody cranesbill is pest-free, but leaf spot can be a problem. Cut back hard to remove infected foliage. Keep soil moist until plant grows back.

RECOMMENDED PLANTS AND RELATED SPECIES:

'Max Frei' has purple-pink blooms on compact plants. 'Album' has white blooms. 'Lancastriense' tolerates heat and cold better than others.

'Max Frei' bloody cranesbill

GEUM HYBRIDS

Geum

- Red, orange, or yellow flowers, late spring through summer
- Zones 4–7
- 12 inches × 12 inches
- Full sun
- Well-drained, humus-rich soil
- Continuously moist

DESCRIPTION AND USES:

Geum makes a showy display of eye-catching colors on attractive, dark green foliage. It is very attractive at the front of the border, backed by the cool blues of delphinium or bellflower.

CARE: The plant performs best in full sun in cool regions. Where summers are hot, afternoon shade is mandatory. Space plants 12 to 18 inches apart. During the growing season, water abundantly.

Deadhead to prolong bloom. Geum has no serious pests or diseases if plants are sited correctly. Division is seldom required.

RECOMMENDED PLANTS AND RELATED SPECIES: Werner Arends geum (G. × borisii) is compact (10 inches tall), with heavy-scarlet-orange flowering. 'Mrs. Bradshaw' (G. chiloense) has brick-red semidouble flowers and grows 1- to 2-feet-tall. 'Mrs. Bradshaw Improved' has larger flowers. 'Lady Stratheden' has buttercup-yellow blooms.

'Mrs. Bradshaw' geum

GUNNERA MANICATA

Gunnera

- Gigantic coarse-textured umbrella-shaped leaves
- Zone 7–10 (Zone 6 with winter protection)
- 7 feet × 8 feet
- Sun or shade
- Moist or wet, fertile soil
- Continuously moist

DESCRIPTION AND USES:
Coarse mounds of enormous 4-foot-wide, umbrella-shaped leaves grow to a colossal 6 to 8 feet tall.

Gunnera is a plant only for mild-winter, cool-summer climates. It is perfect for poolside or as an accent. Combine it with finer-textured perennials, such as astilbe or Siberian iris.

CARE: Grow gunnera in sun or partial shade in moist or wet, fertile soil. It is a good choice to plant near water gardens, bogs, shallow water, and stream banks. If not provided with adequate moisture, gunnera leaves turn brown and dry up. Allow 8 feet between plants. Keep soil moist and fertilize two to three times. Gunnera thrives in cool climates and does not perform well in areas where temperatures top 80° F.

RECOMMENDED PLANTS AND RELATED SPECIES: G. *magellanica* has 2-foot-wide, dark green kidney-shaped leaves and is a favorite swampy ground cover. G. *tinctoria* is slightly smaller, at 6 feet tall, and has reddish flowers hidden among the foliage.

Gunnera

GYPSOPHILA PANICULATA

Baby's breath

- Billows of white flowers, summer
- Zones 3–7
- 3 feet × 3 feet
- Full sun
- Sandy, well-drained soil
- Allow to dry down

DESCRIPTION AND USES:
Baby's breath, a ubiquitous component of fresh and dried floral arrangements, is a charming, easy-to-grow addition in the home landscape. Airy and delicate, it makes a gorgeous backdrop for other summer-blooming perennials and is a perfect complement for foxglove or lilies. It is a definite must for the cut-flower garden.

CARE: Plant baby's breath in lean, alkaline soil (add lime if soil is acidic). Space plants 3 feet apart. Support the plants with grow-through stakes. Division is not recommended.

RECOMMENDED PLANTS AND RELATED SPECIES: 'Bristol Fairy' has double white flowers and grows 2 to 3 feet tall. 'Flamingo' is 3 to 4 feet tall and bears double pink flowers. 'Perfecta' (or 'Perfekta') has large double white flowers.

Creeping baby's breath (*Gypsophila repens*) is a wonderful plant for the front border. It reaches only 6 to 12 inches tall and has white to lilac flowers. It is a good edging plant. 'Rosea' is 8 inches tall with pale pink flowers.

'Bristol Fairy' baby's breath

HAKONECHLOA MACRA 'AUREOLA'

Golden grass

- Colorful leafy accent
- Zones 6–8 (Zone 5 with protection)
- 12 inches × 18 inches
- Half sun to shade
- Rich, well-drained acid soil
- Average water

DESCRIPTION AND USES: This ornamental grass is slow to establish but worth the wait, eventually forming a dense mass. Its bright yellow markings light up shady gardens and are smashing with hostas, especially ones with yellow-bordered, dark green leaves. Golden grass develops a pinkish-red color in fall and turns bronze in fall. Plants are clump-forming and don't bloom.
CARE: Grow golden grass in filtered light in a humus-rich, well-drained acid soil. Space plants 12 to 15 inches apart. Trim back faded foliage in early spring to neaten appearance. Avoid heat and drought.

Golden grass

HELENIUM AUTUMNALE

Helen's flower

- Hot-colored blooms, late summer
- Zones 3–8
- 3 to 5 feet × 3 feet
- Full sun
- Lean, moist rich soil
- Continuously moist

DESCRIPTION AND USES:
Helen's flower is a sturdy, adaptable plant native to wet meadows of eastern North America. It grows 3 to 5 feet tall, depending on moisture availability and variety. Plants bloom for 8 to 10 weeks. Helen's flower lends the border a late-summer color boost and combines well with asters or ornamental grasses.
CARE: Space plants 18 to 24 inches apart. Stake taller varieties. Cut back after flowering to keep disease and insects at bay. Divide plants when crowded, usually every other year. Fertilize sparingly.
RECOMMENDED PLANTS AND RELATED SPECIES: 'Moerheim Beauty' blooms rusty red, changing to orange and then gold on 3- to 4-foot-tall plants. 'Rotgold' ('Red and Gold') has red and gold flowers on 3- to 4-foot plants. 'Brilliant' produces large numbers of bronze flowers. 'Wyndley' is only 2 to 3 feet tall with coppery brown flowers.

'Moerheim Beauty' Helen's flower

HEDERA HELIX

English ivy

- Glossy evergreen foliage
- Zones 6-10
- 2 feet tall as a ground cover; as a vine, it can cover almost any structure
- Shade to sun
- Well-drained, rich soil
- Average water to continuously moist

DESCRIPTION AND USES:

English ivy is among the most commonly used ivies. Many cultivars are available, offering a variety of leaf shapes, sizes, and colorings. Most have lobed leaves in various shades of green. Some have variegated leaves or leaves with splotches of gray and white that may turn pink in winter.

Train English ivy on a wall behind a perennial garden. The dark green makes bright colors pop. English ivy trained on wires in a classic pattern is an outstanding accent to the garden.

Use cultivars with special leaf sizes and shapes where they will be noticed and add to the textural display. Yellow and white variegated ivies brighten dark spots. Interplant English ivy with bulbs, such as daffodils and snowdrops. The dark ivy leaves strikingly set off bright yellow and white blooms and hide fading bulb foliage.

CARE: Grow English ivy in well-drained, rich, fairly moist soil. It grows best in shade but once

'Buttercup'

English ivy

established tolerates full sun if kept watered. In hot, dry regions, all ivies require regular watering. Take care to not overwater them in shady areas where the soil is slow to dry.

English ivies root at every node on a stem and can be invasive. When trained on the wall of a building, prune them regularly to keep the new growth from invading windows and doors and from growing under siding and shingles. In gardens, prune regularly to

'Luzii'

prevent ivy from growing where you don't want it.

Propagate English ivy from seed or softwood to semihardwood cuttings. Leaf spots, snails, and slugs may be problems. Plantings may provide a habitat for small rodents.

Any of the cultivars can "revert" or change back to standard green leaves. If a change in growth occurs,

cut it off before it overtakes the original plant.

RECOMMENDED PLANTS AND RELATED SPECIES: 'Anna Marie' has gray-green leaves with cream variegation. Leaves of 'Buttercup' are pale green in shade, yellow in sun, and maroon in cold weather. Those of 'Fluffy Ruffles' are frilled; 'Glacier' has variegated leaves with white edges. 'Maple Leaf' has deeply divided leaves with pointed lobes.

Among the most hardy—to Zone 4—are 'Baltica' (smaller leaves), 'Bulgaria', 'Rumania', 'Thorndale' (heart-shaped leaves with white veins), 'Wilsonii', and 'Ogalalla'.

'Ann Marie'

NOTE: English ivy is considered an invasive plant and banned in some areas, such as along the West Coast.

'Mathilde'

HELIANTHUS X MULTIFLORUS

Perennial sunflower

'Flore Pleno' perennial sunflower

- Yellow flowers in late summer to fall
- Zones 4–8
- 3 to 6 feet × 3 to 4 feet
- Half to full sun
- Moist, well-drained soil with plentiful organic matter
- Continuously moist to average water

DESCRIPTION AND USES:
Perennial sunflower is a dependable back-of-the-border plant that makes a good backdrop for purple coneflower or butterfly weed. It is valued for its late-season effect and statuesque plants. The bright, 3-inch-wide flowers may be single or double. Plants form a sturdy column that is half as wide as it is tall, gradually becoming wider. The growth rate is moderate to fast.

This coarse, upright plant combines well with ornamental grasses, mounded perennials, and flowers, such as black-eyed Susan, fountain grass, chrysanthemum, azure monkshood, blazing star, cardinal flower, and Russian sage.

CARE: Perennial sunflower grows tolerates half sun, heavy clay, and a wide pH range. Provide 50 percent more fertilizer than the average but spread applications out over the year rather than applying it all at once. Pinch the plant several times from midspring to early summer to restrict height. Deadhead to prolong bloom. Double-flowered forms are seedless. Divide plants every three years in fall or spring. Taller varieties may need staking with individual braces or long crutches

Powdery mildew can be a problem in dry soil and in older clumps. Maintain constant moisture and divide every three years in fall or spring to facilitate air circulation within the clump. Other pests include slugs, aphids, and four-lined plant bugs. Stalk borer is an occasional pest.

RECOMMENDED PLANTS AND RELATED SPECIES: 'Morning Sun' is a single-flowered, 5-foot variety. 'Loddon Gold' is fully double, 4 to 5 feet. 'Capenoch Star' is a lighter yellow, 3 to 4 feet.

HELICTOTRICHON SEMPERVIRENS

Blue oat grass

- An ornamental grass with steely blue blades
- Zones 4–7
- 30 inches × 30 inches
- Full sun
- Well-drained, neutral to slightly alkaline soil
- Average water

DESCRIPTION AND USES: This grass looks a little like blue fescue but forms much larger clumps. It has attractive foliage and a beautiful, spiky form. Oatlike flowers on arching stems start off brownish and turn a golden wheat hue in fall.

Grow blue oat grass as a specimen or in mass plantings. An excellent partner for obedient plant or coral bells, the plant has blue-gray foliage that works well in gardens needing a cool-down.

CARE: Blue oat grass grows best in sites with dry soil and excellent drainage. Space plants 2 to 3 feet apart. In late winter, cut plants back by half; divide them every three years. Plants are prone to fungal attack in humid climates. Winter mulch is recommended in areas colder than Zone 5.

RECOMMENDED PLANTS AND RELATED SPECIES: 'Sapphire Fountain' ('Saphirsprudel') has bluer leaves than the species and is more weather-tolerant.

Blue oat grass

HELIOPSIS HELIANTHOIDES VAR. SCABRA

False sunflower

- Yellow flowers early to late summer
- Zones 3–8
- 3 to 6 feet × 2 to 4 feet
- Full sun
- Well-drained soil with plentiful organic matter
- Continuously moist to average water

DESCRIPTION AND USES:

Bright color, large 3-inch flowers, and long bloom time make false sunflower indispensable in informal borders. Plants are clump-forming and fast-growing.

Use false sunflower as a backdrop or partner for shorter, finer-textured mounded, perennials, such as lavender, catmint, peony, and salvia. It is impressive near spiny bear's breeches, blazing star, or speedwell.
CARE: False sunflower tolerates drought, half sun, a wide pH range, and heavy clay soil. It does not do well in wet or poorly drained soil and needs some midday shade in hot regions.

Deadhead to prolong bloom. Plants self-sow; seedlings will be variable and most likely inferior to the original plant. If stems flop, give the plant more sun, improve drainage, or increase water and fertilizer in the early season. Cut plants back in late fall or early spring. Divide them every two to three years to maintain vigor and full bloom; they have offsets.

Powdery mildew may be a problem; increase water and fertilizer. Aphids, leafhoppers, and four-lined plant bugs can disfigure foliage.
RECOMMENDED PLANTS AND RELATED SPECIES: 'Summer Sun' is a soft-yellow double-flower that grows 3 feet tall.

False sunflower

HELLEBORUS ORIENTALIS

Lenten rose

- Cream, green, purple, or pink flowers, late winter to early spring
- Zones 4–9
- 12 to 18 inches × 18 to 30 inches
- Half sun to shade
- Moist, well-drained soil with plentiful organic matter
- Continuously moist to average water

DESCRIPTION AND USES:

An early delight for winter-weary gardeners, lenten rose is one of the finest perennials in cultivation. Its saucer-shaped flowers are 2 to 3 inches wide in nodding or out-facing clusters. Blooms may be multihued; for example, pink petals may be flushed with purple or green. Buds are borne upward over several days as stems elongate. These evergreen, clump-forming plants have lustrous foliage.

Lenten rose complements perennials with ferny, pale foliage or columnar shapes, such as astilbe, bugbane, bleeding heart, Jacob's ladder, and cardinal flower.
CARE: Provide a shady site with moist well-drained soil. Plants do not grow well in wet or poorly drained soil, windy areas, or warm spring weather. They will take dry and alkaline soils. Lenten rose can tolerate, even thrive, in full sun if the climate is cool and plants have ample water during winter.

Supply 50 percent more fertilizer than for average perennials; apply it as new foliage emerges. Plants do not require deadheading, but they may self-sow. The resulting seedlings are often pleasing. Transplant them before the expanding foliage shades them out.

Prune dead leaves in late winter to make way for new growth and flowers. Divide plants in spring; this allow time for plants to reestablish before winter. They may not bloom the following year. Plants seldom need division once established.

Cut back old growth in spring before the plant blooms. In Zones 4 to 5, provide extra protection if snow cover is not reliable.

Pests include slugs, snails, and root weevils. Leaf spot can occur if soil is very heavy or acid. Remove infected foliage and apply fungicide if sanitary measures do not help. Plants are resistant to rabbits and browsing deer.
RECOMMENDED PLANTS AND RELATED SPECIES: Lenten rose is usually available in mixed but unidentified colors. 'Pluto' and 'Dusk' have dark purple blooms. 'Cosmos' is white. 'Royal Heritage' has a mix of colors from white to red.

Lenten rose

HEMEROCALLIS HYBRIDS

Daylily

- White, yellow, red, purple, and all shades in between, late spring or midsummer
- Zones 3–9
- 1 to 2 feet × 2 to 3 feet in leaf; up to 6 feet tall in bloom
- Full sun to shade
- Well-drained soil with plentiful organic matter
- Average moisture

'Silent Sentry'

'Living Color'

'Spiderman'

DESCRIPTION AND USES:

Daylily flowers may be plain or ruffled, striped or bicolored, single or double. Plant heights range from 10-inch minis to 40-inch giants. Some varieties are evergreen; these do best in southern regions. Flowers may skim the top of the foliage or rise several feet. Most plants are clump-forming with a moderate growth rate. Some spread quickly.

Peak bloom time is midsummer, but some cultivars bloom in late spring; others in early, mid-, or late summer. Repeat bloomers have several flushes each year. A few superstars bloom continuously from late spring to fall frost.

Showy but easy, daylilies blend beautifully with most perennials.
CARE: Daylilies withstand heat, drought, shade, salt, foot traffic, flooding, wind, and competition from tree roots. Grow them in full or half sun. They do best in humus-rich, well-drained, and consistently moist soil. Plant daylilies anytime during the growing season, even when plants are in bloom. Leave about 18 inches to 3 feet between plants, depending on the variety. Fertilize regularly but not heavily. Snap off spent flowers at their base. Divide every three to five years, when the number of blossoms declines.

Slugs, snails, and late-spring frost damage make plants vulnerable to disease. Plants attract rabbits, woodchucks, muskrats, and deer.
RECOMMENDED PLANTS AND RELATED SPECIES: Here is a sampler of cultivars; refer to the photographs for more.

Rebloomers: 'Stella de Oro', golden yellow blooms, spring to frost; 'Pardon Me', vigorous, bright red with a yellow throat; 'Happy Returns', lemon-yellow flowers, reblooms in all climates, hot or cold.

'Raging Tiger'

Extended, day-long bloom: 'Daring Dilemma', creamy pink.

Late spring to early summer bloom: 'Siloam Purple Plum' and 'Lullaby Baby', ice pink with green throat.

Early summer: 'Astolat' and 'Coral'.

Mid- to late summer: 'Cherry Cheeks', 'August Flame', and 'September Gold'.

Fragrant flowers: 'Hyperion', lemon-yellow.

Miniatures (small flowers on full-sized plants): 'Golden Chimes'.

'Dot Pierre'

HEUCHERA SANGUINEA

Coral bells

- Red, pink, or white flowers, late spring
- Zones 3–8
- 6 to 12 inches × 6 to 12 inches; 18 to 24 inches tall in bloom
- Shade to full sun
- Well-drained soil with plentiful organic matter
- Average water to continuously moist

DESCRIPTION AND USES:

Loved for its tiny, wiry-stemmed blooms, coral bells are available with striking foliage. Leaves may be ruffled, lobed, or marbled with contrasting veins. The plants grow in clumps at a moderate pace. They work as bedding, edging, and at the front of a border. Coral bells pair with low, mat-forming evergreens.
CARE: Plants compete with tree roots if topdressed with 1 to 2 inches of compost every fall. Deadhead to prolong bloom. In winter, cover plants with loose mulch, such as evergreen boughs, to prevent frost heaving. Root weevils can be serious. Cut away old or damaged foliage in early spring.

RECOMMENDED PLANTS AND RELATED SPECIES:

Varieties with green foliage: 'Chatterbox', large pink flowers, 18 to 24 inches in bloom; 'Firebird', deep red flowers, 18 inches.

Purple-leaf coral bells (*H. micrantha* and *H. americana* hybrids) (Zones 4–9): 'Pewter Veil' has white flowers and silvery leaf edges with areas between veins; 'Chocolate Ruffles', deep maroon leaves; 'Palace Purple', dark purple brown leaves.

Foamy bells (× *Heucherella*), a hybrid of coral bells and foam flower, (Zones 4–9): 'Quicksilver', white flowers, bronze foliage with silver variegation, 18 inches; 'Rosemary Bloom', coral flowers, 1½ to 2 feet.

Coral bells (right), 'Velvet Night' purple-leaf coral bell (above)

HIBISCUS MOSCHEUTOS

Hardy hibiscus

- Pink, red, and white flowers, mid- to late summer
- Zones 5–9
- 3 to 5 feet × 3 feet
- Full sun
- Rich soil with plentiful organic matter
- Continuously moist to soggy

DESCRIPTION AND USES:

With its large, maplelike leaves and gigantic, dark-eyed, dinner-plate-size flowers, hardy hibiscus adds a tropical look. Plants grow at a moderate pace.

They contrast well with vertical plants and perennials with finer texture or smaller flowers, such as Siberian and Japanese iris, blazing star, fleece flower, Joe-Pye weed, tufted hair grass, turtlehead, cardinal flower, great blue lobelia, obedient plant, and culver's root.
CARE: Plants need heat to bloom well. Native to marshlands, they don't tolerate drought. Plants stand up to wind, although the flowers may be shredded.

Apply 50 percent more fertilizer than for average perennials. Divide hibiscus every 7 to 10 years, using a saw to cut sections of woody root. Plants are easy to start from seed; seedlings bloom their first year. Cut plants back in late fall or early spring. Shoots rise from the old stem bases and roots, emerging late in spring. Japanese beetles and caterpillars are the main pests.

RECOMMENDED PLANTS AND RELATED SPECIES:

Disco Belle Series: 9-inch, pink, red, or white flowers on 20- to 30-inch-tall plants. Southern Belle Group: 10- to 12-inch red, pink or white blooms, 3 to 4 feet tall (Zones 5–10). Scarlet rose mallow (*H. coccineus*) grows 6 to 8 feet tall and half as wide, with large red funnel-shaped flowers (Zones 6–9).

Hardy hibiscus

Hostas

- Lilac or white flowers, midsummer; distinctive foliage
- Zones 3–8
- 6 to 30 inches × 6 to 30 inches; 1 to 3 feet tall in bloom
- Half sun to shade
- Well-drained neutral to slightly acid soil with plentiful organic matter
- Continuously moist to average water

'Francee'

DESCRIPTION AND USES:

Hostas have showy gold, blue, green, or variegated leaves that may be puckered, ruffled, or quilted, and vary from oval to oblong, narrow to wide. Lilac or white bells hang from tall stalks that rise above the mound of foliage in midsummer. For most cultivars, the flowers are not the attraction.

Combine hostas with mat-forming perennials or species that have strong vertical lines or fine-textured foliage, such as Japanese anemone, goatsbeard, turtlehead, bugbane, yellow corydalis, fringed bleeding heart, barrenwort, Jacob's ladder, Solomon's seal, meadow rue, and toad lily.

'Great Expectations'

CARE: Hostas tolerate sun if temperatures are cool and water plentiful. Yellow-leafed cultivars are more likely to do well in sun than blue-leaf ones. Alkaline soil is acceptable, but plants do not take drought. Fertilize plants regularly. Divide them every seven to eight years; they grow from offsets and are easy to move. In late fall or early spring, cut down plants and topdress with compost.

Deadheading depends on the species. Some are weak bloomers with floppy flower stems; cut these off before blooms open. Other species have substantial flowers on sturdy stalks. The big, blue-leaf hostas produce more flowers if the season is long and you remove the first blooms before seed sets.

'Albomarginata'

Slugs, snails, rabbits, and deer can ruin hosta foliage. Voles and root weevils may eat the roots. Hostas with thick leaves and quilted surfaces are more resistant to slugs. Under trees that host heavy insect populations, sooty mold may disfigure leaves. Rinse foliage regularly, and plant smooth-leaved hostas, which self-clean better than quilted types.

RECOMMENDED PLANTS AND RELATED SPECIES:

There are many hosta species, ranging from diminutive 8-inch dwarf specimens, such as *H. venusta*, to giants, such as 'Sum and Substance', with its 3-foot-tall, puckered gold foliage.

Here is a sampler of other hosta species: Blue-leaf siebold hostas (*H. sieboldiana*) include 'Elegans', with large leaves in amber fall color, and 'Frances Williams', with large leaves irregularly edged in creamy yellow. 'Great Expectations' has blue edges around a leaf center streaked cream,

'Mediovariegata'

gold, and green. *Hosta nigrescens* varieties have lance-shaped, gray-green foliage. These include 'Krossa Regal', which forms an upright, vase-shaped clump. Its flower stalks rise 3 to 6 feet; attractive seedpods persist through winter.

H. nakaiana varieties include 'Golden Tiara', which has small, heart-shaped leaves edged in gold. The dense, heavy blooming clumps are 8 to 12 inches tall with purple flowers that are barely taller.

Blue hosta (*H. ventricosa*) has large, smooth, shiny foliage and dark purple flowers. Wide, irregular, creamy white edges mark the leaves of 'Aureo-marginata'.

The heavily scented white blooms of fragrant hosta (*H. plantaginea*) are large, like flaring trumpets. Plants bloom in late summer, after most other hostas

'Sum and Substance'

have finished. They are 18 inches tall in leaf, 24 inches in bloom, and 24 inches wide, slowly spreading wider. The light green foliage is more prone to slug and snail damage than others. Hybrids include 'Sugar and Cream', with fragrant, pale lilac flowers and quilted, slug-resistant foliage in Zones 4–9.

HYDRANGEA ANOMALA PETIOLARIS

Climbing hydrangea

- Deciduous vine with creamy white flowers, late spring
- Zones 5–7
- Can reach 30 feet over time, 2 feet wide
- Partial shade to full sun
- Well-drained soil
- Average water

DESCRIPTION AND USES:
Climbing hydrangea is a deciduous vine that provides year-round garden interest. Its creamy white, lacy flowers float against a background of deep green, shiny leaves in late spring. The foliage provides a dark backdrop for the garden during summer. In autumn, the leaves often turn bright yellow before falling. During the winter months, the dark red, peeling bark provides interest and the dried flower clusters, an attractive tan, stand out with a dusting of snow.

Climbing hydrangea will clothe a wall with white flowers and turn a dull structure into a floral masterpiece. It disguises masonry walls. Or grow it as a large shrub. Plant it away from structures and let it pile on top of itself.

CARE: Although it can grow in full sun, climbing hydrangea thrives with at least a bit of shade. Be patient with climbing hydrangea. Even if you purchase a blooming plant, the vine may put all its energy into leafy growth and you may have to wait up to five years to see flowers. The wait is worth it, and the display will generously increase every year.

Little pruning is needed with climbing hydrangea, but trim it away from windows.

Plants have rootlets on their stems, which they use to attach to structures and climb. Propagate climbing hydrangea by taking cuttings.

In early spring, clip off 6-inch-long shoots that have these rootlets. Bury the bottom two-thirds of the cutting. New growth should start by late May.

Pests include Japanese beetles, which can skeletonize the leaves, especially those in full sun.

RECOMMENDED PLANTS AND RELATED SPECIES: 'Brookside Littleleaf' has small (1½ to 2 inches) leaves and is especially attractive in containers. False climbing hydrangea (*Schizophragma hydrangeoides*) has showy white flowers grows 5 feet tall in Zones 6–8. The gray-green foliage of 'Moonlight' is stunning.

Climbing hydrangea

IBERIS SEMPERVIRENS

Evergreen candytuft

- White flowers, midspring
- Zones 3–9
- 6 to 12 inches × 12 to 18 inches
- Full to half sun
- Well-drained, sandy soil with plentiful organic matter
- Average water

DESCRIPTION AND USES:
In spring, evergreen candytuft forms a carpet of white blooms over a mat of fine-textured, dark evergreen foliage. It is particularly attractive trailing over a stone wall. Plants grow at a moderate pace. Evergreen candytuft complements coarse-textured, mounded, or vertical plants and species with winter interest: rockcress, coral bells, iris, and thrift. It blooms at the same time as columbine and catmint.

CARE: Plants are heat tolerant but do not tolerate wet or poorly drained soil. Cut back or shear by one-half after they bloom to promote dense growth, and to keep plants compact. In long, cool falls, plants may bloom lightly. Divide candytuft every four to five years in spring or fall, and add organic matter when replanting. If snow cover is not reliable in cold regions, foliage will desiccate and branches die back. Protect plants in windy, open areas in Zones 3–5 with a cover of twigs or evergreen boughs. Prune any damage in spring.

Candytuft is basically pest-free. Clubroot may infest older plantings in poor soil. Destroy plants and do not grow any mustard family species in that spot for several years.

RECOMMENDED PLANTS AND RELATED SPECIES: 'Alexander's White' is especially dense and free-flowering.

Evergreen candytuft

IMPERATA CYLINDRICA 'RED BARON'

Japanese blood grass

- Brilliant red foliage
- Zones 6–9
- 15 inches × 24 inches
- Full sun
- Moist, well-drained soil
- Continuously moist

DESCRIPTION AND USES: 'Red Baron' (also sold as 'Rubra') grows in 12- to 18-inch-tall upright clumps. In cooler climates, it gets redder as the season progresses. It is not a good choice for hot, dry areas; the farther south this grass is grown, the less its red color is evident.

Mass it with silver-gray plants, such as lamb's-ears, or grow it in containers with other perennials. Its beautiful red color backed by sunlight is unforgettable, as is its excellent fall red color.

CARE: Grow 'Red Baron' in full sun for best color, spacing plants 12 to 15 inches apart.

NOTES: Plants can be invasive. And in some areas, especially warm climates, the sale and distribution of Japanese blood grass is prohibited. Green forms are especially problematic.

Occasionally 'Red Baron' reverts to its green-leaved parent, and those shoots should be eliminated aggressively.

Japanese blood grass

INULA ENSIFOLIA

Sword-leaf inula

- Long-lasting, narrow-petaled yellow flowers, early summer
- Zones 4–8
- 18 to 24 inches × 18 to 24 inches
- Full sun
- Well-drained soil with plentiful organic matter
- Average water

DESCRIPTION AND USES: The plants grow in a dense mound, spreading by short, shallow rhizomes at a moderate growth rate. The fine-textured sword-leaf inula combines with coarse vase-shaped and columnar plants, such as butterfly weed, yarrow, blackberry lily, clustered bellflower, perennial salvia, blue oat grass, blazing star, perennial sunflower, and speedwell.

CARE: Plants tolerate wind but not the combination of high heat and humidity, or wet, poorly drained soil. Shear plants after flowering for repeat bloom. In early spring, cut them to the ground. Divide plants every four to five years in spring or fall; they have offsets and are easy to move. Add organic matter to the soil when replanting. Plants are basically pest-free.

RECOMMENDED PLANTS AND RELATED SPECIES: 'Compacta' grows less than a foot tall and 12 to 18 inches wide.

NOTES: It attracts butterflies.

Sword-leaf inula

IRIS CRISTATA

Dwarf crested iris

- Pale lilac blue flowers, spring
- Zones 3–8
- 6 inches × 12 inches
- Sun to dense shade
- Well-drained soil
- Continuously moist to average water

DESCRIPTION AND USES:
This lovely, lightly fragrant iris naturalizes well and is a native of the Southeast. Its bright green 4- to 6-inch leaves emerge from a rhizome and spread in fan-shaped sprays. One to two pale blue blossoms are produced on each 2- to 3-inch-tall stem. The handsome foliage grows low to the ground, so dwarf crested iris works well as a specimen or a ground cover, spreading to make a low carpet of bloom. Pair it with bleeding heart or columbine. It looks spectacular when massed in drifts in the woodland garden.

CARE: Plant rhizomes or container-grown plants in spring. Moist, well-drained soils are best, but dwarf crested iris will grow in normal conditions with regular watering. Space plants 15 inches apart in partial sun to deep shade or in a site with morning sun. Divide in fall if desired.

RECOMMENDED PLANTS AND RELATED SPECIES: 'Alba' is a handsome white-flowered variety with contrasting yellow crests that is decidedly less vigorous than the species (and also not as common).

'Alba' dwarf crested iris

IRIS ENSATA

Japanese iris

- Cool blues, purples, pinks, and white, late spring or summer
- Zones 5–9
- 3 to 4 feet × 3 feet
- Full sun or partial shade
- Rich, acid soil
- Continuously moist

DESCRIPTION AND USES:
Japanese iris are excellent eye-catchers for wet areas. Beautiful orchidlike flowers top sturdy 3- to 4-foot tall stems (up to 6 feet in rich, boggy soils in mild climates). Plants are a good companion for queen-of-the-prairie.
CARE: Grow Japanese iris in full sun or partial shade (partial shade required in the South). Provide plenty of water when plants are in bloom; conditions can be drier the rest of the year. Although they do well in wet sites, plants must have good drainage over winter. Space plants 18 to 24 inches apart. Apply an acidifying fertilizer occasionally. Plants rarely require division.

RECOMMENDED PLANTS AND RELATED SPECIES: 'Cry of Rejoice' has deep purple flowers with yellow centers. The white blooms of 'Gekkeikan' are edged in purple. 'Loyalty' has violet-blue blooms marked with yellow on the falls. 'Sapphire Star' is an early bloomer with lavender flowers. 'Pink Frost' bears ruffled 8-inch-wide pink flowers.
Yellow flag iris (*I. pseudacorus*) has beardless yellow flowers on stems that grow 2 to 4 feet tall. It thrives in standing water or very moist soil in Zones 5–9.

Japanese iris

IRIS HYBRIDS

Bearded Iris

- Blooms in a number of colors and color combinations, mid- to late spring
- Zones 3–9
- 6 to 18 inches × 18 inches in leaf; 6 to 40 inches tall in bloom
- Well-drained, sandy soil
- Average water; allow to dry down

DESCRIPTION AND USES: Named for the Greek goddess of the rainbow, irises come in almost every color imaginable except true red and often have contrasting beards. Sizes range from 6-inch dwarfs to plants 4 feet or more.

The shortest varieties bloom earlier in spring than taller types, but all peak by early summer. Plants spread by stout rhizomes on or just under the surface.

Combine irises with mounded and finer-textured plants, such as dwarf aster, yarrow, golden marguerite, pinks, threadleaf coreopsis, catmint, cushion spurge, sword-leaf inula, perennial flax, and black-eyed Susan.

CARE: Bearded irises tolerate heat and alkaline soil. They don't do as well in wet soil or shade. Tall cultivars do not stand up to wind. Stake them in windy locations, or where soil is very rich, and after transplanting. Use individual braces.

Deadhead after plants fade to promote growth of new, clean foliage. Divide plants every four years between the time they finish flowering until August. Their rhizomes have multiple eyes; plants are easy to move.

Iris borers can be a problem. They chew between the folds of the foliage down into the root. Iris soft rot follows their feeding and can devastate a planting. Control borers by removing all old foliage every fall and spring. Apply insecticide as necessary in spring when borer damage is first noticed. Divide in early summer when you can easily destroy borer grubs in the roots.

RECOMMENDED PLANTS AND RELATED SPECIES: Cultivars differ mainly by flower color. 'Argentea Variegata' sweet iris (*I. pallida*) has a wide white stripe on each leaf. It is 12 inches tall and up to 18 inches with lilac flowers. The foliage resists borer damage. 'Aurea Variegata' has a wide creamy yellow stripe up each leaf (Zones 3–10).

'Jane Philips'

'Lime Fizz'

'Tomorrow's Child'

'Oktober Fest'

IRIS SIBIRICA

Siberian iris

- Blooms in a broad range of colors, early summer
- Zones 3–9
- 2 to 3 feet × 2 feet
- Full sun to shade
- Fertile, slightly acidic soil
- Average water to continuously moist

DESCRIPTION AND USES:
The flower show begins just after bearded irises finish. Unlike bearded iris, Siberian iris's grasslike leaves stay reliably green and lush all summer long. Plants are lovely at the edge of a pond or grouped with lady's mantle or hardy geranium.

CARE: Grow Siberian iris in full sun or partial shade. It tolerates almost any soil but grows best in moist, fertile, slightly acid soil. Water to keep plants moist during the growing season. Plant rhizomes in early spring or late summer, spacing them 18 to 24 inches apart.

Plants rarely need division. If clumps become crowded or start dying out in the center, divide them in spring or late summer. They'll take time to recover. Siberian iris is less susceptible to iris borer and soft rot disease than is bearded iris.

RECOMMENDED PLANTS AND RELATED SPECIES: 'Butter and Sugar' is 2 feet tall with white standards (upright petals) and yellow falls (lower petals). 'Caesar's Brother' is the classic, a 3-foot tall cultivar with dark violet flowers. 'Fourfold White' is a vigorous white-flowering form. 'Super Ego' is a blue and lavender bicolor. 'My Love' is a rebloomer in the Midwest. Cut old flowering stalks to the ground before seed set to encourage repeat bloom.

'Butter and Sugar' Siberian iris

KIRENGESHOMA PALMATA

Japanese wax bell

- Large yellow bells, fall
- Zones 5–7
- 2 to 3 feet × 3 feet
- Half sun to shade
- Rich, neutral to slightly acid soil with plentiful organic matter
- Continuously moist to average water

DESCRIPTION AND USES:
Japanese wax bell is a textural delight in shade. It forms a coarse, shrubby mound of maple-leaf-shaped foliage. In fall, creamy yellow bells hang from the tips of its stems. Plants grow slowly in clumps. They pair with fine-textured, short, and columnar plants, such as bugbane, astilbe, goatsbeard, meadow rue, yellow corydalis, cardinal flower, and globe flower. They bloom at the same time as azure monkshood and toad lily.

CARE: Japanese wax bell does not tolerate heat or drought. It takes very heavy soil and most other conditions if its moisture needs are met. Foliage may scorch in sun or dry soil.

Deadhead if desired. In Zones 5–6, frost usually ends the bloom period so seed is rarely set. Plants rarely need division, and staking is unnecessary.

Cut plants back in late fall or early spring. Young plants can be mistaken for maple seedlings, so take care to not weed them out.

Japanese wax bell is basically pest-free.

Japanese wax bell

Crimson pincushion with perennial salvia and yellow lilies

KNAUTIA MACEDONICA

Crimson pincushion

- Deep purple-crimson flowers, summer
- Zones 4–9 (Zone 7 east of the Rocky Mountains)
- 2 feet × 2 feet
- Full sun
- Well-drained soil
- Average water

DESCRIPTION AND USES: Crimson pincushion is a lovely addition to the border, the cottage garden, or wild garden. Though a somewhat straggly plant, it is charming with its 2-foot-tall, long-lasting 2-inch flower heads dancing above low foliage on long, wiry stems. Because the flowering stems may fall over, combine it with more sturdy but open plants, such as perennial salvia, that can prop it up. Then its open sprays will float beautifully over other lower plants. Or try it with other airy bloomers, such as baby's breath and Brazilian verbena (*Verbena bonariensis*).

CARE: Grow crimson pincushion in full sun in well-drained soil. It is not terribly tolerant of warm nights. Space plants 18 inches apart.

Plants start out neat and tidy in spring. In fact, you may believe they are spaced too far apart. But as the summer wears on, the plants spread and can become quite floppy, so be sure to choose good companions.

Crimson pincushion is not usually invasive, but it sometimes self-sows. Deadheading prevents reseeding. Divide clumps if they become crowded.

NOTES: The plant attracts butterflies and bees.

KNIPHOFIA UVARIA

Torch lily

- Towering spikes of flamboyant colors, summer to fall
- Zones 5–7 (Zone 4 with winter protection)
- 3 to 5 feet × 3 feet
- Full sun
- Well-drained soil
- Continuously moist

DESCRIPTION AND USES: Torch lily's electric flower spikes stand 3 to 5 feet tall from summer through early fall. It is a showy accent plant, but it's also great for the cut-flower garden. Plant torch lily at the back of the border. If you feel the setting needs a little cool-down, combine it with a blue bellflower, which also covers the coarse, ratty leaves.

CARE: Torch lily performs best in warm climates. Plant it in full sun in moist, well-drained soil, and avoid windy spots. Space plants 18 inches apart.

After flowering, cut back spent flower stems by half. Plants seldom need division.

RECOMMENDED PLANTS AND RELATED SPECIES: 'Alcazar' bears red flowers with a hint of salmon; it is one of the hardiest cultivars and is a good rebloomer. 'Earliest of All' blooms with orange-red and yellow flowers several weeks sooner. 'Ice Queen' has creamy-white flowers on 5-foot-tall plants. 'Shining Sceptre' grows 3 feet tall with golden tangerine flowers. 'Primrose Beauty' is also 3 feet tall and has primrose-yellow blooms.

NOTES: It attracts hummingbirds.

'Primrose Beauty' torch lily

LAMIUM

Dead nettle

- Colorful foliage and pink, white, or rosy blooms
- Zones 3–7
- 6 to 24 inches × 12 to 36 inches

'Pink Pewter' dead nettle

- Shade to dense shade
- Well-drained average soil high in organic matter
- Continuously moist

DESCRIPTION AND USES: Dead nettles have a 1- to 3-foot spread, rapidly filling a bed, then setting seed and cropping up in other parts of the yard. Some are weeds; several are fine ground covers. Plant dead nettle at the front of the border to draw the eye in shady spots.

CARE: Grow dead nettle in a site with cool, moist soil. Space plants 18 to 24 inches apart. They do not tolerate winter moisture or very dry soil and hot weather. Plants are less likely to be invasive in dry soil. Shear or mow them in midsummer. Propagate by seed or by division of runners in winter, early spring or fall. Or take stem cuttings of nonflowering shoots in midsummer.

RECOMMENDED PLANTS AND RELATED SPECIES: 'White Nancy' dead nettle (*L. maculatum*) has mats of silvery green leaves and small snow-white flowers from late spring to summer. 'Pink Pewter' is similar but with pink flowers. 'Chequers' has mauve-pink flowers and white-striped leaves. Yellow archangel (*L. galeobdolon*) has silvery variegated foliage and yellow tubular flowers in early summer. 'Hermann's Pride' is a clump former in Zones 4–8.

LAURENTIA FLUVIATILIS

Blue star creeper

- Light blue flowers, late spring and summer
- Zones 5–10
- 1 to 5 inches × 24 inches
- Sun to shade
- Average garden soil
- Continuously moist

DESCRIPTION AND USES: Blue star creeper has bright evergreen leaves that hug the ground for a mosslike effect. Star-shaped flowers grow scattered across the surface of the foliage in late spring and summer. As the plant blankets the soil, it seems to flow around rocks and pavers. Use it between pavers or stepping-stones, or among rocks.

CARE: In areas with hot summers, blue star creeper can be grown in shade. Space plants 6 to 12 inches apart. Water regularly to frequently in summer, and fertilize monthly from spring to fall.

NOTES: Taxonomists have recently changed the name of this genus to *Isotoma fluviatilis*. When selecting plants for your garden, you may find it under either name.

Blue star creeper

LAVANDULA ANGUSTIFOLIA

English lavender

- Tiny purple spikes, early summer
- Zones 5–9
- 1 to 3 feet × 1 to 3 feet

'Munstead' English lavender

- Full sun
- Well-drained, sandy soil
- Allow to dry down

DESCRIPTION AND USES:
English lavender is a woody perennial for the senses. Both its tiny purple or gray-white flowers and foliage are fragrant. On a warm day, the scent wafts to people standing nearby. The clump-forming plants grow in a mound of gray foliage at a slow to moderate pace.

Attractive companions include taller plants, plants with coarser textures, or blue-green or maroon foliage, such as ornamental mullein blackberry lily, or purple coral bells.

CARE: English lavender tolerates drought, heat, and wind, but not high humidity, wet soil, or poor drainage. Shear plants after bloom to promote density and repeat bloom. In spring, wait until new growth has broken before cutting plants back; don't cut them down completely. Propagate by seed or tip cuttings in spring. Deadheading is not needed, but you may want to harvest flowers for sachet. Plants rarely need division. Four-lined plant bug may disfigure foliage.

RECOMMENDED PLANTS AND RELATED SPECIES: 'Alba' is a small plant with white flowers. 'Munstead' is blue-violet; 'Hidcote Blue', violet. 'Lavender Lady' is a dwarf and repeats bloom.

LAVATERA THURINGIACA

Tree mallow

- Pink or white flowers, all summer
- Zones 6–9 (Zone 7 east of the Rocky Mountains)
- 5 to 7 feet × 4 feet
- Full sun
- Moist, well-drained, fertile soil
- Continuously moist

DESCRIPTION AND USES:
Tree mallow thrives in heat and humidity. Very showy all summer, it is a shrubby plant with funnel-shaped flowers.

Because tree mallow is sizeable plant, use it in a large area; it's not suited for small spaces. The size of the plant also makes it a good companion for other large perennials, such as Joe-Pye weed, plume poppy, or hollyhocks at the back of the border.

CARE: Grow tree mallow in full sun in most areas and in afternoon shade in the South. It thrives in moist, well-drained, fertile soil. Space plants 3 feet apart. Provide ample water. Handpick Japanese beetles, which might become a problem.

RECOMMENDED PLANTS AND RELATED SPECIES: 'Barnsley' sports fringed white flowers that fade to pink, each with a contrasting reddish eye, from June to frost. 'Bredon Springs' has rich pink flowers with white centers.

'Barnsley' tree mallow

LESPEDEZA THUNBERGII

Thunberg bush clover

- Tiny pink, rose, or white flowers, fall
- Zones 4–9
- 3 to 6 feet × 5 feet
- Full to half sun
- Deep, well-drained soil
- Average water

DESCRIPTION AND USES: Tiny, pretty pealike flowers coat the stems of thunberg bush clover. For most of the summer, the strong columnar shape forms an upright accent in the garden. But when the flowers appear, the plant becomes a fountain of bloom. Plants grow in clumps at a slow to moderate rate. They are excellent paired with ornamental grasses and shorter, coarser, mounded plants.
CARE: Thunberg bush clover tolerates drought, heat, wind, and a wide soil pH range. Cut plants to the ground or to live wood in early spring; doing so delays blooming.

Deadhead to prolong bloom; flowers grow as a multicluster. Luckily, bush clover rarely needs division, a difficult task with this plant. It is basically pest-free, but leafhoppers may disfigure foliage in spring and early summer.
RECOMMENDED PLANTS AND RELATED SPECIES: 'Gibraltar' is a floriferous pink-flowered form. In bloom, it arches nearly to the ground.

Thunberg bush clover

LEUCANTHEMUM X SUPERBUM

Shasta daisy

- White daisies, early summer
- Zones 4–8
- 10 to 36 inches × 24 inches
- Full to half sun
- Well-drained soil
- Average water

DESCRIPTION AND USES: This is the classic white daisy with the yellow center that everyone has used to predict love interests. Columnar in bloom, it reverts to a basal rosette when cut back. The size of the plant in bloom depends on the variety.

Shasta daisies are excellent with spiky flowers, such as speedwell, Himalayan fleece flower, 'Purple Rain' salvia, ornamental mullein, and checkerbloom, and other flower shapes, such yarrow, bee balm, globe thistle, bellflowers, and delphinium.
CARE: Plants grow well in alkaline soil. Deadhead to prolong bloom and prevent excessive self-sowing; they have a branched flower stem. Some varieties repeat bloom if cut back before seed is set. Support taller varieties with grow-through stakes. Supply plants with 50 percent more fertilizer than for average perennials.

Divide Shasta daisy every two to three years in fall or spring to maintain the clump's vigor; they have offsets and are easy to move. Discard the oldest, central portion of plant to help control pest buildup—you'll still have many divisions from each clump.

Aphids can be a problem for Shasta daisies. Four-lined plant bug can disfigure foliage just before bloom. Nematodes, crown or stem rot, wilt, and viral infections occur on older plantings and in wet soil. Stalk borer is an occasional pest. Plants are resistant to browsing deer.
RECOMMENDED PLANTS AND RELATED SPECIES: 'Alaska' and 'Becky' are 24 to 30 inches, with sturdy stems and extended bloom period if deadheaded. 'Becky' performs well in hot, humid areas. 'Silver Princess' is a 9-inch-tall dwarf. Double-flowered 'Marconi' is white; it does best in half sun and grows to 30 inches. 'May Queen' (*L. vulgare* 'Maikonigin') is hardier (Zone 3), blooms in midspring, and reblooms after cutting back. It grows 18 to 24 inches. Its stems are thin and can be beaten down by rain.
NOTES: Some references list Shasta daisy as *Chrysanthemum × superbum*.

'Snowcap' shasta daisy

Blazing star

LIATRIS SPICATA

Blazing star

- Bottlebrushes of purple or white, midsummer
- Zones 3–9
- 3 to 5 feet × 2 feet
- Full sun
- Rich soil with plentiful organic matter
- Continuously moist to soggy

DESCRIPTION AND USES:
A favorite native of prairies and wet meadows, blazing star's bold flowers stand tall. Its unique purple or white flowers are beautiful and long lasting, whether in the garden or a vase. The columnar, moderate to slow-growing plants form clumps.

Blazing star partners well with low, mounded plants, grassy foliage, and daisy-shaped flowers, such as those of pearly everlasting, golden marguerite, purple coneflower, geranium, false sunflower, daylily, patrinia, meadow rue, hardy hibiscus, iris, and tufted hair grass.

CARE: Plants tolerate heat and wind. Prevent drought; it causes reduced bloom and leads to early dormancy. Plants are basically pest-free, though voles may eat the cormlike roots during winter. Clip the flowering stem above the larger, basal foliage as blooming finishes. Blazing star self-sows.

Deadhead to prolong bloom and keep plants neat; they have a top-down spike. Tall varieties need staking in average to dry soil. Use individual braces or water more. Cut down plants in late fall or early spring. Divide them in fall or spring every four to five years; blazing star is easy to move.

RECOMMENDED PLANTS AND RELATED SPECIES: 'Kobold', 18 to 24 inches, is lilac-mauve. 'August Glory', 3 to 4 feet, is purple-blue. The flowers of rough gayfeather (*L. aspera*) grow in tufts along the wands, 3 to 6 feet tall. Kansas gayfeather (*L. pycnostachya*), 5 feet tall, is suited to dry soil. Older clumps often need support. Divide every other year.

LIGULARIA

Ligularia

- Cheerful yellows and oranges, mid- to late summer
- Zones 5–8
- 3 feet × 3 feet
- Full to half sun
- Well-drained soil
- Continuously moist

DESCRIPTION AND USES:
Most ligularias stage their best performance in regions with cool nights. Their large, coarse leaves provide drama in the garden. For visual effect, pair ligularias with sedges and golden grass.
CARE: Plant ligularias in full sun in cool regions but in half shade where weather is hot. Soil that is moist but well-drained is essential. Mix in plenty of organic matter. Space plants 2 to 3 feet apart. Water abundantly and feed regularly. Ligularias will wilt, even when soil seems to have plenty of water.

If the soil is moist, they'll recover at sundown. If not, water the plants. Division is rarely necessary.
RECOMMENDED PLANTS AND RELATED SPECIES: Big-leaf ligularia (*L. dentata*) has large kidney-shaped leaves and daisylike flowers. 'Desdemona' has reddish orange, flowers and deep purple leaves. 'Othello' has orange flowers and mahogany red leaves. 'The Rocket' ligularia (*L. stenocephala*) has impressive spikes of bright yellow flowers.

Rocket ligularia

LIMONIUM LATIFOLIUM

Sea lavender

- Lavender flowers, mid- to late summer
- Zones 3–9
- 2 feet × 2 feet
- Full sun to half sun
- Well-drained, sandy soil
- Allow to dry down

DESCRIPTION AND USES: Sea lavender looks lovely massed in seaside plantings, in the midborder, and in fresh or dried cut-flower arrangements. It has a bushy yet see-through habit and airy, flat-topped flower clusters. Its upright stems rise from a clump of big, leathery, green basal leaves that turn bright red in fall.

Pair it with ornamental grasses, yucca, and prostrate rosemary.

CARE: Grow sea lavender in full sun to half sun in well-drained, sandy soil of average fertility. Avoid overfertilizing because that leads to lanky growth that requires staking.

Do not overwater. Standing water leads to root and crown rots. Space plants 18 to 24 inches apart to ensure good air circulation.

Limonium is both salt- and heat-tolerant.

Sea lavender is slow to flower after planting. The second year, the plant may put up three or four stalks, but it may be two to three years before you see the plant fully flower.

RECOMMENDED PLANTS AND RELATED SPECIES: 'Blue Cloud' has lighter blue blooms; those of 'Violetta' are deep violet-blue. Seafoam (*L. perezii*) is a similar but tender perennial useful in beach plantings in California (Zones 8–11).

Sea lavender

LINUM PERENNE

Perennial flax

- Violet, blue-violet, or white flowers, late spring to early summer
- Zones 5–8
- 18 to 24 inches × 12 inches
- Full to half sun
- Well-drained, sandy soil
- Average water

DESCRIPTION AND USES: This charming, airy, vase-shaped plant is a mass of 1-inch flowers. A fast-growing perennial, use it as filler among earlier and later blooming dense-foliaged plants.

CARE: Perennial flax is tolerant of heat, drought, and a wide soil pH range, but it does not perform well in wet or poorly drained soil. Deadhead to prolong bloom. Remove each flower stem when more seedpods are forming below the open flowers than buds developing above them.

Plants are basically pest-free but short-lived. They do self-sow. Division is difficult, and flax may not reestablish. However, seedlings are easy to move. Cut plants back in late fall or early spring.

RECOMMENDED PLANTS AND RELATED SPECIES: 'Alba' has white flowers. Longer-lived than perennial flax, golden flax (*L. flavum*) has butter-yellow flowers on 18-inch stems. 'Compactum' measures 6 to 9 inches. 'Heavenly Blue' (*L. narbonense*), 12 to 18 inches tall, has white-eyed blue flowers.

Perennial flax

Cardinal flower

LOBELIA CARDINALIS

Cardinal flower

- Red spikes, mid- to late summer
- Zones 3–9
- 36 inches × 12 inches
- Full sun to shade
- Rich soil with plentiful organic matter
- Continuously moist to soggy

DESCRIPTION AND USES: Native to wet woods and low meadows, cardinal flower thrives in moist soil. The plants are short-lived, but they self-sow. Tall spikes of brilliant red flowers top 3- to 4-foot stems anchored by a 12- to 18-inch-wide clump of foliage. A fast-growing plant, cardinal flower makes an arresting vertical accent among mounded plants.

CARE: Cardinal flower flourishes in full sun to shade, but, the more sun it receives, the more water it needs. Plants grow in bogs but languish in ordinary soil and average water. They don't tolerate drought. Deadhead to prolong bloom. Divide it every three or four years; it spreads by offsets. Cut plants back in late fall or early spring. Cardinal flower is basically pest-free.

RECOMMENDED PLANTS AND RELATED SPECIES: More tolerant of dry soil, great blue lobelia (*L. siphilitica*) is 2 to 3 feet tall, with spiky midsummer blue blooms; it needs half sun in Zones 4–8. Hybrid lobelia (*L. × speciosa*) reaches a height of 2 to 3 feet and a width of 1 foot; red-violet, fuchsia, pink, white, and blue-violet flowers appear during its long bloom season in Zones 5–8. 'Ruby Slippers' has beet-red blooms; 'Queen Victoria', red flowers and bronze foliage; 'Pink Flamingo, rosy pink blooms.

LONICERA SEMPERVIRENS

Trumpet honeysuckle

'Magnifica' trumpet honeysuckle

- Deciduous vine with attractive red flowers, spring to fall
- Zones 4–9
- 10 to 15 feet tall
- Full sun to shade
- Any garden soil
- Average water

DESCRIPTION AND USES: Tubular, red flowers open in midspring and continue putting on a show until they succumb to heavy frosts in autumn. Although nonfragrant, individual flowers are borne in showy clusters enjoyed by hummingbirds. The flowers are followed by clusters of berries relished by other birds. Leaves are bluish green; the terminal leaf pairs tend to fuse together into one. Plants grow slowly to moderately, eventually reaching 10 to 15 feet.

Plant trumpet honeysuckle on an arch or an arbor, with a small shrub or a perennial at the base to hide its stems. It is terrific trained on a willow trellis and paired with deep purple blooms, such as those of monkshood. Honeysuckle will also climb trellises, chain link fences, bamboo tripods, even a single strand of rope. Place it where you can observe the hummingbirds without disturbing them.

CARE: This vine tolerates shade but blooms best in the sun. It needs average moisture; avoid drought for best results. Aphids are a major nuisance; they attack heavily in the spring. The plant may outgrow them without sprays by early summer. Spraying one or two times with horticultural oil or an insecticide is effective.

RECOMMENDED PLANTS AND RELATED SPECIES: 'Sulphurea' and 'John Clayton' have yellow flowers. 'John Clayton' is a newer selection and seems to be more floriferous and attractive than 'Sulphurea'. 'Magnifica' and 'Superba' have scarlet flowers; 'Cedar Lane' has long (to 2 inches), dark red flowers.

LUPINUS 'RUSSELL HYBRID'

Lupine

- Wide range of flower colors and bicolors, early summer
- Zones 4–6
- 36 inches × 24 inches
- Full sun to half sun
- Rich, well-drained soil
- Continuously moist

DESCRIPTION AND USES:
Lupine produces fabulous, showy flowers They are best massed in beds or when combined with hardy geranium or shasta daisy.

CARE: Species lupines are tough plants, surviving the poorest of conditions. Hybrids are another story. They perform best in light, sandy soil and where summers are cool—not at all in hot, humid summers or wet, cold winters. Provide rich, moist soil and good drainage. Space plants 18 to 24 inches apart. Water during dry periods. Mulch in summer to keep roots cool. Use an airy mulch in winter where snow cover is reliable. Plants do not need staking. Powdery mildew, rust, aphids, and four-line plant bugs can be problems.

RECOMMENDED PLANTS AND RELATED SPECIES:
Gallery Hybrids, a dwarf series, is 15 to 18 inches tall, with blue, pink, red, and white blooms. Minarette Hybrids, also dwarf at 18 to 20 inches, is a mix of colors. 'My Castle' has brick-red flowers on 2- to 3-foot-tall plants. 'The Chatelaine' (Band of Nobles Series) has pink and white bicolor flowers.

Minarette Russell lupine

LYSIMACHIA CLETHROIDES

Gooseneck loosestrife

- Crooked spikes of white blossoms, late summer
- Zones 3–8
- 3 feet × 3 feet
- Full sun to half sun
- Humus-rich soil
- Continuously moist

DESCRIPTION AND USES:
White spikes arch toward one side on 2- or 3-foot-tall stems. The showy blossoms are most attractive in mass planting. Use alone as a ground cover or combine with blue star or balloon flower. Loosestrife is invasive, especially in moist soil.

CARE: Plants grow in moist, humus-rich soil. Space them 15 to 24 inches apart. Divide in spring as necessary to restrain the size of the clump; they have running roots. Plants are pest-free.

RECOMMENDED PLANTS AND RELATED SPECIES: 'Alexander' yellow loosestrife (*L. punctata*) sports variegated yellow and green leaves, with yellow flowers whirled around each stalk. It grows to 2 feet and is not as invasive (Zones 4–6).

Gooseneck loosestrife

MACLEAYA CORDATA

Plume poppy

- Creamy plumes, early summer
- Zones 3–8
- 6 to 10 feet × 6 feet
- Full sun or half sun
- Lean soil
- Average water to continuously moist

DESCRIPTION AND USES: This huge plant, with its 10- to 12-inch airy plumes and hairy, heart-shaped leaves, is impressive for large gardens. Use it as a living screen, the back of an expansive border, or the center of an island bed. Plants are invasive in almost all areas, particularly if soil is rich and moist. It requires plenty of room. Combine it with other equally gigantic plants, such as Joe-Pye weed.

CARE: Plume poppies require little care where room to spread. Plant them in full sun or half sun.

(Plants decline in full shade.) Allow 6 feet between plants. Install a barrier to keep roots from spreading beyond the allotted area if necessary. Staking isn't needed. Divide plants every two years or as needed to reduce crowding among clumps. Watch for leaf spots.

RECOMMENDED PLANTS AND RELATED SPECIES: 'Flamingo' is a pink-flowered variety on gray-green stems. 'Coral Plume' (M. microcarpa) is similar to plume poppy and grows up to 8 feet tall with showy coral-pink blossoms.

'Flamingo' plume poppy

'Fastigiata' hollyhock mallow

MALVA ALCEA

Hollyhock mallow

- Purplish pink flowers, summer to frost
- Zones 4–10
- 3 to 4 feet × 3 feet
- Full sun to half sun
- Well-drained soil
- Average water

DESCRIPTION AND USES: Hollyhock mallow is an easy, handsome plant that brightens the garden for most of the summer. It is free-flowering, tall and bushy with heart-shaped, scalloped leaves and funnel-shaped purplish pink flowers.

Use hollyhock as a summer hedge, or combine with obedient plant or balloon flower.

CARE: Plant hollyhock mallow in any well-drained soil in full sun in most areas and in half sun in hot ones. Space plants 18 inches apart or sow seeds in spring. Cut back their tops 12 inches after the first flush of bloom to promote continued blossoming and prevent self-sowing, which can get out of hand. Division isn't necessary because the plants are short-lived.

Hollyhock mallow is prone to disease problems in hot, humid areas. Avoid overhead irrigation to prevent powdery mildew. Handpick Japanese beetles as necessary. Spider mites may also occur.

RECOMMENDED PLANTS AND RELATED SPECIES: 'Fastigiata' has attractive deep pink flowers well into autumn; it has a more compact, neat, upright form. 'Zebrina' (M. sylvestris) has strong, erect stems and white to pink flowers with raspberry red markings. The flowers resemble pinwheels all summer. The plant is hardy to Zone 5.

MATTEUCCIA STRUTHIOPTERIS

Ostrich fern

- Large, light green fronds
- Zones 2–7
- 3 feet × 3 feet
- Shade to sun
- Any garden soil
- Average water to continuously moist

DESCRIPTION AND USES: If you want the classic fern look, ostrich fern is your choice. It naturalizes beautifully in dappled shade. Unsurpassed for its dramatic fronds that resemble ostrich feathers, this big, bold, vase-shaped perennial spreads rapidly.

It is wonderful growing in a large mass planting and peeking out from between other perennials. However, ostrich fern has a running root and spreads rapidly through an area. In many gardens, it may be too aggressive to combine with other perennials, unless you have the time to dig out the extras.

CARE: Plants grow well in average to moist soil. Although best in shade, ostrich fern will tolerate sun as long as the soil never dries out. Space plants 3 feet apart.

Ostrich fern does not perform well in the hot summers of the South. And its fronds will scorch if the soil becomes too dry, even in shade.

NOTES: The emerging fronds, or fiddleheads, are edible.

Ostrich fern

MISCANTHUS SINENSIS

Maiden grass

- Ornamental grass with large pink or silver plumes in fall
- Zones 5–9, depending on cultivar
- 3 to 7 feet × 3 feet
- Full sun
- Average to heavy soil
- Average water, tolerates drought

DESCRIPTION AND USES: This outstanding grass—valued for its foliage and flowers—forms dense clumps that may be tall and narrow or fountain-shaped. The flowers begin as drooping purple-tinged fans. These open to long, silky spikelets that mature in late summer to dazzling silvery plumes, which last well into winter.

CARE: Maiden grass will flop in shade. It thrives in moderate to wet conditions and is drought-tolerant. Allow 4 to 5 feet between plants. Divide plants as they outgrow their boundaries. Cut them back in early spring. Maiden grass is pest-free.

RECOMMENDED PLANTS AND RELATED SPECIES: 'Gracillimus' grows 3 to 4 feet tall with narrow, curly leaves. It is best in cool areas. Flame grass ('Purpurascens') has orange-red fall color and silvery plumes. 'Morning Light' has white-striped leaves and 4- to 6-foot flower stems. Zebra grass ('Zebrinus') is upright with horizontal yellow bands on the leaves. Porcupine grass ('Strictus') is similar but more erect. 'Adagio' is a dwarf, up to 3 feet tall and wide.

'Gracillimus' maiden grass

MOLINIA CAERULEA CAERULEA 'VARIEGATA'

Purple moor grass

- Ornamental grass with pink flowers in autumn
- Zones 4–9
- 18 inches × 18 inches
- Full sun to half sun
- Acid to neutral soil
- Allow to dry down

DESCRIPTION AND USES:
Native to acid moorlands, this graceful ornamental grass forms dense tufts and is deciduous. This is one of the most popular garden grasses because of its elegant habit and fall beauty. Use it as a ground cover or a specimen.
CARE: Grow purple moor grass in full sun in acid to neutral, moderately moist soil. Space plants 2 feet apart. In southern regions, grow purple moor grass in half sun. Divide plants when the outgrow their boundaries. Moor grasses are deciduous and lose their leaves in fall, so no need to cut them back.

RECOMMENDED PLANTS AND RELATED SPECIES: Tall purple moor grass (M. *caerulea arundinacea*) has fine-textured foliage only 2 to 3 feet tall, but its flowers, appearing high above, arch out 7 to 8 feet high. They make a marvelous gauzy screen in front of a window. 'Skyracer' is 7 to 8 feet tall, with more erect stems and attractive yellow-orange fall color.

Purple moor grass

MONARDA DIDYMA

Bee balm

- Lilac, pink, red, and white flowers, early summer
- Zones 4–9
- 3 to 6 feet × 2 to 4 feet
- Half to full sun
- Well-drained neutral to acid soil with plentiful organic matter
- Continuously moist to wet

DESCRIPTION AND USES: Bee balm is one of the best plants for attracting hummingbirds and butterflies, but it can be invasive. The fast-growing plants are columnar in bloom, a low mat before bloom. They combine well with maiden grass, goatsbeard, astilbe, hibiscus, and others.
CARE: Bee balm doesn't tolerate drought or high humidity. Deadhead to prolong bloom. Stake with grow-through supports or cut plants back one or two times before they bloom. Powdery mildew can be serious; grow only resistant varieties. Four-lined plant bug disfigures foliage.

Divide or remove excess plants every two to three years; they spread by offsets and are easy to move. Cut back in late winter or early spring.
RECOMMENDED PLANTS AND RELATED SPECIES: Mildew resistant cultivars, shades of red: 'Jacob Cline', 'Colrain Red', 'Raspberry Wine'; shades of purple: 'Violet Queen', 'Petite Delight', 'Vintage Wine'; shades of pink: Marshall's Delight'.

'Cambridge Scarlet' bee balm

MUHLENBERGIA CAPILLARIS

Muhly grass

- Vibrant pink to pink-red plumes, late summer
- Zones 6–10
- 1 to 3 feet × 1 to 2 feet
- Full sun to half sun
- Average to poor garden soil
- Average water

DESCRIPTION AND USES: This fine-textured grass is suited for beds or naturalistic settings. It grows 1 to 3 feet tall and even larger in rich soil. In late summer, the grass sends out light purple plumes that fade to gold in the fall. Grow it as an accent or a ground cover; this well-behaved beauty is at home anywhere you would plant an ornamental grass. Its structure adds interest to the winter garden.

CARE: This tough native plant tolerates wet or sandy soil, sunny or partially shaded sites. It is resistant to salt sprays an basically pest-free. The plant rarely needs division.

NOTES: Muhly grass draws butterflies.

Muhly grass

MYOSOTIS SCORPIOIDES

True forget-me-not

- Tiny, baby-blue flowers, mid- to late spring
- Zones 3–8
- 6 to 8 inches × 8 inches
- Half sun to shade
- Well-drained soil, plentiful organic matter
- Continuously moist to wet

DESCRIPTION AND USES: Carpets of tiny, baby-blue flowers with yellow centers characterize this ground-hugging perennial. It grows very fast growth, spreading 18 inches or more per year.

Use it as an edging for the front of gardens. True forget-me-not also works as a pretty spacer under and between moisture-loving half-sun plants requiring good air circulation: bee balm, tall phlox, globe flower, azure monkshood, meadowsweet, and queen-of-the-prairie. Some cultivars can also grow in the water of a pond or stream.

CARE: This plant tolerates some foot traffic but does not do well in heat or drought. It tolerates full sun only if soil is wet or boggy. Staking and deadheading are unnecessary. Cut plants back as desired each spring to keep them within bounds.

Remove oldest portions every three to four years; plants spread by offsets. Mix compost into the soil and allow remaining plants to recolonize the renewed soil.

Though pest-free, plants can succumb to crown rot, which kills patches in mid- to late summer in very hot areas or where soil is dry.

True forget-me-not

NEPETA X FAASSENII

Catmint

- Blue-violet flowers, midspring to early summer
- Zones 4–8
- 18 to 24 inches × 18 to 24 inches
- Full to half sun

'Six Hills Giant' Siberian catmint

- Well-drained soil
- Average moisture

DESCRIPTION AND USES:
An important source of blue for the front of a garden, catmint produces billowing masses of small flowers for several weeks. The fast-growing plants are mounded clump-formers with scented gray-green foliage.

For effect, pair fine-textured catmint with coarser-textured, taller plants, such as bearded iris, yarrow, blackberry lily, obedient plant, purple coneflower, many-flowered sunflower, and balloon flower.

CARE: Catmint tolerates heat, wind, drought, and foot traffic. But it does not perform well in regions with hot, humid summers. It is basically pest-free, though four-lined plant bug may disfigure the foliage.

Deadhead by shearing after spring bloom. Stake with crutches. Divide plants every five to six years to renew vigor; they grow by offsets and are easy to move.

Cut plants back in early spring. They can be cut to the ground in late fall or early spring; if left over winter, the frost-flattened stems and decomposing foliage act as a weed-smothering mulch.

RECOMMENDED PLANTS AND RELATED SPECIES: 'Blue Wonder' has deep blue-violet flowers and is only 12 to 15 inches tall and wide. 'Walker's Low' is even more compact. Later-blooming 'Six-Hills Giant' is 2 to 3 feet tall. If deadheaded, it will bloom from early to late summer. The plant is upright but may flop toward the end of the season. Stake with crutches and pinch for bushiness in spring; or cut back hard after it collapses and let it regenerate in the cool of late summer and fall. Suited to Zones 3–8, it self-sows.

NOTES: Catmint attracts butterflies and beneficial insects. A sterile hybrid, N. × faassenii is sometimes confused at garden centers with look-alike relatives such as N. racemosa, which is a prolific self-sower. Deadhead to reduce seedlings and consider replacing the plants.

OENOTHERA FRUTICOSA

Sundrops

- Yellow flowers, early to midsummer
- Zones 4–9

Sundrops

- 18 to 24 inches × 18 to 24 inches
- Full to half sun
- Well-drained soil
- Average water to continuously moist

DESCRIPTION AND USES:
A fast-growing, upright spreader, sundrops reach their maximum size within one to two years. Yellow flowers sit on sturdy stems. Their basal rosettes are evergreen and turn maroon in cold weather, making sundrops an attractive off-season ground cover.

Combine sundrops with vigorous spreaders of various heights and textures, such as Siberian catmint, 'Fire King' yarrow, daylily, golden marguerite, bloody cranesbill, perennial ageratum, and tall phlox.

CARE: Sundrops are basically pest-free. Deadhead to prolong bloom and to prevent self-sowing. Then when blooming stops, shear plants back by one-third to encourage vegetative growth. Or cut plants back to their rosette. To keep sundrops under control, dig out excess plants annually.

Divide plants in spring or early fall every four to five years. Remove and discard the oldest, central portion of the clump; the plant grows by offsets and is easy to move. Mix a generous amount of compost into the soil and allow outlying plants to recolonize the area.

RECOMMENDED PLANTS AND RELATED SPECIES: The yellow flowers, red buds, and reddish stems of 'Fireworks' are eye-catching. Ozark sundrops (O. missouriensis) is a sprawling plant with large, long-lasting lemon-yellow flowers. Give it rich, moist, well-drained soil in full sun. Though the plant grows less than 12 inches tall, its stems spread 18 inches in Zones 4–8. Showy evening primrose (O. speciosa), 18 inches tall, has enchanting daytime blooms that open white and fade to pink in Zones 5–8. It spreads deep and wide with underground runners and can become a nuisance in rich soil.

OPHIOPOGON JAPONICUS

Mondograss

- Grassy clumps with small lilac flowers, late summer
- Zones 6–10
- 6 to 12 inches × 12 inches
- Sun to half sun
- Moist, humus-rich, well-drained soil
- Average water to continuously moist

DESCRIPTION AND USES:

Not a true grass but resembling ornamental grasses in appearance and behavior, this unusual foliage plant is a standout, especially when contrasted with brighter colors. It spreads slowly and grows about a foot high. It has slender, shiny, dark evergreen leaves and small, tubular flowers on spiky stalks. Small, blue, pea-size fruit follow the blooms. It is a good edging for beds and paths.
CARE: Mondograss prefers fertile, moist, humus-rich, well-drained soil and can be grown in sun or light shade. Mow or cut it back in spring before new growth begins. In full sun, mondograss needs more frequent watering. Divide plants in spring when they become crowded. Mondograss is usually pest-free. Space plants 12 inches apart.

RECOMMENDED PLANTS AND RELATED SPECIES:

Black mondograss (*O. planiscapus* 'Nigrescens') forms clumps of purple-black foliage up to 9 inches tall. It has evergreen leaves and white or lilac flowers.

Black mondograss

ORIGANUM

Ornamental oregano

- Long-lasting purple to pink flowers, late summer
- Zones 5–9
- 12 to 24 inches × 18 inches
- Full sun
- Average, well-drained soil

DESCRIPTION AND USES: A

mainstay of herb gardens, oregano has some lovely vibrant-blooming cousins. Their foliage is fragrant, but not like that of the herb. Use ornamental oregano at the front of beds and borders or let them weave through other perennials.
CARE: Grow ornamental oregano in full sun in average, well-drained soil, spacing plants at least a foot apart. Avoid wet sites; oregano cannot tolerate wet feet. Keep plants tidy and compact by cutting them back by about half in early summer. No need to deadhead the flowers. Some cultivars may need winter mulch to ensure survival in areas colder than Zone 6.

RECOMMENDED PLANTS AND RELATED SPECIES:

'Herrenhausen' (*O. laevigatum*) is one of the most ornamental, with abundant sprays of maroon flowers and reddish purple-tinged foliage. Hybrids: 'Hopleys', 18 inches tall and wide, lavender to deep blue flowers; 'Rosenkuppel', erect form, bright pink to mauve flowers; 'Nymphenburg', 20 inches tall, pink flowers; 'Kent Beauty', small pink flowers with large, showy, bright pink bracts.

'Kent Beauty' ornamental oregano

OSMUNDA CINNAMOMEA

Cinnamon fern

- Stately, tall fronds
- Zones 3–7
- 36 inches × 18 inches
- Shade to full sun
- Acid soil
- Continuously moist to soggy

DESCRIPTION AND USES:
Robust and elegant in form, cinnamon fern is a good choice for sunny, low-lying spots—ideal at the water's edge or where water stands—and for cool areas. Its fertile fronds emerge in spring, changing to cinnamon-brown, hence the name.
CARE: Plant 2 feet apart in light shade or full sun in constantly moist soil. They are pest-free.
RECOMMENDED PLANTS AND RELATED SPECIES: One of the largest garden ferns, royal fern (*O. regalis*) is typically 4 to 6 feet tall but can grow up to 9 feet in wet areas. It's fairly sun tolerant if it receives good moisture.

Cinnamon fern

PANICUM VIRGATUM

Switch grass

- Ornamental grass with airy, dark purple to pink flowers, fall
- Zones 3–9
- 5 feet × 2 feet
- Full sun
- Light, sandy, moist soil
- Average water

DESCRIPTION AND USES:
This native prairie grass makes an excellent fall and winter display. Its blue-green leaves form an upright column that turns bright yellow or red in fall. One of the finest-textured of the grasses, it is beautiful as a specimen or nice as a living screen.
CARE: Switch grass will tolerate half sun, dry sites, and seaside conditions. In shaded sites, it may need staking. Space plants 3 feet apart. Cut them back in late winter. Switch grass is usually pest-free.
RECOMMENDED PLANTS AND RELATED SPECIES: 'Cloud Nine' forms a cloud of seed heads above the foliage, 6 feet tall. 'Haense Herms' has red fall color, 3 to 4 feet tall. 'Heavy Metal' has upright, metallic-blue leaves, turning amber-yellow in fall. 'Rotstrahlbusch' or red switch grass is the reddest variety, 3 feet tall, with flowers, and 4 feet wide. Tall switch grass ('Strictum') has 5- to 6-foot tall blue leaves.

'Heavy Metal' switch grass

PAEONIA LACTIFLORA HYBRIDS

Peony

- White, pink, red, lilac, and bicolor flowers, late spring to early summer
- Zones 4–7
- 3 feet × 3 feet
- Full to half sun
- Deep, well-drained soil with plentiful organic matter
- Average water

DESCRIPTION AND USES:

A stalwart of the perennial garden, peony provides beauty that lasts a lifetime. The large flowers may be single, double, or one of many intermediate forms.

Substantial plants can easily stand alone but look grand surrounded by low-growing, fine-textured perennials. Peonies have long-lasting foliage that serves as background, filler, and support for later-blooming perennials, such as meadow rue, balloon flower, and Japanese anemone.

CARE: Plants tolerate a wide pH range but are not worth growing in lean, dry soil. Their large flowers are almost too heavy for their stems to hold up. Deadhead to reduce the weight; this won't extend bloom or encourage new flowers. Or stake with grow-through supports or hoops in early spring. Fertilize in spring when shoots are emerging.

Divide plants in fall every eight to 10 years to renew the planting and the soil. Plant the divisions so that the large pinkish buds are only 1 to 2 inches below the soil, spacing them 3 feet apart.

Peonies will not flower until plants have been chilled to below 40° F for several months. For this reason, they do not bloom satisfactorily in regions with warm winters.

Botrytis infection is common; dark spots on leaves, purple-brown streaks on stems, and small, dried, unopened flower buds are symptoms. Good sanitation prevents spread of the disease and eventual decline of the plant. Remove all discolored foliage as you see it and clean up all peony foliage in late fall to avoid infecting new shoots as they emerge in spring. Check roots and discard any that are distorted or soft. Spent petals can host botrytis infection.

RECOMMENDED PLANTS AND RELATED SPECIES: Hundreds of beautiful varieties are available.

NOTES: Plants are not wind tolerant.

Peonies add strong color from late spring to early summer.

'Le Jour', single flowers

'Auguste Dessert', semi-double flower

'Bowl of Beauty', anemone or Japanese-shape blooms

'Souvenir de Maxime Cornu', double

PAPAVER ORIENTALE

Oriental poppy

- Red, orange, pink, or white flowers, mid- to late spring
- Zones 3–7 (8 on West Coast)

Oriental poppy

- 3 feet × 2 feet
- Full sun
- Well-drained soil with plentiful organic matter
- Average water

DESCRIPTION AND USES: These fabulous flowers open in mid- to late spring but finish blooming all too soon. Plants grow at a moderate to fast rate. Because they go dormant after blooming, grow them with late-emerging perennials, to cover fading foliage. Oriental poppy pairs well with Japanese anemone, hibiscus, balloon flower, hardy ageratum, Joe-Pye weed, Russian sage, or butterfly weed.

CARE: Avoid sites with high wind or wet soil; oriental poppies do not tolerate those conditions. They need excellent drainage, especially during winter.

Deadhead to keep the planting neat, or allow seedpods to develop to use in dried decorations. Deadheading will not prolong bloom or stimulate a second flowering. Instead, flower formation requires a warm-season dormancy, then a period of chilling. Hence, Oriental poppies do not bloom reliably in areas with warm winters.

Foliage begins growth in mid- to late summer and persists through winter. Do not cut it back in late fall. Leaves resume growth in early spring and are already dying back by early summer to enter a short summer dormancy. You can cut back the foliage of established poppies after bloom or allow it to die back naturally.

Oriental poppy rarely needs division; the forked taproot is hard to move. To propagate or to control the size of a planting, dig the fleshy taproots after flowering. Watch for wilting after moving. Plants will grow from root cuttings as well as from bits of roots left behind in digging. Removing an old clump can involve several seasons of digging out surviving roots.

Oriental poppies are basically pest-free, although they can have problems from spider mites.

PARTHENOCISSUS QUINQUEFOLIA

Virginia creeper

- Vine with bold texture and scarlet fall color
- Zones 3–9
- 5 to 10 feet per year
- Sun or shade
- Heavy, even compacted soil
- Average moisture

Virginia creeper

DESCRIPTION AND USES: Virginia creeper offers bold-textured five-fingered leaves. Dark green during the summer, they turn a brilliant red in fall, if growing in sun. Flowers are inconspicuous; the waxy, blue-black fruit like clusters of small grapes and are borne on red stalks. The fruit and stalks remain showy for several weeks after leaf drop, and are a favorite of birds.

This tough climber grows almost anywhere and on almost anything, forming a solid mass of foliage. The plant wraps its tendrils around structures and plants, and with adhesive discs at the tips of the tendrils, it climbs easily on rocks and masonry.

Use Virginia creeper in a support role in perennial gardens. It is a good choice for covering unsightly walls and giving the garden a standout background. Trailing stems will creep through the garden and provide interesting textural contrast. But don't let them become established.

CARE: Virginia creeper tolerates soil compaction and smog as well as seaside conditions. To control overly vigorous growth, cut unwanted shoots just above a leaf or a bud as often as necessary. The only pest problem is Japanese beetles, and these tend only to attack plants growing in the sun.

RECOMMENDED PLANTS AND RELATED SPECIES: 'Engelmannii' has smaller leaflets than the species but is otherwise similar. 'Monham' (sold as Star Showers) has white, paint-splattered leaves.

Silvervein creeper (*P. henryana*) is similar to Virginia creeper but is less vigorous and has more attractively colored leaves. Instead of forming a dense mass, this plant is open in appearance and lacy in effect. Use it as an accent plant; it is less likely to overwhelm an area, and the leaves are beautiful up close. It goes well with anything pink or rust-colored, such as granite or other pink stones or perennials. Grow it in half sun in the southern portion of Zone 6 to Zone 9.

PATRINIA SCABIOSIFOLIA

Patrinia

- Yellow-green flower clusters, mid- to late summer
- Zones 5–9
- 4 to 6 feet × 2 feet
- Full to half sun
- Well-drained soil with plentiful organic matter
- Average water to continuously moist

DESCRIPTION AND USES: You can count on this plant to bloom with yellow cup-shaped flowers from summer to fall. It goes well with just about everything in a garden. The airy, flat-topped, flower clusters on sturdy stems look like a grouping of chartreuse Queen Anne's lace.

Patrinia is a clump-forming plant that spreads by stolons at a moderate rate. During summer heat, its blooms recall cool spring green. Combine patrinia with perennials that have dense flowers in hot or cool colors, such as ironweed, blanket flower, perennial sunflower, or cardinal flower.

CARE: Plants tolerate wind, heat, drought, and humidity, but not winter-wet soil. They are basically pest-free. Do not deadhead in the first year. For mature plants, dead-heading prolongs flowering, but the jury is out as to whether the developing seedpods are worthwhile. After observing them, decide whether or not to deadhead in future years. Plants will self-sow. Divide them every four to five years to maintain vigor; plants spread by offsets. Cut plants back in late fall or early spring.

RECOMMENDED PLANTS AND RELATED SPECIES: 'Nagoya' grows 3 feet tall and 18 inches wide. The 12- to 18-inch mound of basal leaves is very different in appearance from the feathery stem leaves. Flowering stems arise from established roots, so newer portions of a clump (outer edges) and new transplants may not flower.

Patrinia with Joe-Pye weed in the background

PENNISETUM ALOPECUROIDES

Perennial fountain grass

- Glossy green blades and bottlebrush blooms, late summer
- Zones 5–9
- 3 to 4 feet × 2 feet
- Full sun to light shade in the South; full sun elsewhere
- Well-drained, fertile soil
- Continuously moist

DESCRIPTION AND USES: One of the most useful grasses for flower gardens, perennial fountain grass is a warm-season grass that looks wonderful throughout the year. Its narrow, fine-textured, glossy green leaves form a dense mass that remains green into fall, then changes to rose, apricot, or gold before bleaching almond for winter. In late summer, foxtail-like plumes open green and mature to silvery pink or white. Robust fountain grass combines attractively with black-eyed Susan and with upright perennials.

CARE: Space plants 3 feet apart. Cut plants to the ground in the fall.

RECOMMENDED PLANTS AND RELATED SPECIES: 'Hameln' is smaller and finer than the species fountain grass. It grows 2 feet tall and wide. 'Little Bunny' is very short and suits rock gardens. 'Moudry' is 30 inches tall, with deep green leaves and black flower plumes in fall. 'Cassian' is a dwarf with 12-inch-tall foliage and 24-inch-tall blooms in Zone 6.

Fountain grass

PENSTEMON BARBATUS

Common beard-tongue

- White, pink, red, purple, blue flowers, early summer
- Zones 3–7
- 4 to 30 inches × 12 to 18 inches
- Full to half sun
- Well-drained soil
- Average water

DESCRIPTION AND USES: Beard-tongues include spectacular western wildflowers as well as species suitable for gardens, even in hot, humid regions. The species have tubular scarlet flowers, while hybrids have larger blooms. Until plants bloom, they form a neat mat.

Combine beard-tongues with artemisias, pearly everlasting, peony, Japanese iris, dropwort, cranesbill, feather reed grass, fountain grass, or catmint. Pair dark-stemmed cultivars with pink-flowered daylilies or hardy hibiscus.

CARE: Plants tolerate heat and wind. Avoid sites with wet soil in winter. Space plants 1 to 2 feet apart, depending on the cultivar's mature size. Deadhead to prolong bloom. Divide plants every four to five years to maintain vigor; they have offsets and are easy to move. Plants self-sow. Seedlings are variable but worth watching for.

Cut plants back in late fall or early spring. Well-grown plants can be sturdy and attractive through winter. Seed heads dry well but have an unpleasant smell.

The plants are basically pest-free; leaf spot and nematodes may trouble older clumps.

RECOMMENDED VARIETIES AND RELATED SPECIES: The Prairie Series of hybrids are evergreen in warm regions. 'Prairie Dusk' has clear purple blooms; 'Prairie Fire' is red; 'Elfin Pink' has pink blooms.

'Husker Red' (*P. digitalis*) has cool white flowers arrayed along tall maroon stems in late spring to early summer. Foliage may fade to bronze or green in summer heat; it grows 2 to 3 feet in Zones 2–7

Tender hybrids: 'Garnet', wine-red blooms, 30 inches; 'Sour Grapes', bunched blue-violet flowers, 18- to 24-inches (Zones 7–10).

NOTES: Beard-tongue attracts hummingbirds.

Above: 'Garnet' beard-tongue
Right: 'Sour Grapes' beard-tongue

PEROVSKIA ATRIPLICIFOLIA

Russian sage

- Tiny lavender-blue flowers, mid- to late summer
- Zones 3–9
- 3 to 5 feet × 3 to 4 feet
- Full sun

Russian sage

- Well-drained, lean soil, preferably sandy or gravelly
- Average water, allow to dry out

DESCRIPTION AND USES: Tiny flowers fleck the fragrant gray stems in mid- to late summer. A shrub with lacy gray-green leaves, Russian sage spreads by natural layering; its growth rate is moderate.

Russian sage creates a silvery effect combined with grasses and other large-scale perennials. On sunny summer days, the plant's airy foliage softens the harsh shadows of coarse-foliage plants, such as perennial sunflower, purple coneflower, queen-of-the-prairie, bee balm, showy sedum, and phlox.

CARE: Russian sage tolerates heat, drought, alkaline soil, and wind, but not shade or poorly drained soil. It is basically pest-free.

Fertilize at half the average rate. Deadheading is unnecessary; the bloom period is very long without help. Russian sage may require staking in rich loam or moisture-retentive clay; use grow-through supports or crutches.

Plants rarely require division. They may need protective winter mulch around branch bases in Zones 3–4 if snow cover is not reliable. Cut last year's branches to their base in early spring for upright new growth and better flowering. Propagate any time by cutting through and transplanting layered branches or by taking tip cuttings in summer.

RECOMMENDED PLANTS AND RELATED SPECIES: 'Blue Spire' (also called 'Longin') has deeper violet flowers and grows more upright than the species.

PHLOX PANICULATA

Garden phlox

- White, pink, magenta, or lilac flowers, mid- to late summer
- Zones 4–8
- 36 to 40 inches × 18 to 24 inches
- Half to full sun
- Well-drained soil with plentiful organic matter
- Average water to continuously moist

DESCRIPTION AND USES:

Today's garden phlox is nothing like the muddy magenta plant found in the wild. Hybridizers have developed plants with spectacular blooms and improved disease resistance.

Fast-growing garden phlox pairs well with balloon flower, speedwell, lobelia, turtlehead, checkerbloom, or bush clematis.

CARE: Plants tolerate and wind and a wide pH range, but not drought with extreme heat and high humidity. Apply 50 percent more fertilizer than average. Stake tall varieties with grow-through supports. If stems flop, thin clumps and increase water and fertilizer the next spring. Divide plants every three to four years; they have offsets. Plants self-sow readily; seedlings are usually inferior. Cut plants to the ground in late fall and remove trimmings.

Problems include powdery mildew, spider mites, and nematodes. In spring, thin stems to five or six per clump in order to help control mildew. Remove any discolored growth.

RECOMMENDED PLANTS AND RELATED SPECIES:

Mildew-resistant cultivars include 'David', white blooms; 'Eva Cullum', bright pink with red eye; 'Franz Schubert', lilac-blue with crimson eye; 'Natascha', pink and white; Robert Poore', purple; and 'Starfire', red.

'Pinafore Pink' garden phlox

PHLOX SUBULATA

Moss phlox

- Masses of pink, red, white or lavender flowers, early to midspring
- Zones 2–8
- 6 to 8 inches × 24 inches
- Full sun
- Well-drained, light, neutral to alkaline soil
- Average water

DESCRIPTION AND USES: Moss
phlox is a magnificent low ground cover that blooms lavishly in sunny gardens from early to midspring. When blooming, these creepers are covered with a mass of color. The foliage is prickly and looks like moss. Moss phlox is ideal as a pretty evergreen edging. It also looks good planted around shrubs. The plant pairs well with daffodils.

CARE: Plant clumps a foot apart in full sun in well-drained, light, neutral to alkaline soil. Thin out the clumps whenever they become crowded. Mulch lightly to protect shallow roots, but avoid smothering the evergreen leaves. Shear plants after they bloom. Divide plants as needed to control their spread.

RECOMMENDED PLANTS AND RELATED SPECIES: 'Candy
Stripe' has white flowers striped with pink. 'Emerald Gem' is light pink with a mounding habit. 'Scarlet Flame' is deep red. 'Apple Blossom' has pale-pink blooms. 'Red Wings' is a heavy-blooming rosy red. 'Snowflake' is the showiest white variety.

NOTES: Creeping phlox is the most fragrant of phloxes.

'Red Wings' moss phlox

PHORMIUM TENAX

New Zealand flax

- Ornamental grass with colorful foliage
- Zones 8–10
- 5 to 7 feet × 4 feet
- Full sun
- Deep, fertile, moist soil
- Continuously moist

DESCRIPTION AND USES:
Native to the swamps of New Zealand, this flax grows in clumps and has foliage that may be yellow-green, dark green, red, rust-colored or variegated with many fine stripes.

Grown for dramatic effect and colorful foliage, New Zealand flax has limited adaptability but is great as an annual where winters are cold. It is perfect for planting at the edge of a water garden, as a focal point in the border, or in a container.
CARE: Grow it in a sunny sheltered spot in deep, fertile, moist soil.

Water regularly to keep soil moist. Divide plants in spring.
RECOMMENDED PLANTS AND RELATED SPECIES: 'Aurora' bears
leaves striped with red, pink, and yellow. 'Burgundy' is a deep wine red. 'Purpureum' has a purple-red sheen to its leaves. 'Williamsii Variegated' has wide yellow-veined green leaves. Mountain flax (*P. cookianum*) is a smaller, 3-foot plant with pendulous flowers. It offers a number of

useful varieties from which to choose, including 'Maori' Chief', which has bronze leaves streaked with red and pink.

New Zealand flax

PHYSOSTEGIA VIRGINIANA

Obedient plant

- Spiky pink flowers, late summer
- Zones 3–9
- 3 to 4 feet × 3 feet
- Full to half sun
- Most soils with plentiful organic matter
- Average to continuous moisture

DESCRIPTION AND USES:
The name of this very fast-growing columnar plant derives from the flowers' tendency to remain obediently in place whether pushed left or right. Plants are beautiful but rampantly invasive; the stolons spread underground.

Use obedient plant as a vertical accent near mounded forms, such as cranesbill, catmint, Japanese

anemone, chrysanthemum, Serbian bellflower, hardy ageratum, tufted hair grass, and fountain grass.
CARE: Plants tolerate shade, but flowering is much reduced. Avoid drought. Deadhead to prolong bloom. You may pinch stems several times before midsummer to reduce plant height.

Stake plants in shade, using grow-through supports. Divide plants every two to three years to restrict their spread. Obedient plant has offsets, but watch for wilting after moving the plants. Cut plants to the ground in late fall or early spring.

Plants are basically pest-free, though four-lined plant bug may disfigure foliage.
RECOMMENDED PLANTS AND RELATED SPECIES: 'Summer
Snow' blooms earlier and grows up to 24 inches. 'Vivid', which is deep pink, reaches 18 to 24 inches. 'Variegata', with pink flowers and cream borders on the leaves, grows to 3 feet but at a slower growth rate. The much less aggressive 'Miss Manners' is white, 24 inches tall, and 2 to 3 feet wide.

Obedient plant

PHYTOLACCA AMERICANA

Pokeweed

- White flower spikes, summer to fall
- Zones 4–9
- 6 feet × 4 feet
- Full sun or half sun
- Lean, moist soil
- Continuously moist

DESCRIPTION AND USES:
Traditionally harvested for its young leaves, pokeweed has been relegated to weed status in much of North America. However, some gardeners appreciate the plant for its bold color, size, and form, and its ornamental use is gaining favor.

In midsummer to early autumn, it bears white to pink flowers. In fall, its screaming red stems and glossy black berries are gorgeous. Pokeweed is an expansive plant for large gardens or for naturalizing in woodland gardens.

CARE: Plant in sun or half sun in lean, moist soil. Plant seeds or space plants 2 or 3 feet apart. Support taller species in open sites. Take care to aggressively root out any seedlings that pop up.

RECOMMENDED PLANTS AND RELATED SPECIES: Chinese poke (*P. clavigera*) is less aggressive and tidier. It has oval green leaves with white midribs and long trusses of pink flowers. This species is likely hardy to Zone 6.

NOTES: The berries are poisonous.

Pokeweed

PLATYCODON GRANDIFLORUS

Balloon flower

- Blue stars of deep blue-violet, white, or pink, early to midsummer
- Zones 3–8
- 36 inches × 18 inches
- Half to full sun
- Well-drained soil
- Average water

DESCRIPTION AND USES:
Balloon flower is a real child pleaser with its inflated blue buds that look like expanding balloons. The buds open into cupped five-pointed stars. This clump-forming plant ranges from columnar to vase-shaped. Growth is slow to moderate.

These elegant, fun, and easy plants combine beautifully with almost any perennial. Their texture and vertical profile complements finer-textured and mounded plants, such as artemisia, yellow yarrow, catmint, pearly everlasting, blue flax, or perennial ageratum. Blooms contrast nicely with daisylike flowers, such as sword-leaf inula, and black-eyed Susan.

CARE: Balloon flower is slow to emerge in spring, so be patient. Surround it with early bulbs and take care to not hoe it down. You may need to stake the tallest forms as well as plants in shade and in very hot regions. Use individual braces for each stem. Deadhead to prolong bloom. Delay bloom by pinching all or some of the stems in early summer.

Plants rarely need dividing and are hard to move. Propagate by cutting pencil-thick side roots from the main taproot. The plant self-sows; seedlings are quite variable. Cut plants back in late fall or early spring.

Plants are basically pest-free, but slugs, snails, and rabbits may take their toll on the foliage.

RECOMMENDED PLANTS AND RELATED SPECIES: 'Mariesii', blue-violet blooms, and 'Shell Pink' have a compact size, 18 to 24 inches tall. 'Sentimental Blue' grows less than 12 inches.

Balloon flower

POLEMONIUM CAERULEUM

Jacob's ladder

- Blue-violet or white flowers, mid- to late spring
- Zones 3–8
- 24 inches × 12 inches
- Half to full sun
- Most soils with plentiful organic matter
- Average water to continuously moist

DESCRIPTION AND USES: Blue-violet or white flowers cluster at the stem tips of this clump-forming plant, which grows at a moderate to fast rate. The fine-textured foliage and upright-arching shape complement coarse-mounded hosta, celandine poppy, fringe cups, lady's mantle, big-root cranesbill, lungwort, and globe flower.

CARE: Jacob's ladder tolerates shade and alkaline soil. It does not perform well in heat, humidity, or drought. Provide continuous moisture and good drainage for plants in full sun; be aware that the flowers are more fleeting when exposed to continuous light.

Deadhead to prolong bloom or reduce self-sowing. As flowering falls off, cut back hard to encourage new foliage. Staking may be necessary; use crutches or individual stem supports. Divide plants every three to four years in fall or spring. They spread by offsets and are easy to move. Do not cut them back in fall or spring, as foliage decomposes rapidly over winter. Plants are basically pest-free, but rabbits may browse.

RECOMMENDED PLANTS AND RELATED SPECIES: 'Brise d'Anjou' has cream-edged leaves; it may be reluctant to bloom, but the foliage is so delightful you won't mind. Leafy Jacob's ladder (*P. foliosissimum*) is taller (30 inches) and blooms later; it is attractive with yarrow and coreopsis.

Jacob's ladder

POLYGONATUM BIFLORUM

Solomon's seal

- Narrow, creamy bells, mid- to late spring
- Zones 4–9
- 1 to 6 feet × 1 to 2 feet
- Half sun to shade
- Most soils with plentiful organic matter
- Average water to continuously moist

DESCRIPTION AND USES: Flowers are soon followed by blueberry-like berries; however, it's the arching foliage for which this plant is prized. The narrow, creamy bells hang in pairs along and underneath the stems. The plants form arching columns that lean toward the strongest light. Their growth rate is moderate.

The upright-arching form contrasts with mounded hosta, fringe cups, lungwort, cranesbill, purple-leaf coral bells, heart-leaf brunnera, and bleeding heart.

CARE: Solomon's seal tolerate drought. They do not do well in very hot summers and are likely to go dormant early. Buy the largest container plants you can find. Small ones are slow to develop a presence in the garden.

Deadheading does not prolong or stimulate bloom; it ruins the plant's profile instead. Divide Solomon's seal every five to six years in fall or spring; plants have offsets and are easy to move. Do not cut plants back as foliage and stems decompose quickly in winter.

Solomon's seal is basically pest-free, but slugs and snails may disfigure the foliage. Scorch may occur on foliage exposed to heat, drought, or full sun.

RECOMMENDED PLANTS AND RELATED SPECIES: Small Solomon's seal (*P. biflorum*) grows 18 to 36 inches tall. Great Solomon's seal (*P. commutatum*) may reach 6 feet. Its foliage turns apricot in fall, so the plant becomes a stately, glowing shrub in the shade garden in Zones 3–8.

Foliage of variegated Solomon's seal (*P. odoratum* 'Variegatum') is delicately outlined in ivory, and grows 12 to 24 inches tall and wide in Zones 4–9.

Variegated solomon's seal

POLYGONUM AFFINE

Himalayan fleece flower

- Deciduous vine with a cascade of white flowers, summer
- Zones 4–8
- 9 inches × 12 inches
- Full to half sun
- Most soils with plentiful organic matter
- Continuously moist to soggy

DESCRIPTION AND USES: Pink or red flower buds on spikes turn white as they mature. Because of the long blooming period, red- and white-flowering spikes are mixed across the same plant. This spreading plant has a coarse mat of overlapping leaves and stolons; its growth is moderate to fast.

Use fleece flower as edging or a spacer between larger plants, or where its persistent chocolate-brown foliage will add interest to the winter scene. Plant near thyme, thrift, soapwort, candytuft, or bigroot cranesbill.

CARE: Plants tolerate some foot traffic and shade, but not drought or high heat. They are pest-free.

Deadhead in midsummer to prolong bloom. Divide plants every four to five years in fall or spring to restrict their spread and promote vigor and free-flowering; fleece flower is easy to move.

RECOMMENDED PLANTS AND RELATED SPECIES: 'Superbum' produces pink flowers that age to red. 'Dimity' is more compact, and flower spikes rarely top 6 inches.

Snakeweed, or bistort, (*P. bistorta*) forms a dense, spreading mound of large leaves in difficult, wet, or heavy soil; it reaches 12 to 24 inches in height.

'Superbum' produces large, pink poker flowers 1 to 2 feet above the foliage over a long season in Zones 4–8. If in full sun, it requires continuously moist or wet soil.

Mountain fleece (*P. amplexicaule*) is a spreading mound 4 feet tall with coarse foliage and thin red or pink poker flowers from early to late summer. This plant performs well in heavy and poorly drained soils. 'Firetail' has bright red flower spikes up to 6 inches tall in Zones 4–8.

NOTE: Also known as *Persicaria*.

'Fire Tail' mountain fleece

POLYGONUM AUBERTII

Silver lace vine

- Deciduous vine grown for its cascade of white flowers, late summer
- Zones 4–8
- 10 to 20 feet in summer
- Sun or light shade
- Most soils, including dry
- Average water

DESCRIPTION AND USES: An old-fashioned twining vine, silver lace vine becomes a froth of pearly-white foam when it blooms in late summer. The individual flowers are small but borne in a profusion of lacy clusters. The thin, arrowhead-shaped leaves have a fine texture and are small (under 4 inches long).

Silver lace vine will quickly camouflage a chain link fence. Train it on netting for a perennial garden backdrop. Or use it to cover a pergola or arbor entrance to your garden.

CARE: Grow silver lace vine in sun or light shade. Give it average moisture. It tolerates drought and city conditions.

Silver lace vine blooms on new wood and can be cut back hard in the spring. Tie the stems to their supports as they grow. Vines are quite vigorous, so cut them to the ground every other year to keep them from overwhelming nearby plantings. Plants also spread by underground runners. Dig up any new plants that pop up.

Occasionally Japanese beetles will attack the foliage.

Silver lace vine

Variegated tovara

POLYGONUM VIRGINIANUM

Tovara

- Colorful foliage
- Zones 4–8
- 2 feet × 2 feet
- Half sun to shade
- Any soil with plentiful organic matter
- Average water to continuously moist

DESCRIPTION AND USES:

Tovaras are sturdy, upright plants. The variegated cultivars bring subtle color to a garden with green leaves splashed with yellow and white. Tiny, pink flowers top whiskerlike flower stalks. Plants spread by rhizomes. The rate varies with growing conditions, from slow in dry, lean soil to fast in moist, rich beds.

A good companion for mounded or fine-textured shade plants, grow tovara with hostas, fringe cups, goatsbeard, astilbe, heart-leaf brunnera, bleeding heart, yellow corydalis, and cranesbill.

CARE: Tovaras are drought-tolerant, but don't do well in drying wind. Because foliage is the main show, not the flowers, deadheading is not a priority except to prevent self-sowing. Remove the entire flower stalk.

There's no need to cut down plants in fall or early spring. Its stems and foliage decompose rapidly during winter. Divide plants every three to five years as necessary to restrict spread. Plants have running roots and are easy to move.

Tovaras are basically pest-free.

RECOMMENDED VARIETIES AND RELATED SPECIES:

The variegated cultivars are more attractive than the all-green species, which is nearly impossible to find. 'Variegatum' has white markings on its foliage. 'Painters Palette' is bright green marked with yellow, white, and rusty pink.

NOTES: This species has been recently renamed *Persicaria*.

POLYSTICHUM

Sword, Tassel, and Christmas ferns

- Sturdy evergreen fronds
- Zones 4–10, depending on species
- 1 to 5 feet × 1 to 3 feet
- Half sun to shade
- Moist, well-drained soil
- Continuously moist

DESCRIPTION AND USES: The lustrous green fronds of these tough, pest-free plants captivate gardeners. Pair with woodland perennials, such as bergenia or corydalis.

CARE: Plant container-grown polystichums in spring. Space western sword ferns 3 feet apart; tassel ferns, 1 foot apart; Christmas ferns, 2 feet apart. Water in dry weather. Divide clumps when crowded. Remove brown foliage as new growth emerges.

RECOMMENDED VARIETIES AND RELATED SPECIES:

An important plant for coastal western United States landscapes, western sword fern (*P. munitum*) is 1 to 5 feet and hardy only to Zone 7; divide in fall. Tassel fern (*P. polyblepharum*) has dark glossy fronds and grows 1½ to 2 feet tall and 10 inches wide; use in Zones 6–8. Christmas fern (*P. acrostichoides*), 1½ to 2-feet-tall, grows best in Zones 4–8; divide in spring. The cut fronds are popular for Christmas decorations.

Tassel fern

PRIMULA JAPONICA

Japanese primrose

- Clusters of flowers in a rainbow of colors, early spring
- Zones 5–9
- 6 inches to 36 inches × 12 inches
- Half sun to full sun
- Rich, deep, well-drained soil
- Continuously moist to soggy

DESCRIPTION AND USES:
There are hundreds of primroses, some easy, some difficult, ranging in size from a few inches to 3 feet tall. All are favorites for their early flowers in the woodland.

Japanese primrose is a prolific bloomer with handsome foliage. It is a candelabra primrose, so named for the whorls of blooms arranged around the flower stems, which rise above a clump of foliage.

Primrose is a good choice for planting with other pond-side beauties, such as marsh marigold.

CARE: Plant in light shade in soil that is high in organic matter. An acid soil pH is best. Space plants about 3 feet apart. Abundantly water during dry spells. Mulch heavily to keep roots cool and moist. Plants may go dormant in summer and reappear in fall. Divide every third year after flowering. Slugs and snails may be a problem.
RECOMMENDED PLANTS AND RELATED SPECIES: 'Album', white, grows to 16 inches. 'Carminea' is rose-red; Redfield Hybrids are cold hardy.

Japanese primrose

PRIMULA VULGARIS

English primrose

- Tubular sulfur yellow blossoms, spring
- Zones 4–8
- 6 inches × 8 inches
- Half sun to full sun
- Well-drained soil
- Average water to continuously moist

DESCRIPTION AND USES: This easy-to-grow primrose is the best species for southern gardens. Deep-veined leaves grow in rosettes from which the flowers emerge on 8-inch stems. They look wonderful massed in moist woodland settings.
CARE: Space plants 12 inches apart. Plant in fall for winter bloom in mild-winter regions. Tolerates full sun if soil remains continually moist. Mulch well. Slugs, snails, and spider mites may be a problem.
RECOMMENDED PLANTS AND RELATED SPECIES: Vial's primrose (*P. vialii*) produces spikes of intense blue-violet flowers on leafless stems late in the spring.

English primrose

'Roy Davidson' lungwort

PULMONARIA SACCHARATA

Lungwort

- Blue or pink flowers, early to midspring
- Zones 3–7 (to Zone 8 in the West)
- 15 inches × 15 inches, 18 inches in bloom
- Half sun to shade
- Well-drained soil with plentiful organic matter
- Average water

DESCRIPTION AND USES:
Valued by early herbalists as a cure for lung ailments, the leaves are shaped like lungs and bear white spots resembling those found diseased lungs. Lungwort is an eye-catching sight in shade. Its coarse foliage anchors taller, arching plants, such as Solomon's seal, great blue lobelia, or Jacob's ladder.

CARE: Lungworts tolerate drought and heat but not together. Do not deadhead, as they bloom just once. Plants self-sow and slowly spread by stolons to form weed-smothering colonies. They rarely require division but are easy to move if you do. Do not cut back in fall; the foliage decomposes over winter. Lungworts are basically pest-free, but powdery mildew can develop.

RECOMMENDED PLANTS AND RELATED SPECIES: 'Mrs. Moon' has silver-spotted leaves and pink buds that open to blue blooms. 'Pierre's Pure Pink' has pink-salmon blooms and moderate spotting.

Hybrids: 'Milky Way' has heavily spotted leaves; 'Excalibur', silvery white leaves with a green margin; 'Majesty', narrow, silvery leaves edged in green; 'Roy Davidson', brilliant blue buds and flowers with handsome, narrow, silver-spotted foliage; 'Sissinghurst White', white blooms; 'Bertram Anderson' (*P. longifolia*), violet-blue flowers and slender silvery spotted leaves— a good choice for the South.

RANUNCULUS ACRIS

Swamp buttercup

- Yellow flowers, late spring to midsummer
- Zones 3–7
- 18 inches × 18 inches
- Full sun to shade
- Any moist soil
- Average water to soggy

DESCRIPTION AND USES:
The easiest way to identify a buttercup is to see the shiny yellow flowers. Those of swamp buttercup are arranged in airy masses 3 feet above the mound of foliage.

Swamp buttercups grow quickly and make good filler between larger, later-emerging perennials in troublesome heavy soils and damp, wet areas. Grow them with Siberian iris, Joe-Pye weed, meadowsweet, queen-of-the-prairie, black-eyed Susan, swamp milkweed, tufted hair grass, and turtlehead.

CARE: Plants tolerate salt, a wide pH range, and windy sites. Heat and drought combined are hard on them. Swamp buttercup is a prolific self-sower. Deadhead plants after the first flush of bloom slows by cutting the flower stalks back to their base. The flowers grow in a branched pattern. Plants will rebloom.

Cut swamp buttercup to the ground in late fall or early spring. It rarely needs division; seedlings are always ready to replace any worn-out clumps.

Swamp buttercup is basically pest-free. Powdery mildew can occur where soil is dry.

RECOMMENDED PLANTS AND RELATED SPECIES: 'Flore Pleno' is a double-flowered variety. Its blooms are not as airy as the species.

'Flore Pleno' swamp buttercup

RHEUM PALMATUM

Chinese rhubarb

- Massive fan-shaped leaves; tall red spikes in summer
- Zones 5–7
- 7 feet × 5 feet
- Full sun or half sun
- Fertile, well-drained soil
- Continuously moist

DESCRIPTION AND USES: This ornamental plant grows just as the rhubarb does in the vegetable garden, but it's prettier and bigger— much taller and nearly as wide. It's perfect where you want a tropical or Jurassic Park effect.

With its 2- to 3-foot-wide leaves and colorful stems, Chinese rhubarb is quite imposing. It is perfect as an accent, especially at the water's edge. Or pair it with fine-textured perennials, such as astilbe.

CARE: Plant ornamental rhubarb in full sun or partial shade in fertile, well-drained, moist soil. Space plants 5 feet apart. Spade in compost or other organic matter before planting, and topdress established plants with it each spring.

Supply ample water in dry weather and mulch to conserve moisture. Division isn't necessary unless performance declines.

RECOMMENDED PLANTS AND RELATED SPECIES: 'Atrosanguineum' has emerging red leaves that gradually turn purple, red stems, and a huge stalk topped with a pinkish red plume.

Ornamental rhubarb (*R. palmatum* var. *tanguticum*) produces fan-shaped leaves of rich purple. Its flower color varies among shades of white, pink, and red. Plants grow 5 to 7 feet tall and 6 feet wide.

Chinese rhubarb

RODGERSIA AESCULIFOLIA

Fingerleaf rodgersia

- Large textural leaves, ivory flowers, late spring
- Zones 5–8
- 2 to 4 feet × 3 to 6 feet
- Half sun to shade
- Rich, even heavy soil with plentiful organic matter
- Constantly moist to soggy

DESCRIPTION AND USES: A foliage plant par excellence, fingerleaf rodgersia bears huge bronze-tinged leaves that resemble the fingers on a hand and dense clusters of ivory flowers held high above the foliage.

The slow-growing plants act as a focal point among other coarse-textured species. Use them as specimens or pair them with other clump-forming shade plants, such as hosta, celandine poppy, snakeweed, and tovara. They also complement large, upright plants such as meadow rue, great Solomon's seal, cardinal flower, bugbane, and azure monkshood.

CARE: Rodgersia does not tolerate heat or full sun. Deadheading will not stimulate additional bloom; self-sowing is not a problem. However, deadheading improves the plant's appearance. Cut plants back in late fall or early spring. Division is rarely needed and plants are difficult to move; watch for wilting. Plants are pest-free.

RECOMMENDED PLANTS AND RELATED SPECIES: Flowers of featherleaf rodgersia (*R. pinnata*) are more spread-out along the flowering stalk, and the foliage looks less like a hand. 'Superba' foliage emerges bronze, flowers pale pink.

Fingerleaf rodgersia

Featherleaf rodgersia

RUDBECKIA FULGIDA

Black-eyed Susan

- Gold coneflower-daisies, mid- to late summer
- Zones 3–8
- 24 to 30 inches × 24 to 36 inches
- Full to half sun

'Goldsturm' black-eyed Susan

- Any soil with plentiful organic matter
- Average water to continuously moist

DESCRIPTION AND USES:
The handsome foliage and brassy gold flowers of black-eyed Susan are a sure sign of summer, and every perennial garden should have a few. Plants are in bloom for much of the summer. Fast growing clump-forming plants, they take care of themselves for the most part.

Black-eyed Susan's coarse texture and mounded shape combines well with finer-textured and upright perennials, such as ornamental grasses, ironweed, culver's root, speedwell, Joe-Pye weed, mugwort, false indigo, delphinium, crocosmia, globe thistle, and blazing star.

CARE: Plants tolerate wet and poorly drained soil, wind, salt, and heat. Deadhead them to prolong bloom and keep the plant tidy. Or leave the first sturdy seed stalks for winter interest. If birds do not eat all the seeds over winter, plants will self-sow to the point of being obnoxious. Flowers are on a branched stem. Staking is unnecessary.

Divide plants every four to five years to maintain vigor, size, and quantity of bloom. Plants have running roots and are easy to move.

Cut plants back in late fall or, if leaving seed heads through winter, in early spring.

Black-eyed Susans are basically pest-free. Leaf spot and crown rot may develop in older, crowded clumps.

RECOMMENDED PLANTS AND RELATED SPECIES: 'Goldsturm' (*R. fulgida* var. *sullivantii*) is a lovely compact plant. 'Viette's Little Suzy' is just 12 to 15 inches tall and wide. 'Herbsonne' grows 5 feet tall and has drooping sulfur-yellow blooms with green cones. Giant coneflower (*R. maxima*) has huge blue-green leaves and yellow flowers with prominent narrow cones. It grows 4 to 8 feet tall and 2 to 3 feet wide in Zones 5–9.

NOTES: The plant attracts birds and butterflies.

RUELLIA CAROLINIENSIS

False petunia

- Tubular blue to lavender flowers, spring to fall
- Zones 7–10
- 1 to 2 feet × 1 to 2 feet
- Full sun to partial shade
- Average garden soil
- Average water

DESCRIPTION AND USES:
Non-stop 1- to 2-inch flowers keep coming from spring to fall. Flowers are borne at the end of long, arching stems.

False petunia is a nice addition to beds, borders, and wildflower gardens. It also does well around water gardens.

CARE: Plants are basically pest-free and easy to care for. Propagate them by cuttings, seeds, or division.

NOTES: Also called *Ruellia hybrida*, the plant attracts hummingbirds and butterflies.

False petunia

SALVIA X SUPERBA

Perennial salvia

- Violet or blue-violet flowers, late spring to early summer
- Zones 4–7
- 1½ to 2½ feet × 1 to 2 feet
- Full to half sun
- Well-drained soil
- Average water

DESCRIPTION AND USES:
Perennial salvia is one of the showiest and longest-blooming of the cold-hardy salvias. Its flowers bloom in densely packed, narrow spikes. Plants grow in a clump at a moderate to fast growth rate.

Use perennial salvia to blend small and large mounded plants, such as candytuft, dwarf aster, and fountain grass, or to contrast with rounded blooms like those of yarrow.
CARE: Plants are tolerant of heat, drought, and a wide pH range. They don't do well in high humidity with heat. Deadhead as aging flower stalks begin to lean; flowers are a standard spike. As the flower stalk is bloomed out, cut it just above the main foliage mass. New flowering shoots develop near stem base. Plants self-sow. Divide them every four to five years to rejuvenate

'May Night' perennial salvia

clump. Plants have a forked taproot which is increasingly resistant to division with time. Cut back in late fall or early spring. Perennial salvia is basically pest-free. Four-lined plant bug may disfigure leaves.
RECOMMENDED PLANTS AND RELATED SPECIES: Dozens of hybrids are available, including 'May Night', indigo blue, and 'East Friesland', deep purple.

'Superba Rose' perennial salvia

SAPONARIA OCYMOIDES

Rock soapwort

- Rose-pink flowers, mid- to late spring
- Zones 3–7
- 6 to 9 inches × 18 inches
- Full to half sun
- Well-drained soil
- Average water

DESCRIPTION AND USES: Rock soapwort is a great perennial for softening the hardscape. Let the bloom-covered trailing mat spill over walls or creep over a brick pathway. It is a good companion for sedum, coral bells, fountain grass, blue oat grass, lavender, 'Silver Mound' artemisia, rockcress, thrift, and big-root cranesbill.
CARE: Plants do not tolerate wet or poorly drained soil or hot, humid summers. Shear them after they bloom to promote density, make the plant neater, and reduce self-sowing. Self-sown volunteers are almost always available to save you the trouble of division. Divide rock soapwort in spring as desired. They have a running root; watch for wilting after moving. Plants are basically pest-free.

RECOMMENDED PLANTS AND RELATED SPECIES: 'Rubra Compacta' is red-violet and not as wide-spreading.

Rock soapwort

Pincushion flower

SCABIOSA CAUCASICA

Pincushion flower

- Blue-violet, pink, or white flowers, early to midsummer
- Zones 5–7
- 24 inches × 18 inches
- Full to half sun
- Well-drained sandy soil with plentiful organic matter
- Average water to continuously moist

DESCRIPTION AND USES: The blue-violet, pink, or creamy white flowers look like wide lace trim around a pincushion. Wiry flower stalks rise up to 30 inches above the mostly basal foliage. Plants grow at a moderate rate.

Because flowers float far above their own insubstantial foliage, combine them with more substantial plants, such as 'Silver Brocade' artemisia, pearly everlasting, perennial bachelor's button, chrysanthemum, and Russian sage.

CARE: Pincushion flower is tolerant of wind and a wide pH range. It does not do well in high heat, high humidity, poor drainage, or wet soil.

Deadhead to prolong bloom, cutting first to side branches with flower buds, then removing the entire flowering stem. The plant readily self-sows, enough to become a weed. Seedling flower color varies. Divide plants every three to four years to maintain good flowering and overall vigor; they spread by offsets and are easy to move.

Pincushion flower is basically pest-free. Four-lined plant bug may disfigure the foliage, and rabbits may browse.

RECOMMENDED PLANTS AND RELATED SPECIES: 'Fama' has large deep blue blooms, 18 inches. New cultivars of small scabious (*S. columbaria*) are more compact, 18 inches, and produce more flowers over a longer period: 'Butterfly Blue' and 'Pink Mist' bloom from May to October if deadheaded.

SEDUM SPECTABILE

Sedum

- Broccoli-like heads of pink, rose, or white, late summer
- Zones 3–8
- 12 to 24 inches × 24 inches
- Full sun
- Well-drained soil with plentiful organic matter
- Average water

DESCRIPTION AND USES: One of the most popular perennials for its foolproof nature and long-season effect, stonecrop is a clump-forming, fast-growing perennial. Good companions include salvia, yarrow, ornamental mullein, golden marguerite, or bellflower.

CARE: All sedums tolerate wind, heat, and high humidity but not wet soil or poor drainage. They are basically pest-free, but aphids or leaf spots can be a problem. Staking is not needed unless clumps are overcrowded or overfertilized. When temperatures reach 70° F in late spring, pinch stems to promote density, or use grow-through supports. Divide plants every four years for thick stems and heavy flowering; it grows by offsets. Leave spent blooms for winter interest. Cut off old stems in early spring.

RECOMMENDED PLANTS AND RELATED SPECIES: Hybrids: 'Autumn Joy' blooms later and has denser flowers with richer color. 'Vera Jameson' is 9 to 12 inches tall with bronze foliage and rose flowers. 'Atropurpureum' has bronze-purple foliage and rose-red flowers.

'Autumn Joy' sedum with New York aster

SEMPERVIVUM TECTORUM

Hen and chicks

- Evergreen succulent foliage with a unique texture
- Zones 4–10
- 1 to 4 inches × 9 inches
- Sun to partial shade
- Any well-drained soil
- Average water to allow to dry down

DESCRIPTION AND USES:

Hen and chicks, sometimes called houseleeks, form ground-hugging rosettes of tough, succulent leaves. The rosettes may be 6 inches in diameter.

Clusters of red, purple, white, or yellow flowers rise above foliage on 15-inch stems. They are a good choice for using in rock gardens, on gentle, dry slopes, or under trees.

CARE: Hen and chicks are adaptable to most soils, even infertile ones, as long as the site is well-drained. They tolerate drought. Water plants occasionally in the heat of summer. Remove dead rosettes to make room for new growth.

Propagate hen and chicks from seed or division. To divide, simply separate the offshoots. Space the plants about 6 to 8 inches apart.

RECOMMENDED PLANTS AND RELATED SPECIES:

'Atropurpureum' has dark violet leaves. Leaves of 'Royanum' are yellow-green tipped with red. 'Sunset' has orange-red leaves. 'Triste' has reddish brown foliage. A naturally occurring variety of of hen and chicks, S. t. calcareum, has broader leaves tipped with reddish brown. The leaves of cobwebbed houseleek (S. arachnoideum) are connected by "cobwebs" at their tips; bright red flowers bloom in July.

Hen and chicks

SIDALCEA MALVIFLORA

Checkerbloom

- Rose, pink, or white hollyhock-shaped flowers, early summer
- Zones 4–9
- 2 to 5 feet × 1 to 3 feet
- Full to half sun
- Well-drained soil with plentiful organic matter
- Average water to continuously moist

DESCRIPTION AND USES:

Looking a little like a hollyhock, checkerbloom has spikes of 2-inch single flowers in rose, pink, or white. It forms a mound of foliage that is topped by tall, straight, unbranched stems. Plants grow at a moderate rate.

Use checkerbloom as a short, vertical element to contrast with mat-forming plants, such as lamb's-ears, soapwort, thyme, silver and woolly speedwells, Serbian bellflower, or pinks.

CARE: Checkerbloom dos not tolerate drought or a combination of heat and humidity. Plants are basically pest-free, but slugs and Japanese beetles may be a problem. Supply plants with 50 percent more fertilizer than the average.

Deadhead for prolonged bloom and neater plants. Flowers are a multicluster; clip their stems to just above a large lower leaf when the stem has more spent blooms than flower buds.

Stake with grow-through supports when necessary.

Divide plants every three to four years to renew vigor; they have offsets. Cut plants back in late fall or early spring.

RECOMMENDED PLANTS AND RELATED SPECIES: 'Party Girl'

has light pink flowers and grows to 30 inches. 'Brilliant' is deep rose and also 30 inches.

Checkerbloom

SISYRINCHIUM STRIATUM

Blue-eyed grass

- Yellow blooms, early summer
- Zones 3–10
- 1 to 2 feet × 1 to 2 feet
- Full to half sun
- Moist well-drained soil
- Continuously moist

DESCRIPTION AND USES: Blue-eyed grass is a charming, floriferous perennial whose foliage looks like that of a gray-green iris. Use it as you would irises.

CARE: This beauty is tougher than it looks and can take many garden conditions, including strong wind. Deadhead to prevent self-sowing. Supply 50 percent more fertilizer than the average. Propagate by seed and division.

RECOMMENDED PLANTS AND RELATED SPECIES: Narrow-leaf blue-eyed grass (*S. angustifolium*) has delicate blue flowers with yellow centers, and grasslike pale foliage. A clump-former, it grows in a bog garden with other moisture-lovers. *S. atlanticum* is similar to it.

Blue-eyed grass

SOLIDAGO HYBRIDS

Goldenrod

- Great summer to fall color
- Zones 4–8
- 12 to 36 inches × 12 inches
- Full sun
- Well-drained soil
- Allow to dry down

DESCRIPTION AND USES: Wrongly reputed to cause hay fever, this plant is a lovely addition to a perennial garden. It combines wonderfully with daisy-type flowers, which bloom at the same time, and especially well with aster or boltonia. Use goldenrod as a cut or dried flower.

CARE: Plant it in full sun in well-drained soil. Space plants 18 inches apart. Water in dry weather. Division is seldom necessary.

RECOMMENDED PLANTS AND RELATED SPECIES: 'Golden Baby' is 1½ to 2 feet with golden yellow blooms. 'Peter Pan' is bright yellow and stands 2 to 3 feet tall. 'Fireworks' (*S. rugosa*) has yellow flowers and red-tinged foliage. Seaside goldenrod (*S. sempervirens*) reaches 6 feet tall in Zones 3–11; true to its name, this plant thrives near the ocean in sandy soil, wind, and salt spray.

Goldenrod

SPODIOPOGON SIBIRICUS

Graybeard Grass

- A bamboolike ornamental grass
- Zones 4–8
- 3 feet (5 feet in flower) × 3 feet
- Full sun to shade
- Well-drained soil
- Continuously moist

DESCRIPTION AND USES:
Also known as frost grass, graybeard grass has bold, dark green foliage that becomes brown with streaks and tinges of deep purplish red in autumn. Its fan-shaped form and long-lasting flowers make it perfect as a single specimen, planted in a group, or in masses.

Graybeard grass looks wonderful with late-season perennials, such as aster and stonecrop. Or, place it in front of evergreens that will highlight its airy flowers. Flowers and foliage look lovely in cut arrangements.

CARE: Plant graybeard grass in full sun or light shade. It will also grow in deeper shade but may require staking. Space plants 4 feet apart.

Graybeard grass is not fussy about soil, but it prefers moist and well-drained sites. It performs best with regular watering or rainfall. Cut plants to the ground when foliage withers after frost.

Graybeard grass

STACHYS BYZANTINA

Lamb's-ear

- Silvery foliage
- Zones 4–8
- 4 to 6 inches × 12 to 18 inches
- Full to half sun
- Well-drained, sandy soil
- Average water

DESCRIPTION AND USES: This low, tufted grass is prized for its 6- to 12-inch long fuzzy-velvet foliage. It offers spikes of tiny lilac-pink flowers in early summer, which people either love or hate.

Plants quickly grow into medium-textured gray mat that is useful for edging beds. The foliage contrasts well with deep greens and blues, such as soapwort, thrift, and 'Vera Jameson' sedum.

CARE: Lamb's ears do not tolerate high humidity, especially in hot areas, wet soil in winter, overly rich soil, or heavy fertilization. The foliage will rot in these situations.

Fertilize at half the average perennial rate. The plant is not grown for the flower, so deadhead as flowering stems appear or grow a nonflowering cultivar, such as 'Silver Carpet' or 'Big Ears'.

Divide plants every three to four years to restrict spread and renew the soil beneath the original planting; they have a running root and are easy to move. Plants are basically pest-free; flea beetle may chew foliage.

RECOMMENDED PLANTS AND RELATED SPECIES: Big betony (*S. macrantha*) is a neat 1- to 2-foot mound of pebbly gray-green leaves with pink, white, or violet flowers on wiry 4- to 5-inch stems. Deadhead to keep plant attractive. Don't prune for winter; cut back in early spring (Zones 3–8).

'Big Ears' lamb's-ear, also known as 'Countess Helene von Stein'

STIPA GIGANTEA

Giant feather grass

- Fine-textured blades and golden flowers, early to midsummer
- Zones 6–10
- 2 feet (foliage) to 6 feet (flowers) × 3 feet

- Full sun
- Light, well-drained soil
- Average water

Giant feather grass

DESCRIPTION AND USES: The golden flowers of giant feather grass, sometimes called needle grass, rise above clumps of 2-foot-tall foliage. In warm areas, plant with late-blooming perennials, such as aster, so they can fill the gap if the cool-season grass turns browns in heat. This grass is excellent in a mixed border. It's best used alone or as a focal point (a specimen plant). The flowers make fantastic bouquets.

CARE: Plant giant feather grass in full sun in light, well-drained soil. Allow 3 feet between plants. Water regularly. It can stand hot, humid conditions and some drought; it does not survive waterlogged soil in winter.

RECOMMENDED PLANTS AND RELATED SPECIES: Mexican feather grass (*S. tenuissima*) has a more fluid look with silky June flowers. It is heat-tolerant and hardy to Zones 7–10.

STOKESIA LAEVIS

Stokes' aster

- Blue-violet, white, or violet flowers, mid- to late summer
- Zones 5–9
- 1½ feet (in flower) × 1½ feet

- Full to half sun
- Well-drained, sandy soil with plentiful organic matter
- Average water

Stokes' aster

DESCRIPTION AND USES: This southern native is a fashionable, long-blooming garden subject, attractive to butterflies. Short, fine petals make up its large, daisylike blooms. Plants are clump-forming and grow at a slow to moderate pace. They combine well with fine-textured companions, such as thyme, artemisia, candytuft, and lavender.

CARE: Stokes' aster does not tolerate drought. Deadhead it to prolong bloom; flowers are on branched stems. After deadheading, only the basal foliage remains. Divide to renew plant vigor every four to five years; plants grow by offsets. Do not cut back for winter. Stokes' aster is basically pest-free.

RECOMMENDED PLANTS AND RELATED SPECIES: 'Blue Danube', blue flowers; 'Omega Skyrocket', white to lilac flowers on stems double the normal height.

STYLOPHORUM DIPHYLLUM

Celandine poppy

- Golden-orange flowers, mid- to late spring
- Zones 4–8
- 18 inches × 12 inches
- Half sun to shade
- Any soil with plentiful organic matter
- Average water

DESCRIPTION AND USES:
Celandine poppy brings gray and gold into the woodland garden. It has gray-green foliage is spangled with yellow flowers in spring. Plants are clump-forming and grow at a moderate to fast pace. Pair celadine poppy with yellow corydalis, gold-variegated hostas, purple-leaf coral bells, 'Brunette' fragrant bugbane, golden grass, Jacob's ladder, columbine, or Serbian bellflower.

CARE: Plants do not tolerate heat or sun. They are basically pest-free. Deadhead them if desired (branched flower cluster), although it's doubtful that will extend the bloom season. Plants self-sow. Transplant them to fill in the bed or weed them out. Division is not needed, nor do you need to cut plants back in spring or fall; foliage decomposes over winter.

NOTES: Celandine poppy may be confused with greater celandine (*Chelidonium majus*), a weed that spreads aggressively by seed.

Celandine poppy

TELLIMA GRANDIFLORA

Fringe cup

- Tiny green cups on long stalks, midspring
- Zones 5–8
- 8 inches × 21 inches
- Half sun to shade
- Well-drained soil with plentiful organic matter
- Average water to continuously moist

DESCRIPTION AND USES: This dense-mounded evergreen perennial makes a fine edging for a shade garden and a gray-green point of contrast among forest greens, bronzes, and blue greens. Its tiny fringed green cups bloom on wiry, naked stems. They age to pinkish green by midspring. Plants grow in a clump at a moderate rate.

Combine fringe cups with blue-leaved hostas, columbine, meadow rue, fringed bleeding heart, dwarf goatsbeard, heart-leaf brunnera, dropwort, purple-leaf coral bells, bugbane, barrenwort, or astilbe.

CARE: Fringe cup tolerates drought and competition from tree roots. It does not do well in wet soil, high humidity, and heat, especially when combined, or with poor drainage.

Deadhead to keep plants neat, unless self-sowing is important for naturalizing. The bloom is a standard spike. Topdress plants with 1 to 2 inches of compost every fall or very early spring. Divide plants every four to five years to maintain vigor and renew the soil; they grow by offsets. Mix compost into the soil when replanting.

Plants are basically pest-free. They are slug-resistant but root weevils may be a problem.

RECOMMENDED PLANTS AND RELATED SPECIES: 'Purpurea' has more flower stalks and distinctly pink flowers.

Fringe cup

Wall germander

TEUCRIUM CHAMAEDRYS

Wall germander

- Shiny green foliage and pink or purple flowers, summer to fall
- Zones 4–9
- 8 to 12 inches × 12 to 24 inches
- Sun to partial shade
- Well-drained soil
- Tolerates drought

DESCRIPTION AND USES: Wall germander has evergreen leaves and bell-shaped, tubular flowers that appear summer to fall. Growth is rapid by spreading underground root systems.

Use it as a dwarf hedge, especially around knot gardens or in other formal settings. Wall germander is also a good choice to use as an edging plant, or to incorporate in rock gardens and low-maintenance sites, or to plant in hot or dry settings.

CARE: Plants grow best in any well-drained soil and full sun, but they tolerate and even thrive in sun, heat, and poor, rocky soil. They are also drought-tolerant and easy to maintain once established. Space plants 18 to 24 inches.

Occasionally water in summer; don't overwater. Shear straggly plants to encourage bushy, compact growth. The plants tolerate heavy pruning but are weakened by it.

Propagate wall germander by seed or terminal cuttings.

RECOMMENDED PLANTS AND RELATED SPECIES: 'Nanum' is a dwarf cultivar. 'Variegatum' has leaves variegated with creamy markings. 'Prostratum' is a ground-hugging cultivar.

THALICTRUM ROCHEBRUNIANUM 'LAVENDER MIST'

Meadow rue

'Lavender Mist' meadow rue

- Pale lavender flowers, midsummer
- Zones 4–7
- 3 to 5 feet × 2 feet
- Full sun to shade
- Rich soil with plentiful organic matter
- Continuously moist to average water

DESCRIPTION AND USES: This meadow rue is a splendid background plant, but it looks best planted in groups of three. The medium to fine texture is fairly insubstantial. Airy pale lavender flowers top the columnar, clump-forming plant in midsummer.

In shade, grow meadow rue for height; in moist sunny sites, for its fine texture. Pair it with hostas, goatsbeard, astilbe, lungwort, rodgersia, and Japanese wax bell in the shade. Grow it with Joe-Pye weed, hardy hibiscus, swamp milkweed, snakeweed, and culver's root in sunny spots.

CARE: The more sun, the more water the plant needs. Meadow rue does not tolerate heat and humidity or drought. It is basically pest-free, although powdery mildew is sometimes seen when conditions are dry. There is no need to deadhead; seed heads are almost as decorative as flowers. The plant may need staking where light is strongly one-directional or soil is dry. Stake individual stems.

Divide after five to six years to renew vigor; divide sooner if decline in height or bloom is noted. The plant has running roots and is hard to move. Watch for wilting after moving. Cut plants back in late fall.

RECOMMENDED PLANTS AND RELATED SPECIES: Tall meadow rue (*T. dasycarpum*) is more drought-tolerant. It blooms in late spring, growing 4 to 7 feet tall. It self-sows. New foliage may have purple highlights. Columbine meadow rue (*T. aquilegifolium*) grows 2 to 3 feet tall and flowers in late spring in Zones 4–8; in bloom, it's like an upright baby's breath for the shade. In Zones 5–8, yellow meadow rue (*T. delavayi*) has lilac flowers with creamy yellow stamen and blue foliage. It grows 4 to 6 feet tall. It has a spreading root and requires staking.

THYMUS SERPYLLUM

Mother of thyme

- Evergreen foliage; white, pale pink or violet flowers, late spring to early summer
- Zones 5–8
- 1 to 8 inches × 12 to 24 inches
- Full sun
- Well-drained soil; prefers sandy soil where winters are wet
- Average water

DESCRIPTION AND USES: From late spring to early summer, these fragrant evergreen mats are covered in tiny flowers. Plants spreads by natural layering and can form large dense colonies. They grow at a moderate to fast pace.

Mother of thyme—and all thymes—makes a fine edging with four-season interest. Or use it as an accent petticoat for larger, vase-shaped, bare-ankle perennials, such as golden thyme, butterfly weed, sweet iris, and speedwell. Mother of thyme's foliage is a good foil for thrift or lamb's-ears. Use it around purple-leaf perennials, such as coral bells, 'Vera Jameson' sedum, and purple sage. Or pair it with other thymes to great a tapestry of color.

CARE: Plants tolerate half sun, shade from deciduous trees as well as light foot traffic, drought, wind, and heat. They are basically pest-free. Fertilize at half the average rate. Shear or mow plants after they bloom to promote density.

Divide mother of thyme every three to four years to renew vigor; they have running roots and are easy to move. Cut out sections, fill the void with compost and sand, then allow perimeter plants to recolonize. Don't cut back hard in fall.

RECOMMENDED PLANTS AND RELATED SPECIES: Many varieties have silver or gold variegation and distinctive scents, such as lemon and nutmeg.

Mixed thymes

TIARELLA WHERRYI

Wherry's foam flower

- White to pink flowers, midspring
- Zones 3–8
- 6 to 12 inches × 18 inches
- Shade to half sun
- Well-drained soil with plentiful organic matter
- Average water
- Tolerates light foot traffic

DESCRIPTION AND USES: Wherry's foam flower (*T. wherryi*) is a lovely small, clump-forming woodland flower. It is aptly named after its foamy clusters of creamy white flower spires. Plants spread 12 inches or more by shallow under- or aboveground stolons, growing at a moderate to fast rate.

They are especially pretty with bleeding heart and offer evergreen winter interest. Pair them with Lenten rose, barrenwort, Serbian bellflower, dropwort, or candytuft.

CARE: Plants tolerate light foot traffic, but not drought. Divide plants every three to four years to reduce their spread; they have offsets. Deadhead clump-forming types to prolong bloom; standard spike. To maintain the vigor of clump-forming types, topdress with compost in late fall. Do not cut plants back in fall.

Foam flowers are basically pest-free; root weevils may be a problem.

RECOMMENDED PLANTS AND RELATED SPECIES: Allegheny foam (*T. cordifolia*) flower spreads by stolons, making a great evergreen ground cover for shade gardens. Many attractive cultivars of both foam flowers are available, with more being introduced every year. 'Dark Eyes' has leaves marked with burgundy; 'Tiger Stripe', light green leaves with red veins.

'Oakleaf' wherry's foam flower

TRACHELOSPERMUM JASMINOIDES

Star jasmine

- Dense evergreen vine covered with white flowers, late spring and early summer
- Zones 8–10
- 15 feet or more
- Shade to half sun
- Well-drained soil
- Allow to dry down

DESCRIPTION AND USES:
Plant this one for your nose. Star jasmine's star-shaped, white tubular blossoms have an intense fragrance. The plant is a vigorous vine that climbs by twining.

Plant jasmine near a patio or anywhere you will enjoy it in the evening, when the flowers stand out with their whiteness and fragrance.

Use as an upright accent in your garden by training it to cover a trellis or arbor. Or grow it to cover and disguise a chain link fence.

In cold regions, grow star jasmine in a container that you winter over indoors. It can be trained on a cage of green mesh.

CARE: Star jasmine vine does best in shade but will tolerate half sun. Provide moderate moisture with good drainage. For the most part, it is not troubled by pests.

RECOMMENDED PLANTS AND RELATED SPECIES:
'Japonicum' has white-veined leaves that turns bronze in autumn and winter. 'Minimum' has mottled leaves and a dwarf habit.

Star jasmine

TRADESCANTIA

Spiderwort

- Purple, blue, pink, and white flowers, spring to fall
- Zones 3–9
- 1 to 2 feet × 3 feet
- Full sun to partial shade
- Well-drained soil
- Continuously moist

DESCRIPTION AND USES:
This foolproof perennial produces abundant, showy three-petaled flowers in a variety of colors from spring to fall. It has grasslike leaves that are nice spilling over the side of a woodland path. Plants do well in moist areas. Pair it with rose mallow, obedient plant, Japanese iris, or columbine for an attractive contrast of textures.

CARE: Spiderwort prefers full sun to partial shade and moist, well-drained soil. After its first bloom in late spring, cut the plant back hard for fresh leaves, more flowers, and a tighter form. Keep it well watered, particularly in sunny locations.

RECOMMENDED PLANTS AND RELATED SPECIES:
Andersoniana Group cultivars: 'Isis', rich blue flowers; 'Concord Grape', intense purple flowers and blue-green foliage; 'Purple Dome', dark purple flowers; 'Sweet Kate', yellow foliage and dark blue blooms; 'Osprey', white with a magenta-pink center; 'Hawaiian Punch', large magenta blooms. 'Caerulea Plena' (*T. virginiana*), double, dark blue flowers.

'Little Doll' spiderwort

TRICYRTIS HIRTA

Toad lily

- White flowers, late summer to fall
- Zones 4–9
- 2 to 3 feet × 2 feet
- Shade to half sun
- Well-drained soil with plentiful organic matter
- Continuously moist to average water

DESCRIPTION AND USES: This is one of the most interesting flowers for the shade garden, particularly in late summer or fall. That's when the purple-dotted, orchidlike flowers appear at each leaf axil. Until then, the plant's graceful, arching stems add an interesting textural note to the garden.

Toad lily's height varies with growing conditions. Plants grow at a moderate to fast growth rate. They are a good contrast for plants with mounded shapes and fine textures, such as dwarf goatsbeard, hostas, and barrenwort. They bloom at the same time as Japanese wax bell and late-flowering Japanese anemones.

CARE: Toad lilies do not tolerate heat, drought, drying wind, or full sun. In cold areas, plant them in half sun rather than deep shade to speed growth and ensure flowering before frost. Apply 50 percent more fertilizer than average. Plants need neither deadheading or staking, even in rich, moist soil. Let stems arch outward as the season progresses to better display the flowers that are borne along the stems.

Divide plants every four to five years to restrict spread and renew plant vigor. They grow by offsets and are easy to move. Mix compost into the soil before replanting. No need to cut toad lilies back in fall or early spring.

The stems and foliage decompose quickly over winter.

Toad lilies are basically pest-free. Rabbits and deer may sample the foliage. Leaf scorch is typical of plants stressed by heat, including reflected heat and sun. Leaf spots may disfigure foliage. Choose anthracnose resistant cultivars, such as 'Togen'.

RECOMMENDED PLANTS AND RELATED SPECIES: Formosa toad lily (*T. formosana*) blooms in mid- to late summer. It has spotted, dark violet flowers (Zones 5–9).

Toad lily

TROLLIUS X CULTORUM

Globe flower

- Lemon yellow globes, midspring
- Zones 4–7
- 2 to 3 feet × 3 feet
- Half sun to shade
- Rich soil with plentiful organic matter
- Continuously moist to soggy

DESCRIPTION AND USES: Globe flower offers beautiful accents in spring. Its blooms are layered globes of lemon-yellow to orange, like large, double buttercups. They rise high above the mounded shiny foliage on strong, nearly leafless stems. Plants are clump formers and grow at a moderate rate.

Plant globe flower with celandine poppy, fragrant bugbane, yellow corydalis, dropwort, golden grass, and lungwort.

CARE: The plant tolerates a wide pH range as well as full sun and wind if soil is well drained and kept constantly moist. It does not do well in drought or where the growing season is very hot. Supply 50 percent more fertilizer than for average perennials. Deadhead after bloom for neat appearance; the plant has branched flower stems. Plants rarely need division. Basically pest-free, globe flower can suffer from powdery mildew where the soil is dry.

RECOMMENDED PLANTS AND RELATED SPECIES: Orange globe flower (*T. chinensis*) is later blooming and taller, reaching 3 to 4 feet by midsummer in Zones 4-8.

Globe flower

VERBASCUM HYBRIDS

Ornamental mullein

- Cream, yellow, or pink flowers, early to midsummer
- Zones 5–8
- 18 to 24 inches × 18 to 24 inches; flowering stems 36 to 48 inches tall
- Full sun
- Well-drained, sandy soil
- Average water to allow to dry down

DESCRIPTION AND USES:
A forgotten perennial just finding a spot in North America gardens, ornamental mullein has outstanding flower spikes that shoot up from a broad rosette of coarse leaves in early summer. Its coarse gray foliage complements blue foliage and contrasts with finer textures. Try it with blue oat grass, fountain grass, cushion spurge, yarrow, aster, mums, threadleaf coreopsis, and catmint.

CARE: Plants are resistant to wind, drought, and heat. They do not do well in high humidity, wet soil, or poor drainage.

Deadhead as seedpods begin to swell at the base of the flowering stalk (flowers are a standard spike). Mulleins are short-lived, so leave the last flowering stalk of the season to self-sow.

Fertilize at half the average rate. Ornamental mullein should not require staking. But if stems flop, cut back on fertilizer or move plants to where they will get more sun. Do not divide ornamental mulleins. To propagate them, take root cuttings in second spring.

In fall, remove the last flower stalk once seed has ripened, but do not cut down basal foliage in fall. Mulleins are basically pest-free.

RECOMMENDED PLANTS AND RELATED SPECIES: The Cotswold Group of cultivars offer a wide range of flower colors.

Ornamental mullein.

VERBENA

Creeping verbenas

- Summer-long purple flowers
- Zones 6–10
- 1 foot × 3 feet
- Full sun
- Well-drained soil
- Continuously moist

DESCRIPTION AND USES:
An easy plant for all-season blooms, creeping verbenas look great cascading over a rock wall, or in a rock garden. There are dozens of cultivars and species. Most form a glossy green, foot-tall mat of foliage that spreads out 3 feet or more. They are suitable for edging, growing as a ground cover, or potting in containers.

CARE: Plant creeping verbena in full sun, spacing plants 18 inches apart. A moist, well-drained soil is essential. You don't need to deadhead plants, but trim them back to keep them looking neat in early spring. Plants are prone to aphids, whiteflies, slugs, snails, and spider mites.

RECOMMENDED PLANTS AND RELATED SPECIES: Rose verbena (*V. canadensis*) has red or pink blooms. 'Homestead Purple', large, dark velvety purple blossoms; moss verbena (*V. tennuisecta*), lavender flowers; 'Sissinghurst', bright pink blossoms with lacy foliage. Brazilian verbena (*V. bonariensis*) bears tiny purple-blue flowers on 3- to 4-foot-tall, wiry stems from summer to fall. It's hardy in Zones 7–10 but reseeds delightfully for year-to-year effect in colder zones.

'Rosea' rose verbena

VERNONIA NOVEBORACENSIS

New York ironweed

- Dark purple and red-violet flowers, mid- to late summer
- Zones 5–8
- 3 to 7 feet × 1 to 2 feet
- Full to half sun
- Well-drained soil with plentiful organic matter
- Average water

DESCRIPTION AND USES: For late-season color, few perennials match New York ironweed. It is a wonderful backdrop plant with large, flat-topped flower clusters that is as at home in informal beds and borders as a wildflower garden. Plants are upright, columnar, or vase-shaped. They have a moderate growth rate.

New York ironweed's coarse, dark green foliage complements ornamental grasses, perennial sunflower, purple bush clover, culver's root, black-eyed Susan, patrinia, and hardy hibiscus.

CARE: Deadheading is not necessary. The tallest plants may require staking; use grow-through supports or individual braces. Stems can be pinched several times between spring and early summer to promote density and reduce height.

New York ironweed is long-lived. Divide plants after seven to eight years to maintain vigor and free flowering. They grow by offsets and are easy to move. Cut back plants in late fall or early spring.

RECOMMENDED PLANTS AND RELATED SPECIES: There are many ironweed species ranging widely in height, color, and size of flowers and leaves. Ironweed is relatively new to gardens and most plants currently on the market are hybrids of uncertain parentage. Watch for growers to begin to sort out and name the many selections. All the species have garden value, so grow any variety you find.

NOTES: It attracts butterflies.

New York ironweed

VERONICA LONGIFOLIA

Long-leaf veronica

- Blue spikes, midsummer
- Zones 4–8
- 24 to 36 inches × 18 inches
- Full to half sun
- Well-drained soil with plentiful organic matter
- Average water

DESCRIPTION AND USES: Veronica is excellent in the middle of a border, ia rock garden, or a clump as a specimen plant. Plants form a columnar clump, growing at a moderate pace.

Use long-leaf veronica as a vertical accent for mounded plants, such as catmint, fountain grass, bloody cranesbill, and black-eyed Susan. The foliage complements artemisia, tufted hair grass, and thyme, while the flower spikes are beautiful paired with yellow daylilies or contrast with round blooms.

CARE: Long-leaf veronica is wind-resistant, but does not tolerate drought, wet soil, or high humidity. Deadhead to prolong bloom; flowers are standard spikes. Divide plants every four to five years to maintain vigor and free flowering; they have offsets. If staking is necessary, use grow-through supports or crutches. Cut plants back in late fall or early spring. Leaf spot and mildew can be problems.

RECOMMENDED PLANTS AND RELATED SPECIES: 'Blue Giant', with lavender-blue flowers, is 3 feet tall. Alpine speedwell (*V. alpina*) is a 4- to 8-inch-tall, mat-forming, spring-blooming miniature. 'Goodness Grows', long-lasting blue, grows 12 inches. Spike speedwell (*V. spicata*) has blue, pink, or white blooms. 'Sunny Border Blue', a hybrid with dark blue blooms, reaches 18 to 24 inches.

Long-leaf veronica

VERONICASTRUM VIRGINICUM

Culver's root

- White to pale pink spires, midsummer
- Zones 4–8
- 4 to 6 feet × 1 to 2 feet
- Half to full sun
- Moist soil with plentiful organic matter
- Constantly moist to average water

DESCRIPTION AND USES:
Culver's root is a giant architectural perennial made for the back of the garden. It grows in clumps at a moderate rate. Use it to provide a vertical accent for mounded plants, such as hardy hibiscus, bachelor's buttons. Its spiky flowers contrast well with those of black-eyed Susan, yarrow, and Joe-Pye weed.
CARE: Culver's root does grow well in hot climates. It may require staking when growing in average to dry soil; use crutches or grow-through supports. Deadhead to prolong bloom. Cut plants back in late fall or early spring. Plants are basically pest-free.

RECOMMENDED PLANTS AND RELATED SPECIES: 'Roseum' flowers have a pink flush.

Culver's root

Sweet violet

VIOLA ODORATA

Sweet violet

- Violet, rose or white flowers, spring
- Zones 5–8 (Zone 7, east of Rockies)
- 6 to 8 inches × 12 inches
- Half sun to shade
- Humus-rich soil, moist
- Continuously moist to average water

DESCRIPTION AND USES:
This is the sweet-smelling violet of literature. Unsurpassed for fragrance, sweet violet is wonderful for naturalizing in the woodland garden or for bordering a path.
CARE: Sow seeds in fall or space plants a foot apart in spring.
RECOMMENDED PLANTS AND RELATED SPECIES: Bird's-foot violet (*V. pedata*), one of the prettiest natives, is heat hardy (Zones 5–8). Labrador violet (*V. labradorica*) has mauve flowers in spring and sporadically the rest of the summer (Zone 3–8). 'Arkwright Ruby' (*V. cornuta*) has 1-inch, dark-eyed maroon flowers; it reblooms if deadheaded (Zones 6–9). Hybrids include 'Rosina', long-blooming pink, and 'Royal Robe', vibrant purple.

YUCCA FILAMENTOSA

Yucca

- Creamy white summer bells
- Zones 4–9
- 2 to 6 feet × 3 feet
- Full sun
- Sandy, well-drained soil
- Drought-tolerant

DESCRIPTION AND USES: Yucca brings a romantic Southwest accent to the garden. The flowers are fragrant and the leaves are evergreen. Huge flower stems rises 3 feet or more above spiky foliage.
CARE: Yuccas are the original easy-care plant. Space them 3 feet apart. Remove spent flowers and tattered older leaves for better appearance. Use a leaf blower to clean up any accumulated debris.
RECOMMENDED PLANTS AND RELATED SPECIES: 'Variegata' has green-and-yellow-striped leaves. 'Bright Edge' bears leaves with yellow edges. *Y. filifera* has smaller leaves. Soapweed (*Y. glauca*) is the hardiest yucca (Zones 3–10).

'Golden Sword' yucca

USDA PLANT HARDINESS ZONE MAP

This map of climate zones helps you select plants for your garden that will survive a typical winter in your region. The United States Department of Agriculture (USDA) developed the map, basing the zones on the lowest recorded temperatures across North America. Zone 1 is the coldest area and Zone 11 is the warmest.

Plants are classified by the coldest temperature and zone they can endure. For example, plants hardy to Zone 6 survive

where winter temperatures drop to –10° F. Those hardy to Zone 8 die long before it's that cold. These plants may grow in colder regions but must be replaced each year. Plants rated for a range of hardiness zones can usually survive winter in the coldest region as well as tolerate the summer heat of the warmest one.

To find your hardiness zone, note the approximate location of your community on the map, then match the color band marking that area to the key.

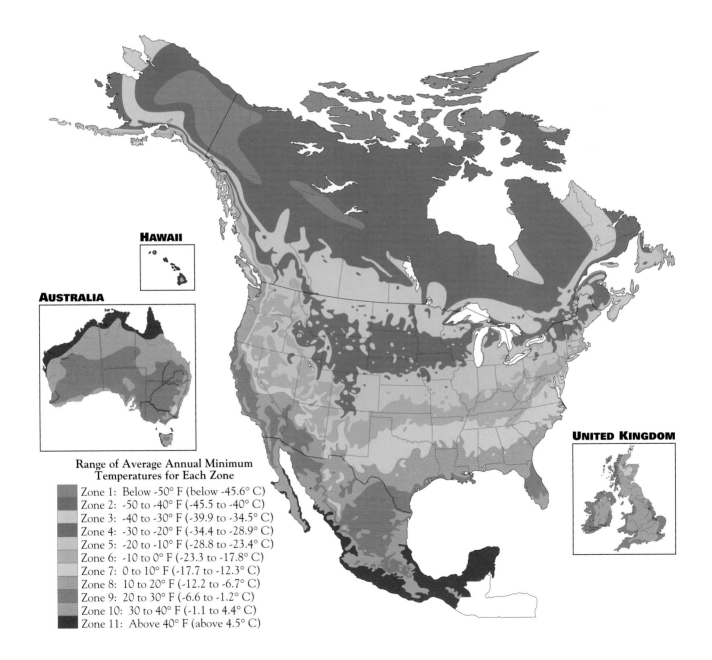

Range of Average Annual Minimum Temperatures for Each Zone

Zone 1: Below -50° F (below -45.6° C)
Zone 2: -50 to -40° F (-45.5 to -40° C)
Zone 3: -40 to -30° F (-39.9 to -34.5° C)
Zone 4: -30 to -20° F (-34.4 to -28.9° C)
Zone 5: -20 to -10° F (-28.8 to -23.4° C)
Zone 6: -10 to 0° F (-23.3 to -17.8° C)
Zone 7: 0 to 10° F (-17.7 to -12.3° C)
Zone 8: 10 to 20° F (-12.2 to -6.7° C)
Zone 9: 20 to 30° F (-6.6 to -1.2° C)
Zone 10: 30 to 40° F (-1.1 to 4.4° C)
Zone 11: Above 40° F (above 4.5° C)

RESOURCES

PERENNIAL PLANTS

Bluestone Perennials, Inc.
7211 Middle Ridge Road
Madison, OH 44057-3096
800-852-5243
www.bluestoneperennials.com
Mail-order and Internet source
of perennials and shrubs

Cooley's Gardens
P.O. Box 126-PE
Silverton, OR 97381
503-873-5463
800-225-5391
www.cooleys gardens.com
Mail-order and Internet source
of bearded irises

High Country Gardens
2902 Rufina Street
Santa Fe, NM 87507-2929
800-925-9387
www.highcountrygardens.com
Mail-order and Internet source
specializing in drought-tolerant
plants

Jackson & Perkins
1 Rose Lane
Medford, OR 97501
800-292-4769
www.jacksonandperkins.com
Mail-order and Internet source of
perennials, roses, and Dutch bulbs

Klehm's Song Sparrow Perennial
    Farm
13101 E. Rye Road
Avalon, WI 53505
800-553-3715
www.songsparrow.com
Mail-order and Internet source of
peonies, hemerocallis, hosta, and
newer perennials

Monrovia
888-Plant-It or 888-752-6848
www.monrovia.com
Wholesale grower and distributor
of container-grown plants under
the Monrovia brand, including
300 patented varieties and cultivars
exclusive to Monrovia

Northstar Nurseries, Inc.
13450 Willandale Road
Rogers, MN 55374-9585
763-428-7601
www.northstardaylilies.com
Mail-order and internet source of
    daylilies for Northern Gardens

Paradise Garden
474 Clotts Road
Columbus, OH 43230
614-893-0896
www.paradisegarden.com
Mail-order source of new and hard-
to-find daylilies, hostas, irises,
peonies, roses, grasses, perennials,
and herbs

Proven Winners
www.provenwinners.com
International marketing cooperative
dedicated to developing and field
testing new hybrid plants sold under
the Proven Winner brand. The
emphasis is on finding colorful, fast-
growing, vigorous, versatile annuals
and perennials.

Spring Hill Nurseries
110 West Elm Street
Tipp City, OH 45371-1699
812-537-2177
www.springhillnursery.com
Mail-order and Internet source of
perennials, roses, trees, and shrubs

Van Bourgondien
245 Route 109
P.O. Box 1000-MGA
Babylon, NY 11702-9004
800-622-9997
www.dutchbulbs.com
Mail-order and Internet source
of more than 1,000 varieties of
perennials and bulbs

Wayside Gardens
1 Garden Lane
Hodges, SC 29695-0001
800-845-1124
www.waysidegardens.com
Mail-order and Internet source
of perennials, bulbs, shrubs, trees,
and gardening aids

White Flower Farm
P.O. Box 50
Litchfield, CT 06759-0050
800-503-9624
www.whiteflowerfarm.com
Mail-order and Internet source of
perennials, annuals, bulbs, and seeds

SEEDS

Ed Hume Seeds
P.O. Box 73160
Puyallup, WA 98373
Fax: 253-435-5144
Mail-order and Internet source
of flower and herb seeds for cool,
short-season climates

McKenzie Seed Co.
30 Ninth Street
Brandon, MB Canada R7A 6E1
204-571-7500
Mail-order and Internet source
of flower and vegetable seeds and
perennial plants; orders shipped
only to Canadian destinations.

Park Seed
P.O Box 31, Hwy 254
Greenwood, SC 29648
800-845-3369
www.parkseed.com
Mail-order and Internet source
of flower seeds and plants, growing
supplies and equipment

Seeds of Change
P.O. Box 15700
Santa Fe, NM 87506
888-762-7333
www.seedsofchange.com
Mail-order and Internet source
of certified organic seeds, bulbs,
and plants

Select Seeds Company
180 Stickney Hill Road
Union, CT 06076-4617
860-684-9310
www.selectseeds.com
Mail-order and Internet source of
flower seeds and plants, specializing
in heirloom flowers

Stokes Seeds
P.O. Box 548
Buffalo, NY 14240-0548
800-396-9238
www.stokeseeds.com
Mail-order and Internet source of
more than 2,500 varieties of seeds
for flowers, herbs, and vegetables,
and for garden accessories

Thompson & Morgan Seedsmen,
    Inc.
P.O. Box 1308
Jackson, NJ 08527-0308
800-274-7333
www.thompson-morgan.com
Mail-order and Internet source
of flower and vegetable seeds,
specializing in rare and unusual
seeds

TOOLS AND SUPPLIES

Charley's Greenhouse and Garden
17979 State Route 536
Mt. Vernon, WA 98273
800-322-4707
www.charleysgreenhouse.com
Mail-order and Internet source of
garden tools, propagation materials,
and greenhouses

Fiskars Garden Tools
780 Carolina Street
Sauk City, WI 53583
800-500-4849
www.fiskars.com
Manufacturer of gardening and
pruning tools designed to reduce
fatigue and strain associated with
gardening activities

Gardener's Supply Company
128 Intervale Road
Burlington, VT 05401-2804
800-955-3370
www.gardeners.com
Mail-order and Internet source
of seed-starting supplies, season
extenders, organic fertilizers and
pest controls, hand tools, watering
systems, and power equipment

Lee Valley & Veritas
P.O. Box 1780
Ogdensburg, NY 13669
800-267-8735 or 800-267-8761
    in Canada
www.leevalley.com
Mail-order and Internet source of
hard-to-find gardening tools and
supplies

OXO International
75 Ninth Avenue, 5th floor
New York, NY 10011
800-545-4411
www.oxo.com
Manufacturer and Internet source of
ergonomic hand tools

SOIL AMENDMENTS AND FERTILIZERS

Canadian Sphagnum Peat Moss
    Association
7 Oasis Court
St. Albert, Alberta
Canada T8N 6X2
www.peatmoss.com
Promotes the value and benefits of
using peat moss and the wise use of
peat-land resources.

Conrad Fafard, Inc.
770 Silver Street
Agawam, MA 01001
800-732-7667 (PEATMOS)
www.Fafard.Com
Manufacturer and wholesale
distributor of peat moss and soilless
potting mix

Mulch and Soil Council
10210 Leatherleaf Court
Manassas, VA 20111
703-257-0111
Conducts a product certification
program to provide consumers with
evidence of a company's
commitment to quality. The
certification logo on product bags
indicates that these products meet
uniform guidelines established by
the Mulch and Soil Council.
www.mulchandsoilcouncil.org

The Scotts Company
800-225-2883
www.scotts.com, www.miracle-
    gro.com, and www.ortho.com
Manufacturer of lawn and garden
fertilizers; soils, compost and
mulches; and pest controls sold
under the brands: Scotts, Miracle-
Gro, Osmocote, Ortho, and Round-
Up. The Ortho Problem Solver, a
1,000-page hardcover book, is
available on the web free at
www.ortho.com.

INSECT AND PEST CONTROL

Gardens Alive
5100 Schenley Place
Lawrenceburg, IN 47025
812-537-8650
www.gardensalive.com
Mail-order and Internet source of
organic lawn and garden products
including fertilizers, pre-emergence
weed controls, organic pest and
fungicide sprays, and beneficial
insects

Tree World, Inc.
10 N. Gates Avenue
Lackawanna, NY 14218
800-252-6051
www.treeworld.com or
    www.plantskyyd.com
Mail-order and Internet source of
Plantskydd animal repellent, an
organic, soluble powder which
protects plants against deer, rabbits,
and elk

MISCELLANEOUS

Effortless Gardening
P.O. Box 2379
Madison, WI 53701-2379
866-394-2733
www.effortlessgardening.com
Multimedia program to help reduce
the pain and strain of gardening
activities

INDEX

Note: Page numbers in **boldface type** indicate Encyclopedia entries. Page numbers in *bold italic type* indicate photographs or illustrations.

METRIC CONVERSIONS

U.S. Units to Metric Equivalents			Metric Units to U.S. Equivalents		
To Convert From	Multiply By	To Get	To Convert From	Multiply By	To Get
Inches	25.4	Millimeters	Millimeters	0.0394	Inches
Inches	2.54	Centimeters	Centimeters	0.3937	Inches
Feet	30.48	Centimeters	Centimeters	0.0328	Feet
Feet	0.3048	Meters	Meters	3.2808	Feet
Yards	0.9144	Meters	Meters	1.0936	Yards
Square inches	6.4516	Square centimeters	Square centimeters	0.1550	Square inches
Square feet	0.0929	Square meters	Square meters	10.764	Square feet
Square yards	0.8361	Square meters	Square meters	1.1960	Square yards
Acres	0.4047	Hectares	Hectares	2.4711	Acres
Cubic inches	16.387	Cubic centimeters	Cubic centimeters	0.0610	Cubic inches
Cubic feet	0.0283	Cubic meters	Cubic meters	35.315	Cubic feet
Cubic feet	28.316	Liters	Liters	0.0353	Cubic feet
Cubic yards	0.7646	Cubic meters	Cubic meters	1.308	Cubic yards
Cubic yards	764.55	Liters	Liters	0.0013	Cubic yards

To convert from degrees Fahrenheit (F) to degrees Celsius (C), first subtract 32, then multiply by $\frac{5}{9}$.

To convert from degrees Celsius to degrees Fahrenheit, multiply by $\frac{9}{5}$, then add 32.

Ortho® Books
An imprint of Meredith® Books

Ortho The Perennials Book
Editor: Marilyn Rogers
Contributing Editor: Nancy T. Engle
Contributing Technical Editor: Robert Polomski
Contributing Writers: Ann Lovejoy, Janet Macunovich,
  Jan Riggenbach, Katie Lamar Smith, Jo Kellum,
  Phillip Edinger
Senior Associate Design Director: Tom Wegner
Assistant Editor: Harijs Priekulis
Copy Chief: Terri Fredrickson
Copy and Production Editor: Victoria Forlini
Editorial Operations Manager: Karen Schirm
Managers, Book Production: Pam Kvitne,
  Marjorie J. Schenkelberg
Contributing Copy Editors: Chardel Gibson Blaine,
  Catherine Hamrick
Contributing Proofreaders: Fran Gardner, Gretchen
  Kauffman, Mindy Kralicek, Terri Krueger
Contributing Illustrators: Mike Eagleton, Lois Lovejoy
Contributing Map Illustrator: Jana Fothergill
Indexer: Kathleen Poole
Electronic Production Coordinator: Paula Forest
Editorial and Design Assistants: Kathleen Stevens,
  Karen McFadden

Additional Editorial Contributions from
  Art Rep Services
Director: Chip Nadeau
Designer: lk Design
Illustrator: Dave Brandon

Meredith® Books
Publisher and Editor in Chief: James D. Blume
Design Director: Matt Strelecki
Managing Editor: Gregory H. Kayko
Executive Editor, Gardening and Home Improvement:
  Benjamin W. Allen
Executive Editor, Gardening: Michael McKinley

Director, Operations: George A. Susral
Director, Production: Douglas M. Johnston
Executive Director, Sales: Ken Zagor

Vice President and General Manager: Douglas J. Guendel

Meredith Publishing Group
President, Publishing Group: Stephen M. Lacy
Vice President-Publishing Director: Bob Mate

Meredith Corporation
Chairman and Chief Executive Officer: William T. Kerr
Chairman of the Executive Committee: E.T. Meredith III

Thanks to
Janet Anderson, Mary Irene Swartz

Photographers
  (Photographers credited may retain copyright ©
  to the listed photographs.)
L = Left, R = Right, C = Center, B = Bottom, T = Top
Lynne Brotchie/Garden Picture Library: 234T; **Patricia J. Bruno/Positive Images:**
93B; **Gay Bumgarner:** 142T; **Gay Bumgarner/Positive Images:** 32, 43TR, 46BR;
Karen Bussolini/Positive Images: 172C; **Brian Carter/Garden Picture Library:**
178T; **David Cavagnaro:** 113TL, 140B, 141CR; **Eric Crichton/Garden Picture
Library:** 198B; **Michael Dodge/gardenIMAGE:** 232B; **Derek Fell:** 36T, 152BR, 205T,
229C; **Catriona Tudor Erler:** 12T, 35T, 37TL, 79, 178BL, 184T, 195T, 200TR,
200BL, 200BR, 205B, 232T; **John Glover:** 6BL, 10BL, 12B, 13B, 14, 15TL, 15TR,
16B, 20, 23R, 24, 25, 28, 44TR,45TL, 45BL, 45BR, 49T, 75, 81, 150T, 173B, 183T,
191T, 191CR, 191BL, 191BR, 193BR, 200TL, 216T, 217BR, 229B, 240T, 242T;
John Glover/Garden Picture Library: 153T, 185BL; **Tim Griffith/Garden Picture
Library:** 105B; **Jerry Harpur:** 31T, 50BL, 56BL, 63T, 159B, 236T(Kettle Hill);
Marcus Harpur: 21, 45CR, 148B(Elaine Munro & Anthony Henn Hampton, Court
Palace Show 2001), 155T, 159T(Beth Chatto. UK.), 172B(Wisley, Surrey. UK.),
197B, 210T; **Margaret Hensel/Positive Images:** 44TL; **Neil Holmes/Garden Picture
Library:** 222B; **Saxon Holt:** 64, 65, 67T, 148T, 149B, 152BL, 153T, 169T, 177T,
183B, 187T, 203T, 215B, 219B, 239T; **Jerry Howard/Positive Images:** 31B;
Bill Johnson: 128TL, 128BL; **Rosemary Kautzky:** 59, 143BL, 217TL, 218T, 220TR,
240B; **Donna & Tom Krischan:** 47L, 63B, 140T, 151T, 154T, 167T, 171BR, 173T,
185BR, 220B; **Lamontagne/Garden Picture Library:** 164B; **Andrew Lawson:**
7BR(Eastgrove Cottage, Hereford), 16T(RHS Rosemoor, Devon), 29R(Waterperry
Gardens, Oxon), 36C, 41, 43B, 46TL, 55B, 61BR(Chilcombe House, Dorset), 80,
159C, 170T, 184C, 189T, 191CB, 193B(The Old Rectory, Sudborough), 196T,
196BR, 201B, 217CR, 217BL, 223, 224T, 227T; **Andrew Lawson/gardenIMAGE:** 11;
Scott Leonhart/Positive Images: 143BR; **Eric Lessing/Art Resource:** 50TL, 50TR;
Lightworker/gardenIMAGE: 61L; **Janet Loughrey:** 10TL, 17, 29L, 33T, 34, 42T,
48T, 50BC, 60, 68, 165B, 170B, 174C, 179B, 186T, 190, 194T, 196B, 206T, 209B,
211B, 215T, 231TL, 231TR, 236B; **Allan Mandell:** 51(Designers: Marietta & Ernie
O'Byrne); **Allan Mandell/gardenIMAGE:** 13TL; **David McDonald:** 37TR;
Michael McKinley: 37B; **Charles Melton:** 67B; **Jeff Morgan:** 74; **Steven Nikkila:**
35B, 78, 87T, 87B, 106, 109L, 113BC, 142B, 150B, 152T, 181B, 206B, 208T, 229T,
237, 244T; **Jerry Pavia:** 23L, 36B, 40, 44BL, 44BR, 50BR, 52, 53, 56BR, 113TC,
113TR, 157B, 163B, 166T, 171TR, 171BL, 176, 177B, 178CB, 179T, 193T, 194TL,
194CBL, 194CBR, 194B, 196CL, 196C, 197T, 199T, 214T, 222T, 224B, 228T, 242B,
244B; **Diane A. Pratt/Positive Images:** 61T, 174B; **Howard Rice/Garden Picture
Library:** 13TR, 151B, 171C, 181T, 182BL, 188T, 195B, 231B; **JS Sira/Garden
Picture Library:** 6T; 46TR, 46BC, 241T; **Richard Shiell:** 15B, 18, 19, 57, 77T, 82, 83,
153B, 154BL, 158T, 158BR, 161, 162B, 163T, 165T, 166B, 167B, 168T, 171TL, 174T,
180T, 182T, 185T, 188B, 195C, 198T, 201T, 204T, 207T, 208B, 209T, 213T, 214B,
221B, 226T, 228B, 238B; **Janet Sorrell/Garden Picture Library:** 213B;
Pam Spaulding/Positive Images: 6BR, 33B, 235B; **Julie Sprott/gardenIMAGE:**
10TR, 47R; **Albert Squillace/Positive Images:** 46BL; **Joseph C. Strauch:** 113BR,
123, 172T, 178BR, 182BR, 192, 230T, 235T, 243T; **Michael Thompson:** 7BL, 37C,
42B, 46LC, 48B, 49B, 55T, 70, 71, 77B, 102, 125, 141BCR, 149T, 154BR, 155B, 156,
157T, 158BL, 160, 164T, 168B, 175T, 180B, 186B, 187B, 189B, 199B, 201, 202T,
202B, 203B, 204B, 210B, 212, 216B, 217TR, 219T, 221T, 225, 226B, 233B, 234B,
238T, 239B, 241B, 244C; **Deidra Walpole:** 31C, 43TL, 243B; **Mel Watson/Garden
Picture Library:** 178CT; **Didier Willery/Garden Picture Library:** 169B;
Justyn Willsmore: 9, 30, 113BL, 162T, 184B, 211T, 218B, 220TL, 227B, 230B

Cover photograph: Donna & Tom Krischan